RHETORICS OF RESISTANCE

Composition, Literacy, and Culture

David Bartholomae and Jean Ferguson Carr, *Editors*

RHETORICS OF RESISTANCE

Opposition Journalism in Apartheid South Africa

Bryan Trabold

University of Pittsburgh Press

Published by the University of Pittsburgh Press, Pittsburgh, Pa., 15260
Copyright © 2018, University of Pittsburgh Press
All rights reserved
Manufactured in the United States of America
Printed on acid-free paper
10 9 8 7 6 5 4 3 2 1

Cataloging-in-Publication data is available from the Library of Congress

ISBN 13: 978-0-8229-6544-2

Cover art: Image of Nelson Mandela from *Weekly Mail*
Cover design: Alex Wolfe

This book is dedicated, with much love,
to my loving family: Kim, Gabriel, and Grace

Perhaps all one can really hope for, all I am entitled to, is no more than this: to write it down. To report what I know. So that it will not be possible for any man ever to say again: I knew nothing about it.
ANDRÉ BRINK, *A DRY WHITE SEASON*, 1979

The newspaper [Weekly Mail] *is one of those which will prevent whites from ever being able to say in the future: "We didn't know."*
ARCHBISHOP DESMOND TUTU, 1988

The result, after the collapse of apartheid, is that South Africans, even the most reactionary whites, cannot say "We didn't know." The only ones who did not know the full horror of apartheid were those who chose not to.
ANTON HARBER, 1994

CONTENTS

ACKNOWLEDGMENTS

I have been working on this book for a very long time. The only way I can think of writing these acknowledgements is to create categories: those who had a direct impact on the publication of this book, those who had an impact on my intellectual and professional development, and those who provided the love, laughter, and encouragement without which this book would not have been possible.

My sincere gratitude to many people at the University of Pittsburgh Press. David Bartholomae and Jean Ferguson Carr, the series editors, who played a central role in allowing me to share this story of these remarkable journalists. Josh Shanholtzer, the senior acquisitions editor, for his professionalism, friendliness, and encouragement during this very long process. Alex Wolfe, the editorial and productions manager, for his inspired idea for the book cover, as well as his assistance during the editing process. Finally, to the readers of my manuscript who provided such valuable feedback, with a very special thanks to Ron Krabill, whose many suggestions and challenging questions improved an earlier draft of this manuscript immensely. My thanks to Shirley W. Logan and Herman Wasserman for their kind words that appear on the back of the book.

To the institutions that provided funding for my research, including the National Endowment for the Humanities, which provided a summer stipend that allowed me to spend several weeks at Harvard University reading on microfilm, once again, copies of the *Weekly Mail* and *New Nation*. My sincere thanks to Suffolk University, which provided me both with a sabbatical and the financial support to make a return trip to South Africa to conduct additional research.

To the many individuals who granted me an interview for this project: Tyrone August, Charlotte Bauer, Clive Cope, Jeremy Cronin, Sarah Crowe, Kerry Cullinan, David Dison, Barry Feinberg, Ryland Fisher, Drew Forrest, Anthony Holiday, Tim Jenkin, Marilyn Kirkwood, Patrick Laurence, Moira Levy, Amrit Manga, Smangaliso Mkhatshwa, Norman Manoim, Sefako Nyaka, Don Pinnock, Benjamin Rabinowitz, Susan Rabkin, Reg Rumney, Pat Sidley, Zwelakhe Sisulu, Charlene Smith, Gabu Tugwana, Phillip van Niekerk, and Janet Wilhelm. A special thanks to those who granted me multiple interviews: Howard Barrell, Shaun Johnson, and Ben Maclennan. And a very special thanks to Anton Harber and Irwin Manoim, who not only granted me multiple interviews but who also graciously responded to my many emails. I hope my admiration for all is reflected in the pages of this book. If not, allow me to con-vey this directly: Their courage to act during one of the darker chapters in their nation's history has been a source of deep and profound inspiration.

To my dear friends in South Africa, who allowed Kim and me to stay with them for weeks at a time when we lived there in 1998–1999. Sandra Klopper and Michael Godby, the times spent talking around their kitchen table remain some of my fondest memories of that glorious period of my life. I cannot thank them enough for their kindness and endless patience answering my endless questions about South Africa. Brenda Schmahmann and Paul Mills, my thanks for their incredible generosity and allowing us to stay at their home for an entire month when Kim and I conducted research in Johannesburg.

To the many people at the University of Wisconsin-Madison. First and foremost, Deborah Brandt, my dissertation director. Her impact on me as a thinker and scholar has been profound. She modeled for me what one must do when writing a book: Ask a question—and then pursue it with dogged deter-mination, regardless of where it may lead, what you must read, and where you must go. Her influence runs through every page of this book. Thanks to the supportive members of my dissertation committee: Michael Bernard-Donals, David Fleming, Rob Nixon, and Marty Nystrand. To the professors who shaped my thinking in the field of writing studies and rhetoric, Stuart Greene and Susan Zaeske. To the singular Brad Hughes, director of the Writing Center, a model of friendliness, good cheer, and tireless work ethic. To Henry Drewal, a preeminent scholar in the field of African art but "Uncle Hank" to me. To Dale Bauer who provided support during that rocky and disorienting first semester of graduate school. To those in the writing studies graduate program who stimulated my thinking both in and out of the classroom, and with whom I shared many laughs: Eli Goldblatt, Nelson Graff, Julie Nelson Christoph, and Rebecca Nowacek. To Tony and Ann Beale, who had heartfelt discussions with me before going to Madison, and to Richard Jacobson and Jacqueline Macaulay, who provided me with gainful employment and friendship when I arrived.

A special thanks to Craig Werner and Tim Tyson, professors in the Afro-American studies department when I was a graduate student at Wisconsin. Brilliant, passionate academics who view institutions of higher learning not as cloistered ivory towers but as an open invitation to all, and whose scholarship engages with the world in deep, meaningful ways. They embody my ideal as teacher and scholar.

To the many special people at Transylvania University, my first job after graduate school, with a special thanks to those with whom I worked most closely: Martha Billips, Ellen Cox, Peter Fosl, Martha Gehringer, Trina Jones, Becky Mills, Louise Penner, and Dave Shannon. To Jay Moseley, dean of the college, who provided generous maternity leaves for Kim when Gabriel and Grace were born, a decision that had such a profoundly positive impact on our family. To the many remarkable students I had the privilege to teach over the years, too many to name, but a special thanks to Spence Witten, who not only provided me with sources about opposition journalists in Iran but who so endeared himself to my children. Finally, to Jack Furlong, who modelled for me with his everyday acts of kindness and generosity a valuable life lesson: the power one has in this life should always be used ethically and to try to help others.

To the many people at Suffolk University, including my amazing colleagues in the English department, with special thanks to those who have invited me to their homes and become good friends, Quentin Miller and Lisa Celovsky. To Rich Miller, a dear friend who always looks out for me and who jams on guitar with my son. To Fred Marchant, who explored the field of peace studies with me at the University of Notre Dame, and whose life decisions, poetry, and kindness enact the very essence of peace studies. To James Carroll, a writer and man of deep humanity who provides me with hope for humanity. To my many wonderful colleagues outside the English department, too many to name, but a special thanks to my friends Nir Eisikovits and Brian Smith. To the many students I have taught over the years, particularly those whom I have had the privilege of sharing my passion about the anti-apartheid movement: their questions and comments shaped in a very real way how I framed sections of this book.

Thanks to the many members of my family. To my mother and father, who provided me with a college education and who instilled in me a way of looking at the world that opened me to the true inspiration of the anti-apartheid movement. To my siblings and their spouses for their love, laughter, and support over the years: JoAnne and Dennis Baxter, Lisa and Larry McGinn, Chris and Sandra Trabold. A special thanks to Jo and Den who supported my move to Wisconsin, without which this journey would have never happened, and for visiting Kim and me in South Africa. Thanks to my brothers and sisters, also, for the wonderful children they have brought into this world: Aimee and Scott Baxter; Michael and Steven McGinn; and Patrick, Laura, and David Trabold. They have provided me with countless laughs and memories; watching them grow up over the years has been one of the great joys of my life.

To my sisters-in-law, Jenny and Kriste; their husbands Dennis and Seth; their beautiful children, Aiden, Greta, and Toren; and to Ronald Warner, who visited us in South Africa. I am truly grateful to have married into a family that has embraced me as family.

To my many friends, too many to list here, whose love and laughter make life worth living. To Gib Jones, my childhood best friend who backpacked through Europe with me and who made the trip to South Africa. To my best friends from George Washington University: John O'Malley, Jim Wodarski, John Gonas, and Harry Kofman. So many memories, so much laughter. To John Duffy, who took me on a long walk around Lake Mendota the day before my pre-lim exams and who has been a source of wise, thoughtful counsel about matters both professional and personal ever since. To my friends here in Massachusetts, Mike LeBlanc and John Partridge, who have kindly inquired about my book and offered words of encouragement the many years I have spent writing it.

To the members of my family who are no longer with us but who remain very much in my heart. My nephew, Scott Baxter, the only person I have ever known who asked more questions than I did and still do. I miss him and his questions dearly. My grandmother, Henrietta Warnken, whose optimism and boundless love of life and people made a deep, profound impression on me as a child. My grandfather, William Warnken, who I know mostly through stories and whom I think of often when cheering for our beloved New York Mets. My mother-in-law, Claudia Miller, a teacher in every sense of the word, passionately committed to helping others, a woman of many accomplishments, the most notable for me: bringing Kim into the world and raising her as she did. My uncle, Albert Trabold, a kind, genuine, good man. I know Anita, his wife, and his children, Paul, Todd, and Nicole, carry him in their hearts every day. My Aunt Ginny, who inherited her love of life from my grandmother; her husband, Curt; and my Uncle Bill and Aunty Judy.

To our rescue dogs, Lucky, a gentle soul, and Luna, with her seemingly always-wagging tail, whom I took on many long walks while thinking about this book.

And finally, my children, Gabriel and Grace, and my wife, Kim. I never feel the limitations of language more acutely than when I try to describe what you mean to me. Gabriel and Grace, you inspire and restore my faith daily: Gabriel, with your kindness and compassion; Grace, with your sensitivity and genuine concern for all people and all living creatures. You both share an endless curiosity about the world and a deep passion for justice. You are already better people than I could ever hope to be.

Kim, our journey together truly began when we packed your black Hyundai and drove across country to Madison, Wisconsin in August, 1993. Since then, we have travelled throughout the country and across the world together. The memories and special moments we have shared in Madison, Cape Town, Lexington, and Sharon: immeasurable and uncountable. It is truly beyond my limited means to thank you for everything you have provided me over the years as we completed our dissertations, found our jobs, and most importantly, started our family. My love for you and the beautiful children we have brought into this world: beyond words.

RHETORICS OF RESISTANCE

INTRODUCTION

I leave it to those more qualified to decide what can be expected . . . "from above"—that is, from what is happening in the sphere of power. I have never fixed my hopes there; I've always been more interested in what was happening "below," in what could be expected from "below," what could be won there, and what defended. . . . The exercise of power is determined by thousands of interactions between the world of the powerful and that of the powerless, all the more so because these worlds are never divided by a sharp line: everyone has a small part of himself in both.
VÁCLAV HAVEL, *DISTURBING THE PEACE*

Most of the political life of subordinate groups is to be found neither in overt collective defiance of power holders nor in complete hegemonic compliance, but in the vast territory between these two polar opposites.
JAMES SCOTT, *DOMINATION AND THE ARTS OF RESISTANCE*

Zwelakhe Sisulu was at his home one evening when masked members of the security forces stormed in, told him to pack a bag, and ordered him at gunpoint to get into a van. Sisulu, the editor of the anti-apartheid newspaper *New Nation*, described during an interview what happened next:

And we drove off. They took me on a very long drive just outside of Soweto, and they did not say, but indicated, that I was going to be eliminated. They spoke on their two-way radios that they were at the spot, a pre-determined spot that they had obviously discussed, and that I was there, and they were ready. They waited and there was a response from the other side, and I couldn't hear what they were saying, but I mean the two-way radio was crackling with life. So we spent probably about thirty minutes at that spot, and they were here as a group, a couple of meters away from me.[1]

At this point, Sisulu slowed somewhat and spoke more deliberately: "I decided that this was it. I just felt that the moment had come. There was nothing I could do. And so I simply waited for the final moment." Sisulu's fears were more than justified, given the number of anti-apartheid activists who had been assassinated by death squads. The security forces, however, eventually told Sisulu to "get in the car" and proceeded to drive him to prison. Sisulu was detained by apartheid authorities for two long years despite the considerable domestic and international outcry calling for his release.[2]

In addition to denying *New Nation* its eloquent and charismatic editor, Sisulu's detention sent a chilling message to those who continued to work for this newspaper: you could be next. For those individuals who had previously been detained and suffered physical and psychological torture at the hands of South African police, this was no idle threat. Other intimidation tactics included sending police to the offices of *New Nation*, where they detained the entire staff and locked the office doors while searching through files for evidence of so-called "illegal activities."

Anton Harber and Irwin Manoim, the cofounders of another anti-apartheid newspaper, the *Weekly Mail*, were never detained, but they too were the targets of intimidation. The Committee to Protect Journalists issued a report in 1990, *Attacks on the Press: A Worldwide Survey, 1989*, which noted the following: "Irwin Manoim—*Weekly Mail*—Johannesburg home of the co-editor and his brother Norman, a civil rights attorney, damaged by a fire-bomb. The assailants and their motives are unknown" (115). During an interview, Manoim described how he had shared a house with his brother Norman, a prominent anti-apartheid attorney, who, coincidentally, provided legal advice to *New Nation*. When their home was firebombed, one of Norman's clients, a political activist, was staying there. Irwin recounted how Norman later discovered who had firebombed their house as he engaged in a legal proceeding:

Many years later there were innumerable commissions of inquiry into all these people who went around blowing things up, and my brother found himself in a position of interrogating a witness on the stand who turned out to be working for some hit squad, run by the local municipality of all things, who had been given instructions, for reasons he never questioned, to go out one night and petrol bomb five houses in Yeoville [a section of Johannesburg]. He couldn't remember which houses. He was told they were "ANC nests," the phrase he used. So he did it.

When the perpetrator was asked who in the house was being targeted, Irwin explained, "He said he didn't know, and you know, he did so much of this, it didn't really matter in his life. He had no idea why he had been told to do it."

Anton Harber, the other founder of the *Weekly Mail*, explained during an interview that he had eventually learned that two members of the security forces, Paul Erasmus and Michael Bellingham, had been "assigned" to certain members of the white Left. Harber had the distinct misfortune of making their list. He described the various forms of harassment he experienced: "We frequently would have a rock thrown [through] the window. In fact, we moved from our house because it was too close to the street. It ended up we couldn't use the front of the house because it had a window in the front, and if you were sitting at the desk there, a brick [could] come flying through. Dead cats strung up on the door. I had a shotgun fired through the front door at one point." Harber eventually met one of these two agents, Erasmus, when he broke with the security police in 1992, and Harber subsequently wrote an article about him. Bellingham, the other agent, testified in front of the Truth and Reconciliation Commission (TRC) that he, together with Erasmus, had harassed Harber because, according to Harber, "they were told I was near a nervous breakdown and they thought they could push me over the edge." At the time I conducted this interview with Harber in 1999, Bellingan was serving a twenty-year prison sentence for murdering his wife.

The experiences of Sisulu, Manoim, and Harber reveal the risks taken by those who used writing as a means of challenging the apartheid government in the late 1980s, a period when most political observers inside and outside the country thought that the country was heading toward a bloody civil war. Levels of resistance in the townships and in rural areas had increased dramatically, and the apartheid government's response mirrored the response of oppressive governments everywhere when confronted with unrest: more oppression. On 21 July 1985 the government declared a state of emergency in what would prove to be the first in a series of such declarations. During these states of emergency, martial law was imposed, and the government not only jailed thousands of activists but also implemented greater restrictions on the media in an attempt to prevent South Africans and the international community from learning about the massive levels of violence it was using to maintain control. The apartheid government thus issued a series of administrative restrictions affecting the press to supplement the more than one hundred censorship laws already in existence.

It was in this context of violence and repression that the *Weekly Mail* and *New Nation* were born. The *Weekly Mail* published its first edition on 14 June 1985, about one month prior to the first state of emergency, and *New Nation*, which published a trial edition in August 1985, began regular publication in January 1986, a few months after the first state of emergency was declared. Writing and publishing in a context of such severe constraints was, at the risk of understatement, challenging. Openly defying the censorship laws and emergency regulations would lead to certain closure and possible imprisonment (or worse); adhering to these restrictions would require those working for these newspapers to abandon their fundamental journalistic principles.

Rather than defy these regulations outright or conform to them completely, those working for the *Weekly Mail* and *New Nation* chose a third way: they developed various tactics to adhere to the letter of these restrictions while simultaneously violating their spirit. In other words, the editors, journalists, and attorneys working for these two newspapers sought to maximize the information they could publish under these restrictions without getting banned. Such an approach was fraught with risks. Both the *Weekly Mail* and *New Nation* subsequently received several official warning letters informing them that they were in contravention of the censorship laws, and the government eventually closed *New Nation* for three months and the *Weekly Mail* for one month. In addition to facing these legal constraints, those working for these two newspapers had to contend with the formidable extralegal constraints described above.

As if these constraints were not enough, the *Weekly Mail* struggled to secure advertising, the primary source of revenue for newspapers, in the free-market media environment of South Africa. The mainstream South African business community was not exactly clamoring to place advertisements in an opposition newspaper targeted by the apartheid government and directed at a readership of black and "radical" white South Africans. Those at *New Nation* did not have to worry about advertising, as the newspaper was funded by the Catholic Church in South Africa, but its editors and staff had to be mindful of white, conservative Catholics who publicly denounced this newspaper as Marxist and openly appealed to the Vatican to shut it down.

In the end, those working for the *Weekly Mail* and *New Nation* not only continued to publish and to reveal information that the media restrictions were clearly designed to suppress, but both increased their circulations over time. The question driving my research therefore was a relatively straightforward one: How, given all of these constraints, did they engage in such successful resistance? My analysis of the tactics they developed contributes, I argue, to two separate and important scholarly conversations. First, analyzing these opposition newspapers provided a case study for theorizing more deeply about the nature of writing and resistance, a central concern for those in the field of writing studies. Second, conducting a fine-grained analysis of these two South African opposition newspapers contributes to the rich body of literature examining anti-apartheid writing.

WRITING SPACE

Many prominent poststructural theorists have offered compelling analysis of the many ways in which power restricts and constrains the ways in which individuals act, write, and even think. This focus, however, constitutes only one part of the equation. Edward Said, who admires the many contributions of Foucault, observes that "[w]ith this profoundly pessimistic view went also a singular lack of interest in the force of effective resistance" (151). Said's observation raises an implicit question, one that has particular immediacy for writing studies, a field that focuses on the writing and rhetorical practices of individuals, on civic participation, and on social justice: What can individuals and collectives accomplish within oppressive contexts of power?[3] By empirically examining the tactics of resistance used by those working for the *Weekly Mail* and *New Nation*, this book aligns itself with others who have theorized about the nature of resistance, including James Scott, Michel de Certeau, and Václav Havel. Writing space, the central analytical framework of this book, not only illuminates the resistance of these opposition journalists in apartheid South Africa but also provides a lens with which to better understand, describe, and analyze writing as a means of resistance in other contexts. Writers face constraints in all contexts; writers also seek ways of resisting constraints in all contexts. David Couzens Hoy perhaps captures the essence of this book when he writes, "The claim that a structural system restricts what an agent *can* do does not entail the claim that such a system determines what an agent *will* do" (128).

The concept of writing space originated from a word that was used repeatedly during interviews with those who worked at these newspapers. Time and again, people referred to their ability or inability to write about certain issues or events in terms of "space": the space that had been closed to them, the space that was available to them, the space that they created, the space that they occupied, and so on.[4] Writing space, as used in this book, is a metaphor to describe the parameters of expression. The editors, journalists, and attorneys working for these newspapers devised various legal, writing, and political tactics to maximize their writing space, whereas the government took steps to constrict it. As Richard Abel observes, "Like other forms of regulation, censorship inevitably becomes a game, if one with unusually high stakes. Each time government proscribed, the alternative media sought a loophole" (304). Similar to the back-and-forth struggle for terrain in war, writing space was constantly changing, as each side would mount offensives in an attempt to gain as much territory as possible. Writing space did not open or close in a linear, predictable manner, therefore, but rather was constantly contracting and expanding.[5]

To continue with the war analogy, each side had various weapons in its arsenal. The apartheid government had overwhelming institutional power, which it used to promulgate and enforce new and increasingly severe restrictions, as well as to detain individuals, harass these newspapers "legally," and engage in various forms of extralegal intimidation. The *Weekly Mail* and *New Nation*, on the other hand, developed a broad range of tactics to resist and subvert these constraints: finding gaps and fissures within the apartheid bureaucracy; developing ways of conveying meanings without explicitly stating them; exploiting legal loopholes; and aligning themselves with various groups and institutions that offered financial assistance, ideological protection, and/or had the potential to adversely affect the regime's interests in some way.

The various means of resistance available to opposition journalists very much resemble Certeau's description of those who lack institutional power and "must play on and with a terrain imposed on [them] and organized by the law of a foreign power" (37). According to Certeau, such individuals must resort to "tactics," an approach he describes as follows: "It operates in isolated actions, blow by blow. It takes advantage of 'opportunities.' . . . It must vigilantly make use of the cracks that particular conjunctions open in their surveillance of the proprietary powers. It poaches in them. It creates surprises in them. It can be where it is least expected. It is a guileful ruse. In short, a tactic is an art of the weak" (37). As Certeau notes, opposition journalists in apartheid South Africa were clearly on unequal footing and were very much playing on terrain "imposed" on them by the government. This, however, did not prevent them from constantly finding, and in many instances creating, "opportunities" to increase their writing space.

In this book, I use the term "writing space" to refer to the struggles that took place within what James Scott refers to as the "public transcript" (13), or the public spaces where the powerful and those with less power interact. The amount of writing space available to writers and their prospects for expanding it, of course, vary dramatically within each society, depending on the government in power. Michael Walzer offers the following observation in his analysis of Foucault, whose theory of power challenges the idea of a "center" and focuses instead on how power and discipline are enacted within various institutions throughout society: "I only want to suggest the enormous importance of the political regime, the sovereign state. For it is the state that establishes the general framework within which all other disciplinary institutions operate. It is the state that holds open or radically shuts down the possibility of local resistance" (66). In terms of controlling writing space, I concur with Walzer and would argue that the power of governments is thus paramount. The more governments shut down writing space within the public transcript, the more those engaging in resistance will utilize what Scott refers to as "hidden transcripts" (4). Scott analyzes a wide range of activities that occur within hidden transcripts, but with regard to writing space this term would refer to the production and distribution of underground literature. Writing as a means of resistance in apartheid South Africa occurred within both the public and the hidden transcripts, a dynamic discussed further below.

In addition to the obvious *spatial* dimension of writing space, there was a *temporal* one as well. In other words, editors, attorneys, and journalists were cognizant that tactics employed to open space in one article had important implications for future articles as well. The fact that each tactic developed by these newspapers had implications for both the present and the future helps in part to explain the intensity of the struggle for writing space. If journalists tried to write about issues or in ways that they knew were risky, and the state did not crack down on them, this meant that they had, in the words of Howard Barrell, a *Weekly Mail* journalist, "occupied that space." In other words, writers had established a precedent that could later be invoked to make it more difficult for the state to crack down should journalists cover that particular issue or use that tactic in the future. Of course, journalists' ability to occupy a certain space never offered any guarantees. As Certeau rightfully notes about those in disempowered positions, "[w]hatever it wins, it does not keep" (xix). When these newspapers did successfully identify a loophole that allowed them to successfully publish information, the government always had the power simply to close that loophole and declare it off-limits for the future. Even though any successful opening of writing space could be short-lived and eliminated by the government, those working for these two newspapers and within the opposition media nevertheless acquired a clear sense of momentum during the late 1980s.

This momentum was created in large measure by another element absolutely crucial for expanding writing space in this and every context: collective action. I certainly do not mean to suggest that individuals did not play important roles in expanding writing space. In fact, my framework seeks to account precisely for the fact that individuals can and do successfully resist oppressive power. Based on the evidence revealed in my interviews, however, it became clear that expanding writing space was due primarily to the cooperative efforts of many different groups of people working together. Several journalists, for example, claimed that they wanted to work for the *Weekly Mail* and *New Nation* because they knew that these editors would allow them greater range of expression than they had been afforded by editors at other newspapers. Moreover, the journalists and editors of these newspapers needed the advice of activist attorneys who were willing to aggressively challenge the law and try to find loopholes. And activist attorneys, of course, needed these journalists and editors who were willing to take the necessary risks to pursue and write the stories that would facilitate the legal challenges they spearheaded. To successfully expand writing space thus required the cooperative efforts of all these groups.[6]

The collective action that took place within each newspaper also existed between various newspapers. While there was clearly a healthy sense of competition between the opposition newspapers, as well as between opposition

and mainstream newspapers, there were also moments of genuine cooperation. For example, the *Weekly Mail* published several articles denouncing the
detention of Zwelakhe Sisulu, the editor of *New Nation*. Moreover, when the
government banned *New Nation* for three months, the *Weekly Mail* featured
on its front page a picture of Gabu Tugwana, the acting editor of *New Nation*
after Sisulu's detention, holding a copy of *New Nation* with the word "BANNED!"
written in white letters on a black background. The following statement
appears beneath the photograph: "They banned the *New Nation* and damned
it to silence because it dared reflect the violence of apartheid. They banned
it because it gave a voice to the voteless majority. They banned it because it
articulated the aspirations of millions of oppressed people. But the spirit of
resistance it was born into remains deeply rooted in a tradition that refuses
to die for as long as apartheid lives. And it will be naïve in the extreme for this
government to believe that banning the *New Nation* will resolve the crisis it is
trapped in" (1). The *Weekly Mail* also published articles written by *New Nation*
journalists in this same edition under this headline: "It's Perfectly Legal—
Only *They* Can't Say It" (2). Beneath the headline the text reads, "*New Nation*
can't publish the stories its journalists wrote this week. But we can—because
they are legal. Below is what the government is trying to hide: what would
have been the paper's Page 3" (2). In addition to these acts of solidarity among
members of the opposition press, editors from some mainstream newspapers,
which were not nearly as aggressive in challenging the censorship restrictions, denounced the government's efforts to try to silence the *Weekly Mail*
and *New Nation*. Writing space expanded, therefore, not because solitary
writers were confronting the vast power of the state on their own but rather
because various groups worked cooperatively with one another to achieve a
common objective.

The concept of writing space, I argue, offers the following insights into
writing as a means of resistance. First, it highlights the complex but very real
relationship that exists between specific "micro" decisions individual writers make and larger, more "macro" forms of power that they can strategically
harness for the purpose of resistance. In other words, the extent to which the
Weekly Mail and *New Nation* were able to expand their writing space was ultimately determined, as Havel notes in the epigraph to this introduction, by the
"thousands of interactions between the world of the powerful and that of the
powerless" (*Disturbing the Peace* 182). In subsequent chapters, I examine the
many South African and international actors who meaningfully and tangibly

helped to increase the writing space of these two newspapers, but a brief list includes the following: the Catholic Church of South Africa; South African political organizations and parties; labor unions; South African businesses (including mining companies); multinational corporations; governments throughout the world, particularly of the United States and Britain; international anti-apartheid organizations; and international media organizations. Despite the many and deep ideological differences that may have existed among this broad array of groups, they all contributed either in helping those working for these newspapers to expand their writing space and/or attempting to prevent the apartheid government from further restricting their writing space.[7]

Writing space also provides, I suggest, a more robust means of capturing and describing the profoundly fluid, dynamic nature of writing and resistance. While the concept of agency conveys the sense, as Said notes above, that individuals can and do effectively resist power, the concept itself can have limited value when trying to assess the success or limitations of writing as a means of resistance. Agency, in other words, seems to imply a threshold, or an endpoint, that writers either do or do not obtain. An examination of the articles published by the *Weekly Mail* and *New Nation* over a period of time, however, reveals that this is in fact more complicated. The stories both newspapers were and were not able to publish regarding apartheid prisons provide a case in point. Both newspapers managed to publish several articles about conditions in apartheid prisons that the censorship restrictions were clearly designed to suppress. Among these articles was a spectacular series in the *Weekly Mail* by a former political prisoner, Thami Mkhwanazi, who reflected on his experiences on Robben Island. Yet, more than one journalist revealed how they had heard accounts of horrifying acts that had taken place in apartheid prisons, such as the repeated rape of women political activists, which they simply could not publish because of the restrictions. How does one evaluate prison-related stories, therefore, in terms of agency? Did these newspapers "achieve agency" because they were able to publish some stories about prisons that successfully circumvented the restrictions? But what about other stories that they were unable to publish because of the restrictions?

Writing space, however, invites us to view resistance as constant and ongoing, never completely stymied, never completely successful, sometimes expanding, sometimes contracting, always dependent on ever-shifting dynamics of power. With the exception of writers operating in the most extreme contexts of oppression, opposition journalists in South Africa reflected a truism of writers in most contexts throughout the world: they were never completely constrained nor were they ever completely free to express themselves. Even though these absolutes were never reached, one can nevertheless identify moments of successful and meaningful acts of resistance in which they successfully expanded their writing space, as well as instances in which constraints clearly curtailed their writing space.

In addition to providing a more robust and nuanced framework for better assessing writing as a means of resistance, writing space also offers a more nuanced means for considering the contexts in which resistance takes place. "Censorship," for example, can at times contribute to thinking about writing, resistance, and constraints in a binary manner. Consider the following statements: "There is no official censorship in the United States" and "There was censorship in apartheid South Africa." Both statements are technically true, and yet both mask important dynamics of power. There are admirable protections for free speech within the United States, and no official entity responsible for censoring the writing of American citizens exists within the US government. But there are also significant constraints that inhibit writing space, specifically, the massive classification of information on the grounds of "national security." Journalists, historians, and other writers do not have access to literally billions of documents that have been produced by the US government, and this lack of access serves to conceal a considerable amount of information from American citizens. At the same time, official censorship *did* exist in apartheid South Africa. As this book chronicles in considerable detail, however, opposition journalists, editors, and attorneys were able to expand their writing space and reveal a considerable amount of information that the apartheid government clearly wished to conceal.[8]

OPPOSITION JOURNALISM AS ANTI-APARTHEID WRITING

In addition to encouraging broader reflections on the nature of writing and resistance, an in-depth analysis of the *Weekly Mail* and *New Nation* also contributes to the scholarly analyses of anti-apartheid writing. There are, of course, many distinguished South African writers who used fiction, drama, and poetry as a means of resistance. In addition to not one but two Nobel

Prize winners, J. M. Coetzee and Nadine Gordimer, a brief and very incomplete list of South African writers who challenged apartheid includes Breyten Breytenbach, André Brink, Athol Fugard, Es'kia Mphahlele, Lewis Nkosi, and Mongane Wally Serote. Considerable scholarship has been devoted to the work of these writers, including Coetzee's *Giving Offense: Essays on Censorship* (which examines censorship both in apartheid South Africa as well as in other contexts), Margreet de Lange's *The Muzzled Muse: Literature and Censorship in South Africa*, and Peter McDonald's *The Literature Police: Apartheid Censorship and Its Cultural Consequences*. All of these works, however, exclude writings by opposition journalists. McDonald mentions that censorship existed for newspapers, but he focuses, as his title indicates, on literature. Lange writes in *The Muzzled Muse*, "Censorship can focus on the media or literature, on political reporting or on publications generally.... This book looks at one particular kind of writing, literature, in one particular, country, South Africa, at one particular time when apartheid was in full development" (1). And Coetzee makes the following claim in his introduction to *Giving Offense*: "Wholly aware that the line between journalism and 'writing' is hard to draw, particularly in the late twentieth century, I nevertheless do not address the situation of journalists practicing their profession under regimes exercising press censorship or otherwise restricting the flow of information" (ix). Given the breathtaking scope of literature that was banned by the apartheid regime, it is certainly understandable that these scholars focused exclusively on this kind of writing.[9]

I would argue, however, that the writing of opposition journalists merits further attention for two reasons. First, the nature of their writing was crucially important for the larger anti-apartheid struggle. André Brink's argument about the importance of literature in his essay "Censorship and Literature" certainly applies to opposition journalists as well:

> For society requires knowledge of itself, but it does not always consciously admit that need: its instinctive reaction may well be to be left in peace, rather than to be forced to acknowledge a state of affairs which will stir it out of the security of inertia into some form of action. It is a hazardous undertaking, not only for the writer, but for the society that permits him to undertake his explorations. He may come up with uncomfortable facts which those in power might have preferred to remain hidden—either to prevent panic, or to strengthen their own position. (40)

Opposition journalists, similar to those who wrote literature, were clearly engaged in a "hazardous undertaking" as they sought to provide South African society with "knowledge of itself," particularly about matters "those in power might have preferred to remain hidden."

As Brink proceeds to argue about the important role writers can play in the anti-apartheid struggle, he lists several examples of the government's "arrogance of power": the forced removal of millions of black South Africans; the war the South African government waged in Angola that was largely hidden from the South African public; and, finally, the numerous deaths in detention, including the "shocking disclosures following that of Steve Biko in 1976" (41). Again, these were precisely the facts and issues opposition journalists were seeking to expose and to disseminate to large audiences on a weekly basis. And when Brink reflects on some of the risks that accompany freedom of expression, he makes the following claim in italics: *"But that is the risk society must take if it allows the artist in its midst"* (40). Brink's claim is equally valid, I propose, if one substitutes "opposition journalist" for "artist."

The writing of opposition journalists was not only extremely important in terms of the larger anti-apartheid struggle, but their objectives and the challenges they faced as writers were in many ways unique. Coetzee, for example, makes the following claims about literary writers: "Censors can and often have been outwitted. But the game of slipping Aesopian messages past the censor is ultimately a sterile one, diverting writers from their proper task" (*Giving Offense* viii). In terms of fiction, drama, and poetry, one can certainly appreciate Coetzee's point. But for South African opposition journalists, devising ways of "slipping" information "past the censor" was *precisely* their proper task.

The challenges opposition journalists faced also differed from the ones faced by those who produced underground literature on behalf of banned political organizations. I had the privilege to interview several people who disseminated material on behalf of the African National Congress (ANC) and the South African Communist Party (SACP), including Jeremy Cronin, Barry Feinberg, Anthony Holiday, Tim Jenkin, and Susan Rabkin. It became apparent during my interviews, however, that the primary constraints facing these writers pertained more to the production and distribution of written texts—acquiring the massive amount of paper to produce pamphlets, producing them so that they could not be tracked by the government, and finding the means to distribute them anonymously—as opposed to the *act of writing* itself. Because what they were doing was by definition already illegal, those who produced underground material were not concerned in the least with the censorship restrictions. As James Scott observes, "If anonymity often encourages the delivery of an unvarnished message, the veiling of the message represents the application of varnish" (152). The tactics developed by those who produced and distributed underground material were both ingenious and admirable, but my primary interest was in examining the ways in which writers, in an attempt to reach larger audiences legally, applied the varnish.

There are many books that focus on the role of the media during apartheid, specifically, that of the opposition press. Some of those that offer important insights into the contributions of South African opposition newspapers include Les Switzer and Mohamed Adhikari's *South Africa's Resistance Press: Alternative Voices in the Last Generation under Apartheid*, Christopher Merrett's *A Culture of Censorship: Secrecy and Intellectual Repression in South Africa*; Keyan Tomaselli and P. Eric Louw's *The Alternative Press in South Africa*; James Zug's *The Guardian: The History of South Africa's Extraordinary Anti-Apartheid Newspaper*; and Irwin Manoim's *You Have Been Warned*. My book similarly focuses on opposition newspapers but offers a more extensive empirical analysis of the specific writing, rhetorical, and legal tactics of resistance developed by opposition journalists. In terms of the scope of this book, some may question the decision to focus on only two opposition newspapers given the numerous publications produced during the long history of resistance to censorship in apartheid South Africa. I readily concede my focus comes at the cost of historical breadth. But I decided ultimately that a narrower focus would allow for a deeper, richer analysis of writing as a means of resistance: how writers read power, how this reading of power shaped what they did and did not write, and how and why certain tactics were or were not successful.

RESEARCH METHODS

Given the many opposition newspapers that existed during apartheid, selecting which ones to examine was challenging. There were, however, certain practical and methodological reasons for selecting newspapers published in the 1980s. First, there was a much better chance of locating and interviewing these journalists and editors, as opposed to those who had worked on newspapers in the 1950s, 1960s, or 1970s. Second, the reliability of memory and the ability of writers to recall with specificity some of the decisions they made when writing articles were already an issue when interviewing journalists who wrote in the late 1980s; it would have only been exacerbated had I interviewed those who were writing decades earlier. Finally, since I was interested in examining how writers negotiate constraints, it made sense to examine those who were writing after 1985, a period in which the states of emergency were declared and governmental repression was at its height.

In terms of other opposition newspapers circulating in the 1980s, *Grassroots* and *Saamstaan* were both very important, but neither was a national newspaper.[10] *South*, which was a national newspaper, had a considerably smaller circulation than either the *Weekly Mail* or *New Nation*. According to one source, *South*'s circulation was approximately 10,800 (Corrigall 9), whereas at their peaks the *Weekly Mail*'s was more than 30,000 and *New Nation*'s was approximately 60,000.[11] *Vrye Weekblad* was a remarkably important, courageous opposition newspaper published in Afrikaans. While I could have studied and learned Afrikaans for purposes of conducting research on this newspaper, I was concerned I could never learn the language sufficiently to determine if and when journalists may have been manipulating the language in order to skirt the censorship restrictions. I thus selected the *Weekly Mail* and *New Nation* because they were national newspapers, were written in English, and had the highest circulations of the opposition newspapers.

I chose to examine both rather than just one because of the considerably different purposes and targeted audiences of each newspaper. The *Weekly Mail* was willing to aggressively challenge the apartheid government but also positioned itself as a newspaper that was not aligned with any particular party or group. Its audience consisted of progressive, well-educated, middle- and upper-middle-class white South Africans, as well as a sizable black readership within the townships. *New Nation*, on the other hand, was clearly and overtly sympathetic to the ANC and the United Democratic Front (UDF), and its readership was overwhelmingly black South Africans. While both were clearly opposition newspapers, I was interested in examining the extent to which their different purposes and audiences may have shaped their tactics of resistance.

I read every available edition of both the *Weekly Mail* and *New Nation* at the University of Cape Town library, beginning with their first editions and stopping at 1990, the year the apartheid government released Nelson Mandela from prison and unbanned the ANC, SACP, and the Pan African Congress (PAC).[12] With this initial reading, I compiled a list of the most regular contributors and photocopied several significant front-page and feature stories. I then contacted as many journalists as I could and arranged to interview them wherever it was most convenient for them: their places of work, their homes, restaurants, and so on.

I certainly did not interview every person who worked for both of these newspapers, but I was able to interview those who played the most significant roles.[13] In terms of my interview script, certain sections were standardized. For example, I tended to ask everyone similar questions about their background, such as, What did you do prior to working for the newspaper? What was your motivation for working on this newspaper? After these initial questions, I would then vary the script depending on the person's specific role and the primary constraint he or she would most likely have encountered.[14] After transcribing, reading, and coding these interviews, I then proceeded to read, once again, every available issue of both newspapers over the same time period, 1985–90, and photocopied hundreds of additional articles for analysis as a result of my more nuanced appreciation of the tactics that I had learned about as a result of these interviews.

In addition to the articles published in both newspapers and these interviews, other extremely rich sources of information included the government legal proceedings involving the *Weekly Mail* and *New Nation*; these records were located in the library at the University of the Witwatersrand. The hundreds of pages of legal briefs and exhibits submitted by both the government and the attorneys representing these two newspapers, as well as the "warning letters" the government sent to the *Weekly Mail* and *New Nation* identifying specific articles "in violation" of the censorship restrictions, were particularly useful.

I had hoped to compare the original drafts of articles written by the journalists with the final drafts published in the newspaper after the attorneys had vetted them. This would have provided a rich source of information for analyzing specific tactics developed to subvert the censorship regulations. None of the writers I asked, however, had saved these drafts, partly because of the time that had elapsed but also because of security concerns. Moira Levy, who wrote for the *Weekly Mail*, explained, "I didn't keep anything like that. I didn't want to keep anything like that because you don't want that on your computer just in case you ever got a visit from the security police. You wouldn't want those records. If the lawyer decided [that you shouldn't] mention this person or don't mention this fact, it's best to eliminate it completely. So I wouldn't have kept that."

The attorney Norman Manoim, Irwin Manoim's brother who did legal work for *New Nation*, described an experience he had that validated Levy's concerns about keeping drafts of material that violated the restrictions.[15] He said,

> We tended to get rid of those things quite quickly. It would have been dan-
> gerous to have them around. I had a bad experience where my client took the
> thing back from us, didn't change the pamphlet, and the police found not only
> the pamphlet but our advice as to what they should remove. And they hadn't
> removed it. It was awfully embarrassing. So I tended to give telephonic advice
> and avoided writing those things down for that sort of reason—it could get into
> the wrong hands. I might have been over cautious, but I was certainly sort of
> chastened by that experience. . . . If there was a police raid, and the *New Nation*
> had a number of police raids—the danger was by no means remote.

The understandable security precautions that attorneys and journalists took to destroy previous drafts thus precluded me from conducting the kind of fine-grained analysis of articles that I had originally planned.[16]

CHAPTER OVERVIEW

The chapters that follow demonstrate the many ways in which the *Weekly Mail* and *New Nation* sought to circumvent the many legal constraints for the purposes of expanding their writing space. Chapter 1, "'That's How Nutty It Was': Media in Apartheid South Africa and the Birth of the *Weekly Mail* and *New Nation*," provides historical context essential for understanding the various tactics of resistance both newspapers used. After examining the apartheid government's obsession with presenting itself to the outside world as "legitimate," this chapter also focuses on the ways in which mainstream newspapers in South Africa engaged in self-censorship. It concludes with an overview of the *Weekly Mail* and *New Nation*: their origins, objectives, and target audiences.

Chapters 2 through 5 focus on the specific tactics of resistance developed by those working for these opposition newspapers. Chapter 2, "'In the Inter-

est of the Public': Utilizing Protected Spaces within the Apartheid Bureaucracy," examines how those working for these two newspapers exploited the
openings available within the South African government itself. Chapter 3,
"'Oblique Speak': Rhetorical Tactics for Constructing Meaning Subversively,"
focuses on the creative ways these opposition journalists used language to
imply certain meanings without explicitly stating them. Chapter 4, "'A Hope in
Hell': The Legal Approach of the *Weekly Mail*," focuses on the very aggressive
legal tactics developed by those working at the *Weekly Mail*. Chapter 5, "'The
Nats Believed in Legalism': *New Nation*'s Legal and Ideological Openings,"
focuses on the ways *New Nation* exploited the legal and ideological gray areas
of apartheid South Africa for the purposes of promoting anti-apartheid resistance more generally and the ANC specifically. Chapter 6, "'Make One Hell of
a Noise': The Struggle of *New Nation* and *Weekly Mail* to Stay Alive," examines when the government targeted these newspapers for closure. Specifically,
it focuses on how the more indirect and legal resistance of these newspapers
shifted at that point to resistance that was more direct and political.

The book concludes with a reflection on the tactics of resistance used by
these opposition journalists, the many accomplishments of the *Weekly Mail*
and *New Nation*, and the implications this story of resistance has for writers
in contexts as diverse as the former Soviet Union, Iraq, Iran, Chile, and the
United States. The fact that similar tactics of resistance have been used in
such disparate contexts reveals the ingenuity, or to use Scott's term, the "art"
of those who engage in resistance. In fact, in his book *Domination and the
Arts of Resistance*, Scott specifically invokes "opposition newspaper editors"
to reflect more broadly on the nature of resistance: "Like prudent opposition
newspapers editors under strict censorship, subordinate groups must find
ways of getting their messages across, while staying somehow within the law.
This requires an experimental spirit and a capacity to test and exploit all the
loopholes, ambiguities, silences, and lapses available to them. It means setting
a course at the very perimeter of what the authorities are obliged to permit
or unable to prevent" (139). This book tells the story of those who worked for
two opposition newspapers, the *Weekly Mail* and *New Nation*, who used writing for the purposes of contributing to one of the most compelling liberation
struggles of the twentieth century. In many ways it is a story of writing and
resistance is unique to that time and place; in many other ways, it is a story
that transcends that time and place as well.

1

"THAT'S HOW NUTTY IT WAS"

Media in Apartheid South Africa and the Birth of the *Weekly Mail* and *New Nation*

The crazy thing is that anybody coming to South Africa reading the news-papers and watching the media in the 1970s and early '80s would not know that somebody named Nelson Mandela existed. I mean, that's how nutty it was.

SHAUN JOHNSON, JOURNALIST FOR THE *WEEKLY MAIL*

For those who have even the most cursory knowledge of apartheid, it might seem obvious, perhaps abundantly so, that the South African government at that time was completely illegitimate. Consider the following. The government allowed only white South Africans to vote, and the white population, which represented only 21 percent of the total at its peak, had dropped to 16 percent by 1978 (Thompson 221). It was illegal for black South Africans, the vast majority of the population, to live in most areas of the country, approximately 80 percent, that had been designated for whites, unless they carried a pass indicating they had permission to do so. These passes had to be carried by black South Africans at all times. Failure to do so and/or failure to have passes in order could lead to arrest and/or deportation to their designated homeland—even if they had been born elsewhere and had never once set foot in their "homeland."

In the process of trying to enact its grand vision of a South Africa completely segregated by race, the historian Nigel Worden claims the apartheid government displaced approximately 3.5 million people between 1960 and 1983 "under Group Areas and Separate Development legislation" (111). He explains that "[f]orced removals on such a massive scale were the crudest signs of state power over black lives. In most cases those relocated to homelands were consigned to barren areas far removed from employment or adequate resources. Critics of apartheid labeled such actions as tantamount to genocide" (111). According to scholar Leonard Thompson, children in the homelands suffered malnutrition by the millions: "An Institute of Race Relations survey revealed in 1978 that 50 percent of all the two- to three-year-old children in the Ciskei were undernourished and that one in ten Ciskeian urban children and one in six Ciskeian rural children had kwashiorkor (a severe protein deficiency) and/or marasmus (a wasting disease ultimately induced by contaminated food" (203). Moreover, the infant mortality rate for black South Africans was extremely high: "[t]he official estimate of the African infant mortality rate in South Africa as a whole in 1974 was 100 to 110 per 1,000, which was worse than every country in Africa except Upper Volta (now Burkina Faso) and Sierra Leone" (203). In contrast to these dire statistics for black South Africans, white South Africans, particularly those with means, had access to some of the best health care in the world.

To maintain this system of vast inequality that caused suffering on such a massive scale, the apartheid government implemented, as noted, the pass system to control the movement of millions of black South Africans; banned entire political parties and countless individuals; arrested and detained thousands; used extensive violence, which included torturing those in detention, murdering activists in detention, and using death squads to assassinate political opponents; and enacted extensive censorship. In what world, one might rightly ask, could anyone possibly view such a government as legitimate?

Yet the apartheid government sought constantly to present itself both to white South Africans and to the rest of the world as legitimate. This idea, stupefying for many during apartheid and one that seems only more so with the passage of time, was nevertheless taken very seriously by white supporters of the South African government and by many of its conservative apologists in the West. True, the apologists argued, there were unsavory qualities of the apartheid government. But it was a government that held elections (for whites), allowed newspapers to criticize the government (within carefully circumscribed parameters), and perhaps most importantly, was virulently anti-communist.

For anti-apartheid activists, the government's efforts to portray itself as legitimate, and the fact that many in the West were willing publicly to accept this image, must certainly have been maddening. But it was precisely this feature of the apartheid government that those working for the *Weekly Mail* and *New Nation* were able to exploit so successfully in their efforts to expand their writing space. Every single tactic these newspapers used to circumvent the censorship restrictions was in some way rooted in the apartheid government's obsession with projecting an image of legitimacy.

In fact, the entire censorship machinery the apartheid government constructed must be viewed through this lens. André du Toit rightly described the nature of the censorship laws that existed in South Africa at the time as follows: "There can be no doubt about the effective function of this legalistic venture: it confers an aura of legitimacy on the workings of publications control which more forthright methods of political censorship lack. The authority of the law, the (apparent) discipline of judicial procedure and the (apparent) constraints of legal precedent and public accountability here serve different ends to that of their normal functions in the practice of the law: they are deliberately employed to give a veneer of legality to what is, and cannot but be, essentially political and ideological decisions" (122). Richard Abel cites a statement made in Parliament by a member of the Progressive Federal Party (PFP) that echoes this sentiment: "We must be one of the few countries in the world where so much pain is taken to clad authoritarianism in the elegance of legalistic jargon" (qtd. on 291). The closure of *New Nation* for three months and the *Weekly Mail* for one month, examined at length in chapter 6, demonstrates the delicate balance the apartheid government sought to strike between restricting writing space and maintaining the façade of legitimacy.

In many ways, the legal system of apartheid bears a striking resemblance to Václav Havel's description of "the law" in communist Czechoslovakia: "Like ideology, the legal code functions as an excuse. It wraps the base exercise of power in the noble apparel of the letter of the law; it creates the pleasing illusion that justice is done, society protected and the exercise of power objectively regulated. All this is done to conceal the real essence of post-totalitarian legal practice: the total manipulation of society" (*Power* 73). There is more than a little irony to the fact that the nature of law in apartheid South Africa and communist Czechoslovakia was so similar, given the South African gov-

ernment's claim, supported by many conservatives in the West, that the apartheid government served as a bulwark against the spread of communism.

Those working for both the *Weekly Mail* and *New Nation* were acutely
aware of the apartheid government's efforts to present itself as legitimate and,
more importantly, how they could actually *use* that official effort to expand
their writing space. Shaun Johnson explained: "There was a strange legalism. It [the government] always thought of itself as legitimate. Now that's
completely different from some kind of crazy dictator who is just murdering
people. They believed they were a legalistic state, and what they did, which
allowed young idiots like us to drive them mad, was that they tried to play it by
the book. Their book. And our lawyers were cleverer at it."

Drew Forrest concurred: "You know, one of the paradoxes of South Africa
is that because it was a limited democracy—democracy for whites—it wasn't
a completely autocratic system, and certain norms, journalistic norms, were
never entirely overthrown or violated. Even though they put in place all these
restrictions, [the fact that] we were still able to get around them sufficiently
for them to shut us down at one point is an indication that there was space—
there was space in which to maneuver." The apartheid government, which disenfranchised the overwhelming majority of South Africans, was of course an
illegitimate regime. But the fact that it was not "a completely autocratic system" for whites provided openings those working for these opposition newspapers used again and again to expand their writing space.

SELF-CENSORSHIP

The apartheid government constructed, in a phrase invoked repeatedly in the
scholarship on South African censorship, "more than 100 laws" designed to
restrict the publication of all kinds of information. Some of the more significant censorship-related laws enacted by the apartheid government included
the Suppression of Communism Act passed in 1950, later amended to become
the Internal Security Act in 1982; the Publications Act; the Police Act; the
Prisons Act; the Criminal Procedure Act; and the Key Points Act. A fuller discussion of each is contained in appendix A and will be discussed at greater
length in subsequent chapters.

These censorship statutes were extremely effective in circumscribing
writing space, specifically by creating a culture of self-censorship. A Commit-

tee to Protect Journalists report published in 1983 identifies this facet of the censorship restrictions: "In South Africa, such self-censorship is no accidental by-product of legal censorship. On the contrary, the government officials with whom the delegation spoke made it plain that they view the laws restricting the press primarily as instruments with which to guide self-censorship. Indeed, the laws of South Africa have fostered the creation of institutional mechanisms through which self-censorship takes place and through which it is regulated" (46). Anton Harber elaborated on this dimension of the censorship laws during an interview: "That was the nature of our censorship—it was postpublication censorship. That was the particular nature of South African censorship. It wasn't that they checked your copy beforehand and said 'yea or nay.' What you had to deal with was you could publish it, but then you had to anticipate the consequences of publishing. That's the way they worked. They made you self-censor by anticipating severe repercussions for publishing." The repercussions for not adhering to the guidelines were significant. Clive Cope recalled the government's actions when it determined that the *Weekly Mail* had not engaged in sufficient self-censorship. The government had issued a confiscation order for a particular edition of the *Weekly Mail* on a Friday morning, but the newspaper managed to get the newspaper out "in fifty to sixty trucks and different airplanes" before the confiscation order actually arrived. Cope and others at the newspaper thought they were in the clear, but as he recalled, this was not the case: "No way they could go and confiscate it out of every shop. But they did. They actually confiscated newspapers from shops." Of course, for those found guilty of repeated "violations," the government could simply close the newspaper.

This system led many in the mainstream media to act out of an abundance of caution. Harber examined this dynamic in an article published shortly after the fall of apartheid: "Inevitably, most of the country's media took the line of most likely survival: self-censorship based on the most cautious interpretation of the rules" ("Censorship" 150). Kerry Cullinan, a journalist for *New Nation*, echoed Harber's analysis: "You have these laws, which are really oppressive, and then people would go even one step below that because they were so scared of the laws." Given the levels of uncertainty and given the stakes, why not err, many reasoned, on the side of caution?

The apartheid government frequently acted in very blunt and crude ways, but its system of censorship was in fact quite shrewd. By cultivating a culture of self-censorship, it allowed the government to severely restrict writing space without showing its hand as overtly as other censorious regimes. In fact, Christopher Merrett notes that the regulations issued under the states of emergency actually "empowered the Minister to place censors in newspaper editors' offices" (*Culture* 121). Merrett's speculation as to why the minister chose not to utilize this power certainly rings true: "This he chose not to do, probably because of the poor international publicity which would have ensued, since it enabled him to argue that there was no censorship under the Emergency, and because he had other effective weapons at his disposal" (121). Even though the apartheid government had passed more than one hundred statutes to restrict the publication of information, and would supplement these laws with additional media regulations during the states of emergency, the fact that the government did not have officials designated to censor information prior to publication allowed it to argue, as Merrett observes, that South Africa had a "free" press: "For instance, Pik Botha, the South African Foreign Minister, appeared on US television in late June 1986 maintaining that the press was free" (262). These were precisely the arguments conservative apologists in the West would parrot to oppose more aggressive sanctions against the apartheid government.

There were, of course, many courageous individuals within the English-language anti-apartheid press who sought to resist self-censorship.[1] But there is a general consensus that even newspapers considered part of the "liberal" mainstream engaged in too many compromises. The Committee to Protect Journalists report of 1983 posed the following question to the National Press Union (NPU), the organization representing mainstream South African newspapers, about its willingness to sign agreements with the government to engage in self-censorship: "Accordingly, though the willingness of the NPU to sign such agreements is understandable, its judgment in doing so is simultaneously questionable. Might it not be better to require the government to use its punitive power to enforce its laws restricting the press? At least then the government would pay some price—in the form of public stigma—for restricting the press" (55).[2] The NPU's actions would seem to confirm André Brink's observation that "the most important ally of the oppressor in the act of oppression can be the collaboration of the oppressed himself" (qtd. in Merrett, *Culture* 144).

The Truth and Reconciliation Commission, quoted at length, was quite harsh in its assessment of the mainstream media during apartheid:

Evidence presented to the Commission tended to support what the Media Monitoring Project noted in its submission: "The English press, whilst predominantly positioning itself independently from the government, and significantly opposing the government in certain instances, continued to report within the political, social, and economic discourse defined by the apartheid state. The state legitimised itself within that discourse, and by not challenging its centrality or providing significant oppositional utterances to it, the English press wittingly or unwittingly validated the apartheid state." Thus, even though some of the media may have opposed the government, the social and political system created by apartheid was sanctioned by the media. The media analysed society from inside that system and did not provide alternative perspectives and discourses from the outside. (vol. 4, 186)

This criticism is particularly stinging. In short, the apartheid government could point to critical articles within the English-language anti-apartheid newspapers as evidence that South Africa had a "free press," but at the same time, these newspapers were ultimately circumscribed within parameters acceptable to the government. Merrett invokes Marcuse's idea of "repressive tolerance" to describe the apartheid government's approach to censorship: "A certain level of dissenting discourse was permitted, enough to encourage an image of a reasonably liberal society, while the influential channels of communication were denied" (*Culture* 7). In some ways, it was the worst of all worlds: the criticism provided by the liberal mainstream press was not sufficient to genuinely challenge or undermine the government and could be used, paradoxically, to enhance its legitimacy.[3]

Several journalists who worked in the mainstream media provided personal anecdotes regarding the timidity of the mainstream press. Moira Levy recalled,

I was at the *Star*. It wasn't only the state repression, it was the *Star*'s mode of operating. The *Star* bought into the censorship completely, very cautious, very conservative. It was staffed by other people who had recently come from Zimbabwe which had just been made independent . . . all conservative white men, who were running the show as they had done in the past. And it was virtually impossible to work under those circumstances. It wasn't only the state repression, it was the repression within the newsroom. It was very frustrating.

Reg Rumney claimed that the "liberal newspapers were slavish in their adherence to the law. Absolutely. I worked on them and I know. It was that kind of slavish adherence to the letter of the law that hampered the mainstream press." Pat Sidley explained why she worked at the *Weekly Mail* and was unwilling to work at the mainstream press: "On the grounds of feeding the crocodile: 'The government is going to do terrible things to us unless . . . ' And they compromised, absolutely, everything, all the way. Not as badly as SABC—I mean, they were just in with it. But the mainstream English press didn't fight hard enough."[4] Charlene Smith, who wrote for the *New Nation*, observed, "Censorship didn't just come from the government. It came from the newspapers."

Several journalists also commented on the working conditions and the racism they either experienced or observed at some mainstream newspapers. Ryland Fisher related his experiences at the *Cape Herald*: "The racism, the conservatism was very great, and I left eventually because I just got frustrated. Working in an environment where people would always look down on you, where your qualities and your abilities were never recognized, where you were always seen as an 'ethnic reporter.' You were never valued as a journalist." Kerry Cullinan, a white journalist, remembered the working conditions for black journalists: "Not to mention the way they used to treat black people. In some, there were even separate toilets in the newsroom."

In addition to the English-language anti-apartheid press that targeted white readers, there were also mainstream newspapers that targeted black readers. These publications, however, were white-owned and did not challenge the apartheid government. Kerry Cullinan described her experiences working at *City Press*: "So to work on a mainstream newspaper, *City Press*, even though it was aimed at black readers, it was owned by Nasionale Pers. They even appointed a 'publisher,' somebody they called a publisher, who was basically an in-house censor. And he would sit there and he would go through all the stories in the queue and all of that. So, to me, even though I was writing for an audience that obviously I would identify with, I didn't have freedom then, and I wasn't prepared to carry on under those conditions." While *City Press* may have focused more on issues relevant to black readers than newspapers targeting whites, it was not a "political" newspaper and actually hired "an in-house censor" to enforce self-censorship.

A tremendous gulf thus existed between the realities of life under apartheid for black South Africans, the overwhelming majority, and what appeared in mainstream newspapers. This gap had different implications for white and black audiences. For white audiences, the newspaper coverage shielded them from the horrors of apartheid and the massive amounts of violence the government was using to maintain it. Mainstream newspapers, for the most part, simply did not address the realities of a country with one of the largest wealth gaps in the world on the brink of revolution. Moira Levy, when comparing the content of the *Weekly Mail* with mainstream newspapers, observed, "The rest of the daily press was somewhere else on another planet."

For many black readers, mainstream newspapers had little credibility. Father Smangaliso Mkhatshwa explained that this was precisely why black South Africans so desperately needed a newspaper like *New Nation*: "We needed an alternative voice. . . . The mainstream media could not in any way be regarded as our voice. Even the English-speaking press, which by and large was regarded as liberal, by no stretch of the imagination could that be regarded as a mouthpiece of the oppressed people." An editorial appearing in the last issue of *New Nation* before it was banned by the government for three months succinctly captured how its coverage differed from that of mainstream newspapers: "For the *New Nation*, rent raids and the killing of unarmed victims of apartheid have weighed more heavily than the birth of sextuplets or an avalanche at a ski resort" ("Campaigning" 5).

Given these dynamics, I use the term "opposition press" in this book rather than "alternative press" or "alternative media." The *Weekly Mail* and *New Nation* were certainly providing an alternative reality than the one provided by mainstream newspapers, but the term "alternative" also carries connotations of "marginal" or "fringy." When one considers the demographics of South Africa and the political dynamics of the time, newspapers that sought to report on conditions affecting black South Africans certainly were not presenting an "alternative view" of South Africa. In fact, from a post-apartheid perspective, it would seem that mainstream newspapers at the time were the real alternative press. Tony Heard, the editor who courageously published an interview with Oliver Tambo and was subsequently charged by the apartheid government for doing so, lamented the gap between the realities taking place and the coverage in mainstream newspapers at the time: "Pictures of rugby and beauty queens have replaced township unrest on many front pages. . . . Now the darkness is almost complete" (qtd. in Merrett, *Culture* 137). Indeed, Shaun Johnson's observation, featured in the chapter epigraph, captures perfectly the surreal nature of mainstream newspaper coverage at that time: "The crazy thing is that anybody coming to South Africa reading the newspapers and watching the media in the 1970s and early '80s would not know that somebody named Nelson Mandela existed. I mean, that's how nutty it was."

STATES OF EMERGENCY AND MEDIA REGULATIONS

While the apartheid government was largely successful in controlling mainstream newspapers, it was not successful in containing widespread political protest. The government was able to maintain firm control during the 1950s, 1960s, and early 1970s, but it was rocked by the Soweto Uprising in 1976, an event that resulted in "at least 575" deaths (Thompson 213). After Soweto, political resistance continued to increase throughout the country, and in 1985 four well-known and respected political activists, the Cradock Four, were assassinated. Despite the government's denials of involvement, it was clear to most who was responsible for these murders. At a massive funeral held to honor the Cradock Four, a communist flag was unfurled as a public display of defiance. Partly in response to this gathering, the government declared a state of emergency on 21 July 1985.[5] The first state of emergency declared applied only to certain parts of the country and was intended as a temporary measure until "order" could be reestablished. Order, however, was never reestablished. Although the initial state of emergency did not include any regulations directly pertaining to the media, some of the journalists I interviewed described the palpable fear they felt at the time.[6]

The initial regulations enacted provided additional powers to the police to detain political activists, but even after thousands upon thousands of activists had been detained, resistance continued. The government, predictably, expanded the scope of subsequent emergencies to apply to the entire country and issued even more restrictions, including restrictions on the media to supplement the more than one hundred censorship statutes already in existence.

One of the primary objectives of these media regulations was to conceal the massive violence the government was using to maintain control. As Merrett observes, "[T]he State of Emergency sought to seal off the realities of apartheid from those who enjoyed its benefits . . . and covered up the truth about the

methods used to sustain apartheid" (*Culture* 117). J. M. Coetzee was particularly scathing in his analysis of how the apartheid government sought to shield
white South Africans from the horrors of apartheid: "The response of South
Africa's legislators to what disturbs the white electorate is usually to order it
out of sight. If people are starving, let them starve far away in the bush, where
their thin bodies will not be a reproach. . . . If the black townships are in flames,
let cameras be banned from them. (At which the great white electorate heaves
a sigh of relief: how much more bearable the newscasts have become!)" ("Into
the Dark" 361). The media restrictions were also designed to help combat
the public relations nightmare the apartheid government was experiencing
overseas, namely, images of white police officers brutalizing unarmed black
civilians.[7]

The media restrictions continued to grow in length, scope, and complexity
with each successive state of emergency. The regulations were several pages
long with some regulations containing sections, subsections, sub-subsections,
and sub-sub-subsections. Some of the many regulations prohibited reporters
from writing articles that did any of the following:

Describe "scenes of unrest"[8]

Contain "subversive statements"

"Promot[e] or [fan] revolution or uprisings in South Africa or other acts
    aimed at the overthrow of the government"

"Promot[e] or [fan] the breakdown of the public order in South Africa" (Coo-
    per et al., *Race Relations Survey: 1987/88* 826)

The very scope of these regulations rendered them virtually meaningless for
anyone who looked to them for actual guidance regarding the parameters
within which they could operate. Moreover, these restrictions, obviously
intended to reduce television coverage, were unfortunately quite successful.
According to Rob Nixon, "While South African resistance during this second
State of Emergency did decline, it fell nowhere near as sharply as American
coverage of the crisis which, by 1987, was a ghost of what it had been a year
before. Issue fatigue, the shutting down of cameras, and institutional timidity
combined to drive apartheid off the small screen" (82).

By 3 September 1986, the government had increased the scope of these
restrictions and actually forbade journalists from even being *present* at "scenes

of security action." The regulation read in part: "The orders also restricted, unless prior consent had been obtained, any journalist; news reporter ... for the purpose of gathering news material for distribution within or outside South Africa, from being on the scene or within sight of any unrest, restricted gathering, or security action" (Cooper et al., *Race Relations: 1986* 839). Sefako Nyaka, a journalist for the *Weekly Mail*, laughed during an interview at the absurdity of this particular regulation:

> Let's say as a journalist you go into a situation, and suddenly, there is stone throwing or looting. You know what was required of you? To turn, face the other way, and run in the opposite direction. That's basically what they said you should do. Now to me it was ridiculous [laughs]. I can't—this is my profession, that's my job. This is what I'm aiming to report—on these things. Now I would be conscious that if I am found on the scene, I may be shot, I may be arrested. And if you're lucky, you're not spotted, you go back to your office, and you write.

As Nyaka's comments reveal, journalists took significant risks simply by remaining at scenes of unrest.

The media statutes and regulations, of course, served a second important function: to silence opponents of the government. The regulation pertaining to "subversive statements" was particularly expansive.[9] Should a publication contain a statement deemed subversive, this regulation provided the minister of home affairs or the commissioner of the South African police with the power to "seize" it (Cooper et al., *Race Relations Survey: 1986* 842). The censorship statutes passed by Parliament, coupled with these media regulations issued during the states of emergency, led J. C. W. van Rooyen, chair of the apartheid government's Publications Appeal Board, to concede that "one is confronted [in South Africa] with the strictest forms of censorship in the Western hemisphere, because of censorship legislation and also because [of] the present emergency situation'" (qtd. in Powell, "Most Censored" 13).

The states of emergency provided the apartheid government with sweeping power, but they also posed the following dilemma: To what extent would the regulations diminish the government's already limited legitimacy? By the 1980s, this was more than just a point of pride for white supporters of the apartheid government; it had profound economic and political ramifications as well. The international anti-apartheid movement, with its threat of economic sanctions, posed a very real threat, and it required the apartheid government, as Drew Forrest observed, to be "sensitive to external opinion."

"LITTLE REASON FOR ANY OPTIMISM"

The political situation in South Africa in the mid- to late 1980s was bleak indeed. As André Brink observed in an essay published in 1988, "There is, in fact, very little reason for any optimism at all in South Africa today" ("Visions" 69–70). Violence within the country was spiraling out of control, international pressure on the South African government was increasing, and the government was digging in its heels. In a speech P. W. Botha delivered in 1985, one in which he was expected to announce important reforms to address the increased violence and instability, he delivered instead what is now referred to as the "Rubicon Speech" in which he blustered that the government would not be intimidated or yield. White South Africans, for the most part, supported Botha's hard line. Edward Perkins, the African American diplomat appointed by President Reagan to serve as the US ambassador to South Africa, observed that in May 1987 "the Nationalist Party put its mandate on the line and said, 'Here is our policy. Do you agree or disagree with it?' The vote was overwhelmingly for the Nats, and P. W. Botha was re-elected president. The message was simple: The Afrikaner government had dug in and would go no further" (361).[10]

To make matters worse, the president at the time was P. W. Botha. There are some historical figures, such as Nelson Mandela, who possess the intelligence, interpersonal skills, and imagination necessary for complex and fraught historical moments. P. W. Botha was not such an individual. As Brink noted in a 1988 essay, "P. W. Botha, ruled by his temper and his whims like any of the less stable emperors in the declining years of the Roman Empire, lacks both the intelligence and the knowledge to cope with an increasingly complex and violent situation" ("Visions" 69–70). The assessments of those who interacted with Botha are almost universally negative.[11]

This political turmoil and instability created extremely stressful conditions for journalists, particularly black journalists. A briefing paper written in 1989 and issued by the Index on Censorship claimed that being a black journalist in South Africa "must currently be one of the most hazardous jobs for any newsman in the 'free world'" (22). A Committee to Protect Journalists report published in 1983 explained why: "Many black journalists—especially those who achieve prominent positions in newspapers reaching large audiences or those who become leaders of the black press union, the Media Workers Association of South Africa (MWASA)—are banned, detained without charges, or prose-cuted and imprisoned. Those detained are treated harshly and, sometimes, they are confined in secret places for months before their families discover where they are held" (8).[12] Sefako Nyaka, a black journalist working for the *Weekly Mail*, explained: "Given the violence of any white policeman, or even black policeman, it would mean nothing for him to take out a black journalist, to kill him. But with a white [journalist], maybe they would think twice."

In fact, the police would not necessarily have had to pull the trigger them-selves if they wanted a black journalist killed. At that stage of the anti-apart-heid struggle, levels of fear and rage were boiling over in the townships, and some youth were engaging in acts of shocking violence against those consid-ered police collaborators.[13] As Nyaka explained, these conditions left black journalists living in the townships particularly vulnerable: "The other thing is that you would live in a community where there is total fear and people would really be so afraid. And given the fact that you now had this information [as a reporter], it would be very easy for [the police] to say, 'So and so is working for the police.' And once that happens, and you live in a township, you're gone. You're gone." Nyaka, in fact, eventually had to leave his home and live with David Dison, the attorney for the *Weekly Mail*: "The reason that I left my home in Soweto to live with David was because on several occasions these guys came to my house to look for me. They were not policemen, but they would leave a message to say I must stop writing all this nonsense or 'we're going to kill him.' That's how I left."

Shaun Johnson of the *Weekly Mail* agreed with Nyaka that white journal-ists, while facing genuine dangers and hardship, were never in as much danger as black journalists: "The security police said that if you put a bullet through Anton Harber's head, it's going to be an international story, whereas at that stage, some eighteen-year old kid, a black reporter, it wouldn't be the same thing. So they bore the brunt of it, the young black reporters. They really, really had it hard." Sarah Crowe also commented on how white South Africans had more protection than black South Africans: "I suppose, looking back, I don't think I was under any huge threat. We were arrested a few times, but it was nothing major. But there were whites, you know, taken in and being tortured. It did happen, but it was unusual, and so you were protected by your white skin in those days, without a doubt."

Although white journalists and activists had a degree of immunity that their black counterparts did not, this immunity was not complete. Irwin Manoim described the experience of Gavin Evans, a white journalist who wrote for the *Weekly Mail*:

> Gavin Evans was reasonably conspicuous in that he was the only person on our staff who drove a motorbike, and when he came down to get on his motorbike, [an assassin] was going to shoot him. For some reason, firstly, he didn't manage to shoot Gavin Evans, it's not quite clear why. And secondly, he suffered complete guilt and went to speak to Gavin Evans and confessed that he had been instructed to kill him. In fact, Gavin Evans wrote a story about confronting [him]: "My interview with the guy who was told to go out and kill me." [The assassin] himself disappeared or was murdered very shortly afterwards, probably because he confessed all to Gavin Evans.

In the case of Evans, it was never entirely clear if he was targeted for his political activities or his activities as a journalist. Again, Irwin Manoim: "In his case, he was also, many of the people were also activists, and it was hard to separate their journalism from their activism. He was very prominent in the anticonscription league, and that might have been a significant factor. Subsequently turned out that he was an ANC guerrilla as well." While the assassination attempt against Evans was not carried out, the government did assassinate David Webster, a white academic activist.[14]

Several journalists, white and black, described the constant fear of detention. Nyaka explained: "Because you know, always, you look over your shoulders. I was working in the streets in Johannesburg. I've heard of people being abducted whilst going to the shops or something like that, and to me, it was always a real threat that one day this would happen to me." Harber concurred: "There was obviously the constant threat of detention."[15] The threat of detention was particularly terrifying. By the late 1980s, torture was rife within apartheid prisons, and while many white South Africans may have chosen to shield themselves from this harsh reality, white and black journalists working for these opposition newspapers would have been keenly aware of the extent and severity of torture in apartheid prisons.[16]

In addition to the possibility of targeting individuals who worked for these newspapers, the government could also target the entire newspaper. Clive Cope explained: "We were lucky. I mean, a lot of institutions were bombed at the time, and we were really scared of bombs. We used to have quite good security on our premises, security companies that robbed us blind, with security guys who used to steal everything in the office. But we had to be wary." In addition to facing the fear of possible bombs, Sarah Crowe of *New Nation* recalled the day the police came to the newspaper's office: "I got in on that day to be met with a closed door. We had this sort of glass door in the office and the door was closed, which was very strange. And so I rattled it a bit and a policeman answered the door. He was very stern faced, brought me in, and closed the door behind him, and locked it, padlocked it, and then I saw some of my colleagues who were in there. We were effectively under arrest in our offices." Surmising that this action was intended to intimidate the staff of the newspaper, Crowe speculates that there were likely two additional reasons for this police action. First, it allowed them to search the files of *New Nation*: "I think the reason for wanting our files was to get names of activists. So they'd look on our computers, they had gone through our computers, that sort of thing, gone through our archives, looking for names of people. And they confiscated quite a lot of material." Crowe and others also assumed that the police were looking for Sisulu.[17]

The entire *Weekly Mail* staff was never detained in their offices in a similar manner, but Janet Wilhelm, a journalist for the newspaper, was visited by Craig Williamson, a member of the apartheid security forces, after she wrote an article in the very first issue of the *Weekly Mail* about the activities of the South African government in Mozambique. When I asked Irwin Manoim about Williamson's visit and whether this article had violated any censorship restrictions or whether this visit was primarily an intimidation tactic, he responded, "No, no, it was an intimidation tactic. There were all sorts of limitations about what you could say, but I doubt that would have fallen under it."[18]

Even if the journalists or these newspapers were not directly targeted by the government, the nature of their job obviously posed certain dangers. In addition to the danger of covering "scenes of unrest" where there was considerable violence, these journalists were constantly trying to interview and interact with the very activists targeted by the apartheid government. Nyaka recalled, "On several occasions, you'd find that you talk to somebody today and you find out the next day this person has been killed." Journalists were thus exposing themselves to considerable danger simply by the nature of the stories they were writing and the sources on whom they relied.[19]

BIRTH OF THE *WEEKLY MAIL* AND *NEW NATION*

It was within this tumultuous and terrifying context that the *Weekly Mail* and *New Nation* were founded. The *Weekly Mail* began publishing in June 1985, one month prior to the first state of emergency declared, on 21 July 1985, and *New Nation* began publishing regularly in January 1986, six months later. At one level, of course, these newspapers shared important similarities. Both sought to defy the censorship restrictions as much as possible to expose the government's use of violence and also to convey the harsh realities for black South Africans under apartheid. But these newspapers were also quite different in terms of their objectives and primary audiences, and this, in turn, led them to develop some distinct tactics in their effort to expand their writing space.

Weekly Mail

The *Weekly Mail* was born shortly after the closure of the *Rand Daily Mail* and the *Sunday Express*, two liberal mainstream newspapers. Their closure, particularly that of the *Rand Daily Mail*, was simply devastating to many progressive white South Africans. There was a pervasive sense that something needed to fill this void, but the central questions were what would fill it, who would do it, and how they would do it. Irwin Manoim, thirty years old at the time, and Anton Harber, twenty-six, were the first to respond. Moira Levy, when reflecting on the founding of the *Weekly Mail* during such a turbulent and repressive time, stated, "I thought the *Weekly Mail* had such chutzpah for trying to come out under those circumstances. The chutzpah appealed to me enormously."[20]

While the *Weekly Mail* very self-consciously sought to position itself as the successor of the *Rand Daily Mail*, there were significant differences. First, the *Weekly Mail* would have fewer pages and reach a much smaller audience. Second, the *Weekly Mail* was considerably more politically progressive than the *Rand Daily Mail*. Prior to joining the *Rand Daily Mail*, Harber explained, he and many of the other younger journalists who came to work at the newspaper had been involved with student political organizations, such as the National Union of South African Students (NUSAS), which were considered part of the white Left. This was something the editors of the *Rand Daily Mail*, in Harber's words, "would have sneered at." He explained: "We went to the *Rand Daily Mail* and the *Sunday Express* because we were given the space. You know they were the open-minded newspapers, but they were definitely positioned in what was then quite a conservative liberal position—still believed that the future lay in parliamentary politics, and politics meant what was in the Progressive [Federal] Party, the PFP. We were to the left of that." According to Harber, while he and others like him worked at the *Rand Daily Mail*, they "were never that comfortable in that environment."

When Harber and Manoim started the *Weekly Mail*, they no longer faced these constraints. Reg Rumney, who wrote for the *Weekly Mail*, stated that the newspaper "wasn't a substitute for the *Rand Daily Mail*—it was one strand of the *Rand Daily Mail* that had been reincarnated, as it were, together with some young blood, fresh thinking." Shaun Johnson claimed that Harber and Manoim took the "liberal" tradition of the *Rand Daily Mail* and "radicalized it." In addition to its more politically progressive orientation, the *Weekly Mail* also engaged in much less self-censorship. Reg Rumney explained: "The *Weekly Mail* pushed the laws as far as it could go and it disobeyed those laws it felt were immoral, which is what was happening in the eighties for those people who had a conscience." Harber attributed this to the impulses guiding the student movements that he and others had participated in: "You must see that we came from a tradition of defiance."

The *Weekly Mail* thus became an extremely attractive newspaper for many journalists in the mainstream media. Some, of course, were motivated by very practical and pragmatic concerns: the newspapers for which they had previously worked had been closed. But there were compelling idealistic reasons as well. Patrick Laurence, for example, explained how he was initially not paid for the articles he wrote for the newspaper but nevertheless continued to write anyway: "I think it would be true to say that I felt, without trying to present myself as excessively motivated solely by idealism, I felt some sort of obligation to help sustain the faith, as it were, in an alternative South Africa. Obviously, there were other factors, but I think that was a factor in my thinking. Surely it related to a lot of people." Moira Levy, when asked why she worked for the newspaper, explained:

> Why write? Because there was a need to cover what was happening, there was a need to try and tell what was happening. I mean it sounds a bit pretentious now, but there was a kind of idealism at that time. This was a very evil country then. Journalism was an exciting thing. I got swept up in the feeling of the

times. And there were things that needed to be written about. During those mid-eighties, when the country was in turmoil, to be there and observing it, and documenting it, was—what's the word I'm looking for? It was an absolute privilege.

Sefako Nyaka, when asked why he wanted to write for the *Weekly Mail*, responded that he wanted to be with a "group of people that championed the cause which I believed was just. So I guess I went to the *Weekly Mail* because I believed that this is one way in which I could help, together with other people, in pursuing a just dispensation for this country." Charlotte Bauer explained: "I was young enough and poor enough to think anything was possible."

This idealism was certainly important given the amount of work necessary to produce this newspaper. As Clive Cope explained, "I think the mission far outstripped any monetary rewards we got. We worked so many hours, it didn't matter. You couldn't measure—I mean, they worked through the nights on these Thursday nights—they worked through the nights, the editors. So that's a Thursday night, and Friday, the paper was out. And then you could just field the calls about problems with distribution."[21]

Despite the incredibly long hours and the extreme stress of working for an opposition newspaper targeted by the government, there was another defining feature of working at the *Weekly Mail*: fun. According to Pat Sidley, "It was what we all believed in. The first state of emergency had been announced as the *Rand Daily Mail* closed, so it was an issue about getting news out. It was a moral obligation." She smiled and then added, "And it was fun!" Despite the extraordinary stress these opposition journalists operated under, it was clear from interviews, as well the pages of the *Weekly Mail* itself, that there was also a spirit of playfulness at this newspaper. Indeed it was one of its defining features.

The *Weekly Mail*'s front page of the 12 December 1986 edition offers an excellent example. Harber explained that as the editors and attorneys were poring over the regulations, looking for loopholes, they kept coming across a statement that it was possible to write about forbidden topics if "permission" was obtained from the appropriate governmental minister. The editors' response: publish the "unlisted phone number of every cabinet minister" (Manoim, *Warned* 72). The first portion of this front-page headline read, "Should you intend discussing any of the following topics: Security force action, Boycotts, The treatment of detainees, The release of any detainee, 'People's courts,' Street Committees," and the second portion of the headline instructed, "Simply phone these numbers to ask for permission" ("Emergency Made Simple" 1). Beneath this headline was a list of all the ministers' telephone numbers, including that of the state president, P. W. Botha; the minister of foreign affairs, Pik Botha; the minister of defence, Magnus Malan; the minister of law and order, Adriaan Vlok; and the head of the National Intelligence Service, Niel Barnard. When asked about this front page, Harber responded, "We were trying to show the ridiculousness of the regulation by being kind of funny about it. I think that's probably what drove it: how to get across the ludicrousness of these regulations without saying that to people." The *Weekly Mail* also used several visual gimmicks as a means of ridiculing the restrictions. Harber describes one in an article he wrote after apartheid: "The *Weekly Mail* once ran a join-the-dots picture of security force action with the caption: '*Don't* join the dots. If you do, you will get an illegal picture'" ("Censorship" 152).

When asked about the pervasiveness of humor within the pages of the *Weekly Mail*, many attributed it to Irwin Manoim. Harber stated, "I think a lot of that is Irwin's sense of humor." Shaun Johnson agreed: "Irwin deserves tremendous credit. He just had an elliptical brain that came up with ways of saying to this scary state, 'Fuck you.' But we did it with a sense of humor, which kind of got some public sympathy for us." James Scott quotes Alexander Herzen regarding the subversive nature of humor in oppressive contexts: "Laughter contains something revolutionary. . . . Only equals may laugh. If inferiors are permitted to laugh in front of their superiors, and if they cannot suppress their hilarity, this would mean farewell to respect" (172). Indeed, its irreverent attitude was one of the *Weekly Mail*'s defining characteristics. As Merrett notes, "The *Weekly Mail* became skilled at drawing attention to censorship without infringing the regulations, and simultaneously raised the spirits of its supporters by adopting a mocking attitude towards the authorities" (*Culture* 142). By all accounts, there was not much to cheer about during those dark days of the emergency. The *Weekly Mail*'s irreverent sense of humor was profoundly encouraging for its readers.

In terms of its purpose, the *Weekly Mail* was quite clear about its role. While it was to the left of the *Rand Daily Mail*, it was politically independent and did not overtly support any specific party. In a letter sent to potential investors, Harber and Manoim emphasized that the newspaper would be "non-partisan and non-polemical. It will not, in general, carry an editorial comment. Its policy will be broadly critical of the status quo in South Africa, but without affiliation to any political party or organisation. It will concentrate on critical, independent analysis, rather than in pursuing a particular 'line'" (qtd. in Manoim, *Warned* 5). Keyan Tomaselli and Eric Louw note that this feature fundamentally differentiated the *Weekly Mail* from other opposition newspapers, including *New Nation*: "In contrast, *Weekly Mail* criticised both the apartheid State and left-wing mistakes. This position inevitably produced tension on occasion between the paper and left-wing activists" (7).

The "tension" that existed between the *Weekly Mail* and ANC was indeed significant and complex. Reg Rumney described most writers for the *Weekly Mail* as "ANC sympathizers in most cases rather than ANC supporters." Shaun Johnson concurred: "I think most of us were ANC sympathizers, but more than anything else, we wanted their views to be reflected. . . . What used to drive us utterly nuts was a world in which particularly whites, but others as well, were living in complete unreality, in denial about who the majority actually was and what the ANC was actually doing." In short, Harber and Manoim were willing to take risks by publishing information about the ANC because they believed that South Africans, particularly white South Africans, needed to know about a political party founded in 1912 that had considerable support among South Africans, particularly black South Africans, and that ANC leaders, such as Mandela, were viewed by many as the rightful leaders of South Africa. The *Weekly Mail*'s intent in publishing stories about the ANC, therefore, was less about "promoting the ANC" and more about promoting reality.

There were multiple, complex layers in the relationship between the *Weekly Mail* and the ANC over the years. As noted in the introduction, Gavin Evans, the *Weekly Mail* journalist targeted by the apartheid government for assassination, was secretly a member of the ANC. Reg Rumney mentioned during his interview that Evans "never told Anton [Harber] about that! [laughs]." Howard Barrell, with whom I conducted several interviews, was also a member of the ANC and consciously sought to use his journalism as a means of promoting the ANC. Harber and Manoim were unaware of this as well, but there was a confluence of interest for both parties concerning the articles Barrell was writing. Barrell wanted to promote the ANC; Harber and Manoim wanted to report seriously about the ANC. As an ANC operative, Barrell was able to write penetrating articles about the organization because of his access to the highest levels of ANC leadership: Thabo Mbeki, Ronnie Kasrils, and Mac Maharaj. These articles were not overtly propagandistic but rather serious reports on the organization, which, from Barrell's perspective, was an indirect but important means of promoting the ANC. Barrell was thus using the *Weekly Mail* to advance his objectives; Harber and Manoim were using Barrell to advance theirs.

To make matters even more complicated, the *Weekly Mail* was the newspaper that eventually exposed the abuses of the so-called "Mandela Football Club" operating under Winnie Mandela's supervision. The shocking revelations of kidnapping, torture, and murder carried out by members of this "club" made international headlines and significantly discredited Winnie Mandela and, by extension, the ANC itself. According to Manoim, the publication of this exposé caused a tremendous amount of bad blood at the time between the *Weekly Mail* and certain prominent factions within the ANC, and those tensions lingered well after South Africa had made its transition to democracy.[22]

Manoim elaborated on how the type of journalism practiced at the *Weekly Mail* differed from the advocacy journalism practiced by other opposition newspapers at the time: "In the South African context, it was about whether you were inside the struggle and a disciplined member of an ANC-aligned organization, or if you saw yourself as outside that."[23] The newspaper may not have been overtly aligned with the ANC, but by publishing thoughtful, serious articles about it, the *Weekly Mail* certainly helped to promote it, especially given the government's cartoonish depiction of the ANC as a terrorist organization controlled by communists. At the same time, however, the *Weekly Mail* probably did more than any other newspaper to damage the reputation of the ANC when it published its articles on the Mandela Football Club. The credibility of these articles was heightened, of course, precisely because the *Weekly Mail* had previously reported about the ANC with such seriousness.

Based on the reader surveys compiled by Marilyn Kirkwood, the newspaper's advertising director, a large segment of the *Weekly Mail*'s audience consisted of politically progressive whites with high levels of formal education, and a significant number of them were financially comfortable. While many South African whites were not interested in reading about the realities of apartheid, there were those who were, and they enthusiastically embraced the *Weekly Mail*. In terms of black readership, the newspaper had no hard data from its reader surveys, as Manoim explains in his book:

> And race? We did not ask the race question. It took days of soul-searching, but in the mid-eighties, asking people their race was akin to making them fill out an apartheid form. A colour-blind newspaper should not care about the race

of its readers. But in truth, we did care, we wanted to know whether we were reaching black readers. It was not until the nineties that we were able to ask the "race" question, and it told us that two out of five readers were black, and they earned the same salaries as their white counterparts. (*Warned* 47)

The findings from the reader surveys conducted in the 1990s support anecdotal evidence that the *Weekly Mail* had a sizable black readership in the early years. Sefako Nyaka shared the following observation in response to my question about the *Weekly Mail*'s audience:

> I think gradually, lots of black people began to see the *Weekly Mail* as the paper that they could trust. You see, in the townships, the life-span of a single copy of the *Weekly Mail* was about a week or two, because it would travel, it really would travel. I wouldn't be surprised if [as many] as fifty people had a single copy of that paper. You'd find people talking to you about a story that they had read, and the economic conditions that this person finds him- or herself in wouldn't allow this person to spend *x* amount of money to go and buy this paper. So obviously this person must have borrowed the paper from somebody.

He concluded, "I think we reached a lot of black people."

Nyaka's observations about the limited purchasing power of many black South Africans identifies a profound structural challenge the *Weekly Mail* and many other opposition newspapers faced. It was the same challenge that contributed to the closure of the *Rand Daily Mail*: attracting "too many" black readers. As Joel Mervis writes in *The Fourth Estate*, between 1957 and 1981, under the leadership of "three liberal editors, Gandar, Louw, and Sparks," the *Rand Daily Mail*'s readership profile "changed radically, from a three to one majority of white readers to a three to one majority of black readers" (495). Mervis notes that this kind of readership spelled financial doom for the newspaper: "The two directors said the problem with the *Rand Daily Mail* was that its readership profile had gone awry. It had too many black readers. It was too strident. It alienated whites, especially businessmen and housewives" (510). Later in the same chapter, Mervis writes, "By October 1982 the picture was gloomier than ever. Surveys in 1981 and 1982 showed that *The Citizen*'s white readership had increased by 8,1 per cent; the *Rand Daily Mail*'s had dropped by 13 per cent. These and other statistical findings forced Kinsley to tell the board: 'The only conclusion to be drawn from all these facts, is that the *Rand*

Daily Mail has ceased to be a viable advertising medium'" (512). And once the *Rand Daily Mail* ceased to be a viable advertising medium for whites, it ceased to be a medium. There has been speculation that the government exerted pressure to close the *Rand Daily Mail*, but even if it did, there was no denying the fact that the newspaper was losing massive amounts of money because of its readership and that the situation had dire implications for its advertising revenue.[24]

Harber discussed how these market forces shaped his role as a journalist at the *Rand Daily Mail* before it closed: "I know certainly in my last year or two at the *Rand Daily Mail*, I was a political reporter and I faced a constant battle with an editor who told me that I was writing too much about black politics." When questioned further about this dynamic, Harber responded, "I suppose it was partly—it [the *Rand Daily Mail*] was under huge pressure, under threat of closure, and so they were really looking to go out to build white inroads, for better or for worse. That was the reality they faced and the strategy they chose to try to survive. It failed, but that gives you an indication of where we were positioned." In addition to the staggering constraints imposed by the government, therefore, newspapers faced significant financial constraints that made it challenging to cover the political, economic, and social realities of black South Africans.

Indeed there was a pervasive sense among many within South Africa at the time that there was a zero-sum game in terms of appealing to black and white audiences: increasing the black audience would by definition decrease the white audience. In one of its earliest editions, the *Weekly Mail* published the following letter to the editor: "Your first issue was uninteresting and irritating: politics, politics, politics, black aspirations, black culture, black politics. Clearly the old *Rand Daily Mail* recipe is being dished out again and will again be the cause of failure. Do me (and the other readers) a favour: reduce your black interest feature to a single page with book reviews, historical features, anthropology, medicine, psychology, music, religious issues, commerce, long letters columns and other topics to engage an inquiring mind" (Goshen 14). Another letter expressed similar sentiments: "I give your paper one year, no more. Because you make the same mistake as the *Rand Daily Mail*. Can't you understand, in South Africa all black people hate all white people and all white people scorn black people? Exactly as French people hate Arabs and Jews in France. You can do nothing. You waste your time" (Paris 10). This racism was not confined to readers of newspapers. Charlene Smith recalled the statement an editor at a mainstream newspaper once made about one of her articles: "Not another kaffirs-in-the-rain story, Charlene."

There were many South Africans, however, who were deeply distressed by this racial divide, as revealed in another letter sent to the *Weekly Mail*: "The communication gap in South Africa was, for me, summed up in a Johannesburg street some weeks ago. A news vendor had tied two posters to a lamp post. One, a well-read 'white' evening newspaper, was represented by the heading about the latest state-of-squabble on the Aussie rugby tour. The other 'black' daily, was represented by the heading 'Cop kills Mayor's son.' Hopefully, the *Weekly Mail* will help bridge that frightening gap" (Judge 10). This situation presented a seemingly vicious cycle to progressive-minded newspapers: advertising revenue was the lifeblood of newspapers, and advertisers sought publications that appealed to readers with purchasing power. In apartheid South Africa, white South Africans possessed the vast majority of wealth— and stories about the experiences of black South Africans to many whites, as the letters above demonstrate, were considered "uninteresting," even "irritating." One of the *Weekly Mail*'s main objectives, therefore, was to "bridge [the] frightening gap" that existed in apartheid South Africa.

New Nation

The birth of *New Nation* was a project years in the making. One of the most important figures in this process was Smangaliso Mkhatshwa, a black Catholic priest who had been harassed, imprisoned, and tortured by the apartheid authorities.[25] During one of his several detentions by the apartheid authorities, Mkhatshwa met Gabu Tugwana, a black journalist who had worked for various South African newspapers. According to Sarah Crowe, who participated in the founding of *New Nation*, "The first person we employed was Gabu Tugwana, who had been in prison with Mkhatshwa and they had shared a cell. So Smangaliso had always said to Gabu that, you know, one day, they'd make a difference. They'd get a paper, they'd do something, and he [Tugwana] would have a part in it. So Gabu started up initially as sports editor and then did other things after that." Indeed he did: after Sisulu was abducted from his home by apartheid security forces and detained for two years, Tugwana essentially served as acting editor.

The plan, in short, was to use money from the Catholic Church to fund an alternative newspaper that would target black South Africans. Mkhatshwa eventually assumed important leadership roles within the Catholic Church hierarchy. He used this position to help secure funding for *New Nation*, without which, quite simply, it could have never survived in apartheid South Africa.[26]

Once the funding had been obtained, it was then necessary to hire an editor. Sarah Crowe explained how Zwelakhe Sisulu was recruited and why he was the ideal candidate for the position:

> Zwelakhe at that stage was at Harvard. So while I was on my fundraising trip to various Catholic and other aid organizations around the world, I stopped in at Harvard and persuaded Zwelakhe to take the job. This was in about May of '85. He returned in August/September and then took up this position. All the other newspapers were edited by white editors who were, although liberal and spoke out, came from a very white WASP, northern suburbs Johannesburg private school type of background and did not, we felt, really understand the struggles that black people were having to face, which is why we felt we needed to get somebody like Zwelakhe as editor.

In addition to his considerable journalism experience, Sisulu came from a political family that, with the possible exception of the Mandelas, was the family most closely identified with the ANC. Zwelakhe's mother, Albertina, had been active in the struggle for decades and had helped to organize some of South Africa's most historic anti-apartheid protests, including the 1956 Women's March. Zwelakhe's father, Walter, had been imprisoned on Robben Island and was Mandela's closest confidant. Many of those interviewed, such as Kerry Cullinan, also commented on Sisulu's impressive personal qualities, specifically noting the impact his detention had on the newspaper: "Taking Zwelakhe was a big blow. He was a brilliant strategist."

Whereas the *Weekly Mail* was a more radical version of the *Rand Daily Mail* with a smaller audience, *New Nation* was something fundamentally new. There were, as noted above, newspapers that targeted black readers, but they were owned by major publishing houses in South Africa that were not political and were very cautious in terms of the censorship restrictions. Because *New Nation* was funded by the Catholic Church, which essentially provided the newspaper with almost complete autonomy, the editors and journalists of this newspaper could more aggressively challenge the censorship restrictions without fear of a crackdown from management and/or fear that the content was "scaring" white readers and advertisers. *New Nation,* therefore, had an editor from one of the most prominent anti-apartheid families in South Africa who had extensive journalism experience running a newspaper that consisted mostly of black journalists who were targeting a black audience. In short, a newspaper such as *New Nation* had never existed before in apartheid South Africa.

New Nation also adopted certain practices that made it unique as a newspaper. There were, for example, no bylines attached to articles to identify the journalist. This was done for two reasons. First, many at *New Nation* noted that the lack of bylines reflected the collective orientation the newspaper sought to promote. The lack of bylines was also related, as Amrit Manga explained, to other concerns: "There was another reason as well, which was security reasons. Intense repression at that point. And we were very careful not to expose ourselves."[27]

Similar to the *Weekly Mail* staff, many journalists working at *New Nation* explained the tremendous appeal of their roles at this newspaper. Manga, for example, had been the economics writer at *Business Times*: "There was certainly a greater scope to express myself in papers such as the *New Nation* than the *Business Times*." He explained how he sought to carve out as much space for himself as he could at *Business Times* concerning labor issues but that it had been quite challenging:

> Even within those confines, I would actually push the limits there and see how far I could go. I would take a view that would be sympathetic to the strikes. Obviously, you had a situation where workers were grossly underpaid, a history of cheap labor policies, and nine times out of ten, the workers were engaged in a legitimate strike. The demand was legitimate for a living wage, and that's the way I would write it. *New Nation* emerged in a situation where there was a need to present an alternative view. And I got a call from Zwelakhe one day telling me, "Why don't you write labor for us?" Great. What gets chucked out of my stories at *Business Times* will get in at *New Nation*.

Manga described the profoundly different experience of working at *New Nation* as compared to other newspapers for which he had worked: "There was absolute freedom. I was never, ever—my work was edited for professional reasons—but never politically. There was never political censorship at *New Nation.* So in a sense, I was spoiled! [laughter]."

Drew Forrest also discussed the latitude *New Nation* provided journalists: "I mean I worked for the *Star*, also as a sub [editor], and they had three people, sort of top-table people, whose sole job was to go through stories and cut out anything which might, you know, which might infringe on the regulations. So there, the idea was to be as safe as possible. At *New Nation*, the idea was to run as many risks as you can get away with." Tyrone August agreed: "All of us, people like Zwelakhe, worked for mainstream newspapers. Gabu [Tugwana] worked for *Rand Daily Mail* at one stage. Amrit Manga, he worked for the [*Business Times*]. We all didn't come from nowhere. We came from other newspapers. And we joined *New Nation* because we saw *New Nation* as giving us space, that room, to publish material that other newspapers didn't publish."

The primary audience of *New Nation* and its multiple objectives were inextricably linked. In terms of audience, *New Nation* was read by some progressive whites but was overwhelmingly read by black South Africans. Kerry Cullinan described the audience of the newspaper: "Well, the readers were mainly black South Africans. I would say working-class people. We never ever were racially specific, though, about who we aimed at. It was people who wanted to know what was happening. But the white readership was very small. The white progressives or liberals tended to read the *Weekly Mail*, and the vast majority of our readers were black." Drew Forrest provides a slightly different perspective regarding the newspaper's white audience but fundamentally agrees that the primary audience was black South Africans, specifically those in leadership positions: "I mean quite a lot of white people did read it. I think the sort of left-wing whites read it. But my impression was that it basically went out to the kind of politicized and intellectual component of the black community: the trade union leadership, community activists, civic leaders—it was probably read by people in exile." Mkhatshwa concurred, noting that the newspaper would have been geared particularly to those "in the leadership of the liberation movement, people involved in the cities, people involved in professional activities, [and] people in the church." Kerry Cullinan added that the newspaper was particularly popular with labor activists: "You know, there were lots of union offices around. [*New Nation*] would be sold on the streets, and you'd see people buying it because there was good labor coverage." *New Nation* thus targeted the leadership within black political and labor circles and consciously sought to position itself as a "progressive" rather than a "populist" newspaper.[28]

Yet another crucial decision for *New Nation*: language. What language should the newspaper use, given the many languages spoken in South Africa? Currently South Africa has eleven official languages: English, Afrikaans, Ndebele, Northern Sotho, Sotho, Swazi, Tsonga, Tswana, Venda, Xhosa, and Zulu. Language, a profoundly politically charged issue in apartheid South Africa, was thus a vexing consideration for *New Nation*. Ultimately, those at the newspaper decided English was the best choice. In addition to the fact that trying to publish the newspaper in multiple languages would increase costs considerably, English was selected, as Amrit Manga explained, for political reasons as well:

> We took the cue from what had happened in Mozambique. FRELIMO (Mozambique Liberation Front), after the liberation there, they made it very clear that they were going to use the colonial language to unite the people. So Portuguese there, a colonial language, was in fact a uniting factor. Ironically. In the same way, English was in fact a uniting factor because English would have been spoken by someone in the Zulu community, would be spoken by someone in the Sotho community, they would all speak English, right? There was a unifying factor. So English, in that sense, we recognized it as a nation builder, which is why we chose it.

Publishing in English, therefore, while not ideal, was considered the least-worst option.[29]

In terms of its objectives, *New Nation* had several. One mentioned repeatedly by those I interviewed was to provide a "voice" for those who did not have one. Smangaliso Mkhatshwa explained that the newspaper was one that could "speak on behalf of the voiceless people." Sisulu noted that *New Nation* had to be "a voice for those people who were voiceless." And Ryland Fisher noted, "It was to give a voice to people who did not have a voice. It was meant to reflect the true story of people whose stories were just not reflected in the mainstream newspapers at the time. The big newspapers in South Africa were traditionally produced by white journalists, for white readers, for white advertisers, etc. They completely ignored the story of the people out in the townships." *New Nation* deliberately and consciously sought to make visible that which had been largely invisible in the mainstream media.

Another important objective of *New Nation*: education. This objective included everything from trying to provide basic academic skills (writing, math, science) and health tips, as well as radically different historical narratives of South Africa. Most of this education occurred within a section entitled "Learning Nation." This educational dimension of *New Nation* was directly tied, as Drew Forrest explained, to the target audience:

> There was a health section [in "Learning Nation"], which was all about health issues and problems that were relevant to black people. So, for example, I can remember writing a column about snakebites. In rural areas, it's an issue for rural people about what to do if you're bitten by a snake and you're miles from the nearest clinic. I don't know how useful it would have been, quite honestly, but it was a gesture in that direction. And you know, I remember we did one on amoebic dysentery. Let's provide—this is a health column for black people. We're not going to write about a quadruple bypass operation and that sort of thing because it's not relevant.

Forrest's reference to a "quadruple bypass operation" is an allusion to the fact that white South Africans, as noted above, had access to some of the best health care in the world at the time. In fact, the first successful heart transplant ever performed took place at Groote Schuur Hospital in Cape Town. For black communities in the townships or in rural areas struggling with diseases often stemming from malnutrition or lack of access to clean water, articles about a successful heart transplant would have been as relevant to their lives as articles about health care procedures on Mars.

The final objective of *New Nation*, and perhaps its defining feature: to actively mobilize resistance among black South Africans against the apartheid regime. *New Nation* embraced "advocacy journalism," which consisted of a variety of tactics. After listing several of the newspaper's objectives, Manga explained how *New Nation* sought "to expose the tyranny of apartheid. What is happening in our prisons, detainees, especially women detainees, as part of their interrogation, getting raped. People getting beaten up. People being detained. So we reflected all those things, that [apartheid] was tyranny, it was a gross violation of human rights."[30] Journalists not only sought to reveal the facts of such abuses but many also described how they actively sought to stir the emotions of readers, a dynamic discussed further in chapter 5. Manga explained that the emotional tone of many stories not only reflected how journalists themselves felt about the situation but it was also used so that readers could "identify with what is happening."

One way the newspaper sought to mobilize black South Africans was by serving as a link for communities throughout the country. Manga commented on this role at length:

> We had to inform people about what was happening. It was important that people didn't have the impression that their struggles were isolated. So you had a community that's struggling around the issue of clean water. They would struggle around the issue and because it's such an isolated community, the struggle seemed specific to them. But people all over the country were struggling around these kinds of issues. And that's what we tried to highlight. People in one factory fighting starvation wages, it wasn't just that factory—there were people elsewhere, in the mines. Expose the working conditions. It wasn't specific to one area. So we tried to give that perspective that this is a national problem. Obviously, that helped bring people together if [they] understand [they] have a common struggle.

Sisulu captured this role eloquently by describing *New Nation* as "a transporter of shared experience":

> And what I mean by that was that there were struggles that were taking place at a very basic level and we wanted people throughout the country to understand that the struggles they were involved in were not as highly localized as they believed but that this, in turn, was a national phenomenon. So I would say that really what the *New Nation* sought to do was basically to get people to share their experiences and understand that in fact what was happening was a national moment rather than a highly individualized or highly localized moment.[31]

Mkhatshwa highlighted this role as well: "The reality is that South Africa is quite a big country. People wanted to be informed about what was happening [not only] in the areas like Johannesburg, Soweto, and so on, but also Durban, Port Elizabeth, and others. So therefore we wanted to disseminate information, to share information about what the activists were doing." *New Nation* thus served as vital communication link for activists operating in different parts of South Africa.

In terms of *New Nation*'s relationship with the ANC, it was much less fraught than the *Weekly Mail*'s. Those interviewed described it as follows: *New Nation* overtly tried to promote the ANC, there was contact between members of *New Nation* and the ANC, but there was never a formal relationship between the two. Sarah Crowe, when reflecting on the ways that *New Nation* differed from other black publications, noted the following: "Where we were coming from, if you like, was a more ANC progressive camp. Having Zwelakhe as its editor, it is inevitably going to look like an ANC newspaper. It was not meant to be an ANC newspaper. But of course, our sympathies, of any political group, it would have [been] with the ANC." Cullinan concurred: "And it was never, ever overtly an ANC mouthpiece, and I don't think anybody considered it that. But the ANC was banned at that stage—it couldn't speak for itself. So we could report on ANC positions and views without saying these are ANC positions and views. *Ja*, it was very close to the United Democratic Front and so on." Other scholars, such as Tomaselli and Louw, have described this as one of the distinguishing features of *New Nation*: "*New Nation* held itself accountable to the UDF and so regularly consulted the Front's leadership on policy" (12).

Sisulu explained the rationale for *New Nation*'s approach: "In the context of our time, there was collaboration or there was revolution. Remember, revolution for us was the thing that would bring all the good things that we wanted: democracy, nonracialism, openness." Ryland Fisher explained his support for this approach: "Because you couldn't be neutral in the face of apartheid. How could you be neutral [about something] which was condemned universally? Something that was considered a crime against humanity? You couldn't be neutral." Tyrone August also commented on this feature of the newspaper, noting that the newspaper clearly supported the ANC, as opposed to other black political organizations, such as the Pan African Congress and the Azanian People's Organisation: "But for me, in my opinion, the paper was honest about it—it didn't hide behind 'objective journalism' and that we must be neutral. It said that apartheid is wrong, we want to take a stand. Firstly, we want to provide a voice for black people, and secondly, ANC, in their opinion, was the main voice of the black community." Those working at *New Nation* were thus clearly aware of the arguments surrounding "objective" versus "advocacy" journalism and were quite comfortable working for a newspaper that practiced advocacy journalism.[32]

Because of the significant differences between the *Weekly Mail* and *New*

Nation, the relationship between them was quite complicated. There were moments of genuine cooperation. Irwin Manoim, for example, helped *New Nation* set up the newspaper's desktop publishing, the cutting-edge technology at the time, which significantly reduced the costs for both newspapers. But there was also, in Manoim's words, "a lot of internal tension" within the opposition press as well: "We didn't see [*New Nation*] as competition in terms of audience. But there was competition in the sense of [pause] credibility. There was an overlap audience, people like you and foreign correspondents and the diplomatic community were reading both and prestige—prestige is the right word. There was a sense of competition and there were huge ideological differences. So the relationship was always very tense." Again, a complex relationship, one of cooperation at times but also a healthy sense of competition.

The *Weekly Mail* and *New Nation* nevertheless had something very important in common: the apartheid government detested them both. It is difficult to overstate the sheer loathing the apartheid government had for the opposition press in general and for these two newspapers in particular. P. W. Botha, president of South Africa until 1989, "accused the opposition press of 'treason and dishonesty'" and later called them "muckrakers" and "little jackals" (Merrett, *Culture* 123). Other prominent government officials at times singled out these two newspapers by name. Pik Botha, the foreign affairs minister, "told the Foreign Correspondents' Association that the *Weekly Mail* was one of the most 'vicious' newspapers he had ever seen and that it 'contributed to more violence in this country'" (qtd. in Cooper et al., *Race Relations Survey: 1988/89* 551). Tense relations between government officials and journalists exist in every country, as they should. But the vitriol between the government and these two opposition newspapers was intense.[33]

While the government and police despised both newspapers, *New Nation* in particular struck a nerve. In fact, it struck three. The three "dangers" that many in the Afrikaner community feared were the threat of communism (*rooi gevaar*), the threat of blacks (*swart gevaar*), and the threat of Catholicism (*Roomse gevaar*). Given that *New Nation* was a newspaper operated by and targeting black South Africans, was funded by the Catholic Church, and frequently voiced enthusiastic support for trade unions and socialist principles, it is perhaps not surprising that the apartheid government developed a particular dislike for this newspaper. In fact, Irwin Manoim observes in his book that "*New Nation* held a mantle of honour among South African newspapers: it was the publication the government hated most" (*Warned* 114).

Technology

While this book focuses on the rhetorical, legal, and political tactics these two newspapers developed to circumvent the censorship restrictions and increase their writing space, a brief discussion concerning the central role that technology played for both newspapers is in order. Manoim explained that one of the major obstacles he and Harber faced when they first decided to start publishing the *Weekly Mail* was that they simply did not have the necessary financial resources: "In those days, the capital outlay to get a conventional facility going was in the region of about 100,000 rands, and there were enormous expenses on things—you had to have a darkroom, and you had enormous expenses on things like film. So the running costs were very high. And basically, we didn't have 100,000 rand to start." How did the *Weekly Mail* overcome this obstacle? By using the cutting-edge technology of the time: the personal computer.

In January 1984 Apple aired a dramatic advertisement during the Super Bowl that invoked Orwell's *1984* to introduce the Macintosh.[34] It was clever, even though conditions for those living in Apple's target markets in no way resembled the conditions of Orwell's *1984*. But this ad was actually relevant for those living in apartheid South Africa, particularly opposition editors and journalists who did not have the financial resources of major publishing houses to start a newspaper. Manoim explained: "What we did was we bought one laser printer and, I can't remember, it was two or three Macintoshes, and we printed on ordinary paper."[35]

Manoim not only harnessed this technology for the *Weekly Mail* but also "helped to set up the systems at *New Nation*, *South* and the *Namibian*" (Harber, "Honour Outs"). Manoim notes the central role technology played for the opposition press in apartheid South Africa: "Media experts have pointed out that within months of the *Weekly Mail*'s launch, there was an unexpected mushrooming of 'alternative' community newspapers. The cause, the pundits say, was the rise of popular resistance to repression. This may even be true. But the real reason was the *Weekly Mail*'s lick 'n' spit production techniques became widely borrowed, lowering the entry barriers to newspaper publishing" ("Voortrekkers" 72). During one interview, Manoim explained how the technology, particularly when compared to today, was incredibly primitive and was the source of considerable frustration. At one point, he stated, "In fact, my memory of those days is not the state oppression and the security police. It's just the sheer drudgery of doing the most simple things." Despite the many limitations and challenges of producing a newspaper with personal computers and laser printers, when asked to provide his overall assessment of the role technology played for the *Weekly Mail,* Manoim stated, "It wouldn't have happened without it. Yes. One can go so far as to say as it wouldn't have happened otherwise."[36]

CONCLUSION

When one considers the censorship that existed in apartheid South Africa at the time—and the technology that did not exist—one simply cannot overstate the importance of the *Weekly Mail* and *New Nation.* By the mid-1980s, news on television and radio was tightly controlled, and the government had largely succeeded in circumscribing mainstream newspaper coverage within certain parameters. Because of the censorship, as well as widespread white indifference and even hostility to news relevant to black communities, mainstream newspapers operating in the free-market media system did not come close to reflecting the realities of black South Africans.

Moreover, while the anti-apartheid movement may seem contemporary in many ways, particularly in terms of its global reach, the 1980s were, in terms of technology, simply a different world. As noted above, personal computers at that time constituted cutting-edge technology. The internet, now such an essential part of our daily lives and so vital for political movements today, was simply not available to the general public. No websites. No blogs. No email. No Facebook. No Twitter. No social media of any kind. National opposition newspapers such as the *Weekly Mail* and *New Nation* were thus part of a very small handful of sources within the entire country committed to challenging the government and covering the realities of apartheid.

In its efforts to control the media, the apartheid government had one notable Achilles' heel: its obsession with maintaining the façade of legitimacy. The chapters that follow explain how both the *Weekly Mail* and *New Nation* capitalized on this opening. To do so would require both newspapers to engage in a series of calculated risks. How far could they go? How would the government respond? Close the newspaper? Detentions? Arrests? Something worse? For the founders, editors, journalists, and lawyers working for these two newspapers, there were no easy or clear answers to these questions. As Shaun Johnson observed, "You may have pushed them this week and you got away with it. But hey, something may have shifted the next week. There was always a sense of—and anybody who tells you different now is lying—we always did this with a real knot of fear."

2

"IN THE INTEREST OF THE PUBLIC"

Exploiting Gaps within the Apartheid Government

It is in the interest of the public that reports of parliamentary and judicial proceedings, and public bodies entrusted with public duties, be protected, provided that they are fair and substantially accurate. Just as every member of the public has a right to be present and to observe what takes place in court and Parliament, so the newspapers, radio, television and other media are entitled to report factually and fairly what occurs in open court and Parliament.

KELSEY STUART, *THE NEWSPAPERMAN'S GUIDE TO THE LAW*

This chapter analyzes how the *Weekly Mail* and *New Nation* took advantage of various gaps that existed within the apartheid bureaucracy to increase their writing space. To fully appreciate this approach, it is useful to analyze the South African government alongside another regime with which it is often compared: Nazi Germany. *Long Night's Journey into Day*, a documentary about the Truth and Reconciliation Commission, begins with the following statement: "For over forty years, South Africa was governed by the most notorious system of racial domination since Nazi Germany." Mark Mathabane, in his memoir *Kaffir Boy*, also addresses the many parallels that existed between apartheid South Africa and Nazi Germany.[1] Indeed, many Afrikaner political leaders were overtly sympathetic to Nazi Germany before and during World War II. When South Africa entered the war to fight with the Allies, B. J. Vorster, South Africa's prime minister from 1966 to 1978, was actually interned because he "opposed South Africa's participation in the war" (Thompson 189). Thompson reveals the sympathies many Afrikaner leaders had for Nazi Germany:

> Other Afrikaners tried to exploit the opportunities created by German victories. German radio broadcasts in Afrikaans were beamed to South Africa. Afrikaner intellectuals who had studied in German universities, such as Nicolaas Diederichs (later president of the Republic of South Africa) and Piet Meyer (subsequently chairman of South African Broadcasting Corporation), wrote articles, pamphlets, and books and spoke to enthusiastic audiences, using ideas from German national socialism. (184)

It is certainly understandable, therefore, why people often associate apartheid and its leaders with Nazism.

It is important to note, however, that the South African bureaucracy that implemented and enforced apartheid was not nearly as centralized as Nazi Germany. Nor, for that matter, did the apartheid government have the degree of centralization of other totalitarian regimes, such as the Soviet Union, especially under Stalin; Iraq under Saddam Hussein; or the communist government of North Korea. Clearly the executive branch within apartheid South Africa was dominant, particularly in the 1980s, but even during the states of emergency there were entities within the apartheid government that could be strategically harnessed by opposition journalists. The judiciary, which ultimately did yield to the executive during the states of emergency, nevertheless was not a complete rubber stamp for the government, unlike the judiciary that existed or currently exists in the countries mentioned above. As noted in chapter 1, this by no means suggests that apartheid South Africa was a democracy in any sense of the word. But in the words of attorney David Dison, the "trappings of a legitimate government" that existed could be used by opposition journalists.

For the purposes of the analysis in this chapter, it is useful to distinguish between a "structure" of power and a "site" of power. Governments, or entities such as the Catholic Church, constitute structures of power. At a certain level, structures of power are purportedly unified to pursue and advance common goals or values. The government of the United States, for example, exists to promote and enhance the interests of American citizens; the Catholic Church seeks to advance a certain interpretation of Christianity. The most cursory examination of these structures, however, reveals that they consist of numerous—and often conflicting—sites of power. For the US government, this division of power, of course, was created by design, namely, the "checks and balances" system contained in the Constitution. In other structures, such as the Catholic Church, various sites of power may have developed more organically over time. Regardless of intent, structures of power consist of various sites of power that often have competing agendas and/or overlapping jurisdictions. Moreover, there are often competing agendas and complex power relations within individual sites of power. Courts within a particular country may constitute one site of power, for example, but there are often profound differences within the judiciary about how best to interpret the law. To refer to the "apartheid government," therefore, has the effect of invoking a monolithic entity that acts with a singular purpose and will, thus obscuring the very real openings that were available to opposition journalists as a result of contending sites of power.

There is a long history of groups using the very institutions that oppress them for their own purposes. Michel de Certeau discusses how those engaged in resistance have often "used the laws, practices, and representations that were imposed on them by force" and "made something else out of them; they subverted them from within" and "made [them] function in another register" (32). In apartheid South Africa, courtrooms, which the government used to convict political opponents, were the same spaces opposition journalists used to acquire and publish information the censorship restrictions sought to suppress. Parliament, which was used for passing the statutes to create and enforce the architecture of apartheid, was the same site used to acquire and publish information embarrassing to the government. The Publications Appeal Board, created to enforce the Publications Act, which was used to ban literally thousands upon thousands of texts, was the same site opposition journalists used in the late 1980s to acquire and publish material that other sites within the apartheid government wanted to censor.

As many individuals made clear during interviews, the tactics they developed over time were ad hoc in nature or, as Certeau observes, "opportunities seized 'on the wing'" (37). There never was a master plan. But this particular approach represents the most logical first step: utilize as much as possible the opportunities provided by the apartheid government itself. Those working for the *Weekly Mail* and *New Nation* certainly did not invent these tactics, but they were particularly aggressive in using them.

COURT RULINGS AND EMERGENCY REGULATIONS

The South African judiciary ultimately failed to curb the many abuses of the executive branch during apartheid. The Truth and Reconciliation Commission provides the following blunt assessment: "the courts and the organised legal profession generally and subconsciously or unwittingly connived in the legislative and executive pursuit of injustice. Perhaps the most common form of subservience can be captured in the maxim *qui tacet consentire* (silence gives consent)" (vol. 4, 101). When J. C. G. "Stoffel" Botha eventually closed both newspapers, for example (a dynamic examined in greater detail in chapter 6), the courts provided no protection.

Despite the genuine limitations of the South African judiciary, which became more apparent over time, there was a handful of independent judges. Norman Manoim, an attorney for *New Nation*, described during an interview the ambiguous nature of the South African judiciary: "You had moments in which certain independent judges were able to kind of give the emergency a black eye. But at the end of the day, because your highest court was ultimately very, very conservative, basically the state was ultimately victorious in most of them." Some of these court rulings by independent judges during the early stages of the emergency provide an excellent example of how these contending sites of power within the government were used by opposition journalists. These rulings also highlight an important dynamic of writing space, namely, that it did not expand or contract in a linear fashion but rather could expand and contract, only to expand and then contract again.

The "black eyes" Norman Manoim is referring to pertain to those court rulings that struck down and limited the scope of some of the emergency regulations initially issued during the state of emergency. These rulings were particularly important given that the emergency regulations, as noted in chapter 1, were far more sweeping than the censorship statutes passed by Parliament. In the case of statutes passed by Parliament, *mens rea*, or intent, could be used as a possible shield. Dison, the attorney for the *Weekly Mail*, clarified this concept when explaining a photograph shown to him from the *Weekly Mail* that featured a spray-painted sign on a doorway that read "Viva ANC." When asked why this photograph would not be considered a breach of the statute that prohibited the promotion of banned organizations, Dison explained,

> You see, the interesting thing here is that you're in the realm of the Internal Security Act, as distinct from the realm of the regulations. This relates to *mens rea*. The Internal Security Act says, "It will be a criminal offense to promote the aims of a banned organization." That's statute, from Parliament. So Mr. Harber would go into court, and he would say, "No, this is a photograph of an entrance. It's a factual occurrence that occurred. This was spray painted and it shows what actually happened here. This was an account, and a representation of the language that was used. This is a news report. This does not per se promote the aims of the ANC. But if you find that it does, if you say that it does, we'll say that we lack the intention of the aims. We are doing this within the context of a newspaper, that is, reporting facts."

If journalists were charged with violating censorship statutes, therefore, there were two important ramifications. First, there was often at least some wiggle room, as reflected in Dison's comments; second, one would argue one's position in court.

This, however, was not the case with the media regulations promulgated during the states of emergency. If one were charged with violating a regulation, one did not go before the courts but appealed directly to the government minister who promulgated the regulation. This is why the emergency regulation that echoed a provision of the Internal Security Act was so significant. In January 1987, the government "gazetted regulations which gave the commissioner of police the power to ban the publication of reports or advertisements 'calculated to improve or promote the public image or esteem' of outlawed organisations" (Cooper et al., *Race Relations 1987/88* 818). If a newspaper were accused of violating this emergency regulation, therefore, it would not have the right to appeal in a court before a judge, where it could use the shield of *mens rea*. Again, Dison is instructive: "The lack of *mens rea* was a refuge, it was definitely a refuge. And again, in ordinary criminal law, it's possible to use that as a defense and writers in oppressive regimes must use that. But once they get to the level of decree, they just cut the intention out and say, 'Thou shall not. Otherwise we'll grab you, we'll detain you, we'll imprison you, we'll close your newspaper down.'" Moreover, the inability to have one's case heard in court precluded the possibility of having one's case heard before a potentially sympathetic or progressive judge.

Several newspapers and organizations thus sought to challenge these media regulations in the courts when they were first enacted. According to Dison, this was an extremely interesting development in the South African context because it provided courts with the opportunity to "review" law. In countries with written constitutions, such as the United States and the current democratic government of South Africa, the constitution represents the supreme legal authority. The apartheid government, however, was a parliamentary system that did not have a written constitution. Laws passed by Parliament, therefore, were supreme; after a statute was passed, there was no entity to which one could appeal.

During the states of emergency, however, Parliament gave the executive the power to impose additional constraints on the media, but the emergency regulations themselves were written by government ministers, not Parliament. As Dison explained, these could then be reviewed by the courts: "When you're reviewing regulations, it's very similar to unconstitutionality because you're dealing with secondary law—it's not law that derives from Parliament. [During apartheid] you were in a context where Parliament was supreme— there was no constitution that could override the laws of Parliament. So for the first time during this emergency, there was reviewability of law." Dison discussed the nature of these legal challenges: "You are going to have to go to the judiciary and say, 'Look, the actual regulation stinks because the regulation, even though the minister's got wide powers, he went beyond his powers. Or he didn't act properly in terms of his powers, he acted unreasonably. Or his regulations were vague . . . [o]r they were overly broad, or they were beyond his mandate.'" For those in the legal community, this represented a new and exciting opportunity.

It should perhaps come as no surprise that activist attorneys, when bringing these court challenges, strategically sought to capitalize on the rifts within the South African judiciary itself. Since one could challenge these decrees only after the state had actually used them, activist lawyers, according to Irwin Manoim, sought to "take up the court challenge in Natal rather than in any other province, because it had the largest proportion of liberal judges, most notably Judge John Didcott, now a constitutional court judge [in 1996]" (*Warned* 76). This tactic did in fact yield some temporary victories.

In July and November 1986, the Natal Supreme Court rendered two important decisions pertaining to media regulations. According to an article in the *Weekly Mail*, these decisions limited the scope of the "subversive statement" regulation: "Gone was the ban on promoting any object of any unlawful organisation and the prohibition on engendering feelings of hostility among sections of the public; and a restricted meaning was given to the prohibition on resisting or opposing the government. Mere criticism was held to be permissible" (Harber, "Five Crucial" 8). Although the court curtailed the broad definition of subversive statements, it nevertheless upheld the state's restriction on any statement calling "for disinvestments, strikes and an end to conscription" (Bekker, "Illustrated Guide" 14). It was, therefore, a mixed ruling, one that upheld many onerous restrictions, modified some, and overturned others.

The *Weekly Mail*, not surprisingly, sought to capitalize as soon as possible on the newfound space created by these rulings. On 21 November 1986, shortly after the second Natal ruling, the *Weekly Mail* published pictures of scenes of unrest accompanying an article headlined "I Saw the Shootings at the MAWU [Metal and Allied Workers Union] Rally." Underneath these pictures was the following statement: "The Emergency regulations prohibit the reporting of actions of the Security Forces and the publishing of certain unrest photographs. However, the *Weekly Mail* can use these pictures and this report because the conduct of the workers and of the Security Forces does not fall within the ambit of the Emergency regulations in accordance with Natal Supreme Court judgements" (Kockott 1). Although it is stated in a confident tone, as if the *Weekly Mail*'s interpretation of the Natal ruling is beyond dispute, this is more than likely an example of the *Weekly Mail*'s use of the "all-clear flag," a tactic discussed at length in chapter 4. In short, this tactic involved attaching an impressive-sounding legal justification to an article for the purposes of intimidating lower-level apartheid bureaucrats from taking action against the newspaper.

The *Weekly Mail* not only capitalized on favorable court rulings in cases initiated by others but the editors, along with the Release Mandela Campaign, challenged some of the emergency regulations themselves in June 1987. The newspaper was fortunate to have extremely capable attorneys representing them. One of those attorneys was Ismail Mahomed, a very talented, high-profile attorney who challenged the apartheid government on several occasions. Mahomed eventually become the chief justice of South Africa in 1996 after the country made the transition to democracy. Dison, the *Weekly Mail*'s attorney, described Mahomed as "the leading administrative lawyer in the country by a long way. Basically, he was the guy I was consulting just about all the time on the regulations." The Pietermaritzburg Supreme Court that heard this case, citing the previous Natal court rulings, provided a partial victory for the *Weekly Mail* and the Release Mandela Campaign in its September 1987 ruling. Specifically, the court "took from the commissioner of police the right to add new definitions of a subversive statement and to prohibit the publication of certain kinds of news and advertisements" (Rickard, "Court Clips" 8).

Although these were indeed victories, they were tempered by the fact that the courts, as with the Natal rulings, ultimately upheld the authority of the state to implement emergency regulations. In an article headlined "Disappointments, but Several Media Restrictions Go Out," a legal expert analyzing this ruling observed that "[a] pattern seems to be developing in which the courts feel bound to acknowledge the virtually limitless powers of the state president, but fortunately, every time the regulation drafters try to delegate similar powers to the commissioner, they get knocked out by the court" (Rickard 8). Dison commented on this dynamic as well. When asked if the legal challenges ever sought to overturn the state of emergency itself, Dison explained, "Mahomed tried that. He would start off his attacks by saying that the emergency is invalid. He would start from that, but he would never win that point."

It was only a matter of time, however, before the government responded to these temporary setbacks. The attorneys working for the government devised new regulations to satisfy the objections of the courts while simultaneously granting the power it sought, a process described in a *Weekly Mail* article headlined "The State's Attorneys Redo Their Homework": "When the new restrictions were introduced last week, it was clear the drafters had been doing their homework. They seem to have studied closely the judgments in those cases which successfully challenged aspects of the Emergency; the new regulations take into account the judge's criticism of the wording in the initial regulations, and the rules are reworded accordingly. This makes the situation far more difficult for lawyers wanting to test the new rules in court" (Rickard 13). This process provides a telling insight into the complexities of the apartheid government. Rather than simply ignore the courts' rulings and assume the power the apartheid government desired, government staff made the effort to rewrite the regulations in order to obtain this power "legally" and maintain the veneer of legitimacy.

As a result of this dynamic, a peculiar situation arose in which the writing space for the media would close as a result of a new regulation, open as the result of a successful court challenge, only to be closed again by a newly revised regulation. While it is true that the media restrictions did become more numerous and onerous as the emergency progressed, this process did not necessarily progress linearly. Instead, the legality of a particular story would depend on the stage of the state of emergency in which it had been written and published.

This dynamic was captured by a series of articles that appeared in the 22 August 1986 edition of the *Weekly Mail*. One of the strategies that the *Weekly Mail* used to great effect, examined at greater length in chapter 4, was to use black lines to cover portions of stories that violated the emergency regulations. Rather than kill a story entirely, the paper would instead convey as much of the article as possible and cover with black lines only those words, phrases, or sentences that were considered in violation of the regulations. This strategy was utilized for several articles published in the 20 June 1986 edition immediately following the first round of media restrictions, including the articles headlined "Some Ironic Pockets of Press Freedom," "Clouds of Teargas above the Mosque Floor," and "Durban: Shopowners Shut the Doors at Noon." One article, written by Sefako Nyaka, about the tenth anniversary of the Soweto Uprising, "The Day That Fell Off the Calendar," was left completely blank because the media regulations "barred journalists from the townships" (12). The fact that this article could not be published under these regulations was ironic, since Nyaka's article explained that there was no violence in Soweto that day. However, after the major English-language newspapers challenged six of the media regulations in court, the state attorneys essentially conceded before the trial even began that two of the regulations were invalid. The two restrictions in question "prevented reports on any action by the Security Forces and prohibited journalists from entering unrest areas" ("Peeling Away" 12). Immediately after the government made these concessions, the *Weekly Mail* reran the same stories it had previously censored with black lines, printing them in their entirety in the 22 August 1986 edition under the headline "Peeling Away Those Black Stripes." A court challenge had opened some space—and the *Weekly Mail* had immediately pounced.

A particularly good example of writing space closing, opening, and then closing again can be seen in the numerous attempts by the United Democratic Front (UDF) to run an advertisement in the *Weekly Mail* calling for the gov-

Images 2.1.A, 2.1.B, and 2.1.C These pages show articles that reveal the dynamic nature of writing space during the state of emergency. Space once closed was opened by a court ruling, which allowed the *Weekly Mail* to "peel away those black stripes" and reveal images and information the newspaper had previously self-censored to comply with the emergency regulations.

The day that fell off the calendar

June 16 did not turn into a day of violence after all. If anything, it was a day of empty streets, closed shops and disconnected phones. SEFAKO NYAKA reports

Church volunteers wrap flowers with memorial cards

Some ironic pockets of press freedom

**By FRANZ KRUGER,
East London**

IN an ironic spin-off from Emergency curbs on the press, the "independent" homelands are now the only places where reporting can take place with relative freedom.

The TBVC states — Transkei, Bophuthatswana, Venda and Ciskei — have rarely been known for their regard for human rights. But none of them has yet followed Pretoria's latest initiative in restricting news coverage in terms of the Emergency regulations.

Transkei has been under a State of Emergency for years, when South Africa's partial State of Emergency was imposed last year. Unrest responded by imposing a curfew throughout the territory.

This time, said Commissioner of Police, General RS Masunga, "we have our own Emergency regulations, and we are not going to follow what is done in South Africa".

Transkei regulations do not target the press, although the frequent deportations of journalists indicate the hazards of reporting there.

In Ciskei, no State of Emergency has been declared, and so if it is from Mdantsane — East London's largest township, but technically in the Ciskei, and subject only to laws and declarations made in B'sho — that some 'of the few direct

reports emerge regarding June 16 events.

The tenth anniversary of the Soweto uprising was marked by numerous outbreaks of violence in Mdantsane, leading to the death of at least one youth, 16-year-old Mdangathini Tipoyo.

Tipoyo died in Cecilia Makiwane hospital in the township after ███████████████████ denominational service in a Methodist church in the township.

According to Rev Gilbert Nyangane, who was leading the service, Ciskei ███████████████ ███████████████████████████████ ███████████████ had given an order that the service would be allowed to proceed.

Nyangane and two ministers went out to relay █████ Vuobono's assurance ████████████████ ███████████████████████████████ ███████████████████████████████ ███████████████████████████████ ███████████████████████████████

About 70 people are estimated to have been taken for medical treatment to both Cecilia Makiwane hospital and East London's Frere Hospital. By Wednesday, only seven remained in the wards, and a hospital spokesman said they were progressing well.

Ciskei government representative, Headman Somomovi said ██████████ had been taken after the service became rowdy, and after a ████████ ███████████████████ Nyangane denied this: "Everyone was behaving well," he said, "and then was re████████".

In other incidents of violence on Monday, the house of Goodwin Makongolo, the senior editor of Umtobomba, a Ciskei government publication, was petrol-bombed. Nobody was hurt, but damage was caused.

A number of buses were attacked by stonethrowers. At least two buses were severely damaged, while a third was burnt out in a petrol bomb attack.

Peeling away those black stripes

THE WEEKLY MAIL

Boycott town under siege

The day that fell off the calendar

Some ironic pockets of press freedom

ernment to "unban the ANC." In early January 1987, the UDF initially sought to place this ad in the *Weekly Mail*, and the attorneys for the newspaper argued the ad was not in contravention of the law. The state, however, issued a new emergency regulation the very night the ad was supposed to be published; it restricted "any newspaper report or advert which promoted a banned organization or explained its strategies" ("That Baffling" 6). The security police called the editors of the *Weekly Mail* to inform them of this new regulation, and "Major Zaaiman warned a confiscation order had been prepared and said the police were ready to seize copies of the newspaper if they contained the advert" (6). After consulting with the newspaper's attorneys, the editors determined that they could not publish the ad. There was one problem, however. The newspaper was already at press, but the state had banned the use of black lines and blank spaces at that stage of the emergency that newspapers had been using to highlight the censorship laws. In a situation that can only be described as Kafkaesque, the *Weekly Mail* had to obtain special permission from the state to run blank pages in place of the ad, thus violating one emergency regulation in order to comply with another (6).

The story, however, did not end there. The committee responsible for placing the ad challenged the government in the Rand Supreme Court—and won. To celebrate this victory, the *Weekly Mail* planned to publish this advertisement on the front page under the heading "We present, courtesy of the Rand Supreme Court, the advert we were prevented from printing three weeks ago" with a big, bold headline in caps: "Illegal Yesterday, Legal Today." As the newspaper was sent to the press with this headline, however, the state issued yet another regulation that made *this* ad illegal. As Irwin Manoim relates in his book, "I phoned our production manager at the press, Phaldi Solomon, and asked him to paint the word WHOOPS! in large letters across the page negative, so as to obliterate the offending words UNBAN THE ANC. He did, but the word WHOOPS! was printed in a light blue ink and the offending words beneath could still be read very clearly. The page must have mystified readers, although the punchline 'There is no accounting for tomorrow' was now more pertinent than ever" (*Warned* 73). As Manoim observes, this edition of the newspaper must have been particularly confusing to readers since the *Weekly Mail* still ran the article entitled "Press Can Report on ANC—under Old Restrictions," which sought to explain the presence of the advertisement on the front page prior to its alteration to comply with the last-minute regulation. Between the time this article was written and could be published, therefore, the space for it had closed.

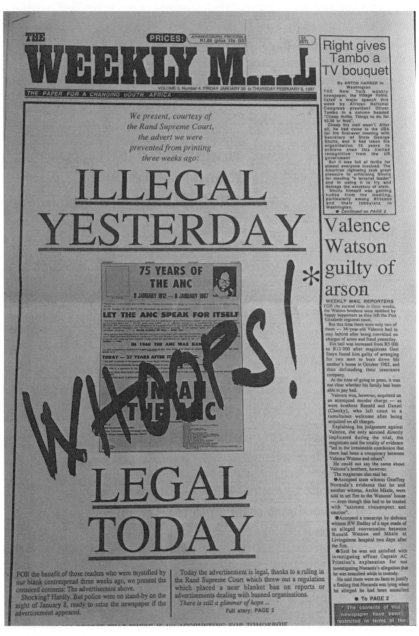

Figure 2.2 The "Unban the ANC" advertisement seen underneath the scrawled "whoops!" provides another example of how writing space could be closed, opened, and closed again—all within a matter of days.

Within the larger structure of the apartheid government, certain courts within the South African judiciary thus proved to be an important site of power. Unfortunately for opposition journalists, the Appellate Division was considerably more conservative than some of the lower courts. As Manoim writes, "The state could always rely on the conservative Appellate Division to reverse the liberal interpretations that hailed from Natal. Some key Didcott judgments did not survive the trip to Bloemfontein" (*Warned* 76).[2] Richard Abel's analysis offers a similar assessment, explaining that the temporary victories were the result of some progressive judges who, in the end, could not withstand the censorship forces within the government:

> If government would not tolerate the press, would the "rule of law" and an "independent judiciary" protect it? Tragically, no. There had been reasons for hope. Courts had interpreted the Police, Prisons, and Defence Acts narrowly, acquitting journalists of violations. . . . The Supreme Court had invalidated other Emergency regulations as overly broad, *ultra vires*, or vague. But the outcome seemed to turn on judicial personality. Occasional victories did not alter the fundamental facts of Parliamentary supremacy and no bill of rights. Government simply promulgated new regulations—often within twenty-four hours—and made them retroactive. (306)

It is important to note that the strategy of challenging emergency regulations in court was used not only by anti-apartheid journalists but by many anti-apartheid activists, including those challenging the detention powers granted to police. Unfortunately, many of these challenges suffered a fate similar to the challenges against the media restrictions: the initial favorable rulings of lower courts were ultimately overturned.

To highlight the absurdity of the ways in which space for articles was constantly expanding and contracting, the *Weekly Mail* published on two separate occasions a fictitious article that revealed how differently it would be censored depending on the particular restrictions in place. In the 6 February 1987 edition, the newspaper published a two-page spread, headlined "An Illustrated Guide to Public Ignorance," written by Jo-Ann Bekker, which displayed eight copies of the same fictitious article, each with radically different notations. Some copies had black lines running through entire paragraphs, other copies had lines running through selected sentences, and some copies had only minor changes to some of the words. Dates and a brief explanation were provided to give readers the reason for either the extensive or limited censorship in each version of the same story. These descriptions, accompanied by the image of a story that was either moderately or extensively censored, were extremely effective for demonstrating the ever-changing nature of writing space in apartheid South Africa.

In terms of resistance more generally, these court challenges highlight Certeau's observation about those who act from a position of weakness: "What it wins it cannot keep" (37). Different people drew different conclusions about this particular dynamic of the courts. Christopher Merrett's assessment was quite pessimistic: "In short, successful legal challenges, at great expense, simply invited harsher controls" (*Culture* 120). Don Pinnock, on the other hand, recognizing the real limitations of this approach, offered a slightly more optimistic assessment: "Another unexpected space which appeared was in liberal judgments handed down by certain sections of the judiciary emboldened by the growth of the mass movements and undoubtedly with an ear to overseas opinion. Although it can be argued that decisions against the state merely helped it to refine legal repression, the presence of judges clearly unwilling to rubber-stamp parliamentary decrees acted as a partial brake on excesses and often forced the state to reveal its hand in key cases against the press and the national democratic movement" (19). Regardless of one's ultimate assessment regarding the value of these legal challenges, this tactic ultimately had a limited lifespan for opposition journalists.

COURTS AND PARLIAMENT AS PROTECTED SPACES

In addition to challenging the emergency regulations in courts, anti-apartheid journalists also used the protected status of courtrooms and Parliament as a means of divulging precisely the information the government took such elaborate steps to conceal. Kelsey Stuart's *The Newspaperman's Guide to the Law*, the veritable bible for many journalists at that time, describes this opening: "It is in the interest of the public that reports of parliamentary and judicial proceedings, and public bodies entrusted with public duties, be protected, provided that they are fair and substantially accurate. Just as every member of the public has a right to be present and to observe what takes place in court and

Parliament, so the newspapers, radio, television and other media are entitled to report factually and fairly what occurs in open court and Parliament" (62). Both the *Weekly Mail* and *New Nation* sought to use these openings as aggressively as possible to accomplish the following objectives: to reveal considerable information about the apartheid government's abuses and also to provide a forum for those the government had banned and sought to silence.

Exposing Abuses of the Apartheid Government

In terms of using the courts, both newspapers were able to publish a remarkable amount of material that chronicled a whole host of governmental abuses. These articles demonstrate how the journalists used a two-part strategy. The first consisted of determining how best to access information within the judicial system. Some of the methods used included the following:

Obtaining information from the testimonies of witnesses
Citing information contained in sworn affidavits and applications before the court
Using information provided during an inquest
Reporting allegations made in civil cases brought before the court
Citing evidence presented at trial
Reporting the decisions rendered by a court in a civil case

There were thus several opportunities within the judicial process in which journalists could access and publish sensitive information.

Once journalists found the necessary opening to report this information, many then used various writing strategies to maximize the impact of the story. For example, journalists could convey as many details as possible, juxtapose competing versions of the same story to highlight the absurdity of the official version, and open or conclude an article with a particularly compelling statement. All of these techniques served to augment what was already highly charged subject matter.

Appendix B chronicles many of the *Weekly Mail* and *New Nation* articles in which journalists used the South African legal system as a means of obtaining and publishing information the government wished to conceal. These articles date from the first edition of each newspaper until February 1990, the point at which the apartheid government unbanned the ANC and other political parties and released Nelson Mandela. These charts are organized based on the kind of governmental abuse revealed in court and/or by court documents: death squad activities, police killings, torture, police links with vigilantes, and various forms of human rights violations by police and military personnel. The first column of each chart contains the headline and journalist (if identified); the second provides sufficient language from the article to demonstrate how the courts and court documents were used to publish this information. There are certainly articles I must have overlooked when reviewing both of these weekly newspapers over a five-year period. These charts, however, provide a sense of the considerable amount of information these newspapers were able to publish using this tactic.

According to Merrett, this tactic was particularly important for chronicling abuses committed in rural areas: "The State of Emergency made the acquisition of information about police activity in less accessible rural areas virtually impossible until court proceedings were instituted. The lodging of affidavits and the bringing of interdicts against kitskonstabels ('instant police,' or hastily trained black police auxiliaries of the Riot Police, in turn the shock troops of the security police) were seen as a tactic which would generate publicity. In this way, information about human rights abuses at KTC (Cape Town), Bhongolethu (Oudtshoorn), Aberdeen, Hofmeyr and Duncan Village (East London) was brought to light" (*Culture* 139).[3] Journalists who used the protection of the courts to reveal information were thus actively assisted by political activists who took the necessary legal steps to facilitate the continued use of this tactic.

In addition to using the protected space of the courtroom, those working on the *Weekly Mail* and *New Nation* also used the protected space of Parliament, which was dominated by members from the National Party but also contained a very small number of opposition party members. These MPs by no means had sufficient power to overturn or challenge the National Party, but they could use their position to ask embarrassing questions on the floor of Parliament. Haber explained: "Not [a tactic] that was used often, but sometimes you would work with an MP. . . . [They could] ask a question or say something that would allow you to cite. Once again, you didn't have absolute immunity, but you had a level of immunity." Ryland Fisher, a journalist for *New Nation*, indicated that "there were other techniques, other tactics that we used. One was using the very people in Parliament who were sympathetic, people like Jan van Eck [and] people like Helen Suzman. We would use people like that to ask questions in Parliament, because Parliament has privilege and whatever you said in Parliament can be reported without fear of you being prosecuted. So we had to be very creative." As Harber notes above, the protected space of Parliament was used less frequently than the courts, but there were nevertheless notable articles published as a result of this approach.

In one instance, for example, the protected space of Parliament was used to circumvent a particularly vexing obstacle for journalists: the difficulty of finding witnesses who would publicly stand by their story. Irwin Manoim recalled,

> You always had serious problems with witnesses, because the way the regulations worked is that you had to have identifiable witnesses who were willing to stand by anything they said, regardless. You could not have the kind of anonymous source stuff that Watergate could get away with. And the significance of that was that it allowed them [the government] to intimidate witnesses and that was always the problem. You always did have witnesses who were willing to tell you things in detail, but the moment their name was going to get involved, then it got problematic.

Manoim proceeded to explain later in the interview how they once used Parliament to overcome this constraint and write an article about the actions of the security forces, one of the more challenging issues to write about, particularly given the difficulty of finding witnesses:

> I mentioned the whole problem of trying to find witnesses who were willing to have their names put to it and how difficult that was. That was the central issue. People disappearing, people being tortured, etc. Lots of stories about these mysterious vans driving around the township with policemen in them, randomly firing at people, just picking people up and abducting them. Every now and then you managed to latch onto—for example, I remember Helen Suzman called a board of inquiry into something, and you could use that as an angle. But generally you just could not find witnesses willing to talk about it.

The article Manoim was referring to was "Suzman's Strange Tale of the Mirror-Glass Mini-Bus," a front-page story in the 4 September 1987 edition. It opens as follows: "All the men and boys in an East Cape township were rounded up and told to file past a mini-bus with one-way glass. Inside it sat an informer who called out the words 'positive' or 'negative' as each person passed. Everyone tagged as 'positive' was promptly arrested. The scene was described in parliament this week by the PFP's Helen Suzman[,] who said she had 37 affidavits in her possession, all 'telling a sorry tale of torture and ill-treatment'" (1). Later in the article, Suzman is quoted at length about techniques of torture used by the police:

> "They have perfected methods which leave no trace of the injuries inflicted."
> Included in such methods is one in which "a wet bag is placed over the head of
> the person being interrogated and it is pulled tight, being released only when
> the person is half-dead. If that doesn't suffice to extract the required confes-
> sion or information, another type of bag with electrodes is used. . . . It seems
> to me that a cast-iron case had been made out for a proper investigation, an
> independent inquiry with special reference to the indemnity clause which I
> have no doubt encourages excesses in the exercise of the powers by the secu-
> rity police." (2)

As a result of Suzman's inquiry, the *Weekly Mail* was able to publish information about activities that would otherwise be challenging if not impossible because of existing regulations and the government's ability to intimidate witnesses.

Other articles appearing in the *Weekly Mail* and *New Nation* used the legal protection provided by Parliament in much the same way courts were used. In the *Weekly Mail* article headlined "An Extraordinary Exchange in the House," the journalist quotes MP Jan van Eck as a means of reporting allegations of torture. In this extended excerpt from that article, note how the journalist provides the most minimal context for Van Eck's statement and then quotes him at length rather than paraphrase or summarize his comments:

> Van Eck referred to the cases of the three detainees in the public gallery,
> Mandla Malgas, 18, Sonwaba Madikane, 17, and John de Vos, 18. Malgas and
> Madikane had been returning home after a meeting of the Institute for a Dem-
> ocratic Alternative for SA (Idasa) in Mowbray. "They were stopped by police
> who wanted to know where they got the brochures of Idasa which were in
> their possession. They were too scared to tell the police where they got these
> brochures and were thereupon beaten with rifle butts and kicked. They were
> taken to Nyanga Police Station. A sack was put over their heads. Little metal
> rings were attached to their little finger, and for four hours they were given
> electric shocks. At about 3am they were sent home without being charged or

even their names or addresses taken." De Vos had been taken to a venue and assaulted by various policemen for six hours, Van Eck said. "When he would not tell them what they wanted to know, he was undressed and both his hands and feet handcuffed. Two tables were brought into the room and he was made to sit on his haunches. A broomstick was stuck through his legs and arms and he was hung from this broom. The broomstick was hung over the two tables with him suspended in the middle. A wet cloth was wrapped around his little fingers, his wrists and ankles. Electric wires were attached to all these areas and electric shock upon electric shock was sent through his body while they kept on asking him questions. His fingers, wrists and ankles were swollen and he had a terrible headache. He was prevented from seeing a doctor and the next day taken to Johannesburg for further interrogation." Van Eck added: "These cases of torture are not exceptions to the rule. The killing of detainees, as used to happen in the old days, seems to have been replaced by torturing. The minister of law and order will have to take the responsibility for these actions and for not taking adequate steps to stop this orgy of violence." (4)

After providing these comments by Van Eck, the journalist includes the denial of these allegations of torture made by Adriaan Vlok, the minister of law and order. Near the end of the article, Vlok is quoted as saying that the youths who had been tortured were given the opportunity to identify the police officers and file a complaint against them but that these teen boys did not because "they would be unable to do so." The journalist cites a question posed by Van Eck: "'May I ask him [Vlok] if he thinks it is possible that people with a sack over their head will recognise the people who torture them? If people can't see, how can they identify the people who are torturing them?'" The article concludes with a short declarative sentence: "But Vlok did not answer him" (4). This particular journalist was thus able to use the protected space of Parliament to acquire information about torture and then structure the article to maximize the impact of these revelations.

The front-page story of the 6 March 1987 edition of the *Weekly Mail*, "2,200 Babies in Jail, Coetsee Says," is another example of reporting information revealed in Parliament that was profoundly embarrassing to the government:

Over 2,200 babies were imprisoned with their mothers last year, according to Kobie Coetsee, the Minister of Prisons. Giving written answers to parliamentary questions yesterday, Coetsee drew a picture of South African prisons that included overcrowding of over 200 percent. And thousands of children and babies are among those in custody. . . . In answer to another question, Coetsee said 2,280 children, of whom 1,880 were black, were held with their mothers last year. At December 31, there were 196 babies in custody. Prison regulations stipulate that a woman prisoner was allowed to have her baby with her "during the period of lactation and for such period as may be necessary." (1)

The issue of children in detention was particularly damaging internationally for the apartheid regime; anti-apartheid activists and advocates of sanctions highlighted it to reveal the barbarism of the state.

The availability of this space provided real opportunities for opposition journalists, much to the chagrin of the government. As Merrett observes, "That this was uncomfortable for the government was suggested by rumours in early 1987 that press coverage of parliament might be limited" (*Culture* 148). The government, however, ultimately did not embark on this course of action most likely for the same reason it did not install in-house censors at newspapers during the states of emergency, as discussed in the previous chapter: doing so would only undermine its already limited legitimacy in the eyes of the world.

Forum for Those Banned by the Government

In addition to revealing information about the numerous abuses of the apartheid government, the *Weekly Mail* and *New Nation* both used the protected spaces of courtrooms for another purpose: to provide a forum to those officially banned by the government. In 1950 the government banned the South African Communist Party, and in 1960 it banned the African National Congress. It was thus illegal not only to belong to one of these two political parties but it was also illegal for any publication, including newspapers, to "promote" them.

The government also banned numerous individuals. Mandela, who was banned before eventually being arrested and imprisoned, describes this process in his autobiography: "My bans extended to meetings of all kinds, not just political ones. I could not, for example, attend my son's birthday party. I was prohibited from talking to more than one person at a time. This was part of a systematic effort by the government to silence, persecute, and immobilize the leaders of those fighting apartheid and was the first of a series of bans on me that continued with brief intervals of freedom until the time I was deprived of all freedom some years hence" (*Long Walk* 144). Once individuals were banned, newspapers were strictly forbidden from quoting them.

Journalists, however, had much greater latitude quoting those who had been banned if they were testifying as part of a trial, which both *Weekly Mail* and *New Nation* did as much as possible. Dison, the attorney for the *Weekly Mail*, commented on what journalists would do: "I mean, you couldn't quote Mandela and you couldn't quote Tambo or you couldn't quote people who were listed, like Terror Lekota and all those other people. But you could use courtroom situations, the texts of what was happening in courts, because it was privileged around a courtroom situation." Amrit Manga provided a memorable example of how *New Nation* used the courts for this purpose:

> I'm talking about this trial of the ANC MK guerrilla that was captured in Swaziland.[4] At his sentencing, he prepared a whole speech which was very useful because he tried to motivate the reasons for the armed struggle and give justification to that. We would not be able to do that under any circumstances in South Africa—justifying that was patently illegal. So he reads this thing out in court and the lawyers gave it to us and we took that and we did a two-page feature on that—"This was why an armed struggle was necessary." Smack dab in the middle of the state of emergency. And they couldn't do a thing to us.

Both newspapers, therefore, covered trials in which they knew, or suspected, valuable information would be revealed.

It is important to note that the *Weekly Mail* and the *New Nation* did not invent this tactic. In fact, there was a long and distinguished history of political activists in South Africa using the courtroom as a means of making statements that would then be covered by the media, particularly progressive newspapers. Mandela, for example, relates the following about his 1964 trial: "At the end of the address, I simply sat down. . . . I had read for over four hours. . . . The speech received wide publicity in both the local and foreign press, and was printed, virtually word for word, in the *Rand Daily Mail*. This despite the fact that all my words were banned" (*Long Walk* 369).

Jeremy Cronin related a similar experience. Cronin was captured by the police in 1976 for illegally producing and distributing underground pamphlets on behalf of the South African Communist Party. He was convicted and served several years in prison for these actions. Cronin, who would subsequently be elected to South Africa's democratic parliament, stated that the distribution of underground pamphlets "probably had some small impact" in the anti-apartheid struggle but that his trial was much more significant:

> But I think our biggest propaganda coup was our trial, if the truth be told. . . . [It] was a rhetorical strategy. . . . Political trialists were making statements from the dock. We were able to make, David [Rabkin] and I, statements from the dock and basically we just tried to convey defiance. . . . So probably in all the early seventies, the most successful thing I did was, you know, take a dive in the court speech. But they were, the thing was very widely reported, so courts created a rhetorical space which our little pamphlets didn't then, and obviously you reach an audience. It was a very widely covered trial, which we knew, and so we knew that we had to use it as best we could.

The courts, as Cronin states, served as a rhetorical space, but only if those in the media were willing to report these statements. It is significant, for example, that it was the *Rand Daily Mail*, the most progressive mainstream newspaper in South Africa at that time, that printed Mandela's four-hour speech "virtually word for word."

Journalists working for the *Weekly Mail* and *New Nation* were aware of this opening, and some had actually utilized it prior to the 1980s. Howard Barrell, for example, who wrote for the *Weekly Mail* and contributed occasionally to *New Nation*, discussed how he had covered the trials of black consciousness leaders in the 1970s. Barrell explained how these trials had been a turning point for him personally because they revealed "how much legal space there [was] that had not been exploited":

> There was daily coverage of this trial, and a lot of the guys on trial had been banned. In other words, they could not be quoted, but in a court they could be quoted. If they were giving evidence under oath, they could be quoted. . . . Justice had to be seen to be done, even if it was South African justice. So Steve Biko comes to give evidence. Steve's been banned for a few years, gives evidence for about five days. . . . It was the first time that Steve had been able to speak publicly in his own name.

Given that the state of emergency resulted in even more restrictions on journalists in the 1980s, *New Nation* and the *Weekly Mail* utilized the protected space of the courtrooms as much as possible. Appendix C contains articles that appeared in both newspapers as a result of this tactic.

PUBLICATIONS APPEAL BOARD

Yet another site of power within the apartheid government that the *Weekly Mail* and *New Nation* utilized to increase their writing space was the Publications Appeal Board (PAB), an entity created by the Publications Act of 1974. The origins of this particular piece of legislation provide a tangible example of the antagonism that can develop between various sites of power within a government. According to the journalist Ivor Powell, "In fact it was a growing rift and conflict between the courts and the Publications Control Board set up by the 1963 Act which led to the passing of the later Publications Act. The new legislation emerged essentially out of a somewhat anarchic situation in which the courts were routinely trashing the decisions of the Board and thereby questioning the legal basis for its decisions. This led to a commission of inquiry under former Police Minister Jimmy Kruger and, unsurprisingly, to the passing of new legislation" ("Most Censored" 17). The system in which the *Weekly Mail* and *New Nation* operated was thus the result of previous conflicts that had taken place within the apartheid government between courts and the Publications Control Board.

According to an article appearing in the *Weekly Mail*, the Publications Act of 1974 became "the principal vehicle for effecting censorship" in South Africa by creating numerous committees that determined whether or not various publications should be censored (Bauer, "How It Works" 15). Another *Weekly Mail* article noted that the work of these committees was "shrouded in secrecy" and that "the names of individuals comprising a particular committee are never revealed and the Act precludes interested parties from a right of audience before them" (Bauer, "In Search of the Light" 15). An official justification for this secrecy was never provided: "Why such levels of secrecy need to be maintained in relation to censoring objects, publications and films has never been satisfactorily explained. The closest I have come to receiving any enlightenment was when a member of the directorate staff told me it was mainly in order to protect the reputations of the people involved and to secure their personal safety" (Powell, "Most Censored" 16). These secretive and conservative committees banned literally thousands upon thousands of "texts" in the course of their existence, including books, films, songs, posters, even T-shirts. During the 1970s, the Publications Act increasingly was used to censor political material.[5]

The Publications Act of 1974 was particularly significant for the *Weekly Mail* and *New Nation*. Mainstream newspapers that were part of the Newspaper Press Union had signed a code of conduct agreement in which they promised to essentially censor themselves in an effort to prevent the government from imposing more onerous restrictions. Newspapers that were not part of the Newspaper Press Union, however, were subject to the Publications Control Board (Stuart 24), which, as will be examined below, had adverse implications for *New Nation*.

The Publications Appeal Board (PAB), as its title indicates, heard the appeals resulting from decisions made by publication committees. During the 1980s, the chair of the PAB, Kobus van Rooyen, was more progressive than previous chairs. The Freedom Charter, for example, a foundational document of the ANC that outlined its political principles and aspirations, had been banned prior to his tenure: "Many editions of the Charter were prohibited under various censorship statutes and in most cases, the mere possession of the Charter constituted a criminal offense. Even quoting from the Charter gave rise to the banning of publications" (Bauer and Johnson 13). In 1984, however, the PAB ruled that the Freedom Charter was no longer an illegal document: "It said that the fact that the ANC had adopted the Charter as part of its constitution was legally irrelevant" (Bauer and Johnson 13). After this decision by the PAB, numerous organizations began to print and openly distribute copies of the Freedom Charter.

To fully appreciate the role of the PAB under Van Rooyen, this entity needs to be situated within the larger censorship apparatus. Because the apartheid government had so many laws designed to censor information, it necessitated the creation of various sites of power within a very large and complex bureaucracy. It was thus entirely possible for different sites within the government to undermine one other in the process of fulfilling their mission. For example, the publication committees and the PAB were not supposed to take into account *other* censorship laws when rendering their decisions but were instead supposed to adhere to the criteria contained within the Publications Act itself. Thus, the PAB allowed the publication and distribution of a book entitled *Apartheid in Crisis*, despite the fact that this book "contraven[ed] the Internal Security Act by quoting 'listed persons,' including Oliver Tambo" (Bauer, "Search" 14).

The Publications Act as such was not necessarily a liberalizing piece of legislation, but Van Rooyen, intent on reform, could interpret its provisions in ways that led to less extreme forms of censorship. For example, he introduced the concept of the "likely reader" of a given publication, which allowed him to argue that *Apartheid in Crisis* was "not undesirable" because "should the book be read by large numbers of blacks it may well incite many of them to violence . . . but this is not a book for the masses" (qtd. in Bauer, "Search" 14). He provided similar reasoning for not banning Gramsci's *Political Thought*: "For the man in the street, the book will hardly be understandable and for the revolutionary, if he can understand it, it will be boring and uninspiring unless he is also a philosopher" (qtd. in Bauer, "Search" 14). As Charlotte Bauer notes, "As he is a great believer in the 'likely reader,' Van Rooyen's judgements often use the 'sophistication' of the viewer or reader as leverage for passing something academic, esoteric, or 'arty'" (Bauer, "Search" 14). Van Rooyen's approach thus seemed to contain a paradox: the rather elitist assumptions informing his concept of the "likely reader" served as a liberalizing force that allowed for the publication of information that otherwise would have been banned.

Richard Abel cited the liberalizing tendency of the PAB under Van Rooyen to highlight the failure of the apartheid judiciary: "The failure of judicial review contrasts sharply with the protection sometimes afforded critical publications by the PAB, even though members lacked lifetime tenure and professional status. . . . They sought consistency, predictability, and certainty. They accepted the defense of truth. They tolerated bias and criticism. They acknowledged ambiguity, refusing to choose the worst of several possible interpretations" (308). An article in *New Nation* at the time headlined "Sensible Voices from the Appeal Board" outlined some additional standards established by the PAB under Van Rooyen's leadership that made it more progressive. Some of the grounds no longer used to censor material included, for example, "sympathy with socialism, communism and prohibited organisations"; criticism of the South African government and military; calls for strikes and the release of Mandela; and objections to conscription. The article also quotes Van Rooyen as noting that "freedom of speech is a mechanism which acts as a safety valve" and that it is important "not to overreact to opposite points of view because that could cause sufficient unhappiness to lead to or contribute to subversion or even violence" (page number illegible). As Bauer notes in one of her articles, Van Rooyen's tenure was "remarkably different from [his] stuffy predecessor, Lammie Snyman" ("Search" 14).

While the PAB under Van Rooyen did soften some of the more egregious effects of censorship, several other constraints continued to stifle genuine reform. Similar to the court system, which consisted of liberal and conservative judges, there were similarly more liberal and conservative publication committees. Although Van Rooyen introduced some progressive criteria, many publication committees remained for the most part very conservative.[6] Moreover, Powell notes the minuscule number of appeals the PAB actually heard: "Only a small fraction of committee bannings ever go before the Publications Appeal Board. On average more than 2,000 objects, publications, entertainments and films are banned each year, but there have seldom if ever been as many as 200 PAB hearings" ("Most Censored" 17). Based on these figures, 90 percent of the decisions made by publication committees, which were mostly conservative, never reached the more progressive PAB for consideration.

There was resistance to the PAB not only from other publications committees but also from other sites within the apartheid bureaucracy. The tensions between the PAB and the rest of the apartheid government were clearly and publicly on display regarding the Hollywood film *Cry Freedom*. Even though a publications committee ruled that the film could be shown in South Africa and even when the PAB upheld this ruling after the minister of home affairs directed a review of this decision, the police nevertheless stepped in and refused to allow the film to be shown. When the information minister confiscated *Cry Freedom* despite the fact that the Publications Appeal Board had not banned it, he merely said that he had "hoped the 'censor board would do its job'" (Abel 295). Bauer and Johnson of the *Weekly Mail* noted the following in an article with the astute title "The State vs. the State": "[T]he [PAB] board operates under state sufferance and if overruled is powerless to do anything about it. As a prominent media lawyer pointed out: 'Where the forces of law and order perceive the security situation to be paramount, they will override the board, time and time again'" (17). Peter McDonald, author of *The Literature Police*, concurs: "Given the larger context in which the government was steadily increasing its powers of direct censorship—not only through emergency legislation but with other statutory instruments like the Internal Security Act, 1982—the beneficial effects of Van Rooyen's reforms were, at best, localized" (78).

Thus, even though the putative role of the PAB was to render the final decisions regarding publications in South Africa under the Publications Act, the police had several other laws they could invoke to ban material not banned by the PAB. Some of Van Rooyen's decisions, particularly his decision not to ban *Cry Freedom*, gave him the reputation of being "an overly liberal reformer" (McDonald 82). In 1990, President de Klerk did not reappoint him because he "considered him a liability" and "because the government was anxious not to alienate its reactionary support base during the uncertain transitional period" (82).

The PAB under Van Rooyen was thus a curious entity. On the one hand, it sought to allow for more freedom of expression by introducing more progressive standards within the censorship apparatus. On the other hand, it was still a censorship board that prohibited the publication and distribution of material that would readily be available in a more open society. In addition, Van Rooyen clearly did not have the support of other publications committees, and other sites of power within the government at times ignored PAB decisions.

Given these complexities, there was considerable disagreement about Van Rooyen's role. Some praised his efforts. A *New Nation* article that examined the PAB's decision to reverse a publications committee's decision banning the children's book *Two Dogs and Freedom* observed, "It would seem there are voices within the Appeal Board which the government would do well to take heed of" ("Sensible Voices"). Others, however, viewed Van Rooyen and the PAB much more skeptically. Merrett argued in a letter published in the *Weekly Mail* shortly after it ran its profile on Van Rooyen, "His liberalising tendencies which come across as endearing may be seen from another angle as simply a shift in the tactics of apartheid, an ideology notable for expediency as well as immorality. What we really need to know about Van Rooyen is whether he supports the scrapping of political censorship; and when he intends to do something about it. Until then he remains an apartheid functionary" (10). Similarly, an attorney who reviewed Van Rooyen's book *Censorship in South Africa* for the *Weekly Mail* offered the following observation: "The author attempts to disguise what is really an exercise in propaganda—a defence of the system of censorship—as an academic work. No amount of legal fancy footwork can disguise the fact that glib lip-service to time honoured legal precepts is the most devastating possible negation of those precepts" ("Erudite" 27). Whether one viewed Van Rooyen's leadership of the PAB as a source of meaningful reform or mere tinkering within a corrupt system was perhaps not as important to those working at *New Nation* and the *Weekly Mail* as the fact that this entity could be used. For *New Nation*, favorable rulings by the PAB were primarily symbolic. Those at the *Weekly Mail*, however, were able to strategically capitalize on various PAB rulings to meaningfully increase their writing space.

The Publications Appeal Board and *New Nation*

New Nation used the PAB to reverse a publications committee's decision to ban four of its editions. In a ruling published in the *Government Gazette* in September 1988, the PAB determined that the committees did not have sufficient grounds to ban these particular editions of the newspaper. In a lengthy article, *New Nation* summarized the key points of the PAB's decision. The PAB's ruling demonstrated the mental gymnastics required to overturn this specific banning order while simultaneously seeking to preserve boundaries that should not be transgressed in the future. "Per se" was clearly a useful phrase for the liberalizing censor:

> The PAB further noted that Sisulu's remarks on the release of Mbeki were emotionally loaded words. The mere use of words like "fighting ranks" and "oppressed and fighting people" is an aggravating factor but not undesirable per se. The excessive use of such words may, however, in certain contexts lead to a finding of undesirability, said the PAB. . . . [T]he PC's [Publications Committee] argument on sympathy for prohibited organisations was also thrown out. The PAB said sympathy with such organisations was not undesirable per se. On the other hand, added the PAB, the situation changes when the views of a prohibited organization are presented and these views contain undesirable statements. (*"New Nation* Now Unbanned" 5)

The remainder of the article explains how the PAB rejected several elements of the initial committee's decision, concluding that "[t]here is no clear indication that a substantial section of the likely readership of *New Nation* will be more inclined to undesirable activities as a result of reading the issue of December 3–December 9" (5). The phrase "more inclined to undesirable activities" is fascinating in that it suggests censors could not only determine who "likely readers" might be but also how they might respond after reading a particular article.

There was a certain symbolic importance to the PAB's ruling. The fact that the PAB undermined a publications committee's reasoning for banning these editions of the newspaper served to bolster the repeated claims of *New Nation* and the *Weekly Mail* that the decision-making process for banning material was arbitrary and irrational. On the other hand, the PAB's ruling merely served to highlight its limited role within the overall censorship machinery. The appeal was actually heard when *New Nation* was already serving a three-month suspension mandated by the minister of home affairs, and the PAB's decision was rendered after the suspension had been lifted. It perhaps provided a moral victory for the newspaper, but it was essentially meaningless in practical terms. It did not, for example, prevent the confiscation of these editions, nor did it in any way affect the three-month closure of *New Nation*. Moreover, given the paper's financial situation and strained distribution system, it was not feasible for *New Nation* to reissue those editions that had been officially unbanned, and even if it could, the events discussed in those editions were no longer timely. In short, it was a moral victory with little practical value.

The Publications Appeal Board and the *Weekly Mail*

The *Weekly Mail*, however, was able to use the PAB on several occasions to actually increase its writing space. This tactic involved capitalizing on progressive rulings of the PAB for the purposes of quoting those who had been banned or of citing information that violated other censorship laws. Perhaps the best example of this was a spread the *Weekly Mail* published after the PAB ruled that the book *The Fifties People of South Africa* was "not undesirable." In two full pages, the *Weekly Mail* published several pictures from this book, including those of Nelson Mandela and other ANC leaders. The accompanying text of the article explains the presence of these photographs, which must have taken *Weekly Mail* readers, as well as the security police, by surprise: "Since Mandela and the other Rivonia trialists were sentenced to life imprisonment in 1964,[7] photographs of them have been prohibited by the notorious Prisons Act. Now a new book on the shelves, *The Fifties People of South Africa*, includes never-before [seen] pictures of Mandela and others—and it has been passed by the Publications Control Directorate" ("It's Mandela" 14). An examination of these two pages reveals the sheer delight the *Weekly Mail* took in publishing these photographs. At the top of the page, the headline reads in big, bold letters "It's Mandela," and in the middle of the page, in equally large letters, "And It's Legal." The pictures themselves are quite large. One depicts a youthful Mandela, in a boxing pose, with the caption reading, "Recognise this sporting young man? His seldom-seen face appears in a remarkable collection of historic pictures, published this week. And, most remarkable of all, the collection is openly on sale—passed by the Directorate of Publications" (14). Beneath the picture itself is the following: "It can't be! Yes it is. In print. In South Africa." On the opposite page is a picture of Albert Luthuli, former president of the ANC and recipient of the Nobel Peace Prize. This picture, as large as Mandela's, shows Luthuli in a suit and tie with his hand over his stomach—laughing.

Eight months after the PAB's decision, an article appeared in the *Weekly Mail* headlined "Test Trial for Mandela Photo" explaining how the government was bringing charges against the publisher and the photographer of *The Fifties People of South Africa* for violating the Prisons Act, which "forbids pictures of prisoners, except under specific circumstances or where permission is given" (5). The article also notes, "However, the book has been passed for

Image 2.3 The *Weekly Mail* gleefully capitalized on a favorable ruling by the Publications Appeal Board (PAB) to publish forbidden images. While the newspaper claimed to be on solid legal ground because these images were approved by the PAB, the government could have invoked other censorship restrictions to declare the *Weekly Mail* was in violation of the law.

publication by the Publications Appeal Board" (5). This situation highlights the complexities and contradictions within the censorship apparatus. It also provides a stark contrast to the experiences of the *New Nation*: whereas the PAB ruling that overturned a lower decision came too late in the case of *New Nation*, precisely the opposite dynamic occurred in this instance. Even though the state eventually brought a case against the publisher of *The Fifties People of South Africa*, the *Weekly Mail* had already published and distributed these photographs to thousands of readers.

In another instance, the *Weekly Mail* used a PAB ruling to publish the words of Steve Biko. Beneath the article headline, "The Quotable Biko: 12 Years Later," is the following heading: "In print, for the first time in 12 years: the words of Steve Biko, extracted from his book 'I Write What I Like,' banned in 1973 and unbanned last week. Readers will note the continued relevance of this extract to the present day" (15). The article itself contains no summary or analysis but rather consists exclusively of excerpts from Biko's book.

The *Weekly Mail* also published excerpts of books prior to their release in South Africa, no doubt realizing the possibility that they could eventually be banned. For example, it published several excerpts in April and May 1986 from a Pulitzer Prize–winning book entitled *Move Your Shadow*, by Joseph Lelyveld, a *New York Times* correspondent who had lived in South Africa. It also published passages from *Thirty Years of the Freedom Charter*, by Raymond Suttner and Jeremy Cronin, which was ultimately banned by a publications committee. This incident provides yet another example of the opening and closing of writing space. In its 28 June 1985 edition the *Weekly Mail* published extensive excerpts from this book. By June 1986, however, the following statement appeared at the end of a *Weekly Mail* review of this same book: "The book was banned soon after this review was written. As a result, sections quoting from the text had to be cut" (Innes 19). Because of its aggressive strategy, therefore, the *Weekly Mail* was able to publish lengthy excerpts from a book in June 1985 that it could not selectively quote from in June 1986.

A GIFT FROM THE BUREAU
OF INFORMATION

Perhaps the most famous instance in which the *Weekly Mail* seized upon an opening provided by the cumbersome apartheid bureaucracy was when it pub-

THE CASE FOR BIG BUSINESS
By GAVIN RELLY

THE CASE FOR STATE CONTROL
By DUNCAN INNES
PAGE 14 & 15

THE CASE FOR AN ALTERNATIVE PRESS
PAGE 10

THE WEEKLY MAIL

Volume 2, Number 22, FRIDAY JUNE 6 to THURSDAY JUNE 12, 1986

THE PAPER FOR A CHANGING SOUTH AFRICA

PRICES: JOHANNESBURG, PRETORIA & REEF R1,00 (plus 12c GST) | ELSEWHERE IN SA R1,12 (excl. GST)

MPs block attempts to ram through Bills

Parliament's Young Turks challenge Le Grange Bills

By JEAN LE MAY in Cape Town and WEEKLY MAIL REPORTERS in Johannesburg and Durban

A SUDDEN surge of opposition by "Young Turks" among coloured and Indian MPs to the two security Bills now before Parliament indicates a leadership crisis for the two Ministers Without Portfolio, the Rev Allan Hendrickse and Amichand Rajbansi.

By deciding to send the two Bills back to the Standing Committee on Law and Order, the (coloured) House of Representatives and the (Indian) House of Delegates have probably stymied Law and Order Minister Louis le Grange's attempts to ram the Bills through parliament before June 16.

But even if the two Bills go back to the standing committee on Monday, there is a chance they could come up for debate again the following week, if they get through the committee in a mutually acceptable form. If they don't, there could be another deadlock.

And given the present mood of the Labour Party and the National People's Party caucuses, this could be on the cards.

If that happens, the Bills could still be sent to the President's Council. But then the government would, in effect, be bypassing parliament altogether — and the National Party would have to consider whether it can afford to do this in the present crisis situation.

The Bills are the Public Safety Amendment Bill, which would enable the Minister to declare "unrest areas", and the Internal Security Amendment Bill, which extends the present 14-day detention of Section 50 to 180 days on the order of a police officer above the rank of Lieutenant-Colonel.

Le Grange's urgency to get the Bills passed, and his banning of indoor commemorative meetings up to the end of June, indicates that he expects an upsurge of violence at mid-month and has given rise to fears of an imminent clampdown on anti-apartheid organisations.

Earlier the Labour Party had earlier tabled several "softening" amendments dealing with access of detainees to relatives and lawyers, proposing judicial supervision of detainees and writing in a safeguard on any indemnity which may be included in regulations which the Minister may gazette.

Solidarity, the opposition party in the House of Delegates, however, joined the Progressive Federal Party opposition in the House of Assembly in refusing to accept the principles of the two Bills.

Solidarity spokesmen said they would propose, when the Bills came up in the House of Delegates, that they should be read "this day six months" — that is, never. It is the strongest form of disapprobation possible, and a considerable body of MPs in both houses, and particularly in the House of Representatives, urged that line be taken.

The point was strongly put in caucus that the Labour Party and the National People's Party had gone into the tricameral system on the platform of destroying apartheid from within, and that what they had achieved so far had been minimal.

Although the two Bills were not apartheid Bills per se, speakers emphasised that if they got any support at all from the coloured and Indian houses, the credibility of MPs would sink lower than it had ever been and there would be no chance of restoring it.

● To PAGE 2

LOUIS NEL'S 'ANC-KNOCKING' BOOKLET INCLUDES THIS MANDELA PICTURE:

The first legal photo of Nelson Mandela in 22 years

(COURTESY OF THE MINISTER OF INFORMATION)

EVERYONE knows his name and what he stands for. But almost no-one knows what Nelson Mandela looks like.

This is because it has been illegal to photograph him or to reprint an old photograph of him for the 22 years he has been a prisoner of the state.

Until this week, that is.

This photograph, right, taken before Mandela was imprisoned for sabotage in 1964, was reproduced this week by the Bureau of Information in their new propaganda booklet, "Talking to the ANC".

It is the first time since 1964 that it has been legal in this country to publish a photograph of South Africa's most famous political prisoner, the leader of the banned African National Congress and by most accounts the most popular leader among blacks.

It is only legal because permission was given by the Department of Prisons. All other pictures, drawings or representations of the man are still illegal.

The controversial Bureau of Information booklet is intended to show South Africans that it is folly to talk of negotiation with the ANC.

●See "UDF calls for ANC unbanning", page 3

JUNE 16 BANS
Lawyers plan to challenge ban in court **2**

WINTERVELD
The man who ordered police to shoot tells why **7**

WITS VIOLENCE
Three angry days as campus erupts **9**

THE FAR-RIGHT
The AWB's anti-semitic streak **11**

Call for press curbs

A CONSERVATIVE PARTY MP, Dr Frans van Staden, yesterday said that more drastic measures might have to be taken in future against "liberal" and "integrationist" publications.

Speaking during the second reading debate on the Publications Amendment Bill, he said the measures might be necessary to check the continued increase in "liberal

Historic Weekly Mail birthday debate

THE Weekly Mail will celebrate its first birthday next week by hosting an historic meeting: the first direct encounter between the two most powerful men in the mining industry, Harry Oppenheimer and Cyril Ramaphosa.

Weekly Mail has organised for these two men to share a platform, meeting each other for the first time.

Oppenheimer, former chairman of South Africa's two biggest mining houses, Anglo American and De Beers, and Ramaphosa, general secretary of

will be meeting at a crucial time — while tense annual wage negotiations between their respective organisations are in progress.

The Weekly Mail will also be holding an exhibition of news photographs that have appeared in the paper in the first year of

leading photographers, including Gideon Mendel, Paul Weinberg and Trevor Samson.

The exhibition will be opened on Sunday night by leading foreign correspondent and former editor of the Rand Daily Mail, Allister Sparks.

The exhibition, at the Market

Image 2.4 The *Weekly Mail* published the first picture of Nelson Mandela in more than two decades by seizing on a picture contained in an obscure government booklet and using an aggressive legal interpretation concerning the "permission" granted for publishing this photograph.

lished the first photograph of Nelson Mandela in South Africa in more than two decades. Anton Harber recalled this particular success during an interview: "[We were] constantly using secondary sources, things said at official press conferences, things said in Parliament, [and] things from government documents, such as the famous Mandela picture, which came from a government booklet." The picture Harber referred to was an eight-inch picture of Mandela published on the front page of the *Weekly Mail*'s 6 June 1986 edition under the headline, "The First Legal Photo of Nelson Mandela in 22 Years." The source for this photograph: a government booklet entitled *Talking to the ANC*, issued by the Bureau of Information. The statement next to the photograph reads, "It is only legal because permission was given by the Department of Prisons. All other pictures, drawings or representations of the man are still illegal. The controversial Bureau of Information booklet is intended to show South Africans that it is folly to talk of negotiation with the ANC" (1). Although it is true that the Department of Prisons granted permission to the Bureau of Information to publish this photograph, it also true that the *Weekly Mail* took a rather expansive interpretation of this permission, arguing that it was "attached to the photograph, not the booklet or the Bureau" (Ludman 86).

Within the vast bureaucracy of the South African government, therefore, a single department, the Bureau of Information, published a single propaganda booklet intended to smear the ANC—and in the process unwittingly opened the door for the *Weekly Mail* to publish the first legal photograph in twenty-two years of the apartheid regime's most prominent enemy. While the *Weekly Mail* often sought to promote the impression that it was earnestly trying to comply with the law, a dynamic discussed in chapter 4, the temptation to gloat on this particular occasion was simply too strong. In large print next to the photograph of Mandela, the editors wrote, "(Courtesy of the Minister of Information)" (1). The publication of this photograph with this particular caption must have been as infuriating to members of the apartheid government as it was gratifying to readers of the *Weekly Mail*.

In the 26 September 1986 edition, the *Weekly Mail* published this same picture of Mandela again, accompanied by a picture of several individuals attending an ANC meeting. Beneath the two photographs was the following explanation: "Invisible Man: The Bureau of Information booklet, 'Talking with the ANC' was a surprise hit in the townships, thanks to a portrait of Nelson Mandela (above), the only photograph the government has allowed since the ANC leader's imprisonment in 1964. The booklet has since been quietly re-issued, with just one change: the picture of Mandela has vanished (below) to be replaced by an innocuous group picture of a 1930s ANC meeting" ("Invisible Man" 7). The *Weekly Mail* thus published this photograph of Mandela not once but twice, and in the process, managed to poke a little fun at the government by noting how the original booklet intended to smear the ANC had in fact been "a surprise hit in the townships."

It is tempting to analyze the ability of the *Weekly Mail* to publish this photograph as a result of bungling apartheid bureaucrats. This incident, however, perhaps more clearly illustrates the ingenious ways in which those intent on resistance can seize upon opportunities presented within complex bureaucracies. For those working in the Bureau of Information, they were given a task: create a booklet to discredit the ANC. Given that Mandela was considered public enemy number one for his role in forming and leading the armed wing of the ANC, it is certainly understandable why those who produced this booklet would include a picture of him. How could those responsible for creating such a publication possibly anticipate that an opposition newspaper would seize upon this one photograph contained within this one booklet, isolate it from the rest of the publication, blow it up, and publish it on its front page? In fact, it would have been remarkable had anyone actually anticipated such a possibility.

The *Weekly Mail* utilized the very same tactic to publish yet another picture of Mandela in its 24 February 1989 edition. On page 6, the newspaper published the famous picture of Nelson Mandela talking in earnest with Walter Sisulu on Robben Island. Beneath this picture is the following: "A rather fuzzy picture of two men deep in conversation. What makes it remarkable is the place (Robben Island) and the people (Nelson Mandela and Walter Sisulu). Is the picture legal? Well, it must be. It comes courtesy of the government's own Bureau for Information, which has reprinted 15 000 copies of a US publication, *Problems of Communism*, containing this rare 1966 photograph, the most recent known picture of the ANC leaders" ("Rather Fuzzy" 6).

Again, one may be tempted to scoff at the apparent incompetence of the Bureau of Information to be fooled not once but twice by the same newspaper using the same tactic. But some questions to consider: Was the same unit of the bureau involved in this second incident, given that it involved "reprinting" a publication from the United States? Were the same people in positions of leadership at the bureau, people who may have had some institutional memory concerning the first incident? These questions are designed not to provide excuses for apartheid bureaucrats but rather to highlight the real challenge of censoring information within a vast, decentralized bureaucracy, particularly when dealing with those who are dedicated to pouncing on any misstep.

CONCLUSION

Staff from the *Weekly Mail* and *New Nation* were thus able to expand their writing space considerably precisely because the apartheid government was not as centralized as other repressive governments. The courts were a particularly valuable site of information. The charts in appendix B demonstrate the vast amount of information both newspapers were able to publish as a result of this particular tactic. As Harber explained, "One would watch trials particularly for the opportunity to publish. . . . We would closely follow the courts as a way of reporting on things." Journalists, in other words, did not simply wait passively for information to dribble out but rather read the institutional landscape to actively seek out opportunities. They attended certain political trials, worked with sympathetic MPs, read publications cleared by the Publications Appeal Board, and strategically used documents produced by the government.

In addition, the *Weekly Mail* and *New Nation* were also able to synthesize information obtained from various court documents to provide an overview of a particular issue. For example, Anton Harber wrote a piece entitled "The Torture File" in which he provided an analysis of torture based on information revealed by a district surgeon in the Port Elizabeth Supreme Court, as well as the applications filed before the Durban Supreme Court. Another *Weekly Mail* article, "Startling Allegations against the Police," used information obtained from students' allegations against the police in Athlone, as well affidavits collected by the Progressive Federal Party. A third *Weekly Mail* article, "SADF in the Dock," began as follows: "The South African Defence Force and its soldiers stand accused in three court cases this week: of murdering civilians in Northern Namibia, of stabbing to death a Swapo leader in Windhoek and of using illegal 'dirty tricks' against its critics. In all three cases, two in Windhoek and one in Cape Town, the SADF and the government tried to keep the details secret. They failed. As a result, the three cases have been heard in public, bringing to light serious allegations about the behaviour of SADF soldiers" (Davis 1). The remainder of the article presents extensive analysis of each trial.

New Nation also used this approach. In the article "Torture: The Pain of Repression," the journalist cites numerous examples of torture revealed in various contexts and concludes, "[b]ut the overwhelming evidence of affidavits, inquests into deaths in custody, allegations in open court, medical evidence and eye witness statements proves beyond doubt that torture is rife in South Africa's prisons and jails" (6). These synthesis articles were extremely valuable. Dedicated readers of these newspapers certainly would have read many stories of individual abuse over time, but these articles effectively connected the dots and demonstrated patterns of abuse on the part of the South African military and police forces.

By adopting this aggressive approach and using sites within the government itself to expand its writing space, those working for these opposition newspapers put the apartheid government in a genuine bind. To allow journalists to continue to exploit these gaps would allow them to write articles that damaged its reputation. To close these gaps and deny public access to the courts or Parliament, however, would also damage its reputation, leaving the government open to accusations that it conducted kangaroo courts and had a phony parliament. In short, the *Weekly Mail* and *New Nation* made it extremely challenging for this illegitimate government to continue its façade of legitimacy; one of the many reasons the apartheid government hated both newspapers with such intensity.

3

"OBLIQUE SPEAK"

Rhetorical Tactics for Constructing Meaning Subversively

Sophisticated newspaper readers learned to read hidden codes that allowed much more to be left unsaid.
IRWIN MANOIM, *YOU HAVE BEEN WARNED*

Tell all the Truth but tell it slant
EMILY DICKINSON

This chapter examines how the *Weekly Mail* and *New Nation* expanded their writing space by constructing meaning subversively with their readers, whereas the subsequent chapters examine these newspapers' legal tactics. These categories of analysis—rhetorical versus legal—are admittedly porous. Rhetorical tactics were developed, after all, with the law in mind and thus had a legal dimension. Similarly, as will be examined extensively in the next two chapters, legal tactics clearly contained a rhetorical dimension in that journalists crafted articles with the government censors in mind. Although the distinction between rhetorical and legal tactics is not absolute, these categories nevertheless provide a useful framework for analyzing the articles produced by both the *Weekly Mail* and *New Nation*.

Legal tactics, according to this framework, consisted of the following two features. First, the government was the primary audience; second, the information conveyed using legal tactics could be grasped by any reader regardless of personal background, such as political affiliation, knowledge of the anti-apartheid movement, and/or beliefs or assumptions regarding the steps the government might take to maintain order. The photograph of Nelson Mandela from the Bureau of Information booklet examined in the previous chapter provides an excellent example of a legal tactic. The *Weekly Mail* seized upon a picture contained within a government publication and then attached a legal rationale to explain why publishing the picture was permissible. Anyone who would have seen this photograph in the newspaper—those who supported or those who opposed the government—would have recognized that the *Weekly Mail* was using a legal loophole to circumvent the censorship restrictions to publish material it was not supposed to.

Rhetorical tactics, on the other hand, depended on the ways in which writers constructed meaning subversively with their intended readers. Allusions, repetition, and arrangement were just a few examples of these tactics. Journalists used rhetorical indirection in hopes that their audience would use their critical reading skills and knowledge of the apartheid government to grasp veiled meanings journalists could not explicitly state. The success of this approach depended on many shared assumptions between writers and readers, including the fact that the government was engaging in extensive illegal activity: torture, targeted assassination, and so on. The writing space these journalists created by using these rhetorical tactics, similar to every other approach they used, was made possible by the government's attempt to create an image of legitimacy. Even though it was using many forms of violence, including the use of death squads, officials publicly denied involvement and perpetrators took active steps to conceal their actions. By doing so, the apartheid government created a significant opening these newspapers could exploit.

"OBLIQUE SPEAK"

James Scott observes that those who face the possibility of adverse consequences for expressing their views openly rely on two basic tactics: "those that disguise the message and those that disguise the messenger" (138). As noted in the introduction, members of the ANC and SACP who distributed material underground fell into the second group. They could write anything they wished since what they were doing was already illegal. The primary challenges for this group were not necessarily during the writing process itself but rather remaining anonymous while producing and disseminating this material.

Those writing for the *Weekly Mail* and *New Nation,* however, sought to operate in what Scott calls the public transcript. Their publications could be sold openly so long as they stayed within the confines of the law. Scott observes, as noted in the introductory chapter, that "if anonymity often encourages the delivery of an *un*varnished message, the veiling of a message represents the application of varnish" (152). He elaborates on the challenges inherent in such an approach: "If the message is too explicit, its bearers risk open retaliation; if it is too vague, it passes unnoticed altogether" (156). The trick for those seeking to communicate publicly in contexts of oppression, therefore, is to walk that precarious line so that the intended meaning is conveyed to one's intended audience in such a way that it is not noticed by the powerful or, as was the case in this particular context, in such a way that it proved too awkward for the government to suppress because of domestic and international power dynamics.

Irwin Manoim coined a term to capture this form of communication: "oblique speak," which he defined as "communication by implication" (*Warned* 74). As he observes in his book, "sophisticated newspaper readers learned to read hidden codes that allowed much more to be *left unsaid*" (*Warned* 74; emphasis added). Oblique speak as a strategy consisted of several different tactics. First, writers could use allusions and words that had ambiguous or double meanings for the purpose of conveying their intended message. Second, writers could describe certain events or facts in an uncoded manner that would allow readers, through either inductive or deductive reasoning, to reach obvious conclusions that were implied but unstated. I refer to this second tactic as the "subversive enthymeme." These two tactics—using coded language and leading readers to obvious but unstated conclusions—were often used in conjunction with one another within the same article.

ALLUSIONS AS CODED LANGUAGE

Allusions were used extensively by journalists at both newspapers. Chaim Perelman and Lucie Olbrechts-Tyteca's definition of allusion is particularly useful in understanding how allusions worked in this context: "There is allusion when the interpretation of a passage would be incomplete if one neglected the deliberate reference of the author to something he evokes without actually naming it; this thing may be an event of the past, a custom, or a cultural fact, knowledge of which is peculiar to the members of the group with whom the speaker is trying to establish communion" (177).[1] Allusions were particularly useful when describing what the apartheid government referred to as "security force action." In short, journalists could "make deliberate references to" these activities "without actually naming" them. The emergency regulations, for example, specifically restricted the publication of any report dealing with "any damaged or destroyed property or injured or dead persons or other visible signs of violence at the scene where unrest or security action was taking or has taken place or any injuries sustained by any person in or during unrest or security action" (Stuart 282). Some of the activities masked by the euphemism "security force action" involved dispersing crowds with massive violence, including whipping them with *sjamboks*, and sometimes using lethal force. The Truth and Reconciliation Commission (TRC) notes that the police often used "deadly force in situations where lesser measures would have sufficed for the restoration or maintenance of public order" (vol. 2, 182). Moreover, the TRC specifically identifies the role that censorship played in abetting these abuses: "Press restrictions ensured the absence of the media during dispersal and unrest situations, further shielding police actions from public censure" (vol. 2, 181). Journalists were not even supposed to be present at "scenes of unrest," and even if they were and observed these events firsthand or if they were told about these abuses by witnesses, the emergency restrictions prohibited them from publishing these accounts.

Journalists, however, figured out ways of circumventing this restriction. Sefako Nyaka, from the *Weekly Mail*, said, "I remember we would describe a certain incident involving a group of people who were traveling in a van. It happened in Orlando West [a township]. We're not saying it's [the police]. These people were traveling in this van, and they then came across another group that was standing idly by, and when this group saw the other group coming, the group ran, and the other group then chased them, you know." Ryland Fisher, a journalist at *New Nation*, described this dynamic as well: "So for instance, one of the emergency regulations that they introduced at some point was that you couldn't write about the actions of security forces. So we never wrote about the police. But we did write about men in blue uniforms, driving yellow

vehicles, engaged in a certain activity, and you know, involving a group of people who are unhappy about something. So it was ridiculous, and if you read
it now, it would seem totally stupid. But people knew what we were writing
about." Readers of these opposition newspapers understood these references
precisely because of the cultural knowledge they shared with the journalists
about the realities of apartheid South Africa at that time. Readers of these
newspapers would know, for example, that the only "van" that would ever drive
through a township would be a police vehicle. Similarly, people who attended
demonstrations, or had friends and family members who did, knew about the
harsh methods used by police. As Fisher explains, "There was a time in that
period from '85 to just before 1990 when there were protest marches almost
every day, and it became so predictable. There would be a protest march, the
police would come, give them five minutes to disperse, two minutes later they
would beat up people. That happened every week, throughout the country. And
people knew those things were happening. Even if we couldn't write about it,
we could allude to it, and people would know what we were talking about."
Journalists could adhere to the letter of the law, therefore, by never directly
identifying the security forces by name but instead using various code words
and descriptions to convey their meaning.

Articles that appeared in the *Weekly Mail* and *New Nation* also utilized
allusions to report on the actions of the security forces. One allusion com-
monly used was to refer to the skin color of the security forces. The article
headlined "Three Arson Attacks in a Night," which appeared in the *Weekly
Mail*, contains the following passage: "According to the night guard on duty at
Khotso House, two white people smashed the entrance door with hammers 'at
about 3am.' . . . The Khotso House attack followed the incident at Ravan Press
house, where the night watch . . . telephoned one of the staff 'at about 2am' after
he saw three white men on the verandah" (3). Readers of these newspapers
would clearly understand these veiled references to "white men," particularly
since Khotso House, which served as the headquarters for the South African
Council of Churches, housed many anti-apartheid organizations, and Ravan
Press was a well-known publisher of anti-apartheid materials. The fact that
two buildings housing anti-apartheid organizations were attacked on the
very same evening would of course have raised suspicions. But the fact that
"white men" were actually observed at the scene provided virtual confirma-
tion of security force involvement. The Truth and Reconciliation Commission
subsequently confirmed that Khotso House was in fact attacked by security

forces and the order had been given by P. W. Botha, the president of South Africa.[2] Although journalists at the time could not have known that the order to destroy Khotso House came from the president himself, they were able to publish an article—during the state of emergency—that very strongly implied government involvement.

Other allusions referred to the clothing worn by security forces. A *Weekly Mail* article, "Uniformed Whites Linked to Firebombing," notes not only the skin color of the men in question but also how they were dressed: "Two uniformed white men were seen speeding off in a blue Ford Sierra immediately after a petrol bomb attack on the home of an Alexandra activist" (Madonsela and Mzimkulu 2). Sometimes journalists referred to the masks security forces wore when they engaged in illegal activities, as in another *Weekly Mail* article, "Balaclava Men Seen at 'Cheeky' Explosion": "Men disguised in balaclavas were seen at the home of the Port Elizabeth Watson family shortly before an explosion[,] heard 10km away, demolished the house" (Bekker 2). Journalists sometimes used multiple allusions within the same article, as demonstrated in the *New Nation* article "72 Hours of Terror," which recounts the kidnapping and torture of an activist living in Moutse: "A Moutse activist this week gave a harrowing account of 72 hours of interrogation and torture at the hands of four hooded white men. . . . The alleged abductors spoke in Afrikaans throughout the ordeal and never removed their hoods" (1). The article explains that these individuals "warned him that they would continue monitoring his activities through their informers" and concludes by noting how this unnamed individual had been detained by the police previously "as a result of his political activities" (1). Although the police are never directly mentioned in this article, the use of so many allusions within a single article demonstrates how oblique speak could at times convey meanings that were not particularly oblique.

Some journalists even included the fact that the individuals in question "identified" themselves as police without ever explicitly claiming that these individuals were in fact the police. Amrit Manga of *New Nation* explained: "But [this is] the way we would do it. The family says, 'People arrived here last night, identified themselves as police.'" The *New Nation* article "Mystery Surrounds Mofolo Night Raiders" provides an example of this approach: "In a sworn affidavit, a Mofolo South resident, Margaret Msengana, described how a band of hooded men in blue overalls carrying weapons raided her house in the early hours of May 4. According to Mrs. Msengana, the men identified themselves as police before searching the house" (1). The article proceeds to describe another incident that occurred at a house owned by the Ngwenya family: "Three hooded men, each carrying two guns—one a pump-action shotgun—entered the house. Ngwenya says they wore rubber boots, while some were clothed in the blue overalls similar to those worn by special recruits" (1). Ryland Fisher may very well have been thinking of articles such as this when he claimed that they might "seem ridiculous" if read today. Not only does this article contain all of the code words for the police—"hooded men," "blue overalls," "carrying weapons"—but it also notes that these men "identified themselves as police." And yet nowhere in the article does the journalist explicitly claim that these men were police.[3]

These examples highlight some fascinating features about both the nature of the restrictions and oblique speak. Again, while there were moments when the full appreciation of oblique speak might depend on one's background and/or cultural knowledge, in other instances the meaning of articles that used oblique speak was apparent to practically everyone. The following absurd situation thus existed in the apartheid context: it was "illegal" to explicitly make certain claims, but it was "legal" to provide enough cues so that virtually any reader could understand the *meaning* of that which could not be explicitly stated.

Coded words and phrases were also useful for conveying calls for action made by individuals and groups in the anti-apartheid movement. For example, Amrit Manga explained, "We would not be able to report on the fact that trade unions had planned a strike." Manga was referring to Regulation 4 of Proclamation R224, which pertained to "subversive statements," that prohibited the publication of statements that encouraged others "to take part in a boycott" or to "stay away from work or to strike unless it was in accordance with the Labour Relations Act of 1956" (Cooper et al., *Race Relations 1986* 841). Manga explained how journalists could circumvent this restriction: "We would then say that the union is 'considering' that its workers not . . . go to work. No final decision had been taken, but there is 'strong support' for the position. It was understood that there would be a stay away on that day." In other words, readers involved in the labor movement would know the restrictions operating on these newspapers and would understand that an article describing "strong support" for a strike was in fact code for "strike."

Howard Barrell made a similar observation about how he used code words when he worked at Capital Radio. As a member of the ANC, Barrell often sought to use journalism to advance ANC objectives, but he could not, of course, overtly reveal this. He recalled how the ANC would "release a pamphlet saying they had a three-day stay away or they're supporting the cause by COSATU, a trade union federation at the time, for a three-day stay away, in connection with some political demand." Barrell was not able to report that the ANC, a banned organization, was in full support of a stay away, particularly in the strong rhetorical terms the ANC would have used in their pamphlets. His solution: use the double meaning of the term "expect." Barrell explained, "Let's just take the word 'expect.' *Expect* can mean 'anticipate' or it can have the connotation of 'demand.' I 'expect' you do to it, I require you do it. It has this kind of ambiguity." When reporting the ANC's position on the stay away, therefore, Barrell would state that "the ANC expects" people to support the stay away in the hopes that ANC supporters and sympathizers would interpret this statement as a "demand" or "requirement." Should Barrell ever be accused by the authorities of seeking to promote the objectives of the ANC, he could always claim that he was simply using the word "expect" to mean "anticipate." When pressed on this example, Barrell conceded that he had no way of actually knowing whether listeners of these statements had constructed the meaning he intended. Both Manga's and Barrell's examples, however, demonstrate the importance of shared knowledge when conveying veiled meanings. Perhaps not every reader or listener of these reports grasped these intending meanings. But the likelihood certainly would have been much greater for those immersed in the labor movement and/or those sympathetic to the ANC.

SUBVERSIVE ENTHYMEMES AND UNSPOKEN CONCLUSIONS

In addition to relying on coded words and phrases to convey unstated meaning, journalists could also rely on readers to reach unstated conclusions based on a series of facts provided. I refer to this approach as the strategic enthymeme, a tactic that I argue represents a variation of the traditional enthymeme. To understand how it functioned, it is useful to recall the classic rhetorical example used to demonstrate the difference between syllogisms and enthymemes:

> Syllogism: Socrates is a man. All men are mortal. Therefore, Socrates is mortal.
> Enthymeme: Socrates is a man; therefore, he is mortal.

In this case, the rhetor expects the audience to supply the obvious missing claim, "All men are mortal."

Imagine a situation, however, in which restrictions expressly forbade anyone from stating the fact that Socrates will one day die. In such a context, one could convey this meaning by emphasizing the claims that naturally lead to this conclusion, trusting that readers would be able to take the final step on their own. In other words, one could use overwhelming evidence to demonstrate beyond a reasonable doubt that Socrates is in fact a man. Then one could provide overwhelming evidence to show beyond a reasonable doubt that all men up to this point in history have indeed been mortal. Rather than relying on the audience to fill in a missing claim leading to the conclusion, as is the case with the traditional enthymeme, a subversive enthymeme instead relies on the audience to fill in a logical conclusion that follows well-established claims.[4]

Some scholars have argued that this conception of the enthymeme as a truncated syllogism is overly restrictive. Specifically, John Gage points to Aristotle's claim that the enthymeme represents "the 'body' of all artistic proofs," to argue the following: "In Aristotle's view, it seems that all choices, including stylistic ones, must be based on a determination of what shared grounds exist for choosing some unshared thing to say that will have the potential to lead to new shared understanding. This dynamic is represented in the structure of the enthymeme, which derives its function from the relationship between a writer's intended conclusions and an audience's pre-existing assumptions. As such, the enthymeme can stand for the rhetorical conditions underlying all compositional decisions" (38–39). There are two significant features of Gage's definition. First, his more expansive definition of the enthymeme is useful for understanding the different forms of subversive enthymemes that were in fact used by journalists. In some instances, such as the two series about death squads that appeared in *New Nation* and examined later in this chapter, the subversive enthymemes developed by journalists adhered to the structure of a traditional syllogism and enthymeme. In other articles, however, the conclusions that journalists invited readers to reach did not fit as neatly into the rigid structure of a traditional enthymeme.

Second, although allusions and subversive enthymemes constitute different forms of oblique speak, they share an important common link: the shared cultural and political knowledge between writers and readers, as well as the fact that writers were keenly aware, as Gage notes, of their readers' "pre-existing assumptions." In other words, these newspapers were not appealing to those who had favorable or even ambivalent feelings about the government. Rather, strategic enthymemes and allusions were used for those who were under no illusions about the steps the government was taking against anti-apartheid activists.

Franz Kruger's article "Arsonists Burn Union Offices" provides an excellent example of how the use of selected facts and description could form a subversive enthymeme. This short article describes how an office building containing numerous anti-apartheid organizations was destroyed: "Office workers said it seemed that the arsonists had moved systematically through the offices, breaking through the offices, breaking down doors and checking through files before piling them on the floor and setting them alight with petrol" (3). The article concludes with the following statement: "Virtually wiped out was a trade union library established by Sached in the building, which is diagonally opposite the main police station in East London" (3). There is not a single allegation made against the police in this article, and yet this last fact, that the library destroyed was "diagonally opposite the main police station," should raise the eyebrows of the careful reader. How could arsonists "systematically" go through a building, "break down doors," and burn offices located next to the main police station—and not be apprehended, or at the very least, chased away? Moreover, some of the specific language used in the article is significant. The fact that intruders "systematically" went through these anti-apartheid organizations while "checking through files" certainly invites readers to conclude that these were the actions of security forces and not, say, random vandals or intoxicated youth.

SUBVERSIVE ENTHYMEMES AND ALLUSIONS RELATED TO DEATH SQUADS

Subversive enthymemes were perhaps most effective for articles focusing on political activists who had been murdered by the apartheid government. The apartheid government's use of violence against the political opposition escalated over time. At first, the government sought to silence opponents by passing various laws: banning individuals and political groups, legally charging and imprisoning individuals, and eventually detaining thousands without even charging them with crimes. As the anti-apartheid resistance continued to grow, the government increasingly resorted to violence, including the widespread use of torture. Torture had several objectives: to obtain information about other activists, to coerce activists to become informers, and to trauma-tize individuals so that they would be wary of engaging in future political resis-tance. The TRC succinctly describes the different forms of repression: "The security forces used both overt and clandestine methods to suppress resis-tance and counter armed actions by opponents of apartheid. Overt methods included bannings and banishment, detention without trial, judicial execu-tions and public order policing. More clandestine and covert forms of control included torture, extra-judicial killings and support for surrogate forces" (vol. 2, 165).

At a certain point in the struggle, members of the apartheid government began murdering political activists. According to the TRC report, "As the levels of conflict intensified, the security forces came to believe that it was no longer possible to rely on the due process of law and that it was preferable to kill people extra-judiciously" (vol. 2, 220). As Maj.-Gen. "Sakkie" Crafford explained in his testimony before the commission, "In some cases it was nec-essary to eliminate activists by killing them. This was the only way in which effective action could be taken against activists in a war situation. . . . To charge someone in the normal court structure and go through the whole process was cumbersome and occasionally totally inadequate and impossible" (vol. 2, 221). Even massive detention, arresting people without going through "the normal court structure," was eventually seen as too limited and potentially counter-productive by those in the government, since the detention of high-profile activists "would give momentum to the liberation struggle" (vol. 2, 221). As one apartheid official noted in his testimony to the TRC, "The security police and the country could not afford a Nelson Mandela again" (qtd. in vol. 2, 221). When banning, imprisonment, and detention failed to contain the anti-apartheid struggle, the government took the next horrifying step.

The government murdered so many activists that the TRC actually devised separate categories for these killings: "The Commission distinguished between four types of extra-judicial killings: targeted killings; killing following abduction and interrogation; ambushes where seemingly little or no attempt was made to effect arrest; and entrapment killings" (vol. 2, 222). In some instances, the bodies were found; in some instances, they were not and activ-ists simply went "missing." This was a particularly harrowing method since it not only resulted in the death of those individuals but also left loved ones in an agonizing limbo. Was there any hope that the person could still be alive? Might they be in hiding? Or were they dead? If they were dead, how were they killed? Who killed them? And where were their bodies?[5]

Significantly, the apartheid government always denied involvement in these murders and disappearances. In fact, members of the government devised implausible explanations, claiming at times, for example, that many of these killings were the result of in-fighting within the anti-apartheid movement. Unfortunately, these claims would sometimes be reported uncritically by mainstream media sources. Tyrone August, when discussing how difficult it had been for him to work in the mainstream media prior to working as a journalist at *New Nation*, provided the following example: "For instance, when Joe Slovo's wife, Ruth First, was murdered, the *Star* sort of unblushingly printed this report linking Joe Slovo to the assassination of his wife because of the kind of sources that they relied on."[6] Those working at the *Weekly Mail* and *New Nation* knew such claims were nonsense and could avoid contributing to the government's disinformation campaign, but they still did not have concrete, tangible proof that the government was linked to these killings. Moreover, they needed to be careful about reporting their suspicions too brazenly, as the government could always claim such an article violated a particular statute or regulation. To write articles about these murders, therefore, journalists relied extensively on both allusions and subversive enthymemes. Allusions were used when eyewitnesses observed what were believed to be members of the security forces perpetrating these crimes, whereas subversive enthymemes were used when there was overwhelming circumstantial evidence to link the security forces to these killings.

Both newspapers published several articles clearly implying that the apartheid government was responsible for murdering activists. One method of doing so was to note that the murdered victim had previously had some connection to the police. For example, "Another Murder Riddle as Former Detainee Stabbed," by Thami Mkhwanazi and Shaun Johnson, begins, "Another young black activist has been murdered in mysterious circumstances only days after his release from police detention" (2). When shown this particular article, Johnson stated, "If you read that, that's really carefully written. I mean, you can't challenge any of those things—they're simply facts. Now, it's a very good example that you've found of how our readers would say, 'Okay, right, the taking out of activists is continuing.'"

The article "A Chilling Pattern to Activist Deaths," by Vusi Gunene, is yet another example. Sicelo Godfrey Dhlomo, an eighteen-year old who "had recently spoken out on detention and torture to international television audiences" (1), was killed in January 1988. Gunene writes, "The Reverend Frank Chikane, general secretary of the South African Council of Churches, yesterday raised questions about 'the co-incidence' of [Dhlomo's] death coming so soon after his detention" (1). Gunene's strategic use of the term "the co-incidence" in quotation marks is masterful in that it simultaneously emphasizes this word for certain audiences, while providing distance for the writer with other audiences. In other words, the readers of the *Weekly Mail* would clearly pick up on the ironic overtone of "the co-incidence," and yet, if ever challenged by authorities, Gunene could simply deny ironic intent and claim that this was a direct statement made by Chikane.

In other instances, journalists could use statements by the police themselves. In the *Weekly Mail* article "Missing," which chronicles the alarming number of Port Elizabeth political activists who had disappeared, the journalist provides a lengthy discussion of the individuals who had gone missing, as well as some of the responses offered by family members. The journalist describes the information provided by a daughter of one of the missing men: "[She] testified in an affidavit that during her 11-month detention in solitary confinement, security police had told her on two different occasions that her father was the cause of the unrest in the Eastern Cape. One of the policemen had said her father was inviting problems for himself and that he was going to get what he was asking for. The day after her father's disappearance, her home was surrounded by policemen, two shots were fired, the house was raided, furniture was broken and people in the house were arrested" (14). The journalist utilized a tactic described in the previous chapter and quotes information from a legal affidavit to reveal sensitive information. Given the statements made by the police prior to his disappearance, as well as their actions the day after his disappearance, it does not require a significant leap to link this particular disappearance to the police.

The article "Dad Won't Believe His Son Escaped," by Phillip van Niekerk, also uses statements made by police to implicate them in the killing of activists. The article, as the title indicates, focuses on the skepticism of a man by the name of S. S. Mahlalela concerning police reports that his son had escaped from jail. Van Niekerk describes the reasons for Mahlalela's suspicions and then provides a statement offset by a bulleted point directly beneath the article: "The mother of Sonny Boy Mokoena, found hanging in the police cells at

Pilgrim's Rest in September last year, Hilda Mokoena, said she was first visited by police who told her her son had escaped" (4). The information contained within the article itself invites readers to share this man's suspicions about his son's "escape," and these suspicions are heightened further when one reads about the experiences of Hilda Mokoena in the bulleted point at the end of the article.

Highlighting the fact that murders of political activists were never solved and that they were never thoroughly investigated by the police was yet another means of suggesting government involvement. In the article "A Murder That Raises the Spectre of Death Squads," Patrick Laurence writes, "Suspicions persist in the extra-parliamentary opposition circles that police are less than thorough in their investigations" (11). In the article "'Death Squad' Spectre Haunts UDF," the journalist writes, "Because of the lack of progress in the investigations, popular belief in the townships is that certain people in authority may somehow be implicated, the spokesman said" (1). The fact that none of these murders was solved was particularly striking, given the scale on which they were occurring. In "The Odd Cases of the Activists Who Vanished," Jo-Ann Bekker notes, "But in this year of probably unprecedented mass resistance, the killings and disappearances occurred on such a scale that observers began talking about South American–style death squads" (6).

Journalists thus found several ways of linking the government to these murders. Because they did not have direct proof and because they were writing in a climate of censorship, journalists wrote about "suspicions," "popular beliefs," and the fact that people were "talking about" government involvement. Shaun Johnson, when shown the article discussed above, "Another Murder Riddle as Former Detainee Stabbed," explained the purpose of these articles: "We're going to record this. We're going to put it on the public agenda. We can't prove this—but we're making the links."

NEW NATION AND THE DEATH SQUADS FEATURES

In 1987 and then again in 1988, *New Nation* ran two extensive features on death squads. Both utilized allusions and subversive enthymemes extensively in the process of synthesizing the known facts about the many individuals who had been murdered. As noted above, there were different types of subversive enthymemes—those that used the structure of the traditional syllogism and enthymeme, and those that did not necessarily adhere to that rigid structure. The two features about death squads that appeared in *New Nation* contained both kinds of subversive enthymemes. Readers could readily conclude that the South African government was using death squads to murder activists because of the multiple subversive enthymemes, allusions, and repetition within these two series.

Each series consisted of three separate articles, which, when read together, formed a subversive enthymeme utilizing the traditional enthymeme structure. To best understand how this particular subversive enthymeme is formed, consider the syllogism and traditional enthymeme that writers could use in a context free of censorship. The formal syllogism would read as follows:

Death squads in South Africa are targeting opponents of the apartheid regime and acting with impunity.
All death squads throughout the world targeting opponents of a regime and acting with impunity have been shown to have links to their respective regimes.
The death squads in South Africa targeting opponents of the apartheid regime and acting with impunity must be linked to the apartheid regime.

The enthymeme would thus read as follows:

The death squads in South Africa targeting opponents of the apartheid regime are acting with impunity; they must be linked to the apartheid regime.

It simply would not have been possible, however, for the journalists working for *New Nation* to make such a direct and forceful claim.

The journalist(s) who wrote the three articles of these two features never explicitly linked the death squads to the apartheid government. But they did make the following claims very explicit:

Death squads targeting opponents of the apartheid regime are acting with impunity.

All death squads throughout the world targeting opponents of a regime and acting with impunity have been shown to have links to their respective regimes.

When the three articles are read together, the subversive enthymeme is formed, and the obvious link between the South African government and the death squads becomes clear. In addition to the subversive enthymeme created *between* the three articles, there are subversive enthymemes *within* each article as well.

1987 Feature

In its 30 July 1987 edition, *New Nation* ran the first two-page spread on death squads. It consisted of the following articles: "Death Squads Waging War in the Shadows," "The Secret Slaughter without Boundaries," and "Killings Didn't Stop Liberation." Below is a brief summary of each:

"Death Squads Waging War in the Shadows": chronicles the history of death squads in two Central American nations, El Salvador and Guatemala. In this long article, the journalist discusses the purpose of death squads, their victims, and, most importantly, explicitly links them to the governments of those two countries. In this entire article, there is not a single reference to the South African government.

"The Secret Slaughter without Boundaries": focuses primarily on the numerous ANC members assassinated over the years. As in the first article, no statements directly link the South African government to these murders.

"Killings Didn't Stop Liberation": discusses how the use of death squads in Zimbabwe, Guinea Bissau, and Mozambique ultimately failed to quell the revolutionary movements in those countries.

After reading the first two articles in the series, "Death Squads Waging War in the Shadows" and "The Secret Slaughter without Boundaries," one is immediately struck by the strong similarities between death squads in other nations and those in South Africa, specifically in terms of their purpose. In the first article, for example, the journalist claims that death squads in El Salvador and Guatemala have sought to "to neutralise anti-government opposition as

Image 3.1 Without explicitly claiming that the apartheid government was using death squads to target political activists, this *New Nation* feature that appeared in 1987 contains allusions, repetition, subversive enthymemes, and overwhelming evidence to allow readers to draw this obvious conclusion.

swiftly as possible" ("Death Squads" 6) and later spells out this broader objective more specifically: "Firstly, it is an attempt to prevent the development of an unarmed opposition. Secondly, it is an attempt to prevent any support for the guerrilla movements" (6). Compare this to the second article, which focuses on the purpose of death squads in South Africa: "to neutralise key members of the opposition, prompt a breakdown in organization, prevent the maintenance of an open political presence, and to spread terror generally" ("Secret Slaughter 7). The objectives of death squads in El Salvador, Guatemala, and South Africa, therefore, are fundamentally the same, and the link between them is made even stronger by the repetition of several terms in both articles, such as "neutralise" and "opposition."

The first and second articles also describe the similar targets of death squads in all three countries. In the first article, the journalist notes that the victims in El Salvador and Guatemala include trade union leaders, students, priests, and journalists. The second article, which focuses on targeted ANC members and sympathizers, includes a leader of a trade union, a university president, academics, and a priest. The purpose and targeted victims of death squads in all of these countries, therefore, are essentially the same.

While the death squads described share these similarities, they differ in a significant way. In the first article, the link between death squads and the governments of El Salvador and Guatemala is made explicitly and repeatedly. There is a brief description of the origins of death squads and their overall objective in the first two paragraphs, and the next section reads as follows: "The silent executions enabled right-wing governments to stand aside with folded arms and deny any responsibility. They wanted to convey the impression that these squads were renegade groups beyond their control. However, it has since become common knowledge that the squads were set up by right-wing governments" ("Death Squads" 6). Later in this same article, the journalist again establishes this link in El Salvador: "Since then, death squads in El Salvador have been linked publicly to high-ranking military officers and other allies of the ruling group" (6). Later the journalist notes, "These squads are made up of soldiers, policemen, and private gangs recruited by right-wing businessmen and farm-owners. They are commanded by high-ranking army officers, and act on intelligence reports provided to them by the army" (6). The journalist notes that the murders of government opponents in Guatemala were at one point committed openly by the military, but eventually they were committed by "shadowy groups . . . linked to the army and police" (6). When discussing the "disappeared" in Guatemala, the journalist informs the reader that "the Guatemalan government's complicity has been proved in at least 75 percent of these disappearances" (6). After outlining the similar purpose and targets between the death squads of El Salvador, Guatemala, and South Africa, the explicit links made between the death squads of El Salvador and Guatemala with their respective governments are obviously significant.

The third article in the series, "Killings Didn't Stop Liberation," which focuses primarily on the futility of death squads in other contexts, also establishes the link that existed between death squads in Zimbabwe, formerly Rhodesia, and the Rhodesian government. Specifically, the journalist writes about the assassination of one leader in the Zimbabwe African National Union (Zanu), Herbert Chitepo: "Although there was widespread suspicion at the time that Chitepo had died as a result of internal problems in Zanu, a book has recently been published in Zimbabwe—which draws on former Rhodesian intelligence sources—saying it was in fact carried out by Rhodesian agents" (7). In this article, the journalist also describes the assassination of Jason Moyo, a leader in the Zimbabwe African People's Union: "Rhodesian security police admitted in interviews after independence that they had got news that the parcel was to be sent to Moyo by tapping a phone. They had intercepted the parcel and inserted an explosive device" (7).

The links established in this article between the death squads and the Rhodesian government would have perhaps resonated even more strongly with a South African audience. In addition to the many similarities between the white supremacist governments of Rhodesia and apartheid South Africa, the specifics provided in this third article are directly applicable to the South African context. The fact that Chitepo was assassinated by Rhodesian agents despite the "widespread suspicion" he was killed as a result of "internal rivalries" directly mirrors the disinformation campaign surrounding the murder of Ruth First noted above. Moreover, the fact that Rhodesian security forces assassinated Moyo with a letter bomb is significant given that the second article in this series, "The Secret Slaughter without Boundaries," chronicles the numerous ANC members who had been assassinated in a similar manner. The first and third articles of this series, therefore, provide considerable evidence to establish the second premise of the subversive enthymeme: all death squads throughout the world targeting opponents of a regime and acting with impunity have had links to their respective regimes.

If the facts in these articles are not sufficient for the reader to see the connections between the death squads in South Africa and those in other countries, the journalist strengthens the connection by using similar phrases in the conclusion and introduction of each article. The conclusion of the first article, for example, which repeatedly links the death squads in El Salvador and Guatemala to those governments, reads, "The war in the shadows has failed. The struggle continues" ("Death Squads" 7). The opening line of the second article, which examines ANC targets of death squads, reads, "Former University of the North SRC president Ongopotse Tiro was the first victim of South Africa's war in the shadows in 1974" ("Secret Slaughter" 7). The journalist is clearly inviting readers to see the second article as a continuation of the first.

The second article, "The Secret Slaughter without Boundaries," not only completes the subversive enthymeme formed when reading the three articles in their entirety but also contains an important subversive enthymeme within the article itself. When describing the assassination of Joe Gqabi, an ANC leader living in exile in Harare, Zimbabwe, the journalist informs the reader, "The white Zimbabwean detective who headed the investigation into the murder—and blamed it on internal rivalries within the ANC—was subsequently exposed as a South African secret agent" (7). In this sentence, the journalist conveys a fact that begs an obvious question: Why would the apartheid government engage in such activities if it had nothing to do with this assassination? Moreover, this information provides evidence concerning the disinformation campaigns utilized by the apartheid government that readers could link to Ruth First's killing, as well as to the many other murders the government blamed on the anti-apartheid movement.

Later in the article, after describing how eleven ANC members had been murdered in Swaziland, the journalist makes the most explicit reference to the South African government: "The ANC believes South African agents have used Swaziland as a thorough testing ground for clandestine assassinations

Image 3.2 Another feature published by *New Nation* in 1988 that uses an approach similar to that of the 1987 feature to link death squads in South Africa to the government.

and attacks. Now that they have seen the tactic work well there, the ANC expects it to be more widely applied" ("Secret Slaughter" 7). While this is a fairly clear reference to the involvement of the South African government, it is important to note that this statement is buried in the article, appearing in the twenty-fourth paragraph of a thirty-two-paragraph article and that, consistent with journalistic writing, merely cites a speculative statement made by the ANC.

The second article by itself, with its subversive enthymeme contained in the description of the Gqabi assassination, coupled with the speculation by the ANC source, strongly implies a link between the death squads and the South African government. The subversive enthymeme formed by reading the three articles together, however, conveys the real persuasive power of this series. By explicitly linking the death squads in other nations to their respective governments, and then revealing the many similarities between those death squads and those targeting opponents of the apartheid regime, the conclusion becomes chillingly obvious: the South African government was using death squads to murder activists.

1988 Series

The 1988 series on death squads shares similarities with the 1987 series in that it, too, uses three separate articles to form a subversive enthymeme, in part by comparing South African death squads to Chilean death squads during the reign of Augusto Pinochet. The three articles in this series consist of the following:

"Hit Squads on the Rampage in Chile": examines death squads within Chile and, similar to the article in the 1987 series that focuses on El Salvador and Guatemala, does not mention the South African government anywhere in the article.

"Apartheid Death Squads": examines the killings of several South Africans but does not overtly claim the government is responsible.

"The 'Disappeared Ones': Ten Years of Stabbings, Shootings and Abductions": provides a brief biography of several South Africans who have been murdered or who have gone missing.

As in the 1987 series, these articles examine the similarities between South

Africa and other countries. In the first article, "Hit Squads on the Rampage in Chile," the journalist describes some of the characteristics of death squads in that country: "The death squads are highly organised and have considerable financial backing"; "They have their own communications equipment and sophisticated training facilities"; and "They also possess detailed information about their victims" (6). The final sentence of the article reads, "Sufficient evidence has emerged over the years to conclude that these squads are composed of members of the security forces" (6).

In "Apartheid Death Squads," the journalist never makes an explicit link between the South African death squads and the apartheid government but does observe the striking similarities with those in Chile: "Whatever their affiliations, these right-wing agents remain highly organised and trained. Their information networks seem to be precise and up to date" (7). In addition to highlighting these logistical similarities, this article also focuses on the very similar political context that existed in each country. The journalist's description of the conditions in Pinochet's Chile—mass arrests, detention, torture, and the declaration of a state of emergency—presents a mirror image of the conditions that existed in apartheid South Africa during the late 1980s.

In addition to the subversive enthymeme formed between the articles, the journalist also utilizes several subversive enthymemes within each of the articles. In "Apartheid Death Squads," the journalist writes, "The declaration of the state of emergency two years ago is an open admission by the government that extraordinary legal means were necessary to restore order. But even these seem to have failed, with the government admitting that a revolutionary situation continues to prevail. It is against this background that the political killings and abductions have occurred. The identities of the killers remain mysterious. Given the choice of their victims, it is certain which side of the political spectrum the killers come from" (7). After strongly hinting at the involvement of government but not explicitly stating so, the journalist formally invites readers to complete this subversive enthymeme by writing, "But that is as far as anyone would venture in trying to identify the killers without fear of reprisals" (7).

Later in "Apartheid Death Squads," the journalist provides yet another subversive enthymeme. The passage reads, "Given the form of repression that has emerged, mass intimidation and the systematic removal of popular leadership seem to be the answers pro-apartheid forces have come up with. At a legal level, this has been achieved to a certain extent by the detention of key leaders. But there are clearly elements which have opted to operate outside the confines of the legal system" (7). A close analysis of this subversive enthymeme reveals how subtle, implicit references serve to construct meaning. In the first sentence, the writer never specifically identifies the South African government but refers rather to amorphous "pro-apartheid forces." In the second sentence, the author describes the actions occurring at the "legal level," primarily the "detention of key leaders," but, again, never refers specifically to the South African government, despite the obvious fact that the government was taking these steps. In fact, the South African government openly acknowledged it was detaining anti-apartheid activists, justifying these measures as necessary to maintain order. Thus, the journalist has not yet explicitly mentioned the government at this point, but readers have essentially "filled in" this meaning for themselves. What else or who else could the journalist possibly be referring to? What other entity operates at the "legal level"? The reason for not explicitly referring to the government becomes apparent in the final sentence: "But there are clearly elements which have opted to operate outside the confines of the legal system." Given that readers have already determined that the journalist is referring to the South African government in the previous sentence, they in effect "carry" this meaning to the next sentence, perhaps not even consciously, making the "elements" referred to in this final sentence quite clear: elements of the South African government.

This series also employs a similar tactic used in other articles discussed above, namely, describing the previous connections that existed between victims and the police. The following facts are provided about the murder victims:

Siphiwe Mtimkulu had been detained in 1981 ("'Disappeared Ones'" 6).
Mxolile Eric Mntonga "had been detained four times since 1981" (7).
Sicelo Dhlomo "had been detained a few days before his death and had once
    been convicted on a charge of illegal possession of a firearm. He said at
    the time he carried the gun because he feared for his life" (7).
Rick Turner "was killed a few weeks before his banning order expired" (6).

The victims, therefore, were not random South African citizens but those who had been targeted in the past by the apartheid government. The journalist also provides this leading bit of evidence regarding Matthew Goniwe, a political organizer from the Eastern Cape who was murdered in 1985 on his way home from a United Democratic Front meeting: "Goniwe had promised his wife before they left that the only person they would stop for would be uniformed policemen" (7).

Moreover, this series used another tactic described above: highlighting the fact that none of these murders had been solved. This fact provides a veritable drumbeat running throughout "The 'Disappeared Ones'":

"His killers have never been found" (6).

"Her assailants were never found" (6).

"[T]he cameraman's killers have never been found" (7).

"[L]egal observers predicted that the mystery of the Ribeiro slayings would probably never be solved" (7).

"Police claimed they knew one of the suspects and expected to make an arrest soon. No arrests have been made" (7).

"His killers remain unknown" (7).

"His killers have not yet been brought to book" (7).

"No one has yet been arrested for the killing" (7).

This repetition clearly supports the claim that the apartheid death squads are acting with impunity. In "Apartheid Death Squads," the journalist writes, "Not one of these murders has been solved" and then includes the statement of a church group: "But unless the killers are brought to book, speculation as to who was responsible for the senseless slayings and bombings will abound, the SA Council of Churches (SACC) warned last week" (7). While the fact that not a single murder had been solved could suggest raging incompetence on the part of the South African police, the alternative interpretation seems much more plausible given the other evidence provided in these articles.

The 1988 series also employs several allusions and coded descriptions of security forces. These allusions appear both in "Apartheid Death Squads" and in "The 'Disappeared Ones'":

"Nkosinathi Solomon Shabangu . . . was gunned down in front of teachers and students on June 5 by three unidentified men, one in a balaclava" ("'Disappeared Ones'" 7).

"Their son, Chris Ribeiro, said two gunmen appeared to have 'dark, black faces,' but as he tried to pull one of the gunmen out of their getaway car he saw from the driver's hand that he was a white man. He thought the driver had worn something over his face to make himself look black" (7).

"Armed vigilante gangs based in the townships have been responsible for
some of the killings. But there have also been some highly organised killings involving white men" ("Apartheid Death Squads" 7).

These allusions would have been quite clear on their own, but they are
even more significant when used in articles containing so many subversive
enthymemes.

Finally, the journalist uses another ingenious tactic that is not necessarily a
subversive enthymeme or an allusion but instead relies on the blurred usage of
a single word: apartheid. In addition to the phrases such as "defenders of apartheid ideology" and "pro-apartheid forces" that appear throughout the articles, the second article is actually entitled "Apartheid Death Squads." While
"apartheid" is technically the name of the *system* within South Africa that regulated everything on the basis of race, it was obviously a system enforced by
the South African *government*. There was, and still is, considerable slippage
between "apartheid" and "the South African government" when discussing
this period of South African history. In this book, for example, I have engaged
in the common practice of prefacing the description of the government that
existed at that time with either "South African" or "apartheid." The journalist clearly relies on this blurred distinction between system and government
when using the word "apartheid" in this series, particularly in the title.

Remarkably, the journalists who wrote these two series managed not only
to link the death squads to the South African government but also to cultivate
a sense of defiance. It would not be unreasonable to assume that a sense of
tragedy and loss would pervade a series focusing on death squads: the horrific
deaths experienced by the victims, the fact that so many young victims were
killed in the prime of their lives, and the suffering of their loved ones. Both
series, however, offer the best strategic response to the death squads: collective resistance.

The 1987 series makes the point repeatedly that death squads have always
failed to accomplish their ultimate objectives. In the article examining the
death squads in El Salvador and Guatemala, for example, the journalist
describes the continued resistance in those countries: "But this coordinated
campaign of violence and terror has so far been unsuccessful in crushing
resistance. It is unlikely it ever will" ("Death Squads" 6). The article concludes
with a simple declaration: "The war in the shadows has failed. The struggle
continues" (6). Similarly, "Killings Didn't Stop Liberation" focuses exclusively

on this idea, citing the successful struggles in Zimbabwe, Guinea Bissau, and Mozambique. The 1988 series even creates a tone of defiance, primarily through its use of imagery. A large photograph of Matthew Goniwe, the young, charismatic activist, appears in the middle of this series. No picture of his casket surrounded by mourners, no close-up of his grief-stricken widow and children, but rather a picture of Goniwe, full of life, in a stirring pose of defiance: arm uplifted, fist clenched, standing in front of a microphone with his mouth wide open, as if rallying a crowd. The death squads may have murdered this one individual, but, as the articles make clear, the mass-based political organizations opposed to apartheid and the memories of those murdered survive.

The defiant attitude these two series promote is linked to the only strategic response to death squads available to those in the anti-apartheid struggle, namely, mass-based political organization. Given the sophistication of the South African security forces, once a person had been targeted for assassination, the well-trained, well-armed, well-informed death squads would more than likely carry out their mission. Mass-based political organization, therefore, was the only possible solution, a point made in both the second and third articles in the 1987 series. "The Secret Slaughter without Boundaries," for example, concludes, "The fact that other national liberation movements survived assassinations was the result of the fact that they had sufficiently strong political organisation within their ranks to ensure that no individual could be indispensable" (7). This point is reinforced in the conclusion of "Killings Didn't Stop Liberation": "But these national liberation movements had all successfully developed political organisations strong enough to ensure that no individual could ever be indispensable to their struggles" (7). The defiance promoted by both series, in words and imagery, is not simply an attempt to put a brave face on a desperate situation but rather a concerted effort to convey a strategic message: mourn, yes, but also mobilize.

In this political context, the subversive construction of meaning between journalists and readers must have been particularly charged. Readers would not only realize the extent to which the South African government had been using death squads but would recognize that this same government was preventing *New Nation* from making this allegation directly. The fact that journalists and readers were able to construct meaning concerning this issue, despite restrictions expressly designed to prevent them from doing so, must certainly have strengthened the claim in these articles regarding the inevitable success of the anti-apartheid struggle.

HOW AND WHY THESE TACTICS WORKED

At this point, it is necessary to address what may be some obvious issues. First, those who developed these forms of oblique speak were not thinking in terms of rhetorical theory when they devised these tactics but rather were creatively and imaginatively thinking of ways to convey their meaning in a very fraught situation. Journalists may have been using allusions consciously, as demonstrated by Ryland Fisher's comment that he and other journalists could "allude" to certain situations. But when journalists employed what I refer to as a "subversive enthymeme," they would not, of course, have been consciously utilizing a variation of the traditional enthymeme. This concept merely provides a framework for analysis. Rhetorical terms in this context, perhaps in most contexts, are more useful for analyzing the results of the invention process rather than understanding the invention process itself.

Second, readers of the not-so-oblique examples of oblique speak examined in this chapter may very well ask: How did these newspapers get away with this? Didn't apartheid officials realize what these journalists were doing? Of course they did. It is certainly gratifying to reflect on situations in which members of an oppressed group are able to develop messages so subtle, so coded that they can be conveyed under the very noses of the oppressors. This was not the case here. Those within the apartheid government may have been supporting a completely immoral and unjust system, but they weren't stupid. At issue was not whether government officials could "figure out" what these journalists were doing but rather which acts of resistance they would grudgingly tolerate and which ones would prod them into action.

There were significant constraints on the government in terms of acting against these newspapers, including those that the government created itself by trying to maintain the appearance of legitimacy. It is highly significant, for example, that the government not only denied its involvement with the death squads but actually engaged in elaborate disinformation campaigns to do so. As Robin Renwick writes in his memoirs, the apartheid government adopted the following approach: "In order to be able to state publicly that South African Defence Force personnel were not involved in assassination attempts against ANC members or sympathizers at home and abroad, military intelligence had created the infamous 'Civil Co-operation Bureau'—a bunch of killers who continued to be financed from secret funds. The names of several of these agents were known, including that of Colonel Eugene de Kock, who commanded the unit at Vlakplaas which was responsible for numerous atrocities" (*Unconventional* 140). The creation of this separate "bureau" indicates the lengths the apartheid government would go to shield its criminal behavior and to present a mask of legitimacy.

Moreover, the TRC revealed the considerable effort the government took to conceal its role in these killings. Regarding those individuals who were murdered while in prison, one apartheid official, T. J. "Rooi Rus" Swanepoel, stated in 1982 that these prisoners had committed suicide, which was part of an elaborate "communist plot": "'If they commit suicide, they can cast doubts on the security forces'" (vol. 2, 206). Indeed, some of the specific denials provided by the apartheid officials to explain the numerous people murdered in detention were often completely absurd. At the conclusion of the film *Cry Freedom*, there is a long list of names and dates of those killed in detention along with the "official" cause of death: "slipping in the shower," "falling down stairs," "falling out of the window," "epilepsy," and "thrombosis."

For those who were not murdered in detention and whose bodies were not burned to ash, the security forces used various means of distancing themselves from the killings. According to the TRC, "Extra-judicial killings were often accompanied by the deliberate placing of weapons on or near the bodies of victims after they had been killed" (vol. 2, 288). This, of course, would make it appear that the murdered individuals had been engaged in armed resistance. After the murders of Jackson Maake, Andrew Makope, and Harold Sefolo, "[t]he three bodies were loaded into a minibus and, somewhere on a road in Bophuthatswana, were placed on top of a landmine, which was detonated. The aim was to create the impression that they had blown themselves up, thus performing the dual function of turning suspicion away from the security forces and making MK soldiers look incompetent" (vol. 2, 239).

In other instances, the security forces, as described earlier in the case of Ruth First, sought to portray these killings as the result of other anti-apartheid organizations or other black South Africans. In the case of the Cradock Four, discussed earlier, "an attempt was made to suggest that their deaths were a result of ongoing and violent conflict between the Azanian People's Organisation (AZAPO) and the UDF in the Eastern Cape" (vol. 2, 228). The amnesty application of Sampina Bokaba regarding the death of an "unknown ANC operative" who was strangled to death by Paul van Vuuren revealed how a "tyre was then put around his neck, he was doused with petrol and set alight" (vol. 2, 239). As Bokaba explained, "[O]ne of the purposes of 'elimination' was disinformation; 'It was painted to be a struggle between blacks.... Voters were once again persuaded to vote for the National Party in the light of the black onslaught'" (vol. 2, 239).

The hypocrisy, the vast gulf that existed between the apartheid government's rhetoric and actions, must certainly have been infuriating. But this pose of legitimacy could be *used*. As Anton Harber explained, "Sometimes you would describe an incident without saying it was the security forces. It would be clear that it was probably security force action, but you would talk about 'masked men' or 'unidentified people' so that you could say, 'Oh, we didn't know it was security force action because we didn't think security forces acted that way.'" The performance described by Harber, a variation of what Manoim called "wide-eyed innocence," examined in the next chapter, was a brilliant way to exploit this mask of legitimacy the apartheid government sought to wear. As one of the articles in the 1988 series on the death squads explained, "The government has repeatedly denied that its forces have had anything to do with the bombings or political killings" ("Apartheid Death Squads" 7). After making so many public denials and taking such elaborate steps to attribute these murders to other groups, how could the government respond to a performance such as Harber's, "Oh, we didn't think security forces acted that way"? The government could not very well concede, "Well, they do." If the apartheid government was going to pretend to be legitimate, journalists could pretend to accept that legitimacy. Even though the allusions in these articles are obvious, in order to prosecute these newspapers the government would need to concede that the unnamed individuals and groups mentioned in these articles were in fact members of the security forces and police. The apartheid government's refusal to embrace publicly the violence it was in fact using thus made it vulnerable to these forms of oblique speak.[7]

Eventually, the story of the death squads and their links with the government was revealed. The *Weekly Mail* published an article in its 20 October 1989 edition that included an interview Ivor Powell had conducted with a police officer from the feared Vlakplaas Unit, which had been responsible for many of these assassinations. A prominent member of the apartheid security forces, Dirk Coetzee, also shared his story with the Afrikaans opposition newspaper, *Vrye Weekblad*, edited by Max du Preez, one of the outstanding and courageous opposition journalists of that time. This feature blew the story wide open, and the revelations about death squads thus broke publicly within

South Africa shortly before the government unbanned opposition political parties and freed Mandela.

The *Weekly Mail* and *New Nation* were thus able to publish articles focusing on the many abuses of the apartheid government, including the use of death squads, which would all be verified in detail by the Truth and Reconciliation Commission a decade later. And they managed to do so during the states of emergency, a period in which censorship within the country was at its height. The space available to reveal this information was due in large measure to the secrecy, deception, and lies of the apartheid government in its attempt to present itself as legitimate. But it ultimately required the creativity and courage of those at the *Weekly Mail* and *New Nation* to seize upon this space to convey this information to South Africans and the world.

"A HOPE IN HELL"

The Legal Approach of the *Weekly Mail*

In the mainstream media, the lawyers would approach the question by saying, 'Is there any chance that this transgresses the law?' Our lawyers would say, 'Is there any chance that this does not *transgress the law?' There's a huge difference. So we would say we're going to do this—have we got a hope in hell in court? A hope in hell. A hope in hell was good enough.*

SHAUN JOHNSON, JOURNALIST FOR THE *WEEKLY MAIL*

Typically the trickster makes his successful way through a treacherous environment of enemies out to defeat him—or eat him—not by his strength but by his wit and cunning. The trickster is unable, in principle, to win any direct confrontation as he is smaller and weaker than his antagonists. Only by knowing the habits of his enemies, by deceiving them, by taking advantage of their greed, size, gullibility, or haste does he manage to escape their clutches and win victories.

JAMES SCOTT, *DOMINATION AND THE ARTS OF RESISTANCE*

One means by which the apartheid government sought to maintain control, while simultaneously projecting a sense of legitimacy, was to construct rule after rule regarding what was and what was not permissible. Such an approach, however, provided opposition journalists with many opportunities to expand their writing space. Written rules, after all, are ultimately subject to interpretation—and aggressively interpreting the rules was one of the defining features of the *Weekly Mail*.

The sheer number of restrictions enacted to regulate the media was staggering. Don Pinnock, a journalist and political activist in the Eastern Cape in the late 1980s, recalled the effect of such a system: "I mean there's no 'law'—there's no law at all. What happened was that South Africa at that point became so overlegislated that we just didn't operate in terms of the law. We operated in terms of what we could get away with, because everything was illegal—unless you got away with it. Then it was legal. That was how we operated." There were thus activists such as Pinnock, as well as those at opposition newspapers such as the *Weekly Mail* and *New Nation*, who were determined to aggressively challenge the law. But if one were determined to stay within the letter of the law, one would always be able to find some statute or restriction to justify inaction.

In addition to the fact that there were so many laws, many of these laws were also extremely harsh. Reg Rumney, a journalist for the *Weekly Mail*, noted the draconian punishment for violating some of these laws: "But the laws were very, very punitive. And in my area particularly, the area of fuel—oil sales, oil procurement, anything to deal with nuclear energy—we weren't allowed in the mainstream press to reflect how much fuel the country consumed, how much petrol was consumed. You didn't want to touch it. I mean ten years is a long time to be put inside for something which wasn't that important." Rumney's statement raises an important question: What rational person would risk ten years in prison to write an article about oil consumption? .

To make matters worse, the restrictions, especially the emergency regulations, were extremely unclear. While it is possible that the government was guilty of drafting sloppy regulations because of incompetence or haste, a more likely explanation is that this vagueness enhanced its power. Norman Manoim, an attorney for *New Nation*, explained: "They deliberately wanted the law to be vague. There are many people who criticize these laws and said, 'The guys who wrote these are stupid, they can't write a decent law.' That's in fact not the case. The people who wrote these things deliberately made them vague because they wanted people to not know where the edge of the cliff was, and if you didn't know where the edge of the cliff was, you were naturally cautious. You would stay very far away from it. A lot of people did." Many emergency regulations, therefore, were never designed to draw clear red lines that people knew they must not cross but rather for precisely the opposite purpose: to make the "edge of the cliff" unclear.

Many also emphasized during interviews that those charged with enforcing these vague and poorly written regulations had the power to interpret them anyway they pleased. Amrit Manga from *New Nation* noted, "Because the emergency regulations were so wide and so broad that whether we contravened these regulations or not depended on a subjective interpretation of a group of people who we would never know." Harber commented on this dynamic as well: "And another thing I constantly said to Irwin [Manoim], whatever precautions we take, we think that this article is the one that's going to draw them this week. Inevitably, it'll be something we didn't think of that's on page 24 that we hadn't even shown to the lawyers. And we thought, 'Why this one?' So you have to understand that there was an element of complete unpredictability and irrationality. That was the nature of the emergency regulations."[1] There are several possible explanations for these random and subjective interpretations on the part of the government. Norman Manoim speculated on a few: "I'm not sure who they had reading these things. Clearly the minister wasn't doing it, and he obviously had people who were doing it [and they] had their own thing that set them off or they didn't do a very thorough job. And it may well have been that they didn't really care. They wanted, in a sense, to start intimidating these newspapers, making life difficult for them." Those at these newspapers never knew the people in charge of enforcing the regulations or the reasons for some of their mystifying interpretations: personal idiosyncrasies, sloppiness, a determination to crack down on the newspaper, or some complex combination of all of these reasons.

In the final analysis, the censorship statutes and particularly the emergency regulations were not "law" in any meaningful sense. In addition to the fact that there were so many restrictions, some of which overlapped with one another, they were overly punitive, poorly drafted, and inconsistently applied. But these media restrictions were never designed for the purpose of being good law; they were designed to restrict writing space while projecting an image of legitimacy.

JOURNALISTS' RELATIONSHIP TO THE RESTRICTIONS

The journalists of the *Weekly Mail* and *New Nation* provided fascinating responses when asked to describe their relationship to the censorship restrictions. All of them, of course, shared the same objective: to challenge the restrictions as much as possible without jeopardizing the survival of the newspaper. As Ryland Fisher from *New Nation* explained, "The strategy was to get as much information out as was possible. Obviously, the idea was to push the laws as far as we could. Because there was this balance of trying to push but still protect the paper—you didn't want to be absolutely reckless, even though we all agreed that the laws at the time were unjust, unfair. If there is such a thing as illegitimate laws, we had them. Really. So it was a balancing act." To accomplish this "balancing act," journalists developed different approaches, particularly with regard to knowing the intricacies of these restrictions, and at what point they would think about them: before, during, or after they wrote their articles.

Many journalists stated that they had a very clear sense of the restrictions. When asked how well she and others knew the laws, Pat Sidley said, "Backwards and inside out. You knew about the laws. If you didn't know about the laws, you found out quickly enough." Shaun Johnson agreed: "Every journalist had to become an amateur lawyer. You just had to learn it, you just had to imbibe it. Every story that we wrote, particularly during [a] state of emergency, we could recite the state of emergency pat. We knew every single rule and law." Sefako Nyaka said, "*Ja*, I knew them very well. I had to because it would be very frustrating if one didn't know that, because you'd go out and get yourself in trouble."[2] Finally, Howard Barrell explained how the training he received from someone in the mainstream media about the restrictions provided him with the means to circumvent them: "He gave me the formal, legal training and he gave me a very good grounding. In fairness to him, he might be the world's most boring person, but he taught me all the rules, and as he taught me the rules, he taught me how to break the rules. He didn't know it. He didn't intend by telling me the rules that he told me how I could break them and find my way around them."

Others, however, claimed much less confidence about their knowledge of all the restrictions and their nuances. Janet Wilhelm, who wrote for the *Weekly*

Mail, stated, "They were too complicated. They were far too complicated and they just got vaster and vaster. And so, certain things you just knew—okay, you can't write about this, and you can't write about that, but it just got more and more complicated. You would just leave it up to the instinct of the editors and the sub-editors, the specifics of it. I never bothered to acquaint myself with the very specifics." Wilhelm stated at another point of the interview, "There was something called *The Newspaperman's Guide to the Law* and it just got thicker and thicker and thicker. Now I never bothered to know the ins-and-outs of that." Ben Maclennan, a journalist who did not write for the *Weekly Mail* or *New Nation,* agreed with Wilhelm: "I never had any terribly clear understanding [of the restrictions]. There was, I think, there was a *Newspaperman's Guide,* a book written by an advocate named Kelsey Stuart, that was around by then. But I never, I can't ever remember sitting down with a copy of that." Kerry Cullinan, who wrote for *New Nation,* expressed similar sentiments: "We didn't have a firm sense. They kept on changing anyways. I wasn't going to waste my time. I just knew, if you have a prison story, you must send the whole story to the prisons and then you're obliged to print their entire comment back. So you would learn from that." She stated at another point, "So you knew the biggies. But as far as getting into the minutiae of the laws, no, forget it. It's just a waste of time." Phillip van Niekerk suggested that there might be a strategic dimension of not being too familiar with the nuances of the restrictions: "I think you're kind of aware of them. But you don't like to get into the details because once the details get too far into your head, embedded into your head, then you're actually kind of doing, you're actually self-censoring yourself. And I think that on the whole, we fought to avoid that."

The differences among journalists in terms of how well they knew the intricacies of these restrictions may not have been terribly significant. Journalists who claimed not to know all of the nuances of these laws nevertheless were aware of the "biggies" and certainly knew enough to consult with someone when treading on dangerous terrain. For those who claimed to know these restrictions very well, that knowledge may have been only marginally useful given that no one could predict with any real certainty how these restrictions would ultimately be interpreted and enforced.

Journalists also provided very different responses when asked about the stage of the writing process when they first thought about these restrictions. Did they, for example, think about these restrictions before they started writing? As they were writing? After they had written an article? Tyrone August of

New Nation, who frequently wrote about arts and culture, offered this insight: "But for me self-censorship is something very insidious. I can never remember going to the computer and censoring myself. It may have been a given, and I may have just worked from a particular framework. I mean, it must have been there, because we were operating in quite a dangerous period. But I can't really recall it ever being a conscious thing, you know, 'Okay, don't say this, don't say that.'" August's response raises a compelling question: To what extent can writers even consciously articulate the extent to which censorship shapes their choices as writers and to what extent do writers simply internalize restrictions after operating within a "particular framework" for an extended period of time?

Sefako Nyaka claimed that he did not allow the censorship restrictions to affect him before or while he was writing. He stated, "Now I used to write almost as if there was no restriction. Yes, I'd just write what I want, tell the story as I saw it, and then later on, say, 'Listen, this is what I wrote.'" Nyaka then explained the responses he would receive from the editors who would tell him, "But you can't say this and you can't say this," and Nyaka would respond, "Yes, I know. But I'm giving you this because this is what I saw and this is what happened." After that, he said, "[t]hey would then call David [Dison] and we could then go into doctoring it." Clearly Nyaka's approach had strategic value: rather than self-censor and eliminate information from his articles that the editors and attorneys might never see, he would instead include everything in the hopes that they could then figure out ways to "doctor" the sensitive information.

Moira Levy, when asked when she thought about these restrictions—before, during, or after—responded, "All three really, if I think back." She then explained, "You would always have at the back of your mind what was possible in terms of the range of laws, and so you'd choose your stories with that in mind. . . There's no point in interviewing someone who's not going to be quoted." Levy then provided a concrete example of a story that she never even tried to write. She was in London at the time and was called to a meeting with Jacob Zuma, who became the third president of South Africa after Nelson Mandela and Thabo Mbeki, along with another person who was a member of the ANC:

> It was a very distressing meeting because they had important information for me, something about the military in Kwa-Zulu Natal, and I knew it couldn't be run. I knew no one would even touch it—it was just outside the bounds the

law would permit, and I felt very frustrated and guilty. . . . They kept thinking
there must be a way, but I just knew, and I even called a friend of mine, an experienced South African journalist who was living in London, and I said, "Can
you see any angle to this story that I can slip it through?" There was no way to
write this story.

Some stories, regardless of how much creativity was used, were thus beyond
doctoring and could not be published given the scope of the restrictions.

Anton Harber agreed with Levy and argued that it was essential to have a
firm sense of the restrictions at all stages of the writing process. Harber specifically stressed the importance of recognizing the limitations imposed by the
restrictions before one wrote a single word: "[t]he principle we worked on is
that you had to know from the moment of reporting, witnessing, or interviewing somebody how to handle it because if you were naïve at that point, you may
lose your way of dealing with it." In other words, one might be able to maximize
the information one could ultimately publish by knowing how to frame certain
questions when conducting an interview.

When I asked Harber if he had a little censor in his head when he was actually writing, he initially responded, "Absolutely," but he then qualified his
remarks somewhat: "Certainly, in the beginning, we would have had to say to
people, 'Just write and we'll handle it,' and that would be like on the first day of
emergency, when the reporter hadn't actually read the regulations. But thereafter, no, it would be a case of *as* you're writing, *before* you're writing." According to Harber, therefore, the extent to which journalists had the ability to monitor what they were writing when they wrote may have depended in part on
how long a particular restriction had been in existence.

Finally, it was fascinating how many of those interviewed described the
censorship restrictions in physical terms. Ben Maclennan described these
regulations as "a thing, a structure in the middle of the road that you worked
around, you went over, you dug tunnels underneath." At another point during
his interview, Maclennan explained how journalists would be writing an
article and would "bump up against" these restrictions. Others, such as
Janet Wilhelm, conveyed a similar sense of physicality. She explained that
journalists experienced many situations in which restrictions prevented
her from writing about certain topics and how she needed to "find a way to
write through it." David Dison, an attorney, described how "you [would] work
your way around it." Maclennan used a darkly humorous metaphor when he

described writing in this context as "blundering optimistically through a minefield."

Due in part to the *Weekly Mail*'s and *New Nation*'s different objectives, each newspaper took a slightly different approach to the law. Accordingly, this chapter focuses on the *Weekly Mail* whereas the next chapter focuses on *New Nation*. The *Weekly Mail*, which viewed itself as the "free speech" newspaper, developed legal tactics primarily for the purposes of conveying as much information as possible. While those at *New Nation* pursued this objective as well, they also sought to exploit legal gray areas for the purposes of promoting the ANC.

GUIDING PRINCIPLES FOR SUBVERTING THE LAW

Anton Harber described the prevailing attitude at the *Weekly Mail* when discussing how it differed from the culture that existed at other mainstream newspapers:

> I think you must also see that we came from a tradition of defiance. I mean, I'm not pointing any fingers. I think after twenty years of censorship, newsrooms developed ways of coping, and they developed them in the repression of the sixties and seventies—when you can't publish, you just don't. The 1980s brought a wave of defiance, the United Democratic Front. What we felt we were doing was bringing that attitude, the eighties attitude of defiance, into the media, into newspapers. So there was a fundamental shift in attitude where we were keeping with that spirit.[3]

The approach developed by many South African mainstream newspapers in the 1960s and 1970s was perhaps in some ways quite predictable: people will actively challenge what appears to be an immovable system for only so long. Opposition newspapers such as the *Weekly Mail* that came to life in the defiant decade of the 1980s, however, began to challenge assumptions regarding the limits of the possible.

The *Weekly Mail* did not challenge the government, as Harber explained, "head on," because the newspapers were certain to lose. He explained: "Okay, so how did we do it? We never took a 'fuck you' attitude. I mean that was our

attitude, but strategically, we never said, 'Fuck the law.' We said we will understand the law, we will identify gray areas where we believe there's room for
maneuver, and occasionally we'll go beyond that into defiance of the law. But
we would develop strategies. We will choose which laws and what time, and
we would never take it head on." This approach, perhaps best described as
strategic defiance, consisted of several steps.

First, it was imperative that the newspapers be absolutely certain that their
stories were factually accurate whenever they entered forbidden territory. In
fact, Dison went so far as to claim that this was the "touchstone" for all articles on sensitive subjects: "And the point was, when you're using the legalisms,
you want ultimately to be able to prove your facts. I mean that was our touchstone. Our operating notion was we get the facts right. The facts—that'll get
you through the hoops. If the facts can't be substantiated, or the information
can't be substantiated, then you're talking about them really being able to close
you down. Because then you're talking about major defamation or criminal
suits." Shaun Johnson also commented on this issue, saying that "the responsibility is to the reputation of what is a very vulnerable title." He elaborated:
"[The *Weekly Mail*] doesn't have major financial backing, it has a readership
that is very loyal but is also, by definition, out of power. It's a real opposition
readership. So if you sensationalize something and you're wrong, you really
are opening the paper up to big damage." Of course, confirming one's facts is
essential for journalists in all contexts, but the stakes were particularly high
in a context in which the government was looking for an excuse to close opposition newspapers.

Second, when considering whether to publish risky stories, the editors and
attorneys realized that the "law" ultimately provided them with only a rough
guide for making decisions, given the vagueness of the laws and subjective
interpretations noted above. As Harber explained, other factors had to be
taken into account:

> I want to emphasize that it often required not a strictly legal view or approach,
> because you could well look at something and say, "Well, this is in breach, but
> they're not going to pay any attention," and it would go. Or you would look at
> something else and say, "Well, technically, it's okay, but this is going to freak
> them out." So the decision was often about how you played things—the con-
> text, the headline—what mattered more in their minds than other things. So

there were certain infringements that they would scream and shout about and certain [ones] they would let go.

When asked if the editors ever rejected Dison's advice and published articles that he advised against, Harber replied, "More likely I would have said, 'Well, can't we rewrite the intro? Or what if we bury it inside the paper? Or what if we change the headline?' That would have been a more likely conversation where I said, 'What if we did this?,' to the point where he said, '*Ja*, that works.' That's a much more likely scenario. Or he would say, 'This is the risk. It's your decision.' So it's not going against his advice. It's him acknowledging that it's not a purely legal decision." Given the nature of the censorship restrictions, "purely legal" decisions did not really exist.

Because of this uncertainty, final decisions were often made on the basis of what several people described as "gut feels." Harber, when explaining the overall approach of the newspaper, claimed, "It was a reading of the times. It was a reading of how far what one could be defiant about. More gut-felt than anything else." Shaun Johnson emphasized this uncertainty repeatedly during his interview: "What's going to be so important when you write this is that you're just going to have to strike the right tone in not giving the impression—I'm sorry to keep repeating myself—that we were a bunch of highly trained mature people who knew exactly what we were doing. A lot of this stuff is instinctive." The final decisions about what to publish and how to present the material, therefore, were largely a product of instinct and, as noted above, defiance.

Once they decided to publish a risky article, those at the *Weekly Mail* then engaged in a calculated public performance that Irwin Manoim describes in his book *You Have Been Warned* as "wide-eyed innocence" (74–75). This consisted of stating to the authorities with a straight face that the editors and attorneys had genuinely tried to adhere to the law. Harber elaborated on this performance during an interview: "It was always an argument that we knew we could present in court, even if we had to hide our sniggers. For example, the first thing they would do if they thought there was contravention was they'd come and take a statement from us. Now a lot of people would have had the attitude, 'I'm giving no statement. Prosecute me. Stuff you, you pigs.' We didn't. We would say, 'No, of course this is legal. Here is the logic, here is the argument, and here is the statement prepared by our lawyers.'" Dison commented on this approach as well: "These arguments, this legalism, were really just a shield. I mean we knew we were in breach of the law, if you know what I mean. But the logic was it [the law] was illegitimate."[4]

The editors and attorney for the *Weekly Mail* were well aware that their approach to the law was risky and born out of desperation. As Irwin Manoim stated, "It wasn't a case of 'Is this good law? Is this breaking the law?' This is a matter of pure strategy—how are we going to get away with this?" The private deliberations of those on the *Weekly Mail* staff were thus considerably different from their public performance. In private, they consciously and deliberately sought to undermine the censorship restrictions, which they viewed as illegitimate, and often were uncertain about their possibilities of success. The public performance, on the other hand, consisted of striking an earnest, sincere pose of adhering to the letter of the law and asserting with confidence that they had successfully done so.

A COLLABORATIVE APPROACH FOR EDITORS, JOURNALISTS, AND ATTORNEYS

To fully appreciate the roles and relationships of the journalists, editors, and attorneys at the *Weekly Mail*, it is useful first to examine the nature of these relationships that existed in the mainstream press at that time. At mainstream newspapers, many editors were quite cautious and would rely on their attorneys to determine whether or not a particular article violated the restrictions. Anton Harber made the following observation: "The practice we had learned at the *Rand Daily Mail* was to phone the attorney, and you would read the attorney the story and they would say, 'You can publish that' or 'You can't publish that.'" Harber explained that he and Irwin Manoim had a different relationship with David Dison: "We fundamentally said to David: Be part of our strategic planning. What we want you to do is come tell us: Can a story work? So the lawyer's function was entirely different—it was to find a way to publish. That was a key element." Manoim confirmed Harber's observation: "It tended to be traditional on newspapers to treat the lawyers as the enemy, as it were. We had a very different situation where, (a) the lawyer happened to be one of the founders of the paper and was on the board, and (b) had a grasp of what we were trying to do and make it possible. So it was very, very important. We spent an awful lot of time with the lawyers working on strategies." Dison

elaborated on the importance of this difference when he contrasted his experiences working at the *Weekly Mail* to the work he did for the *Sunday Times*, a
mainstream newspaper:

> I was also advising people like the *Sunday Times* after the closure of the *Rand
> Daily Mail*, so that when the emergency came around in '86, '87, [the editor]
> would say to me, "I want a 100 percent guarantee that what we're publishing
> here today is not in contravention of the emergency regulations." And I'd say
> to him, "I can't give you that." I would sit in the *Sunday Times* every Saturday
> afternoon, and I would sit at the *Weekly Mail* every Thursday, and the differ-
> ence was like chalk and cheese. Because basically, the *Weekly Mail* wanted to
> publish, and the *Sunday Times* didn't want to break the law.

This fundamental difference between the level of risk the mainstream and
opposition newspapers were willing to tolerate is captured by Shaun Johnson's
observation that "[i]n the mainstream media, the lawyers would approach the
question by saying, 'Is there any chance that this transgresses the law?' Our
lawyers would say, 'Is there any chance that this does *not* transgress the law?'
There's a huge difference."

Dison's observations indicate that attorneys working for mainstream
newspapers may have assumed a more cautious role because editors directed
them to do so. The *Weekly Mail* was unique, therefore, in that it consisted of
aggressive editors working with aggressive attorneys. As Clive Cope, the manager of the *Weekly Mail*, observed, "And I mean that was the beauty of having
David Dison and Laura Jacobson. We were pushing it to the edge, and they
believed in it. They weren't just these professionals that we employed. They
were people very close to us and were part of the struggle with us."

In addition to their shared desire to challenge the restrictions together,
the relationships among the journalists, editors, and attorneys at the *Weekly
Mail* were much more collaborative and much less hierarchical than at other
papers. Harber explained: "Dison's advice was terribly important. . . . But I've
always had the view that lawyers are there to give advice, not decisions. And
that's fundamental to the point that I was making previously, that it was the
lawyer who said, 'That's illegal. You can't run that.' So it's saying the lawyer
is there to advise and guide, but the decision on whether or not to break the
law is an editorial one." This more collaborative relationship between editors
and attorneys also extended to the *Weekly Mail* journalists. When asked if any

of her articles had ever been fundamentally altered in order to be published, Moira Levy responded,

> I never thought my story was unrecognizable at the end. There'd be a process of consultation. I'd submit a story and I'd say to Anton, "I'm a bit worried about this," and then maybe he'd come back to me and say, "Look, we're going to take it out," and I would say, "*Ja*, we have to take it out." You know, I wouldn't feel frustrated. It wasn't like the *Star*, where part of my stuff was just taken out and there wasn't [that] kind of consultation. The *Weekly Mail* was different. There was more consultation, and I could see the point.

At the *Weekly Mail*, therefore, the attorneys were not "the enemy," as Manoim observed, but rather collaborative partners committed to working with editors and journalists to circumvent the censorship restrictions.

THE ALL-CLEAR FLAG AND BLACK LINES AS LEGAL TACTICS

The *Weekly Mail*'s strategic defiance of the law, coupled with the unique relationship between editors, journalists, and attorneys, led to the creation of some truly innovative legal tactics. The first was one that Irwin Manoim described as the "all-clear flag" (*Warned* 75). The second tactic was extremely risky and one that the *Weekly Mail* is perhaps best remembered for to this day: its use of black lines within articles as a means of engaging in subversive self-censorship.

All-Clear Flag

The all-clear flag was developed for very high-risk articles, the ones Manoim described as "somewhat tenuous." This tactic consisted of providing a legal justification next to or within the article itself. This particular tactic required the editors of the *Weekly Mail* to play both smart and dumb, depending on the audience in question. A brief description of the censorship process is necessary to appreciate the nuances of this tactic.

At a certain stage in the emergency, police would arrive at the printer of the *Weekly Mail* to determine if the contents of the newspaper were in violation of any of the emergency regulations. If they determined that it contained illegal or legally suspect articles, they had the power to prevent distribution of the newspaper. Making it past this first obstacle, however, did not necessarily mean that the newspaper was entirely in the clear. If the minister of information later determined that the newspaper contained illegal material, he could order the police to confiscate it from newsstands and/or bring charges against the editors.

There were thus two objectives in using the all-clear flag. The first was to deceive the security police sent to read the newspaper the night before distribution; these individuals were not necessarily highly trained in the legal nuances of the censorship restrictions. As Manoim observes, "We would write in a sentence advising an imagined faceless security policeman on the other end as to the correct legal position, thus saving him the trouble of thinking about it himself" (*Warned* 75). Harber identified how important it was to get past this first hurdle: "Or sometimes it would be the only way they could act on this one is not to confiscate but to prosecute. That's fine. That takes years. We can deal with that in the court." In other words, even if the authorities were going to take action against the newspaper, Harber and Manoim wanted it to get out on the streets. The second objective of the all-clear flag was to facilitate possible "wide-eyed innocence" performances should the newspaper make it past this first hurdle but later be challenged by the Office of the Minister of Information.

The all-clear flag was particularly effective for circumventing the emergency regulation forbidding coverage of security force action. The multiple layers of this tactic are captured by Sefako Nyaka's article "Behind the Barricades," which describes several acts of violence and abuse on the part of security forces when they surrounded and then stormed the headquarters of the Congress of South African Trade Unions (COSATU) in April 1987.[5] During the crackdown on anti-apartheid activists during the state of emergency, it was very common, as noted in previous chapters, for security forces to use excessive violence. The facts and descriptions contained in this particular article, made possible by the use of the all-clear flag, were precisely those that the censorship restrictions sought to conceal from the South African public and the international community.

The *Weekly Mail* published this particular article on the front page of its 24 April 1987 edition, and it was accompanied by a large photograph showing the exterior of Cosatu House and individuals with their hands aloft and their bodies pressed against the windows. The caption beneath the photograph reads, "Up against the wall ... Cosatu House on Wednesday evening, the night of the police siege." Immediately beneath the headline of the article, the following statement appears in bold print: "*Weekly Mail* staffer Sefako Nyaka was trapped in Cosatu House during this week's police siege. The *Weekly Mail* is able to publish details of what he saw because it is satisfied that the acts of police conduct he has described are true and, because of their excessiveness, do not constitute 'security action' as defined in the Emergency regulations. Insofar as his report contained 'security action,' it has been censored, as indicated in the copy" (Nyaka, "Behind the Barricades" 1). Knowing that this article would clearly raise red flags for the police who would read the newspaper the night before distribution, the editors and the attorney of the *Weekly Mail* were essentially trying to bluff their way past this obstacle. This dynamic is examined more extensively at the end of the chapter, but it is important to note that the average police officer had only a vague sense of the numerous and ever-changing media restrictions. Given the extremely hierarchical nature of South African society, particularly within institutions such as the police and security forces, an impressive sounding legal justification would carry considerable weight.

This legal justification, however, also contains the basis for two "wide-eyed innocence" performances before the Office of the Minister of Information. The first is contained in the second sentence, noting that the actions of the police were so "excessive" that they "do not constitute 'security action' as defined in the Emergency regulations." According to Harber, this was all part of the performance: "If a policeman acted illegally, does it constitute security force action? It couldn't have been the intent of the law to protect a policeman doing something illegal. So because it was illegal, it became publishable. You know, those were the kind of convoluted arguments one would use step by step." Harber's comment provides yet another example of how the *Weekly Mail* was able to exploit the apartheid government's attempt to present itself as a legitimate government. The lawyers and editors would have had to struggle mightily to "hide their sniggers" by claiming "it couldn't have been the intent of the law to protect a policeman doing something illegal" when everyone knew that this was precisely the intent of the media restrictions.

The statement also contains the basis for yet another wide-eyed innocence performance. Harber explained that if the *Weekly Mail* was confronted for publishing material in violation of the regulations, they would respond by saying, "[Pretends to be addressing a governmental official] 'That's not how we understood the regulation. . . . We cut out what we thought was the problem in good faith. We, our lawyers told us it wasn't proper, and we cut it out.'" Although they would indeed excise some information from the article, Harber said that they would also "leave in some stuff" that they knew was in violation of the restrictions. In other words, the material that they cut became the evidence that they were, in all earnestness, trying to comply with the restrictions. The final sentence of this legal justification is an example of this tactic: "Insofar as this report contained 'security action,' it has been censored, as indicated in the copy."

As one reads "Behind the Barricades," the term "censored" appears several times. Two sentences read, "The drama at Cosatu House started shortly after a group of workers had (censored) in Davies Street near the Doornfontein Station, Johannesburg," and "I could clearly see how people, some bleeding profusely from head wounds, were being (censored)" (1). Two quotations read, "'We tried to indicate that we were not fighting, but (censored)'"; the other reads, "'At that moment we retreated, but (censored),' one worker said" (1). In two sections of this article, "(Censored)" appears between paragraphs, suggesting that entire paragraphs had been deleted. The all-clear flag, accompanied by these selectively "censored" sections, thus would allow the editors and attorneys to claim that they had, in good faith, tried to comply with the law.

These legalisms provided the editors, in Dison's words, with the "shield" to publish a considerable amount of information. The following quotations from this article provide examples of material that the apartheid authorities, concerned about their image at home and abroad, clearly did not want publicly revealed:

[Beginning of the article] "I saw a badly injured and handcuffed man pushed down the stairs of Cosatu House in central Johannesburg during this week's police siege. After hitting the bottom of the stairs head first with a dull thud, he lay still. A young policeman moved up to him and hit him once on the ribs with a rubber pick-handle. The man didn't stir. He was dragged on the ground to a police truck before being thrown in head first" (1).

"The workers retreated to Cosatu House, leaving a trail of blood on the pavement. I saw two workers lying on the pavement in Davies Street. It was clear that they were dead. One had apparently been shot in the head" (1).

"The man in the red shirt had blood streaming down his face which was
contorted in pain. All the time, truncheon blows were raining on the two
men" (3).

"On looking through the opening in the back of the truck I could see both
men lying on their backs. The semi-naked man's eyes were heavily swollen and closed" (3).

"The man in the red shirt was groaning and one of the policemen told him to
shut up and kicked him in the ribs. The man rolled over" (3).

"Our view was then blocked by two Casspirs [police vehicles] and all we
could hear were screams and sounds of breaking glass and wood" (3).

The all-clear flag, accompanied by selective censoring, allowed for the publication of information that mainstream newspapers would never have dreamed
of publishing.

The all-clear flag is also featured in another article written by Nyaka,
"Shooting Victims Buried in Secret." Appearing in bold print next to this
article is the following statement: "Although General Johan Coetzee prohibited the reporting of 'security action' in a special gazette on Wednesday
night, the *Weekly Mail* has been advised that this only applies to a limited
category of Security Force actions, because of the narrow definition of 'security action' in the gazette. We can accordingly give you an account of yesterday's events in Soweto including certain actions of Security forces." The
Weekly Mail, again, was trying to bluff its way past the police sent to read
the newspaper the night before—police who more than likely had not read
the "special gazette" published "on Wednesday night." Even if they had, what
position would they be in to challenge the confident interpretation of this
provision provided by the newspaper's attorney? A portion of this all-clear
flag, which implies self-censorship, was also directed at the minister of
information. Note the use of the word "certain" in the final sentence, implying that the article does not convey information about "*all* actions of security
forces," but rather "certain actions."

The all-clear flag could also be used for the purposes of constructing subversive enthymemes, discussed in the previous chapter, particularly for stories concerning calls for certain kinds of political action. Two articles written by Thandeka Gqubule provide excellent examples of this approach. In
"Church Conference Defies Regulations," published on 1 July 1988, Gqubule
writes, "Twenty-six South African church leaders yesterday defied Emer-

gency regulations in a press conference called to discuss the October municipal elections. The current regulations make it illegal to call for a boycott of the
elections and prevent the *Weekly Mail* from reporting the contents of the press
conference in full. It can, however, be reported that the decision to defy the
regulations was made on Wednesday night" (5). The article thus contains an
all-clear flag for the authorities to signal that the *Weekly Mail* was "adhering"
to the restrictions. It also serves as a signal to readers that they must reach
conclusions that cannot be explicitly stated. Given the way this article is written, it is abundantly clear that the South African church leaders had in fact
called for a boycott of the elections.

This fact was reinforced the following week when Gqubule wrote a second
article, entitled "Defiant Churches Await State's Response." This article opens
as follows: "South African church leaders this week apprehensively awaited
government response to their defiance last Thursday of Emergency regulations" (2). The article concludes with the following information in a bulleted
point: "It is illegal under Emergency regulations to call for a boycott of elections and for journalists to report such calls" (2). By using the wording of the
regulation itself, this article ingeniously conveys information to readers about
the very action the regulations sought to suppress.

"'We Started Riding a Donkey and Ended on a Tiger,'" an article by Vivienne
Walt, provides yet another example of how an all-clear flag could be used to
form a subversive enthymeme. This particular article focused on a group of
prominent South African whites who had traveled abroad and met informally
with members of the ANC in exile. Walt writes,

> "Do you really trust these whites?" the young reporter from Ghana's *Daily
> Graphic* snapped aggressively at Thabo Mbeki, African National Congress
> information chief, glancing at the 52 white delegates sitting around the VIP
> lounge at Accra airport, who had just arrived on the last leg of their West Afri-
> can tour. Since Mbeki—an ANC executive member and head of the ANC's del-
> egation to Dakar—is banned in South Africa, his unhesitating response cannot
> be quoted here. But his words instantly silenced the packed airport room and
> reinforced what some of the Afrikaners had begun to express, as they and six
> ANC delegates went on safari last week through Burkina Faso and Ghana—
> that the ANC might be their best hope of acceptance in a hostile world. The
> airport interview was not the only occasion for the ANC to jump to the defense
> of their white fellow travelers. (14)

As noted by the all-clear flag in this article, Thabo Mbeki could not be quoted at that time because he was banned. Even though readers may not know specifically what Mbeki said, Walt writes her article in such a way that readers can conclude he obviously spoke out forcefully on behalf of the white South Africans with whom he and other members of the ANC were about to meet. The question impugning these white South Africans had been "snapped aggressively" and Mbeki's "unhesitating response . . . instantly silenced the packed airport room." If those descriptions do not provide sufficient cues, Walt also notes that this was "not the only occasion for the ANC to jump to the defence of their white fellow travelers."

The all-clear flag was also used for the purposes of circumventing the restrictions about quoting individuals who had been banned. One approach consisted of using quotes of banned individuals that had been previously released by the government itself. As Christopher Merrett notes, the government would sometimes allow the media to quote speeches of banned individuals if it served their interests: "The government itself quoted selectively from the banned in order to reinforce its own propaganda and gave permission for others to do so when the ANC could be cast in a poor light" (*Culture* 101). Journalists, however, could use these permitted quotes for precisely the opposite purposes. Patrick Laurence, for example, used quotes from Oliver Tambo that had been previously approved by the government to write an article about the ANC entitled "A 75-Year Thorn in the Flesh of White Power." Beneath this headline in bold print is the following statement: "Oliver Tambo is banned and may not be quoted. All quotes in this article are from excerpts of his speeches released by government officials." Rather than simply use Tambo's statements out of context for the purpose of advancing the propaganda of the government, Laurence instead wove together selected quotes for the purposes of writing a thoughtful analysis of the ANC.

Another loophole that the *Weekly Mail* exploited was to use quotes by individuals before they had been officially banned. Beneath the headline "By Zwelakhe," for example, is the following statement: "We quote the unquotable editor. Legally. Our rulers hope to have silenced Zwelakhe Sisulu, editor of *New Nation*, moved last week from a detention cell to imprisonment in his own home. Our rulers are mistaken. Sisulu's eloquent pen lives on . . . on this page" (13). After a few introductory paragraphs, the article consists of statements written by Sisulu when he was editor of *New Nation* "before he was restricted." While the editors of the *Weekly Mail* claim confidently that they are engaging in legal activities, this article may in fact have been slightly more complicated, particularly in the context of the state of emergency. Simply because the *Weekly Mail* was quoting words Sisulu penned prior to the date he was restricted does not necessarily mean that some of these quotes were safely within the unclear parameters pertaining to "subversive statements."

An even riskier use of the all-clear flag was to have nonbanned individuals summarize the speeches and writings of banned individuals. The *Weekly Mail* published several articles using this approach. In the article "The Slovo Line on Private Investment," the *Weekly Mail* explained how it was "legally" circumventing the restriction that forbade quoting Slovo directly: "Since Joe Slovo is banned and may not be quoted, we asked Dr. Tom Lodge, an authority on the ANC and SACP, to assess the speech" (Lodge 13). After a brief introduction, Lodge writes, "In summary, what Slovo had to say was this," and he then proceeds to paraphrase the central claims of Slovo's speech. Carmel Rickard's "Gwala Sjambokked, Say Lawyers," is another example of this strategy. Rickard describes the physical abuse "veteran African National Congress politician Harry Gwala" suffered at the hands of the police. Rickard manages to convey this story as follows: "Gwala, 70 . . . is restricted and may not be quoted on this incident. However, his version, communicated through his lawyer and family representatives is that . . ." (3). The remainder of the story then summarizes Gwala's version of events as told to others. In the article, "What Winnie Would Have Said to Wits (If They'd Let Her Talk)," Mono Badela opens the article as follows: "If police had not stopped Winnie Mandela from speaking at the University of Witwatersrand this week, she would have told white voters that although this week's election was a non-issue, 'each vote cast by white South African opposition will be a vote of hope, a vote to save the country from the Nationalist political quagmire'" (10). The entire article is essentially a summary of her speech that, according to Badela, "was given to the *Weekly Mail* after the meeting had been banned and she was prevented from speaking" (10). A final example: "Mbeki Would Have 'Urged Unity,'" by Gaye Davis, contains the following: "Freed African National Congress leader Govan Mbeki would have used last weekend's banned rally in Cape Town to urge unity among all South Africans so that apartheid could be destroyed, according to his lawyer, Priscilla Jana" (3). According to the article, Jana conveyed the contents of Mbeki's speech at a press conference where she described "the kinds of things she believed Mbeki would have said at the rally, had it not been banned" (3). These arti-

cles thus adhere technically to the restrictions while simultaneously subverting their intent.

The apartheid regime did in fact take selective action against some newspapers for using this tactic, including Max du Preez, editor of the Afrikaans
anti-apartheid newspaper *Vrye Weekblad*. According to Merrett, "In the Slovo
case ... *Vrye Weekblad* editor Max du Preez was found guilty of summarising
(not quoting) a contribution to the Leverkusen Conference to which Soviet
and South African academics contributed" (*Culture* 149). In the process of
making its case against du Preez, the government stated quite bluntly the
objective of restricting individuals: "the prosecutor argued that the aim of the
list was to silence completely anti-government individuals" (149). Two significant issues are noteworthy about the case against Max du Preez. First, the
Weekly Mail was clearly venturing into dangerous terrain when using the all-
clear flag for these purposes. Second, if the intent of this regulation was really
"to silence completely anti-government individuals," the fact that the government prosecuted du Preez and not the *Weekly Mail* for the many articles cited
above clearly demonstrates selective enforcement.

Black Lines

The tactic for which the *Weekly Mail* is most famous was the use of black lines
as a form of subversive self-censorship. It consisted of publishing an article
that contained material violating the censorship restrictions and then placing black lines over the "illegal" words, phrases, sentences, or paragraphs. This
tactic was developed during a particularly stressful evening the night before
the newspaper was to be distributed.

Immediately following the state of emergency, the minister of information
declared that the *Weekly Mail*'s first edition published under the new emergency regulations contained subversive material and ordered police to confiscate all copies of the newspaper from newsstands across the country. It was
a devastating blow to the *Weekly Mail* and revealed the lengths to which the
government was willing to go under the state of emergency.

The night preceding the publication of their next edition, David Dison, the
Weekly Mail's lead attorney, was out of town, and so Harber and Manoim met
with other members of his firm. These attorneys were not as bold as Dison
in interpreting what could and could not be published under the emergency
restrictions, particularly with regard to what constituted a "subversive state-

ment." They proceeded, therefore, to underline within various articles all of the problematic passages that could not be published. In some instances, they claimed that entire articles could not be published (Manoim, *Warned* 62–63). Manoim and Harber objected, but the attorneys argued that the material was simply too provocative. Manoim recalled during an interview,

> Our usual lawyer David Dison was not available. One of his partners, who was infinitely more cautious, was available and he was sitting there, red-lining everything left, right, and center, and Anton [Harber] was having a screaming match with him. What kind of newspaper are we going to have under the circumstances? As someone who was in design, I suddenly realized here's a visual metaphor. Let him do it. Let him do it. We're going to end up saying nothing anyway. So we just let him go ahead and wreck the paper and everything he put a line through with a ball point pen we got a guy to follow after him putting tape on the pages.

It was now up to Manoim to invent a headline suitable for this edition. His first few attempts were squashed by the attorneys, which in turn led to his epiphany. Manoim relates: "I was beginning to feel some sympathy for the still smarting Harber, to whom I complained: 'The lawyers reckon we can say absolutely nothing critical of the Emergency.' Then I realised that this was a headline: 'Our lawyers tell us we can say almost nothing critical about the Emergency. But we'll try.'" (*Warned* 66). The *Weekly Mail* proceeded to use black lines on this front page and in other articles within this particular edition, and the editors used this tactic in several subsequent editions as well.

This approach actually accomplished several important objectives. First, it was a means of revealing information that otherwise would not be revealed. Rather than killing an article completely or reframing it so that it essentially conveyed nothing, the process of keeping the original copy with only sections missing allowed readers to acquire a considerable amount of information. In some rare instances, it was even possible to determine the word or phrase that had been blacked out.

The short article "Journalists [black line]" provides one such example. It reads, "Three journalists and photographers who regularly contribute to the *Weekly Mail* are among those [black line] under Emergency regulations. They are [black line] a Port Elizabeth reporter, [black line] and [black line] both Afrapix photographers from Johannesburg. Also [black line] are two

Image 4.1 The *Weekly Mail's* most famous front page. It was the first time the newspaper used black lines as a form of subversive self-censorship. A picture of this front page received international attention when it was featured in both the *New York Times* and the *Times of London*.

people who have been responsible for *Weekly Mail* distribution. They are [black line] of East London and [black line] of Oudtshoorn" (2). Given that this article appeared when the government was detaining literally thousands of individuals under the recently declared state of emergency, it is fairly obvious that the blacked-out word in the title, as well as in the text of the article, is "detained." Although it is impossible to determine the identities of the individuals who had been detained, publishing the article in this manner allowed the *Weekly Mail* to convey the fact that individuals who regularly contributed to this newspaper and assisted with its distribution had in fact been seized by the police.

Publishing the names of those who had been detained was in fact a vexing issue at the beginning of the state of emergency. Before newspapers began to defy the government and publish lists of detained individuals on a regular basis, the editors of the *Weekly Mail* used black lines. They published, for example, the story of a seventeen-year-old youth who had been detained and assaulted by police. Although his name is covered by a black line, every other aspect of his story is revealed: how his attorneys informed the court that the youth had been threatened by the police, how his mother had filed an application with the courts to prevent the police from assaulting her son, how subsequent medical examinations of the boy "showed that he could not move any of his limbs due to bruising and swelling," and how "the District Surgeon found swelling at the base of his tongue and soft palate and bleeding from the left ear drum" ("I Was Threatened" 9). Rather than simply kill this article in its entirety because they could not publish the youth's name, the editors used selective black lines, thus allowing the newspapers to convey an important story involving police abuse.

The *Weekly Mail* used this tactic in a slightly different way when they provided a partial list of those detained under the state of emergency and used the following headline: "Persons Known to Be in Detention since June 12" (4). The entire page is full of prison numbers with black lines next to each one. The following excerpt from beneath the headline explains the meaning of this page: "Below is a portion of the Detainee Parents' Support Committee list of people detained under Emergency regulations. The list—covering only the Transvaal and the Cape—was provided with names blacked out to comply with the law. The full list includes over 1000 names" (4). The effect created by so many black lines on a page provided, in Manoim's words, a visual metaphor to convey the scope of the government's actions, and it has a much more powerful impact than simply stating in a single sentence that "thousands have been detained."

Readers might not know the names concealed by these black lines, but they are aware that each black line represents an actual person.

In the vast majority of articles, the exact word or words covered by black lines remains a mystery to the reader; sometimes entire sentences, and in some instances entire paragraphs, are covered. Sufficient information is provided, however, to determine the basic premise of the article. One such example is "We're Backing ANC, Say Greens," by Hans Brandt, which describes how the Green Party of then West Germany "came out in full support of the ANC" (6) after a delegation of Greens visited South Africa. In this article, two major sections are blacked out, including a statement by Annemarie Borgmann, the party's spokesperson: "Borgmann expressed her [black lines]" (6). The black lines cover six full lines of text, thus making it impossible to determine what she said. In the final analysis, however, the exact wording of her quote is not particularly significant. Given that her party is supporting the ANC, it is clear that the statement covered by the black lines is highly critical of the apartheid regime. While this may very well have been an eloquent and forceful statement, it is doubtful that anyone from outside of South Africa was going to articulate something about the apartheid government that readers of the *Weekly Mail* were not already painfully aware of. Moreover, the essential facts of this article are conveyed to readers even with this portion blacked out: a small political party with parliamentary representation in a major industrial country had decided to publicly support the ANC.

Other articles in which readers are able to determine the central message of the story despite the fact that entire sentences or paragraphs are blacked out include the following: an interview with a United Democratic Front (UDF) leader in hiding that provided the UDF analysis of the state of emergency; an article that described how the South African Council of Churches continued to oppose the government despite the detention of several of its members; an article about the number of deaths due to recent violence; and an analysis of how the state of emergency was affecting the South African economy and the sanctions movement.

One unintended feature of this strategy was that it may have led some readers to look at those mysterious black lines and assume that something worse had actually occurred. Harber explained this phenomenon in an article he wrote about censorship: "When the public knew that security force action was being hidden from them, they did the natural thing, which was to imagine the worst. Often what people believed the authorities had done in secret was far worse than what they had actually done" ("Censorship" 150). He elaborated on this idea during an interview: "You know if a word is missing, you think of the worst. It might say 'hit,' but you'd assume it said 'shot,' 'killed.' . . . If it said 'injured' and you couldn't see the word, you'd think 'killed.' So my overriding impression was that actually people read things, much worse things, because they used their imagination. You read half a story, you fill in with your imagination. You imagine the worst [laughs]. So I think that was a real ironic effect." Given the pervasive violence used by authorities, it is entirely understandable why many readers would "imagine the worst."

Finally, these black lines had significant political implications. Even in those instances in which large chunks of information were lost under black lines, they nevertheless provided a stark and graphic reminder that the press was severely constrained, a fact the apartheid government sought actively to conceal. Christopher Merrett explains: "The overall plan [of the government] was to keep the public ignorant of the extent of censorship itself" (*Culture* 118). These black lines thus served as a stark reminder to South Africans that other articles that might not contain black lines were nevertheless produced and published in a context of censorship, a point Manoim emphasized in an article that appeared in the *Weekly Mail*: "For in an age in which the real news is all too often the stuff that doesn't appear in the papers, readers need to develop a special set of reading skills. They must cultivate the ability to read between the lines, to interpret silences, to grasp the meanings of tangential phrases" ("Worst Monsters" 18). One way that the *Weekly Mail* constantly sought to remind readers about the censorship restrictions was to put the equivalent of a "warning" label on many of its pages: "RESTRICTED: Reports on these pages have been censored to comply with the Emergency regulations."[6]

These black lines had important international political implications as well. The *Weekly Mail*'s first use of black lines provided concrete, tangible evidence to both opposition journalists and to the apartheid government that the international community was indeed watching. In what must certainly have exceeded Harber and Manoim's wildest expectations, a picture of their front page featuring these black lines was carried by both the *New York Times* and the *Times* of London, extremely prominent newspapers in the two most powerful countries with active anti-apartheid movements (*Warned* 65).[7]

DOMESTIC AND INTERNATIONAL
POWER DYNAMICS

The use of black lines, particularly the first time they were used in the *Weekly Mail's* now-famous front page, was an inspired example of strategic defiance. The editors were in essence both adhering to and ridiculing the censorship restrictions at the same time. It was an extremely risky approach. The fact that the state's security forces actually allowed the *Weekly Mail* to publish and distribute this edition, as well as subsequent editions using black lines, was a source of amazement to both Harber and Manoim. Harber stated, "I can remember one occasion where we put a newspaper to bed and I said to Irwin, 'Well, I think that's it. We'll never get away with this one.' It was the black stripes one, the first one where we blacked out large spots. I remember [I said] to Irwin, 'I think, this is probably our last edition.' But I was wrong precisely because they saw that we blacked stuff out, [and] they accepted that." While it is indeed remarkable that the *Weekly Mail* was able to "get away with this," an analysis of the domestic and international power dynamics of that time reveals how this form of strategic resistance created formidable dilemmas for those in the apartheid government.

First, the hierarchical nature of South African society and its rigid attitudes toward "the law" provided the *Weekly Mail* with an important opening. One must be careful about making sweeping generalizations, but this adherence to rules and the law seemed particularly strong for those in the lower echelons of the bureaucratic pecking order. This attitude is captured, for example, in the amnesty application Capt. Frank McCarter submitted to the Truth and Reconciliation Commission. McCarter, who had murdered political activists at the behest of his superiors, made the following statement: "We were fighting a war where the enemy was not bound by any rules. . . . I had to do things that went against my grain sometimes. . . . I did not regard them as morally wrong, although I realise that my acts were illegal" (vol. 2, 240). In other words, this individual who murdered people because he was ordered to do so did not wrangle with the moral implications. But he did acknowledge that these acts were "illegal."

Those at the *Weekly Mail*, aware of these attitudes, used them to their advantage. As Harber explained, "For example, one thing we learned over time that David [Dison] taught us was that the kind of bureaucrats you were dealing with, if you said you were acting in terms of the law, that's half of what they are looking for. If you say this has been passed by our lawyers, they would seldom know any better." Irwin Manoim concurred: "And very often we would play the game of soberly following the correct procedure. 'This is the procedure and we are following it to the last T.' Very often, that would play absolutely fine with the average policeman who had no sense of irony to demonstrate how you were going out of your way to keep track of these regulations. And they were quite impressed." The police, particularly those sent out to examine copies of the *Weekly Mail*, were charged with enforcing laws that must have seemed complex and mysterious to them, and in apartheid South Africa, with a judiciary that occasionally exerted independence, it was at least plausible that these individuals could be held accountable if they did not have, in Manoim's words, "some piece of paper to back them up" (*Warned* 57). The security personnel who came to inspect the newspaper that fateful evening when the black lines were first used were more than likely given instructions to make certain that the newspaper was not publishing subversive information. If one interprets these directions literally, and if one has, in Manoim's words, "no sense of irony," the presence of black lines would seem to indicate that the newspaper had fulfilled this requirement. For this particular audience, black lines constituted evidence the police could cite when explaining to their superiors that the newspaper did not publish subversive material.[8]

If appeals to the law did not work, those at the *Weekly Mail* could engage in what Manoim described in an interview as "legal bullying." In *You Have Been Warned*, Manoim recounts the night the police sought to confiscate an edition of the *Weekly Mail* after another state of emergency had been declared. In the week prior to the declaration of this particular emergency, the *Weekly Mail* had celebrated its one-year anniversary, and to commemorate the event it sponsored a debate between Cyril Ramaphosa, the leader of the National Union of Mineworkers and who became the fourth president of democratic South Africa in 2018, and Harry Oppenheimer, head of Anglo American, one of the major mining companies of South Africa. According to the description of this event in Manoim's book, as well as the comments made by others during interviews, this was an extremely stressful occasion. Marilyn Kirkwood, who had the unenviable task of trying to secure advertising for the *Weekly Mail*, recalled this event, unprompted, during an interview: "On our first birthday party, we had Cyril Ramaphosa and Harry Oppenheimer. They had never met each other before. It was terrifying. It was absolutely terrifying. Ramaphosa came with a whole lot of trade unionists, who were toyi-toying and singing these trade union songs and surrounding Harry Oppenheimer. And [Oppenheimer's] P.A. [personal assistant] got fired for getting him into that. I've always felt bad about that."[9] Manoim includes in his book the photograph that appeared in the *Weekly Mail* edition commemorating this event, the one the colonel subsequently reviewed and tried to confiscate. The photograph accompanied the article describing the debate between Ramaphosa and Oppenheimer, and it shows the two men ascending some stairs, presumably before their debate, with Harber following close behind, situated in the middle of these two.

On the night that Dison was arguing with the colonel about this particular edition of the *Weekly Mail*, Dison first sought to use the wording of the emergency regulations, specifically section 11, to argue that the colonel did not have the authority on his own to confiscate the newspaper. Dison also argued that if the colonel seized this paper and it was later determined to be an "illegal" seizure, the *Weekly Mail* would then have the right to sue for compensation, which could run into hundreds of thousands of rands. Both of these arguments, however, were ineffective. As Manoim writes, "The colonel was unmoved" (*Warned* 58).

What did move the colonel? Dison observed that the colonel at one point was looking at the picture of Harry Oppenheimer in the newspaper, and according to Manoim's account, Dison informed the colonel that Oppenheimer was one of the newspaper's "key supporters" (*Warned* 59). While it is true that Oppenheimer had some nice things to say about the *Weekly Mail* when he attended its first birthday party, it is more than a slight exaggeration to describe him as a "key supporter," particularly given the unpleasant experience he had just had with the toyi-toying labor activists. But the fact that Oppenheimer was featured in a photograph, with Harber, clearly had an effect on the colonel. The leaders of the South African mining industry had real power in South Africa. As Manoim writes of Oppenheimer, "royalty is royalty" (59). After seeing this picture and listening to Dison, the colonel called his superiors, came back to Dison, Harber, and Manoim, and said, "You've got me on a technicality this time.... But we'll come back next week better prepared" (59). In fact, the government did not even wait until the next week. They responded the next day. Police proceeded to go to newsstands throughout the country and confiscate copies of the *Weekly Mail*.

Although the government ultimately was able to exert its power over the newspaper, this moment of legal bullying on the part of Dison represents a fascinating insight into power relations at that time. First, it should be noted that it was technically not even "legal" bullying. Dison's initial attempts to use legal arguments failed. But as Irwin Manoim noted during one of his interviews, South Africa was a "very hierarchical country" at that time, and one effective strategy when interacting with officials at the lower end of that hierarchy was to "to drop important names to make them nervous." Cope, the manager of the newspaper, provided additional insights into this relationship when he recounted the many battles that took place at the printer: "And it happened on three or four occasions, where I had to call them to come, and David had to deal with them from a legal point of view and say, 'Look, you can't take this newspaper because you have to have orders signed by the minister.' The security police who arrived last minute had papers that hadn't been signed by the minister but had been signed by the local commander. So you know, on every edge, we were taking it right to the final limit." Because the judiciary had not completely lost all independence and because apartheid South Africa was so hierarchical, those at the newspaper could invoke power that was either real or imagined when interacting with rank-and-file police officers.

Of course, the government could use legal bullying of its own. Cope also described instances when the police would stop drivers who were carrying copies of the *Weekly Mail* and say, "'Hold on, we've got this piece of paper.' And they just intimidated the drivers who didn't know what it was and basically just diverted them just to miss the airplanes." All of these examples support Don Pinnock's claim that apartheid South Africa became "so overlegislated" that very few people actually knew the intricacies of the laws. Both sides could thus engage in legal bullying with sufficient bluster by referring to a "piece of paper" that either was or was not in their possession to justify a particular course of action that may or may not have been "legal"—to the extent that anything was firmly legal in apartheid South Africa.

Another interesting dynamic revealed in the course of interviews was that some of the police sent to inspect the newspaper may not have been particularly invested in their role as censor. Parliament could pass all the statutes it wished and the executive branch could enact all the regulations it wanted, but in the final analysis, the government had to find the means of enforcing these restrictions. Harber described the attitude of one police officer assigned to review the newspaper's contents before distribution: "And [we] got quite friendly with the policeman who was on the case. He would come by about once a week. We got quite friendly because he found it terribly exasperating. He was a kind of guy who felt this wasn't proper police work. So you know, whenever he took a paper, he would say, 'You know, this is wasting your time, this is wasting my time. I'd much be rather be catching thieves and robbers.'" Thus, while those at the *Weekly Mail* may have outsmarted or "bullied" some members of the police responsible for reviewing the newspaper, it is also clear that some of them did not believe that their role as censor constituted "proper police work."

For those higher in the bureaucratic pecking order, this legal tactic exploited the gap between the image the apartheid government wanted to promote of itself and reality. As Dison explained, those at the *Weekly Mail* were constantly challenging the government to behave in ways consistent with legitimate governments:

> So that's the point about the lawyer. Well, this might technically be a breach of the regulation, but the regulations are so bloody badly drawn, they're so crude, they're so illegitimate, they come from such a weird base, they don't come through Parliament, they don't have the status of primary statutory law, they could be reviewed, they could be voided, they could be vague, and they could be unreasonable. So basically, every time we wanted to publish something that was in contravention of the regulations in the [*Weekly*] *Mail*, we looked for a reason why it could be published and some kind of attack on the regulations. And Stoffel Botha [a government minister] realized that was what we were doing because he was a lawyer. I mean, he understood that we were basically flouting the regulations.

Dison's claim that Botha knew "what we were doing" echoes a point made in the previous chapter concerning the rhetorical tactics used by these newspapers. It was never a question of whether those in the government "knew" what those in the opposition press were trying to do. They knew. Rather, the decision about whether or not to take action was based on a cost-benefit analysis. As noted in chapter 2, some progressive and independent-minded judges within the judiciary did, as Norman Manoim explained, give the government a "black eye" by declaring some of the emergency regulations invalid. Given that the government was seeking to promote itself as legitimate, however, it could not simply ignore these court rulings without giving itself an even bigger, blacker eye. The government thus accepted these rulings, and rewrote another censorship restriction based on the legal ruling.

These power dynamics allowed those at the *Weekly Mail* to engage in multiple performances. When discussing some of the convoluted logic they used to devise the rationales contained in their all-clear flags, Harber admitted that they often realized that "it was complete hogwash." Shaun Johnson of the *Weekly Mail* recalled that the potential success of these arguments depended on the judge:

> It was like a damn lottery. We worked under the assumption that it was possible that we could get a liberal judge. We always worked on that possibility. We knew that if we got one of the hanging judges, we were dead. [But] say we got Judge Goldstone on this case. Would he be sympathetic to the argument—I mean we were young, innocent-looking kids—of us saying [assumes sincere and earnest voice]: "Your honor, we did this two months ago and there was no problem then." He would know exactly what we were doing, but he would go with us.

Progressive judges such as Goldstone would *need* the *Weekly Mail* to engage in this kind of performance.[10] If those at the *Weekly Mail* entered the courtroom and said, "This is an illegitimate government. We do not recognize any of its laws and do not feel bound to follow them," no judge, regardless of how sympathetic he may have been, would be in a position to help.[11]

Consider, therefore, all of the performances involved—and the fact that every participant was keenly aware of the performance of the other. The government was pretending to be a legitimate government, one that adhered to the "rule of law." Opposition journalists recognized this performance and took steps to exploit it by engaging in a performance of their own, that is, pretending to adhere to the law. In turn, those in the government, whether it was the minister of information who was seeking to crack down on this newspaper or a liberal judge like Goldstone who sought to provide legal cover for this newspaper, were aware that those at the *Weekly Mail* were engaged in this performance and were not actually trying to adhere to these restrictions, despite their public claims to the contrary.

If all the players involved were aware of one another's performances, then who was the audience? For the apartheid government, it was most certainly the international community. As Manoim rightly observed, freedom of expression was used by the US government during the Cold War as a means of justifying its opposition to certain governments: "The U.S. Congress had recently turned against Nicaragua because it closed down a single newspaper" (*Warned* 70). The editors of the *Weekly Mail* were acutely aware of these international dynamics and used them to their advantage. As Harber explained at one point, "It would be a gut feel in the end. It would be knowing, Are they feeling international pressure on the media? If you know sanctions are about to come before Congress, you know they're going to be cautious. They're not going to act against you." Harber's comments support a claim made in the introduction about the complex relationship between "micro" decisions of writing and "macro" dynamics of power. The decisions about what to include or exclude in a particular article could depend in part on political debates occurring within one branch of a powerful government thousands of miles away.

One article, "Inside the Kine Consulate," by Shaun Johnson, provides a tangible example of how the *Weekly Mail* used international dynamics to its advantage. Murphy Morobe, Mohammed Valli, and Vusi Khanyile, the so-called "Kine 3," had been detained by the apartheid authorities for more than a year because of their political activism. They eventually escaped and fled to the US consulate for protection. After receiving advice from several members of the anti-apartheid struggle, including Nelson Mandela, with whom they communicated using Winnie Mandela as an intermediary, they decided that staying in the US consulate was not a viable long-term strategy. Rather than flee the country, they would instead remain in South Africa and continue their political activities. The article published by the *Weekly Mail*, according to the accompanying caption, constituted "the first interview with one of the Kine fugitives" (1).

Those at the *Weekly Mail* thus had to make a decision. It had an important article to publish, but how would the government respond? Johnson, and perhaps Harber and Manoim, could be in a precarious position since apartheid officials could question them and ask where Johnson had interviewed Mohammed Valli. When shown this article, Johnson explained, "It definitely would have gone to Anton, Irwin, and David, and we would have had a discussion and said, 'What are the chances of them subpoenaing me and the editor?' and [the government] saying, 'Where did you see this guy? Where is he now?'"

In fact, the prospect of the government taking such a course of action was by no means remote. Moira Levy, a *Weekly Mail* journalist, described a situation in which she had been summoned by authorities concerning a particular article she had written. The people she had interviewed were wearing masks at the time, so she could state with complete honesty that she did not know who they were. She explained, "And at the end, they [the police] just asked me, "If you did know, would you tell us?" And I said 'no,' and it was true. I wouldn't tell them." Fortunately for Levy, the government did not take further action against her. Other journalists, however, were not so lucky. The *Weekly Mail* article "Journalist Jailed for 'Silence'" describes how Keri Harvey was sentenced to serve thirty days because she would not reveal the names of a doctor and a nurse "on grounds of 'the journalistic code of conduct'" (3). Another article, written by Johnson himself, "Showdown as Editors Face Subpoena Threat," describes how Ken Owen, editor of *Business Day*, and Harvey Tyson, editor of the *Star*, had "been served with subpoenas under section 205 of the Criminal Procedure Act. The section is designed to force journalists to reveal their sources—or face imprisonment" (3). Janet Wilhelm commented on this issue as well during her interview: "You could be imprisoned for not revealing names. So you had to be absolutely sure that this is going to be a story that is worth taking a chance on."

Clearly, those at the *Weekly Mail* believed this article was worth the risk, and fortunately for Johnson, he was never contacted by the government about this article to ask him where he had conducted his interview and whether he knew the current location of the Kine 3. Johnson speculated as to the reason why:

> And we would have taken the view, and clearly we were right, that for whatever reason, politically at that stage, that they wouldn't go for us. Probably our reasoning at that stage, and this is where it is not legal, it's instinctive, is that the state had taken such a beautiful hammering on this issue. They really looked like idiots. The US consulate was involved. I mean, it was just a propaganda nightmare for them. They would have probably looked at it [the article] and said, "Well, now if we arrest the journalist—Jesus, it's not worth it."

Reading the political dynamics of the time thus led those at the *Weekly Mail* to conclude that the government would not take legal action, even though it of course had the power to do so.

The publication of photographs of Mandela in the *Weekly Mail*'s 9 December 1988 edition provides yet another example of when the newspaper's leadership calculated that political dynamics would prevent the government from taking legal action. A passage within the article headlined "At Last: A Face Not Seen in 25 Years" reads as follows: "The government first announced last week that Mandela would not be going to prison. On Wednesday that week he was moved from his bed in the Constantia Clinic, where he had been recovering from TB, to a house adjacent to the Victor Verster prison farm in Paarl. This is the first step in a tortuous process the government is using to release Mandela gradually. Their hope is to defuse excitement over his release, and make it as quiet as possible by doing it in stages" (3). Why did this dynamic lead the *Weekly Mail* to conclude it could publish photographs of Mandela? According to a statement featured beneath the headline, the editors claimed, "Since he was jailed in 1962, pictures of Mandela have been prohibited because he was a prisoner. . . . But the government has now told us that Mandela is not going back to prison. If that is true, he is no longer, legally speaking, a prisoner—and photographs of him may be lawfully printed" (3). This argument, that Mandela was no longer a "prisoner" because he was being transferred to a facility that was technically not designated as a prison, is almost comical. Given that Mandela was still clearly in custody and had not been officially released makes the argument that he was no longer a prisoner more than a little specious. The *Weekly Mail* could not realistically have expected a court of law to uphold this argument. Although I did not ask Manoim, Harber, or Dison about this specific example, it seems likely that the *Weekly Mail* calculated that a government crackdown on a newspaper for publishing photographs of a man they appeared to be preparing to free would send a curious signal. In short, the decision to publish these photographs was based less on the strength of the legal argument and more on the political dynamics of the time.

In conclusion, the *Weekly Mail*'s approach shares many similarities with Havel's observations about how dissidents in communist Czechoslovakia used the law. It is worth quoting Havel at length, given the applicability of his words:

> A persistent and never-ending appeal to the laws—not just to the laws concerning human rights, but to all laws—does not mean at all that those who do so have succumbed to the illusion that in our system the law is anything other than what it is. They are well aware of the role it plays. But precisely because they know how desperately the system depends on it—on the "noble" version of the law, that is—they also know how enormously significant such appeals are. Because the system cannot do without the law, because it is hopelessly tied down by the necessity of pretending the laws are observed, it is compelled to react in some way to such appeals. Demanding that the laws be upheld is thus an act of living within the truth that threatens the whole mendacious struc-

ture at its point of maximum mendacity. Over and over again, such appeals make the purely ritualistic nature of the law clear to society and to those who inhabit its power structures. (*Power* 76)

Similarly, those at the *Weekly Mail* were acutely "aware of the role" that "the law" played in apartheid South Africa. They pretended to adhere to it while knowingly transgressing it. Such an approach not only allowed them to publish more information but also forced the government to respond in ways that served to unmask the hollow, even farcical nature of their "laws."

Perhaps nothing better exemplifies this dynamic than the regulation the apartheid government eventually issued forbidding the use of black lines and blank spaces in publications. The wording of the regulation speaks for itself: "Reg 3(3). No person shall publish any publication in which any blank space or any obliteration or deletion of part of the text of a report or of a photograph or part of a photograph appears if that blank space, obliteration or deletion, as may appear from an express statement or a sign or symbol in that publication or from the particular context in which that blank space, obliteration or deletion appears, is intended to be understood as a reference to the effect of a provision of these regulations" (qtd. in *Warned* 64). Although the apartheid government clearly had massive institutional power, the legal approach of those at the *Weekly Mail* required officials to make difficult choices. Allowing the newspaper to continue publishing articles with black lines would undermine the government's attempts to conceal the full extent of its censorship; forbidding the use of black lines required the government to enact utterly ridiculous regulations, as quoted above. Similar to the approach described by Havel, constantly challenging the government to adhere to its own laws served to expose "the whole mendacious structure at its point of maximum mendacity."

5

"THE NATS BELIEVED IN LEGALISM"

New Nation's Legal and Ideological Openings

The Nats [National Party] believed in legalism. What they could say was, "There are a bunch of communist terrorists who have infiltrated these organizations backed by Russia and China, and therefore we need laws to protect ourselves against the communist threat." So they would get those laws through Parliament, but they still had to be laws that were rational and that said, "Okay, you've got to actively be promoting the aims of the ANC."

DAVID DISON

As any ideology does, this ideology not only excluded certain forms of activity as illegitimate, it also, perhaps inadvertently, created a small niche of opportunity that was utilized by the mothers of the desaparecidos.

JAMES SCOTT, ON THE MOTHERS OF THE PLAZA DE MAYO

Given its objectives as a newspaper, *New Nation* faced even more constraints than the *Weekly Mail* when devising its legal approach. Both newspapers sought to expose the violence of the apartheid government as much as possible. But *New Nation* also engaged in advocacy journalism, or, as

Amrit Manga noted, it actively tried "to agitate." Specifically, this newspaper sought to promote both anti-apartheid resistance more generally and the ANC specifically. To accomplish these objectives, *New Nation* exploited various vulnerabilities of the apartheid government. As noted in previous chapters, the attempt by the government to present itself as legitimate provided various legal openings. *New Nation*, however, had a second opening as well. Because the government also sought to present itself as a Christian bulwark battling the communist onslaught, it created an ideological opening or, as James Scott notes, "a small niche of opportunity" (166) that this Catholic Church–funded newspaper successfully utilized.

LEGAL OPENINGS

The relationship between journalists at *New Nation* and their attorneys was not as close and cooperative as the one between journalists and attorneys at the *Weekly Mail*. In fact, Manga explicitly compared *New Nation* to the *Weekly Mail* in this regard: "Our lawyers were very conservative, strictly a matter of law, so it was difficult working with them. Not so with the *Weekly Mail*—they had lawyers who were a little more innovative, who wanted to push the limits of the law." Several factors contributed to this tension.

First, while Anton Harber, Irwin Manoim, and many journalists at the *Weekly Mail* noted that they occasionally worked with other attorneys, they described mostly working with one attorney, David Dison. Those at *New Nation*, however, described a process that involved constantly working with different attorneys. Tyrone August explained: "To be fair, our lawyers, they did see their primary role as trying to help us to see legally and creatively how you can get around certain laws. But because they would take turns, you know, it all depended on the individual. One individual may be more conservative or real-istic in his/her approach." Kerry Cullinan concurred: "There was one woman who was just impossible. She was the most conservative and I would hate to deal with her. Then there was Norman [Manoim], who was better, and there was another woman who worked a little bit with us and she was also better." When asked if she ever purposely tried to work with Norman Manoim or the less conservative woman attorney, Cullinan laughed and responded, "Oh yeah, of course!" In the end, however, she ultimately had to work with "whoever was assigned, so it didn't work out."

In addition, Cullinan acknowledged the inherent conflict of interest that existed between journalists and their attorneys: "We would have quite a few fights with the lawyers, in fact, because they felt their professional reputation was on the line. If they were our lawyer, and then we got banned, after they were advising us, it would reflect badly on them. And we felt very strongly that some stories just had to be told, even if the paper were taken off of the streets after a few days. So, natural conflict." Cullinan's insight certainly helps to explain the cautious approach many attorneys took when working with *New Nation* journalists. Norman Manoim reflected on this conflict of interest from an attorney's perspective: "It's very difficult, and I think one ultimately doesn't resolve it all that well because there is a conflict between your professional duty to a client and a sense of your understanding where that client is at. My colleagues would say that it's always easy to be very conservative and very cautious. But clients don't want that, particularly those clients [*New Nation*]. They'd say, 'Anybody can tell us that we shouldn't do it. We want to know how far we can go.'"[1] Norman Manoim's analysis concerning the professional duty lawyers have to their clients stands in stark contrast to the closer, more personal relationships that existed between journalists and attorneys at the *Weekly Mail*. As Clive Cope observed, noted in the previous chapter, the attorneys at the *Weekly Mail* "weren't just these professionals that we employed" but rather were "people very close to us and were part of the struggle with us."

The different objectives of the *Weekly Mail* and *New Nation* also played a significant role in this more strained relationship between journalists and attorneys at *New Nation*. The *Weekly Mail* viewed itself as a politically independent newspaper seeking to challenge the censorship restrictions as much as possible. Consider, for example, Sefako Nyaka's description concerning his objectives as a journalist at the *Weekly Mail*: "What I wanted to do was to inform people about what was happening, without saying to them, 'this is bad'—but just inform them. They would make their own judgments." Compare this with Amrit Manga's response, quoted at length, when asked to describe the overall purpose of *New Nation*:

> To aid the liberation of the country. Very simply that was it. I must admit that there were occasions in which we also consciously attempted to agitate, and I think newspapers do that all the time. We just were more blatant in the way we did it. Because the task at hand was a lot more urgent. If there was a huge stay away because someone was getting hanged out at Pretoria Central Prison,

we would write that story in a very emotive way so that people could identify with what is happening. You know, this is an intense human rights question—the right to life, which has been blatantly violated, and something had to be done about it. People who worked at *New Nation* had come from communities which were repressed and they identified with these things, and there were people that you knew who got hanged—perfectly normal, useful human beings, you know. So we got very emotionally involved with what we were doing.

Whereas *Weekly Mail* journalists sought primarily to convey facts for the purposes of informing readers, many journalists at *New Nation* incorporated more emotion for the express purpose of moving readers to action. Preventing people from being moved to action, of course, was one of the primary objectives the censorship restrictions.

This fact was not lost on attorneys such as Norman Manoim. When reflecting on the primary source of tension between *New Nation* journalists and their attorneys, he indicated that most disputes arose because of "tone":

We were always saying to reporters, "You can probably say a lot of what you're saying, but in a different language." Certainly I found at the time, particularly amongst younger [journalists], a very polemical style. And you would try to say to people, "You can actually be a lot more subtle about saying that." . . . A lot of it, in a sense, the tension between us lawyers and the reporters, was over that. Reporters wanted a strong tone. They wanted to bring people into the article—they wanted to make them angry. They wanted to say what they were feeling. And we were saying, "You're acting under these conditions. Conditions are tough. It's important that people get the message. People aren't stupid. They can get the message without the language being so strong." So a lot of our battles were over trying to achieve that. Tone is almost, to me, 90 percent of what it's about.

In terms of rhetorical intent, therefore, there was very little middle ground between journalists and the attorneys. Writers for *New Nation* deliberately sought to incorporate more pathos in their articles, whereas attorneys, more concerned with the restrictions, frequently sought to distill this emotion to prevent a government crackdown.[2]

Despite these differences between the *Weekly Mail* and *New Nation*, attorneys at both newspapers ultimately faced the same situation: dealing with frustratingly vague emergency regulations that did not constitute "law" in any meaningful sense. This dynamic, according to Norman Manoim, fundamentally altered the role of attorneys:

> In a sense, you kind of remove yourself from being a lawyer to almost a kind of a political spin doctor. . . . One is at a level of dealing with ideology. So you're far beyond your conventional lawyer's terrain and your own comfort zone trying to advise these things. It was very difficult. You'd have to say, "Look, I think this might be a contravention. I think we're close to the edge on this one, but I don't think it's something they're very likely to be upset about. I think they're going to leave you alone on this thing. On the other hand, that particular one, that talks about children in detention. They're up in arms—there's a spotlight about that. That they don't like."

Because the restrictions were more political than legal, attorneys could never advise with any real confidence. In fact, Norman Manoim used language identical to those who worked at the *Weekly Mail* when describing his decision-making process: "And those are gut feels." Despite the uncertainty and the guesswork involved, attorneys could, over time, begin to make more educated guesses. Again, Manoim: "Just saying, this is how this beast reacts, and you need to be able to read its reaction. Its reactions are unpredictable, but if you watch them closely, you can sort of make an informed call about how it is going to behave, which has not that much to do with their own law, but the political dynamics."

Norman Manoim, similar to Dison, specifically noted that stories that were inconvertibly and factually true provided a degree of political cover. This was particularly relevant for stories that may have been carried by other media outlets:

> So in other words, if we had alleged that this security policeman had tortured somebody and we knew we could never call that person and that was the only witness, there was no other objective evidence, then we'd be very, very careful about doing that. Whereas on the other hand, if we'd said, "The police had open fired on a crowd," and there was film footage, which police knew was available—BBC had run it—they might not like that story, and it might have contravened something, but it's less likely they would have gone for us. They knew we could back that up because we had objective evidence to do that.

Manoim provided a compelling insight into the government's political calculations. It was, he claimed, "embarrassing for them to censor something that has proved to be true." He explained: "Part of prosecuting people here is propaganda. The government never wanted the public to know that newspapers were writing the truth about them and it [the government] was stopping the truth. They wanted to say, 'These people are lying. If we don't curb their lies, you're going to be very despondent. You're going to think this country is going to pieces and it's not. That's why we're censoring, not because they're telling the truth—these people are liars.' If you look into that logic, you're going to understand how they operate." Of course, the censorship restrictions, particularly the emergency regulations, were designed precisely to prevent people from learning that the country was "going to pieces" and that the government was using extraordinary levels of violence to maintain power. But it could not publicly acknowledge these realities and maintain legitimacy.

Public statements made by apartheid government officials at the time confirm Norman Manoim's analysis. Leon Mellett, chief liaison officer for the minister of law and order, claimed at one point, "We cannot allow these propaganda efforts by the MDM [Mass Democratic Movement] to tarnish South Africa's image abroad where a destructive view is being created by totally slanted rumors emanating from South Africa. We do not want to suppress the news, but we are determined to withhold MDM propaganda from the outside world" (Index on Censorship 8). By creating this distinction between "news" and "propaganda" to justify its censorship, the apartheid government thus provided an opening for factually true stories that could not be dismissed as "slanted rumors."

This fact-based approach to circumventing the regulations was also used to help accomplish *New Nation*'s objective of promoting the ANC, an opening provided by both the Internal Security Act and some of the emergency regulations pertaining to banned organizations. Drew Forrest explained: "Zwelakhe's [Sisulu] purpose was to produce a newspaper which would, as far as possible, within the legal and other limits of the time, provide [a voice for] the ANC in the country. . . . It [*New Nation*] saw itself, obviously couldn't say so at the time, as an advocate of the ANC, when in fact, any open advocacy at that time was very, very risky. Well, it was a criminal offense. I mean, no newspaper that did it in an open way could possibly have survived." *New Nation* did not directly coordinate with the ANC but rather was part of what Howard Barrell described as the "informal underground" within the country. In other words, even if people within South Africa were not part of formal ANC structures, they nevertheless had a sense of ANC objectives and could act accordingly. When asked about the extent of Sisulu's contact with the ANC in exile, Forrest noted, "I mean, look, there was obviously contact. There was contact. But the point is no organization could survive in the country if the security forces knew that there was some sort of formal connection between them and the ANC. So in fact, that's the way the UDF operated. You have a sense, a knowledge of what the ANC's agenda was, and that informed everything. That informed all your decisions and ultimately informed the editorial line of the *New Nation*." Father Smangaliso Mkhatshwa, when asked about the relationship between *New Nation* and the ANC, echoed Barrell's and Forrest's analyses. He stated, "I don't think there was any official relationship as such." He then explained why: "Because sometimes people can find themselves supporting the same cause without officially [laughs] either saying so or reaching an official agreement. But in practice, they may find themselves on the same side. And I think this was the situation."

To fully appreciate *New Nation*'s efforts to promote the ANC, one must consider how much the perceptions and fates of both the ANC and Nelson Mandela have changed since the 1980s. The ANC, once banned, has since become South Africa's dominant political party. Nelson Mandela won the first democratic election with close to two-thirds of the overall vote in 1994. The ANC has lost considerable popularity in the intervening years, with critics claiming it is not sufficiently addressing the nation's problems due to incompetence and/or corruption. While the ANC experienced setbacks in the 2016 municipal elections, it nevertheless remains the dominant political party in South Africa.

The change in fortunes for Nelson Mandela after apartheid was even more dramatic. Toward the end of his life, Mandela was arguably the most revered political figure in the world. Shortly before he died, the United Nations actually created Nelson Mandela International Day. The ways in which people invoke religious figures to describe the man demonstrates the reverence and admiration he generated. When explaining why he wanted to make the film *Invictus*, for example, Clint Eastwood, a white, politically conservative American who supported both Mitt Romney and Donald Trump for president, described Mandela as follows: "The stories of how he forgave his jailers, and spending 27 years in prison, instead of coming out of prison and starting a civil war, which he could've done, and probably got people behind him, he got out and he used a very creative solution to bring reconciliation. . . . I thought, what a wonderful story, how could a guy be like that, he's like Christ-like or something. There's just no people like this on the planet" (qtd. in Ryzik). Compare this with the discussion featured in the film *Amandla* between Sophie Mgcina and Dolly Rathebe, two black South Africans who lived under apartheid. Rathebe says of Mandela, "He's a messiah," to which Mgcina says, "Yes, he's Solomon." Rathebe replies, "He's Moses." Mgcina then laughs and agrees, "He's Moses!" (qtd. in Hirsch).[3] Mandela's ability to appeal intensely to people across vast divides was also evident in a brief film I watched at a museum in South Africa in 2013. In one clip, Mandela was shown riding in a carriage waving to the crowd with a smiling queen of England; in another, he was hugging a smiling Fidel Castro. The attendance of world figures at his funeral provided a tangible measure of his tremendous appeal. Leaders from several countries, including four US presidents, attended, and speakers ranged from Barack Obama to Raúl Castro. By the end of his life, Mandela's appeal seemed to transcend virtually every conceivable divide: race, gender, nationality, even ideological orientation. It may be difficult, therefore, to recall a time when Nelson Mandela was viewed by many white South Africans as the country's number one "terrorist" and the ANC, now the dominant political party within the country, was banned.[4]

In the mid- to late 1980s, the ANC had been banned since 1960, and Mandela had been imprisoned since 1963. Unless South Africans were actively reading banned underground literature to educate themselves about the ANC or Mandela, they would have had very little knowledge of either. How could they? School curricula certainly did not focus on the history of the ANC or Mandela, and the mainstream media, for the most part, avoided focusing on them for fear of being charged with "promoting" a banned organization and individual. When or if South Africans heard about the ANC and Mandela, therefore, it would have been through the distorting lens of government propaganda.

Salman Rushdie explains what happens when voices are silenced over an extended period of time: "But the worst, most insidious effect of censorship is that, in the end, it can deaden the imagination of the people. Where there is no debate, it is hard to go on remembering, every day, that there is a suppressed side to every argument. It becomes almost impossible to conceive of what the suppressed things might be. It becomes easy to think that what has been suppressed was valueless, anyway, or so dangerous that it needed to be suppressed" (39). Don Pinnock's analysis of a delegation consisting of South African academics and business executives who traveled to Dakar in 1987 to meet with members of the ANC confirms Rushdie's analysis. According to Pinnock, a French journalist "was quoted as being astonished at their [the South African delegation's] political ignorance of the context of political struggles in South Africa. 'It brought home,' she wrote, 'that Pretoria's first weapon is ignorance'" (23).

The ignorance concerning the ANC and Mandela ran deep indeed, including at the highest levels of the South African government. In his memoir, Mandela recalls when Jimmy Kruger, the minister of prisons, visited him on Robben Island:

> I then began to tell him a bit about the history of our organization and why we had turned to violence. It was clear that he knew almost nothing about the ANC, and what he did know was gleaned from the propaganda of the right-wing press. When I told him the organization was far older than the National Party, he was dumbfounded. I said that if he considered us Communists he should reread the Freedom Charter. He looked at me blankly. He had never heard of the Freedom Charter. I found it extraordinary that a cabinet minister should be so uninformed. (482)

Most white South Africans would have viewed the ANC and Mandela as dangerous, and while most black South Africans would have overwhelmingly rejected that view, they did not have access to accurate, credible information about them. This was the context in which *New Nation* began publishing in January 1986.[5]

In their attempt to promote the ANC within the confines of the censorship restrictions, those at *New Nation* utilized an opening within the very statute designed to stifle favorable coverage of the ANC. Section 13(1)(a)(v) of the Internal Security Act of 1982 read as follows: "No person shall ... advocate, advise, defend or encourage the achievement of any of the objects of the unlawful organization or objects similar to the objects of such organization, or perform any other act of whatever nature which is calculated to further the achievement of any such object" (qtd. in Stuart 125). David Dison of the *Weekly Mail* invoked the Internal Security Act when contrasting how statutes passed by Parliament differed from the media regulations promulgated during the state of emergency:

Remember the Nats had to take these laws, like the Internal Security Act, through Parliament. There was massive opposition, and they would always be saying to the outside world, "We are a legitimate government. We pass our laws. Law making was preserved in Parliament." And law making means that you can't do things that you write down in decrees: "I hereby decree that you shall not report anything about an emergency situation or you cannot report about unrest." You could never get that law through a parliament because it's just a joke. So the Nats believed in legalism. What they could say was, "There are a bunch of communist terrorists who have infiltrated these organizations backed by Russia and China, and therefore we need laws to protect ourselves against the communist threat." So they would get those laws through Parliament. But they still had to be laws that were rational and that said, "Okay, you've got to actively be promoting the aims of the ANC."

In terms of the Internal Security Act, therefore, it was not sufficient for some petty bureaucrat simply to skim the pages of a newspaper to determine whether or not a particular banned organization had been mentioned. Instead, the government needed to show that the publication was trying to "advocate, advise, defend or encourage the achievement of any of the objects of the unlawful organization." This, of course, was remarkably subjective. Where and how does one draw a meaningful distinction between "reporting on" a banned organization and "promoting" it?

The regulations, as Dison explained, were more sweeping than the statutes, but even these provided a similar opening. One regulation forbade publications from printing "subversive statements," defined as those "which incited or encouraged members of the public or [were] calculated to have the effect of inciting or encouraging members of the public to . . . take part in any activities of, or to join, or support, an organization which was an unlawful organisation in terms of the Internal Security Act of 1982" (Cooper et al., *Race Relations Survey, 1987/88* 821). While this language is quite broad, particularly in terms of trying to determine the extent to which an article could lend "support" to a banned organization, it is significant that even this regulation does not entirely forbid publications from mentioning banned organizations or talking about them. It was precisely this gray area that those at *New Nation* sought to exploit in its attempt to promote the ANC.

New Nation was not the first newspaper to try to promote the ANC. At one point during his interview, Sisulu observed, "One of the things about *New*

Nation you will find is that *New Nation* actually had very few original ideas. What we were good at was, I think, finding existing ideas." Sisulu, who served as a news editor of the *Sunday Post* in the 1970s, may very well have been referring to the similar ways that *New Nation* and the *Sunday Post* used indirection to promote the ANC.

Howard Barrell, who worked as a journalist for the *Sunday Post* in the 1970s, described the newspaper's large black readership and those who worked there: "Zwelakhe Sisulu came from a well-known ANC family. . . . The rest of the white guys amongst us all sympathized, to the extent that we knew anything at all—very few people in those days knew much inside the country—we were all sympathetic to the ANC, Communist Party." In addition to their similar political orientation, the members of the *Sunday Post* staff quickly discovered that they could exert quite a bit of influence because, according to Barrell, the editor of the newspaper delegated considerable responsibility to them: "I mean, [we were] much more powerful on that paper than I've ever known subs [sub-editors] to be on any paper. So we control the paper—between the news editor, Zwelakhe, the chief sub, and Bruce Cohen, we control the paper. But the question was clear to all of us: What do we do with this newspaper?"

The approach they ultimately utilized was inspired in part by the writings of the cultural theorist Stuart Hall. Graham Watts, who Barrell described as the group's "media theorist," read Hall's articles about how publications "set an agenda." Barrell explained: "Stuart Hall wrote one or two little short papers in which he had this notion of setting an agenda. Basically what he said, I'm crudifying it a bit now, but what he said basically was any publication of any seriousness whatsoever, even if it has no seriousness, in effect sets an agenda. It transmits a message about what is the most important issue of the day. . . . Basically, the theory, to the extent that we had any theory, was: If a newspaper unwittingly does this, why don't we wittingly do it?"[6] Barrell described how those at the *Sunday Post* used a two-pronged approach: first, report seriously about the ANC, and second, "transmit conflict."

In terms of reporting seriously about the ANC, those at the *Sunday Post* were capitalizing on the opening described above. According to Barrell,

> What we had to try and do was to find a gap. And we found a gap. And the gap we found, the space we wanted to create, was if we report on the ANC, are we furthering its aims? The state may well try to make out we were, and we should expect them to try to do so. But we should develop a cogent argument for saying

that there was no way that that can possibly apply, and we can hope that the courts would take a similarly intelligent view. Not guaranteed, but we could hope.

At another point during the interview, Barrell reiterated this point: "We're not allowed to 'further the aims of the ANC,' but that's not what we're going to do. We can mention it and we can report seriously on it."

Barrell described the second part of the *Sunday Post*'s strategy, to "transmit conflict," as follows:

> So then, to the extent that we are transmitting an agenda, we transmit con-
> flict. We transmit conflict—that's the agenda. Now we don't need to try and
> make out that the ANC or the black consciousness movement or whoever it is
> that's providing this opposition are "the good people." We don't need to go into
> that kind of shit because we're going to get wiped out immediately. We need
> to survive. So what we decide to do is if the minister of law and order at that
> time, I think it was Louis le Grange, he had a little Hitler mustache, if Louis le
> Grange stands up on a platform and says [mimics an Afrikaans accent], "The
> ANC is the anti-Christ. It is the worst enemy in the world. This is the commu-
> nist onslaught on the nation. We must fight them with everything," whatever,
> whatever, we'll report him saying that. We'll even give him the front-page fuck-
> ing lead. Because our readers, they're going to see Louis le Grange saying it, and
> they're going to say, "Hooray for the ANC. Hooray for the Communist Party."
> That's what they're going to say. And that's what they did say.

Barrell's discussion of the ways in which the newspaper sought to "transmit conflict" offers a fascinating insight into the ways in which meaning was con- structed by the vastly polarized audiences within apartheid South Africa. If an attack on the ANC by Louis le Grange was featured on the SABC, widely viewed as the propaganda mouthpiece for the government, it would have one meaning for its intended white audience. This same statement contained within the pages of the *Sunday Post*, however, would convey an entirely differ- ent meaning for its many black readers. By highlighting the passionate hatred the apartheid government had for the ANC to an audience that had a passion- ate hatred for the apartheid government, the *Sunday Post*, in effect, was pro- moting the ANC.

The following anecdote from Barrell supports his claim that readers understood what journalists at the *Sunday Post* were trying to accomplish. When Barrell was living in Zimbabwe at one point, he recalled an encounter he had with a fellow South African who had fled the country. To fully appreciate his story, it is necessary to know that *Sechaba* was the official publication of the ANC. *Sechaba* was banned in South Africa, of course, but it was sometimes smuggled successfully into the country and shared underground by readers. Barrell recalled, "Now we were the biggest black audience paper in the country. I think we had a circulation of about 150,000 and a readership of well over a million. So, you know, when I subsequently met some exiles, young guys, when I told them I worked for *Sunday Post*, one [said], '*Sunday Post* was our *Sechaba!*'" More evidence would be required to draw any definitive conclusions, but the fact that this individual compared the *Sunday Post* to the official publication of the ANC clearly indicates that some readers recognized that the newspaper was trying to promote the ANC.

While *New Nation*'s approach was somewhat different than the *Sunday Post*'s, particularly in terms of "transmitting conflict," it was similar in that it, too, promoted the ANC through indirection. One approach *New Nation* used was to associate the ANC with both known and lesser-known political and historical figures. The most significant person *New Nation* used in this capacity was Mandela. Both Howard Barrell and Drew Forrest explained how journalists had more space when writing about Mandela as an individual than they did when writing about the ANC as an organization. Forrest discussed this dynamic in relation to his experience working at the *Star*, a mainstream newspaper, which he eventually left to work at *New Nation*: "I mean that was a newspaper which was sort of mildly, a kind of mildly liberal sort of tinge. The editor at the time, for example, campaigned for the release of Mandela, and somehow in his mind, and in the minds of the white media establishment at the time, there was a difference between the ANC and Mandela. Somehow they made some kind of a distinction. So while it was perfectly respectable to campaign for his [Mandela's] release, they never called for the unbanning of the ANC." Howard Barrell claimed that there had been a conscious attempt on the part of activists and sympathetic journalists to separate Mandela from the ANC, which would then allow those advocating for the release of Mandela to claim that they did so without supporting the ANC per se. When relating his experiences working at the *Sunday Post*, Barrell explained, "We also started the Free Mandela campaign. That was the one that really got their goat. In the midst of all this, we started the Free Mandela campaign. Again, it was plausible defensibility. We could say, 'Why not, you know? The bugger's been in jail for twenty years now. Give him a break! We're not pushing the ANC. We're only saying give the bugger a break! He needs a break!' [laughter]." Mandela could thus be used for different purposes in different contexts. For ANC activists outside the country, he was the face of the ANC. For ANC activists and sympathizers within the country, Mandela became a means to promote the ANC indirectly because he was viewed in some circles as distinct from the ANC, something Mandela himself would never have subscribed to.

The article "Mandela: Man of Mystery," featured in one of the very first editions of *New Nation*, reveals precisely this dynamic. On the one hand, the article seems to seize upon the distinction between the ANC and Mandela; on the other hand, it depends on this link as a means of conveying information about the ANC. After the introductory paragraph, the journalist writes, "The name of Nelson Mandela has become synonymous with the struggle for liberation, equality and justice, not only in South Africa but throughout the world. To many he is the one person who could set this country on a course of peace and democracy" (6). The fact that the journalist is capitalizing on the distinction between Mandela and the ANC is evident in the fact that the ANC could never be described in this manner. The following sentence, for example, which substitutes "ANC" for "Mandela," simply could not have been published at the time: "The ANC has become synonymous with the struggle for liberation, equality and justice, not only in South Africa but throughout the world. To many it is this political organization that could set this country on a course of peace and democracy." The writer of this article, therefore, promoted Mandela in ways that simply were not possible if one was intent on promoting the ANC.

After seizing upon this distinction, the journalist also links Mandela with the ANC by describing the important role he played within the organization. The unnamed author(s), for example, describes Mandela's role in the Defiance Campaign of the 1950s; the first trial for treason, in which he was exonerated; and his subsequent trips abroad to garner support from other nations for the ANC. For those readers sympathetic to the ANC, who already knew about Mandela's background, this article would be understood as an effort to promote the ANC. For those readers who knew less about the ANC, this article not only provides valuable information about the history of the organization but also creates a link: Mandela = the ANC, and the ANC = Mandela.[7]

The very different ways *New Nation* used the photograph of Mandela published by the *Weekly Mail* illustrates the ways in which the newspaper sought to promote Mandela. As noted in chapter 2, the *Weekly Mail*'s lawyer, David Dison, had used a bold legal interpretation to argue that the permission granted by the Prison Service to publish Mandela's photograph in a government booklet applied to the picture generally and not to that specific booklet. The *Weekly Mail* published this photograph of Mandela on two occasions: first, when they obtained this government booklet containing this image, and again when the government reissued that same booklet without Mandela's picture. The text that accompanied the publication of Mandela's picture on both occasions demonstrated that the *Weekly Mail* viewed this as an opportunity to defy the regulations (and gloat) the first time they did it and to poke fun at the government (and gloat) the second time. When the apartheid regime failed to take action against the *Weekly Mail* for publishing this photograph, *New Nation* realized that they had, in Barrell's words, "occupied that space." *New Nation* subsequently published this same photograph on at least four occasions, and each time it was accompanied by an article about Mandela and/or his role in the ANC. For *New Nation*, this photograph was significant not necessarily because it represented a triumph over the censorship restrictions but rather because it could be used to promote the man himself.

The importance of the *Weekly Mail* and *New Nation*'s publication of Mandela's image on several occasions cannot be overstated. Mandela relates in his autobiography how government officials openly drove him around Cape Town prior to his release so that he could see how much South Africa had changed during his imprisonment. He writes, "I often tried to see if people recognized me, but no one ever did; the last published picture of me had been taken in 1962" (533). The apartheid government had clearly succeeded in erasing Mandela's image from the memory of South Africans after he was imprisoned. While the *Weekly Mail* and *New Nation* were never able to obtain and publish more recent photographs of the man, the fact that they published any at all constituted a victory. In the 1970s, people risked prison sentences trying to disseminate underground literature featuring images of Mandela. In the late 1980s, during the states of emergency, both the *Weekly Mail* and *New Nation*, sold legally across the country, repeatedly published a photograph of Mandela.

On other occasions, *New Nation* promoted the ANC by featuring profiles of individuals who were not as prominent as Mandela. The writer Sol Plaatje, for example, was featured in an article after he received the Isitwalandwe Award from the ANC. Drew Forrest remembered this article specifically and that its explicit purpose was to promote the ANC:

You see, you could not write an article praising the current leadership of the ANC, you know, an article in praise of Oliver Tambo or anything like that. But you could indirectly promote the organization through Sol Plaatje, a literary figure. He'd been dead for fifty years, sixty years. So you could afford to then run, and I forget who the other two were, but they were also historical figures. . . . But I mean, you could then run long profiles of them, and you could make it clear in the blurb or the headline that these people had been singled out by the ANC. That's the kind of thing that you could get away with.

Forrest was referring to a two-page feature that ran in the 15 January 1987 edition of *New Nation*. A statement in bold above these profiles explains their significance: "As part of its 75th anniversary celebrations, the ANC will be giving the Isitwalandwe Awards. Based on the traditional custom of bestowing a feather of the high flying Isitwalandwe on warriors, the awards are made to past leaders for recognition of their services" ("Sol Plaatje" 6). After explaining how Plaatje wrote about the experiences of black South Africans in the early 1900s and struggled against the unjust Natives Land Act, the final paragraph reads, "Verne Stent, the veteran journalist, wrote in *The Star*: 'Rest in peace, Sol Plaatje. There are some of us who will not forget you, and the seeds you have sown, so few, upon such stony ground, may yet bear fruit a hundred-fold.'" (6).

Amrit Manga related how he used a similar tactic to promote the ANC by highlighting figures who were not well known to most South Africans:

The way we then do it, we would do a profile on someone at the ANC. I remember I did a whole series of them which were called "Worker Leaders," and a lot of these workers would come from the ranks of the ANC and often the Communist Party. And you would write about what they did, where they came from, their social backgrounds, why they got drawn into the struggle, what was their motivation. So it would be a very simple profile on someone who had died a long time ago. Write about J. B. Marks and we'd get away with it.[8]

Lesser-known artistic and political figures, therefore, were invoked for the express purpose of promoting the ANC.

New Nation also promoted the ANC by publishing articles about the Freedom Charter, the document that contains the guiding principles and goals of the organization. Publishing articles about the Freedom Charter in apartheid

South Africa to promote the ANC would be the equivalent of publishing articles about the Declaration of Independence in a context in which it was illegal
to promote the US government. *New Nation* highlighted and celebrated this
document in two separate features, both of which consisted of several articles
that covered two full pages. In its 8 March 1987 edition, it published "All Eyes
on the Charter," and in its 25 June 1987 edition it published "Long Live the
People's Charter!"

An analysis of a massive, several-page advertisement placed within *New
Nation* by the Release Mandela Campaign offers another example of how the
Freedom Charter was used to promote the ANC. This ad contains the name
of the organization at the top of the page, "The Release Mandela Campaign,"
along with its logo: people marching and carrying a flag reading "Mandela."
The headline reads, "The Freedom Charter in Seven African Languages," and
the ad consists of the entire Freedom Charter written, as the title indicates,
in seven languages. The Release Mandela Campaign, therefore, ran an ad that
did not even call for the release of Nelson Mandela but rather promoted the
Freedom Charter. This particular ad would have further extended the chain of
associations for readers: Mandela = the Freedom Charter, Mandela = ANC, the
ANC = the Freedom Charter, and so on.

In terms of focusing directly on the ANC, *New Nation* published short, fact-
based articles about the organization's official activities and positions. "ANC
Hails Shultz Talks" and "Tambo Visit," were two such articles, each only four
to five paragraphs long. Neither article overtly praised the ANC but rather
described meetings that took place, formal requests made, or formal proposals considered. Yet these short articles were clearly significant in that they
provided the ANC with an official status that the apartheid regime constantly
tried to deny. In "Tambo Visit," for example, readers learn that the ANC participated in a summit of the Non-Aligned Movement, consisting of 101 nations
(8). In "ANC Hails Shultz Talks," readers learn that the ANC engaged in direct
talks with members of the Reagan administration (8). These short, informative articles implicitly raise important questions: If the ANC consisted only of
terrorists and hardcore communists, why were so many governments around
the world, including the Reagan administration, willing to meet with them?
Appendix D provides some headlines and brief summaries of the short, informative articles *New Nation* published about ANC activities abroad.

On certain occasions, *New Nation* sought to convey official ANC policy to its readers. It seized, for example, on the trial of Ebrahim Ismail Ebrahim, a case in which South African courts granted permission to three exiled ANC leaders living in London to provide testimony. As Christopher Merrett notes, this "provided more material for a South African public starved of information about ANC activity" (*Culture* 140). *New Nation* used the protected space of the courtroom analyzed in chapter 2 to quote Jacob Zuma and Ronnie Kasrils at length. Both individuals took pains to explain that the ANC did not deliberately target civilians as a part of its armed struggle. The opening of one *New Nation* article, "ANC Men Tell Court of War," clearly reveals its pro-ANC orientation. Note in the excerpt below how long it takes the journalist even to mention the fact that this information was provided as part of official courtroom testimony. In fact, the first three sentences read almost like an official press release from the ANC itself: "The African National Congress (ANC) has never had a policy on soft targets, nor has it ever declared one. It has also never spoken of soft targets, although the media have often referred to the concept as part of the ANC's policy. It would therefore be unthinkable that an instruction on soft targets would be given in any way by the ANC. This is according to ANC National Executive Committee (NEC) member Jacob Zuma, who gave evidence in commission in London in the trial of three alleged ANC members" (1).[9] Kasrils, also cited in the article, made the following statement, which appears above the headline on the front page: "Our morality as revolutionaries dictates that we respect the values underpinning the humane conduct of war" (1).[10]

The short article "ANC Denial" reveals how *New Nation* also sought to communicate official positions of the ANC in exile to supporters within the country. On the front page of its 9 October 1986 edition, the newspaper published the following article, quoted here in its entirety: "The African National Congress (ANC) yesterday denied that it had sent a message of support regarding the launch of a new federation in Johannesburg. The Johannesburg occasion marked the merger of Council of Unions of South Africa (Cusa) and Azanian Congress of Trade Unions (Azactu). In a statement, the organisation said its general secretary, Alfred Nzo[,] only directed the message to the Cusa conference and not to a meeting of Cusa and Azactu" (1). Compared to the ANC's policy on soft targets, this matter is considerably less significant: the ANC is clarifying that it supports Cusa, but it does not support an alliance between Cusa and Azactu. Given the difficulties the ANC in exile experienced in terms of communicating its official positions to sympathizers within South Africa, this small blurb would usefully inform them about the ANC's official position.

In other instances, *New Nation* served as a kind of surrogate spokesperson, particularly regarding some of the most significant political issues of the day, including elections, negotiations, and the government's assassination of ANC leaders. In its 7 May 1987 edition, for example, the newspaper ran a massive two-page feature providing historical background on many jailed leaders of the ANC. "The Main Men" was clearly a response to the whites-only elections that had recently taken place. A caption reads, "White voters went to the polls yesterday—while many authentic leaders of South Africa's voteless majority languish in jail. Foremost among them are Nelson Mandela and six others. The *NEW NATION* looks at the 'Rivonia Seven' and at the Release Mandela Campaign, which seeks the release of all South Africa's political prisoners" (7). The names of Nelson Mandela, Walter Sisulu, Govan Mbeki, Ahmed Kathrada, Andrew Mlangeni, Raymond Mhlaba, and Elias Motsoaledi appear in bold print, beneath which are several paragraphs providing readers with background information on each. In addition, there is an article providing a historical overview of the Release Mandela Campaign. The timing of this feature is obviously significant. The ANC could not take part in this election, nor could they denounce it publicly in a way that South African newspapers could publish. *New Nation*'s response was to use this moment as an opportunity to inform readers about the political leaders who would be running the country if all South Africans were allowed to vote. The informative summaries of each individual do not explicitly endorse or promote the ANC—but for this audience, in this context, of course they promote the ANC.

Indeed, it is useful to compare this series to the efforts of those in the ANC underground during the 1970s to distribute banned literature. Susan Rabkin, who was arrested with her husband, David Rabkin, along with Jeremy Cronin for distributing underground literature on behalf of the SACP and the ANC, described one particular initiative she had worked on.[11] She explained, "When we first got to Maputo, 1978, we were going to do a campaign, 'Release Our Leaders.' This was one of the ongoing campaigns, [and] there'd be all these photographs of the Rivonia Trialists." The material produced as part of this campaign, located in the archives of the Mayibuye Center, featured pictures of several Rivonia Trialists and a paragraph or two summarizing their involvement in the struggle. The summaries that appeared within the pages of *New*

Nation in 1987 and the illegal literature produced underground during the 1970s are strikingly similar. In fact, there are only minor differences between the two. Whereas the underground literature featured pictures of all of the Rivonia Trialists, the *New Nation* article contained only one: the photograph of Mandela first published by the *Weekly Mail* (discussed above). In addition, the language in the *New Nation* summaries is toned down slightly. The phrase "Release Our Leaders," for example, does not appear. Otherwise, the contents of the *New Nation* series and this underground literature produced a decade earlier are essentially identical.

The extremely fraught issue of negotiations between the government and the ANC was also addressed by *New Nation*. Prior to de Klerk's release of Mandela and the unbanning of the ANC, SACP, and PAC, both the apartheid government and the ANC made various demands concerning the preliminary steps the other side must take in order for negotiations to begin. In its 26 November 1987 edition, *New Nation* ran a three-article feature, accompanied by a political cartoon, the very same week the government portrayed the ANC as an organization not interested in negotiations. One long article outlines the official position of the UDF—widely viewed as the internal arm of the ANC— concerning the prospects for negotiations. Throughout the article, the UDF excoriates the apartheid government on many issues, and it concludes with a "set of absolute minimum measures to be implemented if a climate for genuine negotiations is to be created" ("Talk to Botha" 7).[12] The timing of this series is significant: immediately following the apartheid government's attempt to depict the ANC as an organization reluctant to engage in negotiations, *New Nation* responded with a two-page feature making the ANC case about the steps the government needed to take.

Finally, *New Nation* provided the ANC response to the assassination of its leaders. Following one assassination, *New Nation* published an article entitled "Hit the Hit Squads." The article opens as follows: "The African National Congress has vowed to avenge the hit squad–style death in Swaziland last Thursday of one of its top military commanders, Cassius Make" (2). The entire article is framed from the ANC perspective. It does not, for example, include the apartheid government's perfunctory denials about its role in the murder but instead includes strong circumstantial evidence concerning the government's involvement in this and previous assassinations. When describing Make's death, the journalist writes that he was killed "with two others when the taxi in which they were traveling was forced off the road by a South African–

registered BMW containing three heavily-armed men" (2).[13] There is also an attempt to humanize Make. We learn that he "was one of the ANC's most experienced and promising guerrilla commanders" and that Make, along with one of the other victims, Dikeledi, "are each survived by a wife and two children" (2). Finally, although this assassination is described as brutal and tragic, this article nevertheless conveys defiance: "ANC swears revenge." Consider how differently this incident could have been reported: an ANC leader, a member of its violent armed wing, had been killed; the South African government denied any involvement; the ANC now vows revenge, only confirming its violent orientation. Instead, everything about this *New Nation* article—the headline, the content, the framing—reveals a pro-ANC orientation.

IDEOLOGICAL OPENINGS

In addition to the legal tactics they used, *New Nation* journalists exploited another significant opening. Specifically, the apartheid government's efforts, in the words of Drew Forrest, "to project themselves as a Christian bulwark against communism" provided a layer of ideological protection for those at this newspaper, something that was not available for other opposition newspapers. Indeed, the dynamic in apartheid South Africa was strikingly similar to the opening provided to the Mothers of the Plaza de Mayo in Argentina. In that country's "Dirty War," the military junta executed and tortured with impunity thousands of individuals from every segment of society. As James Scott observes, the Mothers of the Plaza de Mayo, a courageous group of women who publicly protested the disappearance of their children, had a degree of protection from the junta:

> Their *relative* immunity from summary violence sprang, I believe, from their structural appeal to just those patriarchal values of religion, family, morality, and virility to which the right-wing regime gave constant lip service. In a public ideology that implicitly respected women, above all, their roles as mothers or virginal daughters, these women were demonstrating as mothers on behalf of their children. An open attack on women acting in this particular capacity and disavowing any other motive would have been quite awkward for the public standing of the regime. As any dominant ideology does, this ideology not only excluded certain forms of activity as illegitimate, it also, perhaps inadver-

tently, created a small niche of opportunity that was utilized by the mothers of the *desaparecidos*. (166)

Scott emphasizes that the immunity of the Mothers of the Plaza de Mayo was by no means absolute. While they did successfully congregate in the public space of the Plaza de Mayo to march silently with pictures of their disappeared children, a form of public protest not available to other groups, they still did not openly criticize the regime. Moreover, some mothers were in fact targeted and killed by the junta.

A very similar situation occurred in apartheid South Africa in terms of Christianity. While there were some admirable dissidents within the Dutch Reformed Church, many Afrikaners viewed their support for the apartheid government as entirely consistent with Christianity. In *Long Night's Journey into Day*, a documentary that focuses on the Truth and Reconciliation Commission, Eric Taylor, one of the police officers who participated in the murders of the Cradock Four, tried to explain why he, along with other police officers, seized four political activists from their car at night, killed them, and then set their corpses on fire after dousing them with gasoline:

> I joined the police force when I was 18, straight from school. I accepted that we are there to uphold the present government and apartheid was part and parcel of the government at the time. There were a lot of values that I felt we had the responsibility to protect, and Christianity was, of course, one of those values. All the people that I worked with were Christians. You must remember that one of the elements of communism is atheism and that is the outstanding point, as far as I'm concerned, that actually justified the kind of work that we were doing. (Reid and Hoffman)[14]

For many white South Africans, Christianity and apartheid were inextricably linked. Not only did they view the system as consistent with the Bible, but opponents of apartheid were frequently described as communist atheists or those allied with communist atheists.[15]

By justifying itself within a Christian framework, the apartheid government, in Scott's words, "inadvertently created a small niche of opportunity." Father Mkhatshwa observed, "[With] the government, as fascist as it was, there was still some kind of respect for religious organizations. That's why our Bishop Tutu could say the kind of things that he said without being locked up."

Sarah Crowe, a young activist journalist at the time, explained why she wanted to work as a press officer for the Catholic Church in the fight against apartheid: "I thought it was an interesting and challenging way to get in the fight. And the church was [a] vehicle that you could do it through. They could hardly ban the churches." There were, of course, many secular avenues for anti-apartheid resistance within the country, including the UDF and the unions. But there was also considerable involvement on the part of the churches. According to Merrett, "Churches became meeting and information centers, and Allister Sparks argues that only in Poland was the church so identified with the freedom struggle" (*Culture* 147).

Similar to the Mothers of the Plaza de Mayo, those who framed their resistance to apartheid in terms of Christianity had "relative" but not absolute immunity. Father Mkhatshwa, as previously noted, had been detained and tortured by apartheid authorities, as had other Christian anti-apartheid activists. Drew Forrest's analysis during an interview of the government's crackdown on Christian activists strongly echoes James Scott's analysis of the Mothers of Plaza de Mayo: "You know the church, particularly because of the nature of the system of that government, had a certain degree of immunity. They did start detaining church members, but I mean, they were extremely uncomfortable with that because they were projecting themselves as a Christian bulwark against communism—that was the whole justification. So when members of the church started to get detained, it got awkward for them." Cracking down on those who justified their opposition to apartheid in terms of Christianity led to some public relations nightmares for the government. Merrett describes one incident during the states of emergency that made international headlines: "In court in 1987, the security police used part of Psalm 5 as evidence of the illegal nature of Maja's documents, and, when cross-examined, put forward the view that extracts from the Bible could be construed as subversive under the Emergency. Orwell's *1984*, it appeared, had surfaced in South Africa just a couple of years late, and even the conservative overseas press recognised in this situation the stripping away of a thin veneer of civilisation and sophistication. Dan Rather of CBS described the situation as 'Alice in Wonderland'" (*Culture* 116). For the government, cracking down on resistance rooted in Christianity, as compared to resistance rooted in politics (the UDF) or economics (the trade unions), was, in the words of both Scott and Forrest, "awkward."

When the Southern African Catholic Bishops' Conference (SACBC) decided to fund *New Nation*, therefore, they were providing not only financial support but political cover as well. Drew Forrest explained: "But the idea was to use church money and use the protection, kind of the ideological protection, afforded by the church to promote a revolutionary agenda." Shaun Johnson, who worked for the *Weekly Mail*, described the feasibility study he helped to write for *New Nation* before it was launched: "[The feasibility study] was done under the auspices of the Catholic Bishops' Conference. I'm not religious. I'm not a member of the Catholic Bishops' Conference. This was a mode of journalistic struggle which was really interesting. We used this as a shield."[16]

Those at *New Nation* actively utilized this ideological protection provided by the Church within the pages of the newspaper itself, specifically its "religion page," the one apparent non-negotiable demand of the SACBC. In a *Weekly Mail* article that announced the upcoming publication of *New Nation*, it specifically mentioned this religion section in its final sentence: "He [Sisulu] said *New Nation* would be mainly a secular paper, although there would be a page devoted to religion" (Rickard, "New Catholic" 9). Sisulu, of course, would have never dreamed of including a religion page on his own had the newspaper not been funded by the Catholic Church. Perhaps the bishops genuinely wanted a religion page. Perhaps they recognized the political cover it might provide for them and/or the newspaper. Perhaps it was some combination of all of these reasons. In any event, the message was clear: *New Nation* needed to include a religion page.

It usually appeared somewhere in the middle of the newspaper, usually between pages 12 and 18. Prior to this page, readers would find no religious iconography or characteristics that would in any way identify *New Nation* as either a Catholic or a Christian newspaper. It is thus surprising to come across a page labeled "Religion" and featuring a logo of a man, a woman, and a child standing underneath a cross. On many of these pages in editions of *New Nation* there is a heading, "Church News," beneath which would be listed some important upcoming church events, as well as a Bible reading. Moreover, this page frequently featured photographs of clergy, both Catholic and Protestant, in their religious attire.

Despite the initially jarring transition from the previous sections, one quickly realizes that this page is entirely consistent with the rest of the newspaper. Sarah Crowe described how Sisulu made it clear from the outset that this page would be integrated within *New Nation*'s overall mission:

I remember Zwelakhe joking about the religious page, and he was very strong with the bishops, right from the word go, that it was not going to be, you know, like a parish newspaper. It was going to be very much on the contextual side. There would be the kind of religious articles that we, that I, elicited from theologians, or from analysts that would be giving context and comparing our struggle to South America. So there was quite a lot of what happened in Brazil, what happened in Argentina, what the churches did there, and trying to make comparisons and see how we could learn from what they'd done.

True to Sisulu's word, this page did not read like "a parish newspaper" but rather was used to advance Christian doctrine consistent with liberation theology.

The Bible readings, for example, were clearly selected to resonate with the current political situation. One was Psalm 78:11: "Listen to the groans of prisoners, and by your great power free those who are condemned to die." Another was Psalm 54:3: "Proud men are coming to attack me; cruel men are trying to kill me—men who do not care about God." Appendix E contains a more comprehensive list of Bible readings that *New Nation* published and the dates when they appeared.

Moreover, the religious section featured many articles arguing that apartheid is fundamentally unchristian and a violation of Christ's teachings. Not only was it acceptable to resist and oppose such a system, it was actually one's Christian duty to do so. The following headlines provide a flavor of the kind of articles that were published: "'S.A. Has Made a Curse of God's Blessing'"; "The Church Can't Stand Aloof"; "God Wishes His People to Be Freed"; "'Christians Should Reject Apartheid'"; "Catholics Should Be Involved"; "Priests 'Should Go to the People'"; "How YOU Can Work for Christian Liberation"; "'Less Talk— More Action'"; "'Faith Calls for Action'"; and "No Action Means Religion Is Opium." Other articles reflected on what Jesus Christ would do if he lived in apartheid South Africa: "'If Jesus Lived in SA, He Would Be in Detention'" and "If Jesus Lived in SA Today, Would He Be on Hunger Strike?" One religion page featured a drawing of Jesus in chains standing on a map of South Africa under the headline "Jesus on Trial Today." Beneath the picture is the following statement: "Arrested, imprisoned, interrogated, tortured, mocked, put on trial, sentenced to death, executed . . . but he rose up again" (12).[17]

New Nation sought to convey that it had the strong support of the Vatican, even though the relationship between the Vatican and leftist movements during the Cold War was extremely complicated. *New Nation*, for example, published any actions of the pope that could possibly be construed as supporting either the newspaper or the anti-apartheid struggle. The 3 December 1987 edition, for example, features a picture of the pope shaking hands with Father Mkhatshwa with this caption: "'An experience of profound joy,' was how the secretary-general of the Southern African Catholic Bishops' Conference, Fr Smangaliso Mkhatshwa, described his meeting with Pope John Paul in the Vatican last week. Mkhatshwa said the Pontiff had 'a very sympathetic understanding of the South African situation,' and had expressed his special support for South Africans working for peace and justice" ("Experience of Profound Joy" 12). The 28 January 1988 edition featured an article entitled "Pope Pledges Solidarity," which contained extended excerpts from the pope's address at a meeting of the SACBC held in Rome. The message *New Nation* sought to convey with these images and this article was clear: the pope was on their side.[18]

New Nation, it should be noted, framed every section of the newspaper, not just the religion page, in terms of the anti-apartheid struggle. Drew Forrest explained: "That was one of the other things about the *New Nation* is that every single section of the newspaper, from the sports section to the culture section, was about trying to promote change, the kind of change that the ANC supported." Later in his interview, Forrest again discussed this tactic: "The idea was, whatever it was that you were covering, whether it was foreign affairs, whether it was sport and culture, or religion, was to try to deal with the issues from one coherent perspective. That was the idea. And I think we were probably fairly successful in doing that." The rationale for such an approach was clear: if every aspect of South African society was shaped by apartheid, then every aspect of society could serve as a potential site of resistance. Forrest's claim that *New Nation* was "fairly successful" in accomplishing this objective was certainly confirmed in an analysis of five years of this newspaper's coverage, from 1986 to 1990. Indeed, it was striking how consistently each and every section of the newspaper was framed through the lens of the anti-apartheid struggle.[19]

While every section of *New Nation* may have been framed in terms of opposition to apartheid, the religion page was the most strident in terms of challenging the government. The articles in this section made overt arguments directly attacking the fundamental basis of apartheid and argued forcefully that true Christians should resist such a system. Perhaps one of the boldest articles featured in this section, "It Could Have Been Drawn from the Bible," actually used Christianity to promote the Freedom Charter and, by extension, the ANC. One passage from this article reads, "'The Freedom Charter is compatible with Christianity,' says Fr Smangaliso Mkhatshwa of the SA Catholic Bishops' Conference" (14). The article later quotes Mkhatshwa as saying that "the document can teach the Church much—even about itself'" (14). Appendix F provides the headlines of many political articles that appeared in the *New Nation*'s religion section over the years.

Religion was clearly the central ideological opening *New Nation* exploited, but it also capitalized on what Norman Manoim described as the apartheid government's "racial arithmetic." In short, Manoim explained, *New Nation* had greater latitude reporting on the abusive behavior of black as compared to white authorities: "The black local authorities sometimes had their own police who did some work and those were generally quite thuggish guys. But they weren't in the mainstream of the establishment, and somehow the regime didn't mind those guys looking like thugs. So you could perhaps get away with saying things about them. But allegations made about the security police and that they might be torturing people—they were very sensitive about that."[20] He explained why this tactic was successful: "In other words, to turn back to the racial arithmetic of the way the apartheid regime worked: They might be less concerned about allegations made against a junior black policeman of atrocities than a senior white policeman. They might not have been worried about the black policeman's problem, but they didn't want [it suggested that] the white colonel is a guy who acts unlawfully." The government had the necessary regulations to crack down on articles exposing abusive behavior of black police, but, politically, these were viewed as less threatening.[21] There was thus an important difference between this tactic and the legal and ideological openings previously examined. Whereas the legal and ideological openings exploited the gap between the image the apartheid government tried to promote and reality, this approach capitalized on the government's overt racist reality.

CONCLUSION

The legal and ideological openings *New Nation* exploited were quite similar to the *Weekly Mail*'s and *New Nation*'s uses of oblique speak (examined in chapter 3). In other words, it was quite clear that *New Nation* was using the financial resources and political cover of the Catholic Church to promote anti-apartheid resistance and the ANC. The government was certainly aware of this. In a meeting P. W. Botha had with Gabu Tugwana, who served as acting editor of *New Nation* after the detention of Sisulu, he expressed his open contempt for *New Nation*: "That newspaper is not worthy of any church belief. It is nothing but communism" (qtd. in Abel 262). The apartheid government, however, was operating under constraints largely of its own making. Because it wanted to appear legitimate, it crafted laws that facilitated the forms of indirect support for the ANC described above. And while it certainly had the institutional power to act against a newspaper financed by the Catholic Church, it was awkward for it to do so given the image it promoted of itself as the Christian defender against godless communism.

In terms of promoting the ANC, *New Nation* was one small part of a much larger political movement that had its origins in the late 1970s and 1980s. Howard Barrell described the efforts of South Africans at all levels of society to "legalize" the ANC on their own:

> Now in the case of Zwelakhe and *New Nation*, you know, people are trying to create their own space. They are doing what Mac Maharaj and some others in the ANC recognized as a very important thing, which is that they are, in effect, legalizing the ANC. The ANC is legalizing itself. The enemy doesn't know what to do, because people are legalizing the ANC. They walk around with the flag, they're singing the songs, they're saying "Oliver Tambo" and all that sort of stuff. And every young black guy in the country considers himself part of the ANC. Whether he knows a single thing about ANC policies, he believes he's ANC. And why not?

Pinnock's description of a political gathering that took place in 1981 provides a tangible example of this movement: "The audience of about 1,000 was soon aware that this meeting was somehow different. Marshals who ushered people to their seats wore khaki uniforms with green, black and gold ribbons [the colors of the ANC]. Around the walls, in huge stenciled letters, were the words of the banned Freedom Charter. . . . As the meeting ended a large ANC flag unfurled behind the rostrum" (24). The cycle that existed within South Africa was thus mutually reinforcing: popular support for the ANC by activists helped create a degree of writing space for *New Nation*, which the newspaper used to publish ANC-slanted articles, which, in turn, were read by hundreds of thousands of South Africans throughout the country. George Orwell commented on the complex relationship that often exists between the will of the people and "the law": "If large numbers of people are interested in freedom of speech, there will be freedom of speech, even if the law forbids it; if public opinion is sluggish, inconvenient minorities will be persecuted, even if laws exist to protect them" (qtd. in Abrams xxi). The South African government, in short, had considerable resources at its disposal and was quite willing to use extensive force to outlaw the ANC. But it simply could not control every individual singing pro-ANC songs, every political meeting, every publication, and so forth.

Because of this dynamic, South Africans were able to generate considerable momentum for the ANC within the country over the course of the 1980s. By the time the apartheid government released prominent political prisoners such as Govan Mbeki in 1987, *New Nation* was celebrating his release with a massive picture of him on its front page and the headline "Welcome Home Govan Mbeki!" It also used this opportunity to overtly praise the ANC in an extremely long article entitled "Mbeki: Still Steadfast as Ever." After some introductory paragraphs about Mbeki's past, as well as reactions to his release, the remainder of this article paints the ANC in glowing, almost propagandistic terms. In addition to highlighting some of its more prominent military accomplishments, such as the bombing of the SASOL plant, the Voortrekkerhoogte military base, and some police stations throughout the country, the article is strewn with phrases of support: "In the years that followed the Soweto revolt, the ANC emerged with great support in the townships"; "Throughout, the ANC has been gaining ground both internally and externally"; and "It [ANC] has attracted the best of those recruits who left the country following the '76 uprisings" (5). Publishing an article that contained such overt praise for the ANC simply would not have been possible in the early 1980s.[22]

According to Smangaliso Mkhatshwa, the leadership of the ANC was extremely pleased with *New Nation*. He recalled, "When I was allowed to travel overseas and so on, and when I met some leaders of the ANC, they would always express their deep appreciation of this. Thabo Mbeki for instance, even Oliver Tambo—they always expressed their deep appreciation of the work of the *New Nation*." He observed at another point in the interview, "I'm quite aware that lots of the ANC people, you know the leadership, the membership outside, they loved it [laughs]. I think they read it very avidly, and they really appreciated it."

Amrit Manga, who assumed an important leadership role at *New Nation* after Sisulu was detained, also met with ANC leaders in exile and expressed similar sentiments. One observation ANC leaders made to Manga was that they thought the newspaper's advocacy of the ANC was at times too strident. When *New Nation* was eventually banned by the government for three months, Manga explained how this became a period of reflection and regrouping for those at the newspaper:

> Inside the country, we consulted with a whole range of people—we consulted trade unions, we consulted the UDF, we spoke to lawyers, and we also felt that there were people in exile that we would have to speak to. . . . So we [he and Gabu Tugwana] went out to Lusaka, spoke to Thabo Mbeki and Joe Slovo, and said, "What would you advise?" And they had a debate about it and gave us a strategic sense of their advice. Joe Slovo's advice was [that] he felt we were being a little too brave, and he thought we ought to back off.

When asked about the advice provided by Thabo Mbeki, who would eventually become South Africa's second democratically elected president, Manga responded, "Similar. That it was important that we had a newspaper that was there to expose the human rights abuses and everything the apartheid regime was up to, and promoted values which we held in South Africa. So that was important—that we needed that medium, and if it means that you need to stop writing about the ANC, then you might just have to do that." Manga described how Slovo cited one particular piece *New Nation* had published to argue that the newspaper had been too direct in its support of the ANC:

> [Slovo] recalled that we had written a piece which was taken from the African Congress. . . . They thought it was a foolish thing we had done, that anybody would know where it would have come from. It *was* foolish. But we were young, you know, and there was an incredible vibe in this country. The struggle was gaining momentum. It was the right thing to do at the point. We did it. But his view was that we shouldn't have—we should have been a little more strategic about it. We walked right into it. And the view was that we shouldn't do that kind of stuff. We had to tone down. I mean, that was the message—that we had to tone down.

The irony of Slovo's response was rich indeed. Here was Joe Slovo—leader of the banned South African Communist Party, "radical," number one white bogey man of the apartheid regime—providing the same advice given by the attorneys for *New Nation*, advice that had been the source of such consternation for journalists: tone it down. But one can also appreciate Manga's insistence that publishing this article that Slovo mentioned was "the right thing to do," given the momentum within the country.

The seemingly infinite variables to consider in a context of such vast uncertainty provide a deeper appreciation for the constant references to "gut feels" and why James Scott refers to resistance as an "art" rather than a science. The outermost point of resistance the government would tolerate was simply unknowable. The chapter that follows explores at length when the apartheid government did, in fact, temporarily close both *New Nation* and the *Weekly Mail* in an effort to silence these newspapers for a time and to convey the message that they needed to be more cautious and adhere more closely to the censorship restrictions once they resumed publication. It proved to be a considerable miscalculation.

6

"MAKE ONE HELL OF A NOISE"

The Struggle of *New Nation* and the *Weekly Mail* to Stay Alive

When they were trying to close us down, the primary strategy was to make one hell of noise and embarrass them.

IRWIN MANOIM

At a certain stage during the states of emergency, the apartheid government signaled that it would no longer tolerate the defiance of opposition newspapers and was prepared to close them down. The question for those at *New Nation* and the *Weekly Mail* was thus no longer how best to increase writing space but whether there would be any writing space at all. This chapter focuses on the tactics both newspapers used in their attempt to survive, an analysis of which reveals the ways in which those engaged in resistance must constantly adapt and devise new tactics when responding to power.

In terms of adjusting their overall approach, both newspapers became more openly confrontational when threatened with closure. Prior to this time, both had engaged in considerable masking by publicly pretending to adhere to the law while devising ways to undermine it. Once the government threatened them with closure, however, both newspapers shifted from an approach that was more legal and indirect and embraced an approach more political and openly confrontational.

While this conscious shift in tactics was something those at the *Weekly Mail* and *New Nation* could control, this chapter also illuminates what they could not control. First, these closures highlighted the central role of what James Scott refers to as the "hidden transcripts" of power. Power brokers speak and act among themselves in ways that are not accessible to those within the public sphere. And yet the decisions rendered as a result of the battles waged within these hidden transcripts of power have profound implications for those engaged in resistance. It is precisely the unknowability of what transpires behind the closed doors of the powerful that accounts for the constant guesswork and uncertainty among those engaged in resistance.

This time period also highlights a second challenge for those engaged in resistance: the profound difficulty of assessing in real time the extent to which certain defeats are in fact genuine defeats and the extent to which they may in fact represent long-term gains. When faced with closure, those at the *Weekly Mail* and *New Nation* did everything in their power to survive, and when they were closed, both staffs were obviously disheartened. *New Nation* was closed first, on 22 March 1988 for a three-month period, and the *Weekly Mail* was closed on 1 November 1988 for a one-month period (Merrett, *Culture* 124). An analysis of the power dynamics reveals what some working at these newspapers may have perhaps suspected but could not know for certain: in the long-term struggle for writing space, the overall momentum was on their side.

THE GOVERNMENT'S CONSTRUCTION OF THE LEGAL FAÇADE

Providing a cloak of legality for the use of raw political power was built into the very DNA of the apartheid government. Such an approach, after all, was how the government slowly, methodically, and "legally" engaged in ethnic cleansing, which, according to Leonard Thompson, resulted in the forced relocation of 3.5 million people during apartheid (111). The term "ethnic cleansing" often evokes images of streams of refugees fleeing their homes during times of war. But the apartheid government engaged in ethnic cleansing over the course of several decades. First, it passed the necessary legislation to provide the government with the power to designate areas within the country on the basis of "race"; then it invoked these laws to do so; then it provided official notices to residents to inform them that they could no longer live in those areas; finally, it used force to remove those residents who refused to obey "the law." The approach to shutting down defiant newspapers would be similar. Rather than simply announce through a decree that it was closing certain newspapers, the apartheid government would do so slowly, methodically, "legally."

The system to close newspapers created in the late 1980s represented the culmination of a much longer history of the apartheid government's efforts to balance domestic and international pressures with regard to the media. In short, certain constituencies within the country would call for increased restrictions on the media, whereas powerful actors in the international community would exert pressure to prevent the implementation of these restrictions. These dynamics were clearly evident in 1977, one year after the Soweto Uprising, an event that shook the apartheid government to the core and thrust apartheid South Africa once again back into the international spotlight.

In the wake of the Soweto Uprising, a "newspaper bill" that would have imposed considerable restrictions on the media was introduced in Parliament. According to the Committee to Protect Journalists report of 1983, this bill would have created a new "press council," largely appointed by the government, which "had the power to suspend publication of newspapers in addition to the power to fine journalists and editors" (48). Faced with this threat, the Newspaper Press Union agreed to a tougher "press code" that "require[d] that newspapers deal with care" with "subjects that may cause enmity or give offense in racial, ethnic, religious or cultural matters in the Republic or incite persons to contravene the law" (48–49). The mainstream South African media thus agreed to censor themselves in an attempt to preempt the passage of legislation that they believed would have been even more restrictive. Certain elements within the government, apparently not satisfied with the levels of self-censorship resulting from this new press code, created the Steyn Commission, which ultimately issued a 1,367-page report calling for even greater restrictions on journalists (49).

The role that the international community subsequently played in response to these proposed restrictions provides tangible evidence of how international pressure could restrain the impulse to censor. After the Steyn Commission's report was issued, the US State Department held a press briefing and claimed that it "would monitor developments closely and that

it was concerned about the impact of the proposed legislation on 'the continued ability of correspondents to keep the American public fully informed of
events there'" (Committee to Protect, *South Africa* 78). Perhaps even more
significant were the actions of Ambassador Herman Nickel. When proposals
from the Steyn Commission report were debated in Parliament, Ambassador
Nickel "paid an unusual visit to the gallery to watch the debate" (78). As a
result of these actions, Nickel was "effective in making clear the interest of
the United States," and according to the Committee to Protect Journalists
report, this visit "was widely reported in the South African press and was
regarded as a significant factor in the failure of the Parliament to enact the
legislation at that time" (78). When considering repressive measures, therefore, the apartheid government engaged in the following calculus: To what
extent would the costs of an international backlash outweigh the potential
"benefits" of increased repression?

This was precisely the dynamic at play in the mid- to late 1980s, when the
government began imposing the states of emergency. In fact, P. W. Botha, the
president of South Africa, openly acknowledged this dynamic in an address he
delivered to Parliament on 12 June 1986: "The Government is well-aware of
the fact that stricter security action will elicit strong criticism and even punitive measures from the outside world. The implications and prices of these
have also been taken into account. The call for sanctions presently heard in the
USA is a cynical political move to buy Black votes in the USA at the expense
of job opportunities for Black people in the Republic of South Africa" (236–
37).[1] Botha, therefore, publicly and explicitly acknowledged the ways in which
international pressure factored into the government's thinking.

An examination of the government's actions reveals that it adopted the following approach: impose as many restrictions as needed to constrain writing
space without raising high-level condemnation from the international community. For example, the government at one point had rejected "nearly half the
visa applications by foreign journalists" (Abel 260), and Stoffel Botha himself,
the minister of home affairs, rejected 186 visa applications of foreign journalists (293). This action allowed the apartheid government to prevent specific
journalists from entering the country who they suspected would write stories
critical of the government without raising a significant outcry on the part of
foreign governments.

But if certain restrictions either caused an international outcry or had the
potential to do so, the government often balked. Richard Abel relates that at one

point the government considered regulations "requiring most 'news agencies' to register and empowering [the government] to deregister those threatening public safety and law" (294). This proposal, however, created opposition from powerful actors in the international community: "[t]he outcry by the United States government, the American and German Chambers of Commerce, and the Inter-American Press Association persuaded Stoffel Botha to repudiate this interpretation and then withdraw the regulations" (294). Another example previously noted: the emergency restrictions provided the government with the power "to place censors in newspaper editors' offices" (Merrett, *Culture* 121), a power they never actually used for fear that it would undercut their claims that they did not engage in direct censorship. There was thus a curious symmetry between opposition newspapers and the government: whereas opposition newspapers sought to defy the censorship restrictions as much as possible without triggering a response from the government, the government sought to impose as many restrictions as possible without triggering a response from the international community.[2]

Given this history, government officials were quite mindful that if they were going to take the extraordinary step of actually closing certain newspapers, they needed as much "legal" and political cover as possible. The government's first step: providing itself with the official power to close newspapers. During the third state of emergency, it issued Regulation 7(1), which read in part, "[T]he minister of home affairs might, if he deemed it necessary in the interest of the safety of the public, the maintenance of public order or the termination of the state of emergency, issue a notice in the Government Gazette prohibiting the publication of a periodical for a maximum of three months" (Cooper et al., *Race Relations Survey 1987* 825).

Second, the government engaged in a high-profile public relations campaign. Stoffel Botha, the minister of home affairs, convened a meeting with the editors of South African newspapers to explain the new press restrictions. He sought to present himself to members of the press as reasonable, even conciliatory. News reports at the time noted that Botha was "affable" at this meeting and "strove to dispel the image of outright State censorship" (Plessis). He claimed, for example, that his "door . . . was always open to editors" and that "much could be settled by discussion" (Plessis). Botha at one point publicly stated "the Government and I respect freedom of the press as much as anyone else" and then added, apparently without irony, that "democracy is what we stand for" (qtd. in Abel 292).

Perhaps the most important part of Botha's public relations campaign, however, was his argument that opposition newspapers such as *New Nation* and the *Weekly Mail* were not just different in degree from mainstream newspapers but different in kind. Given the timidity of most mainstream South African newspapers, discussed in chapter 1, Botha was to a certain extent correct in his analysis. But he then carried this analysis to the next step: since these opposition newspapers were fundamentally different from mainstream newspapers, they were not newspapers at all. According to Botha, newspapers such as the *Weekly Mail* and *New Nation* were "as much a part of the onslaught as the murdering gangs of the ANC" and were "not an informant or watch-dog but an instigator and advocate of violence" (qtd. in Abel 298). He elaborated upon this idea in an interview conducted shortly after these regulations were issued: "But some publications—mainly the so-called alternative press—have been publishing propaganda of a revolutionary nature. I am not referring to normal criticism, even severe criticism, by anyone who disagrees with government. I am referring to propaganda promoting the violent overthrow of the existing order, not the evolutionary replacement of government by constitutional means" (qtd. in Schneider 24). Botha conceded that the international community had a different view of opposition newspapers: "What the Government views as propaganda, is often seen by its critics as acceptable viewpoints and criticism. This is a pity'" (qtd. in Abel 297).

Given the "revolutionary" nature of the opposition press, Botha argued that the government was forced to take extraordinary measures. He claimed, "I would much rather use the courts in order to obtain action against the Press. But we will flood our courts" (qtd. in Schneider 26). According to Botha, the government was taking these steps reluctantly and, in doing so, creating specific rules and a clear process to prevent abuses of power. Botha conceded that such a process could be quite onerous—for him. When addressing Parliament, he claimed that, "in administering and implementing the media emergency regulations, I take the utmost care and the process which I devised and which I am obliged to adopt, is a pain in the neck, I have to give so many notices and listen to so many representations, which I do" (qtd. in Abel 299).

Botha's attempts to explain how he could distinguish between "permissible" and "impermissible" forms of expression were, quite simply, preposterous. According to an article appearing in the *Citizen* at the time, Botha argued, again without irony, that there "had been scientific studies which enabled one to determine whether criticism was permissible and whether it was part of a multifaceted plan to overthrow the government by force and to encourage violence" ("New Body"). These "scientific evaluations," according to an article appearing in *Pretoria News*, would be performed by a panel of "experts" that would include "political scientists, psychologists, sociologists, journalists, and lawyers" (Plessis). As this same article noted, "Mr. Botha was not prepared to name any of the experts who would be helping" (Plessis). But one expert who would assist Botha, according to an article appearing in the *Star*, was an individual who held "a University of Pretoria MA degree specialising in 'human motivation'" ("Censors Will Use").

Since this entire process was a farce with no legal or intellectual foundation, it was not surprising that Botha frequently contradicted himself when trying to explain his powers. When asked at the meeting with editors to clarify the parameters of these regulations, Botha stated that "this is something you cannot pinpoint by way of describing it in legislation" ("New Body"). But in response to other questions, he would claim with confidence that "science" could be used to make such determinations. Another example: when an interviewer stated that these regulations created an environment in which the media "can only report government's version of an event," Botha replied, "No, that isn't true" (Schneider 23). Later, in the *same* interview, Botha claimed that police "at times do not want people to be at particular places and they do not allow journalists into townships during unrest." The interviewer then asked, "So journalists are not free to report on what is happening?" to which Botha responded, "That is correct" (24).

While Botha's explanation of the new media restrictions was not particularly clear, his target was. An article that appeared in *Pretoria News* noted the following about Botha's meeting with members of the press: "Editors of the so-called 'alternative Press'—at whom, it became clear at the briefing, the new measures are most specifically aimed—also attended the briefing" (Plessis). Botha claimed that while these regulations allowed the government to take action against any newspaper, he "'confidently expressed' that this would not be necessary against newspapers which actively subscribed to the code of conduct laid down by the Media Council" (Plessis). The reason, as rightly noted by Abel, was quite clear: "[b]ecause [Botha] expected compliance by 'the organised conventional media,' the regulations were designed for the 'unconventional revolution-supportive Press'" (Abel 266). The government's message to the opposition press was clear: since you have not sufficiently censored yourselves, we will do it for you. It was not a coincidence, therefore, that

Botha used *New Nation* as his "hypothetical" example during one interview: "I cannot merely say, *New Nation*, I dislike you; I now close you down. I must indicate right from the start to the publisher that that article, and your next one, and your next one incited violence'" (qtd. in Abel 268). *New Nation*, which Irwin Manoim described as the newspaper the government hated most, was clearly in the government's sights. And now it had the tools to shut it down—"legally."

To no one's surprise, Botha's first warning letter was sent to *New Nation* on 1 October 1987. True to his word, he cited "that article, and your next one, and your next one." Botha's initial letter cited several items, including articles, photographs, advertisements, and even a poem, that had appeared in *New Nation* over a three-week period. Other newspapers, including the *Weekly Mail, Sowetan, South, Work in Progress*, and *Die Stem*, would subsequently receive letters as well (Abel 282). Botha objected to various articles, images, and even a poem that appeared in *New Nation* for the following reasons:

Five items were "calculated to have the effect of promoting or fanning revolution or uprising in the Republic" (Botha, "State of Emergency" 1–2).
Four items were "calculated to have the effect of promoting or fanning the breaking down of the public order in any area of the Republic" (2).
Nine items were "calculated to have the effect of stirring up or fomenting feelings of hatred or hostility in members of the public towards a security force or members of a security force or towards members of the Afrikaans population group or section of the public" (2–3).
Nine items were "calculated to have the effect of promoting the public image or esteem of an unlawful organisation, to wit the African National Congress and the South African Communist Party" (3).

Some items, such as the poem "To My Son," were listed under more than one category.

The government's objections are particularly fascinating to read in relation to the tactics, examined in previous chapters, that these newspapers used to expand their writing space. First, several articles cited by the government pertained to the issue of "tone." When discussing how journalists at *New Nation* deliberately sought to stir the passions of readers, Amrit Manga had specifically cited articles protesting the execution of political prisoners. In its warning letter the government cited precisely these articles: "Save the Thirty-One

Patriots" and "'Save the 32' Launched in Western Cape." The government claimed such articles were "calculated to have the effect of promoting or fanning the breakdown of the public order in any area of the Republic" (Botha, "State of Emergency" 2). When *New Nation* questioned the government's objection in its written response, the government responded in its letter dated 6 November 1987 that these articles "reinforce the campaign with regard to the so-called patriots sentenced to death for deplorable capital offenses linked with unrest and ANC terrorism" (Botha, "New Nation" 3). The poem "To My Son" was cited because, the government argued, "it fans uprising in the Republic in that people who have partaken in resistance are inter alia depicted as 'selfless sons of the soil'" (5). The government also objected to "Lift Ban on Cosas," because, as it explained in its written response to *New Nation*, "[t]he article . . . seems to be an attempt to stir up or foment feelings of hatred or hostility in members of the public towards a security force" (2). It was difficult for *New Nation* to challenge the allegation that these articles sought "to stir up or foment feelings of hatred" against the security forces because, of course, that was exactly what they were designed to do.

The government also objected to articles that employed subversive enthymemes, the tactic by which readers were invited to reach certain unstated conclusions. This tactic, as previously noted, was particularly useful for implying that the security forces and police were involved in illegal activities, specifically the murder of activists, based on the fact that these crimes were never solved. The government objected to the article "New Fear Grips Hambanathi" because it "reflects the 'unwillingness' of the police to act" (Botha, "State of Emergency" 2). The government thus conveyed to *New Nation* and others that it was quite aware of journalists' attempt to convey meaning indirectly concerning illicit police activity.

Moreover, the government cited several articles it claimed promoted the ANC, including an article examined in the previous chapter, "Tambo Visit." Another article cited was "ANC Women Hold Major Conference" because it "tends to promote the image of the ANC by publishing the activities of this unlawful organisation and its symbols" (Botha, "State of Emergency" 3). The government cited "the photograph of Mr. Oliver Tambo and caption on p. 8" (3) because it sought "to promote the image of the ANC." And it cited another article for promoting the South African Communist Party because "mention is made of a pamphlet *said to be issued* by the SACP to salute the striking workers" (Botha, "New Nation" 2; original emphasis). The government revealed it was quite aware of the attempt to exploit the gray area that existed between "reporting on" and "promoting" banned organizations.

Finally, one government objection revealed the seemingly endless loop of the censorship restrictions. Specifically, the government argued that "the advertisement on p 4 infers that there is torture throughout the country. This statement read in context is clearly aimed at the security forces and is made without any facts to substantiate it" (Botha, "New Nation" 5). Newspapers, therefore, could not claim the government engaged in torture without the necessary facts to support the allegation—but the censorship restrictions were designed expressly to prevent newspapers from publishing any facts to support such allegations.

WEEKLY MAIL'S LEGAL RESPONSE

Shortly after *New Nation* received its first warning letter, the *Weekly Mail* received its own. Since the government's letter was framed in legalese, Anton Harber and Irwin Manoim responded in kind. They would continue their legalistic, indirect form of resistance by promoting a public posture of earnestly trying to adhere to the restrictions. To craft their response, they hired one of the most impressive legal minds in South Africa, Ismail Mahomed, discussed in chapter 4.[3] The end result of Mahomed's efforts: a 111-page document entitled "Representations to the Minister of Home Affairs and Communications Concerning the *Weekly Mail*." If a legal brief could ever be described as enjoyable to read, this was it: brilliantly argued, ruthlessly methodical, peppered with the occasional grandiloquent statement. Quite simply, Mahomed devastated the "legal" arguments contained in the government's warning letter to the *Weekly Mail*.

Mahomed was particularly forceful in rejecting the notion that the articles appearing in the *Weekly Mail* would have the kinds of effects on readers the government claimed.[4] He does so in part by providing a larger context for the articles cited: "the articles or reports to which objection is taken [do] not constitute more than 5% of the contents of any one publication and the particular portion of the article objected to would never exceed more than 1%" (16). Mahomed observes that "this reference to percentages and proportions is not simply a mitigatory plea" but is rather important for determining how this material would affect "the reasonable, rational and balanced reader": "Such a reader reads the newspaper as a whole, absorbing in a relaxed way the totality of the news, the commentary and the advertisements manifest to him. To such a reader must not be attributed a myopic and obsessive and stuttering attention on some phrase in the middle of a lengthy analysis through which obsession everything else in the newspaper dissolves from his brain and his mind becomes singularly concentrated to the manner in which he could endanger the safety of the public" (18). Mahomed's ornate prose comically exposes the absurdity of the government's claims that these articles could actually pose a "threat" to the "safety of the public."[5]

Mahomed also devastated the government's claim that a meaningful distinction could be made between "reporting" on and "enhancing the image" of a banned organization. He argued that the political realities within apartheid South Africa made it impossible for a journalist to know when an article focusing on a banned organization crossed such a line: "The problem is an inherent problem arising from the fact that the ANC is an unlawful organisation but that it does enjoy support and the dilemma which arises from living with both of these facts and conveying commentary and reports which [deal] with these realities and still seeks to avoid in some way the consequence that such a report might objectively or subjectively enhance the image of the unlawful organisation in the reader concerned" (45). Mahomed illustrates this dilemma with his analysis of several articles.

First, he dismissed the government's claim that the short article about Tambo's seventieth birthday "gives positive publicity to the ANC" by stating that such a claim is "to ignore perspective, context and reality" (32) since Tambo "is in fact not ignored and cannot be ignored by any of the news media including the SABC" (35). In terms of the *Weekly Mail* articles on the release of the famous political prisoner Govan Mbeki, Mahomed rightly notes that "[t] he release of Mr. Mbeki was undoubtedly one of the major news events of the year and was treated as such by all the news media in South Africa and several of the leading news media abroad" (55). In terms of the government's objection to the article "UDF's Culture Desk Prepares to Emerge from the Silence," Mahomed notes that this article was actually quite critical of the ANC: "The references to the ANC are not complimentary. They are not even neutral. It is pointed out that the ANC had adopted a 'crude solution' to the problem and later realised this. It points out that the ANC has been caught in 'contradictions and ironies' which 'could no longer be glossed over'" (87). Mahomed thus makes a compelling case regarding the confusion surrounding references to

the ANC. If the *Weekly Mail* published articles that described a factual occur-
rence, such as the seventieth birthday of Oliver Tambo or the release of Govan
Mbeki from prison, it was accused of promoting the ANC. And if it wrote an
article containing criticism of the ANC, it was accused of promoting the ANC.
The government claimed it was not illegal to mention or write about the ANC
so long as the publication did not promote the organization, but newspapers
ran the risk of being accused of doing precisely that regardless of an article's
content or focus.[6]

With hindsight, the most compelling section of this brief is where
Mahomed compared the advertisement from the Release Mandela Campaign, which the government cited, with an article written by Howard Barrell, which the government did not. He writes, "The purported reason is that
the advertisement gives positive publicity to the leaders of the ANC. This
motivation would have equally applied to the other articles referred to as
well as to another article on page 8 and 9 by Howard Barrell to which no
objection is taken" (Mahomed 78). Mahomed's claim had even more significance than he, those at the *Weekly Mail*, or those in the government could
have known at the time. As noted in previous chapters, Howard Barrell was
in fact a member of the ANC underground and was intentionally writing
articles as a journalist for the purposes of promoting the ANC. Nothing better illustrates the limitations of the emergency regulations and their application than this particular example. In the process of citing articles that they
claimed "promoted" the ANC, apartheid officials were unable to identify
those that had been written by actual members of the ANC for that express
purpose.

Mahomed also provided overwhelming evidence regarding the selective application of the emergency regulations. This selective application,
Mahomed argued, had two significant and interrelated effects. First, there was
no clear, discernible, and rational principle involved for citing certain articles
and not others; second, this in turn provided no guidance regarding what articles could and could not be published in the future.[7] Mahomed cited specific
examples from several different newspapers as evidence: the *Star, Sunday
Star, Herald, Sowetan, Citizen, Business Day, Eastern Province Herald,* and
Cape Times. This evidence was compelling not only because he provides so
many examples but also because he drew from such a broad range of newspapers in terms of readership and political orientation.[8]

The overwhelming evidence, in turn, allowed Mahomed to make his central argument: these emergency regulations and the manner in which they were applied lacked any rational basis. Indeed, Mahomed hammers the government over and over again throughout his response with this line of argument: "The difficulty is to find a rational basis for discrimination which does not ultimately rest on the mere opinion of the Minister[,] however bona fide" (49). If there is no rational basis for these regulations, then they are not, in the final analysis, "law."

There is no denying the brilliance of Mahomed's legal mind and the merit of his arguments. But Mahomed also had a distinct advantage. Any time governments seek to censor information, it is difficult, if not impossible, to provide specific guidelines. The opinion of US Supreme Court Justice Potter Stewart regarding pornography illustrates this dynamic: "I shall not today attempt further to define the kinds of material I understand to be embraced within that shorthand description ['hard-core pornography']; and perhaps I could never succeed in intelligibly doing so. But I know it when I see it, and the motion picture involved in this case is not that." Stewart's claim, "I know it when I see it," is perhaps the most frequently cited portion of this statement, but his explanation for why he would not try to "further define" pornography is the most significant for this analysis: "perhaps I could never succeed in intelligibly doing so." Had Stewart tried to outline the specific parameters of what did and did not constitute "hard-core pornography," lawyers would have been able to challenge his language endlessly: questioning the precise meaning of certain words and phrases, highlighting the confusion caused by identifying certain material as pornographic and not others, and so on. The opposition press, particularly the *Weekly Mail*, had great fun depicting Botha as a buffoon and a dolt. But he was tasked with the impossible. In an attempt to provide itself with political cover to close newspapers, the government sought to create a "legal" system. As Justice Stewart had observed, however, no one could "succeed in intelligibly doing so."

Moreover, there was also more than a little performance in Mahomed's response, specifically in the ways he reinforced the *Weekly Mail*'s "wide-eyed innocence" approach to the law. In several sections, Mahomed notes the sincere efforts on the part of the *Weekly Mail* to follow the law: "[S]o anxious is the WEEKLY MAIL to maintain these fierce standards that it retains and has the active and permanent assistance of a skilled firm of press lawyers whom it constantly consults and is guided by. The sole purpose of this exercise is always to ensure that the law is never contravened, wittingly or unwittingly" (22–23).

In another section, he writes that the newspaper had a "sedulous determination" to remain "within the confines of the law" (21). To describe such claims as exaggerations would be generous; to describe them as completely untrue would perhaps be more accurate. As has been demonstrated at length, those at the *Weekly Mail* had complete contempt for the censorship restrictions and dedicated considerable energy and ingenuity—along with considerable assistance from their "skilled firm of press lawyers"—to very wittingly undermine and defy them as much as possible.

The confusion the *Weekly Mail* expressed about its inability to understand the emergency regulations was in fact quite layered. When asked whether the *Weekly Mail*'s claims that they did not understand Botha's objections were genuine, Harber responded, "Well, come on! I mean, we knew we were getting up his nose!" The *Weekly Mail*, in short, knew that they were constantly entering gray areas the government wanted newspapers to avoid. At the same time, the articles Botha selected to include in his warning letters were genuinely confusing. The *Weekly Mail*'s claims of confusion, therefore, were not a matter of "either/or" but "both/and": they were sincere to the extent that the articles cited by Botha did not make sense when compared to other articles he could have cited, *and* their claim of confusion was part of their larger, wide-eyed innocence performance.

Moreover, Mahomed's recurring question throughout his brief regarding the confusion of those at the *Weekly Mail* about how to avoid future sanctions from the government was also rhetorical and part of the overall performance. Those at the *Weekly Mail* knew exactly what they needed to do in order to avoid future warning letters: when in doubt, don't publish a particular article, and engage in levels of self-censorship practiced by the mainstream media. The *Weekly Mail*'s approach, however, was precisely the opposite: when in doubt, publish—and then claim that the regulations were unclear.

LEGAL RESPONSE OF *NEW NATION*

When *New Nation* continued to receive additional warning letters and it became clear the government was going to close the newspaper, the attorneys for *New Nation* "sought an interdict against closure" (Abel 282) from the courts. Abel cites one of the attorneys at *New Nation* who explained the rationale for this approach: "The name of the game quite honestly was staying alive. And we felt that we wanted to adopt legal strategies that were designed to achieve that result. To allow the newspaper to remain on the streets for as long as humanly possible, in the knowledge that we were up against very drastic emergency powers coupled with an immensely restrictive interpretation. ... The Minister had already made up his mind to close down the newspaper ... two days previously. . . . We bought something like six months of time for the *New Nation*" (Abel 282–83). Rather than send letters directly to Stoffel Botha in response to the warning letters they received, therefore, the attorneys for *New Nation* appealed to the courts.

While *New Nation*'s appeal to the courts did contain a number of legal arguments, its defining feature was its extremely strident tone. Abel cites one of the attorneys working for *New Nation* who acknowledged the appeal's true intent: "[the representations] were designed, let me put it bluntly, to embarrass" (Abel 278). Those at *New Nation* were quite aware that the government was going to close the newspaper; this appeal was simply a legal tactic to stall and buy more time. There was thus less emphasis on pretending to conform to the restrictions and more emphasis on legal ridicule.

Toward the beginning of their affidavit, for example, *New Nation* attorneys noted that even Botha himself claimed he did not know the precise boundaries of these regulations: "[a]t the meeting of editors convened by the second respondent [Botha] shortly after the promulgation of Proclamation R123 . . . the second respondent was unable to provide specific guidelines on what sort of material would be considered to promote violent revolution" (Orsmond, "Replying" 32). They observed, "I submit, with the greatest respect, that if the person responsible for the implementation of the regulations is unable to provide clarity and definition as to the precise parameters of the regulations, it is plainly impossible for those bound by the regulations to know and to be able to predict with reasonable certainty what they may and may not publish" (32). In other sections, the attorneys display a contemptuous attitude toward Botha and the government. Toward the end of the appeal, they write, "Some of the objections, particulars of which appear from the representations, border on the frivolous and the absurd. They are the type of objections which could not conceivably have been taken by any person properly applying his mind to the matters at issue" (60). They further note, "Some of the objections are so patently bad, whether by reason of an error of law or a failure by the second respondent to apply his mind, that they taint his discretionary process as a whole" (60). Indeed, at times, it almost seemed as if the attorneys were laughing at Botha: "The second respondent [Botha] now suggests, however, that it must have been clear that what he had in mind was the cumulative effect of all the articles. I reiterate, with respect, that it cannot be expected of the applicant to speculate as to what the second respondent may have had in mind despite what he said" (20).

Botha was not amused. According to Abel, he "found the *New Nation*'s representations 'pugnacious, contemptuous,' bordering on 'bad faith'" (305). Perhaps Botha genuinely believed his own rhetoric about the merits of the process he had developed. Perhaps, as an attorney, he realized at some level that this process was impossible to defend intellectually. Regardless, Botha clearly bristled at *New Nation*'s blunt and forceful legal response.[9] The court ultimately rejected *New Nation*'s appeal for interdiction against closure. As will be examined at length below, the court's decision exposed quite bluntly the illegitimacy of the apartheid government. In short, while the decision that allowed the minister to close *New Nation* constituted a short-term defeat for the newspaper, it served, paradoxically, as a kind of victory in the long term.

THE *WEEKLY MAIL*'S POLITICAL FIGHT

The closure of *New Nation* was obviously significant for other opposition newspapers, particularly the *Weekly Mail*, whose staff realized they would probably be next. What lessons did Harber and Manoim learn? First, they concluded that it was futile to continue to use the tactic of legal indirection and masking. The time had come to engage in a direct political fight. Harber recalled this decision during an interview: "When they threatened us with closure, Ismail Mahomed would produce eight hundred pages of intense legal argument. And I remember the very last time, we said to Ismail, 'It's just not worth it, you know. We're going to produce a ten-page document.' So we actually backed off from our traditional legalistic [approach]. And he was furious. But we stood by it, rightly or wrongly." Manoim recounts this decision as well: "We had now abandoned the idea of yet another long set of legal representations—only Ismail Mahomed continued to believe in the power of reasoned discourse with the government" (*Warned* 109). Harber essentially announced the *Weekly Mail*'s new approach publicly at an Idasa conference: "We no longer see the courts as a useful arena in which to fight the state. . . . It is now a question of having a quick defence, quick feet and trying to slip nimble punches in between raised fists. . . . Although Stoffel Botha still dresses up his actions in legalistic finery, this is only a thin cover for his naked power. The law is now based on his whim, his personal intolerance, and his individual narrow-mindedness" (Abel 296). If the fight against the government depended on the power of rational argument, the *Weekly Mail* would have had an excellent chance to prevail, especially with Mahomed in its corner. But it was now clear to everyone that "naked power," not rational arguments, would determine the fate of the *Weekly Mail*.

Harber and Manoim both concluded that domestic political dynamics were driving the government's attempt to silence the opposition press. Harber said at the time, "Stoffel Botha is trying to win votes in the forthcoming municipal elections" (qtd. in Abel 295). Manoim observed at that time, "What matters is that the newspapers are useful witches to burn and right now P. W. Botha needs to find witches" (qtd. in Margolis 4). In short, closing down these "revolutionary" newspapers would have been politically popular at the time among whites who supported the National Party and those even further to the right.

Harber and Manoim realized that they needed to counter these political dynamics. As Manoim notes in his book, "Our plan was to convince Botha that the price for closing the *Weekly Mail* would be too high" (*Warned* 102). To accomplish this, Harber and Manoim orchestrated a campaign to win support from powerful constituencies both within South Africa and, perhaps more importantly, abroad. They decided to engage in a very different political campaign than the one orchestrated by *New Nation*. Manoim writes, "The staff of *New Nation* blamed white racism for the world's indifference to their plight. Our interpretation was that their tactics were wrong. They had organised a township-based self-defence campaign which promoted solidarity among UDF affiliates, community organisations and union branches. These were undoubtedly dependable allies, but they were in no position to change Botha's mind" (102). The political campaign the *Weekly Mail* would organize, therefore, would rely on appealing to constituencies who might not necessarily be considered "dependable allies" but would instead possess the following qualities. First, they would be sympathetic to the issue of press freedom. Second, and perhaps more importantly, they would be genuine power brokers. As Manoim writes, "We would lean on people who could lean on Botha. Many of those people would be wealthy, white and fairly conservative . . . just the kinds of people *New Nation* was not willing to lobby" (102). As noted in chapter 1, the *Weekly Mail* positioned itself as politically independent within the overall anti-apartheid struggle and, as a result, had much more flexibility in terms of appealing to various constituencies for support.

Manoim describes how Harber and Shaun Johnson took the lead in this political campaign. Harber would focus on domestic constituencies, Johnson would use his international contacts, and both would visit as many embassies as possible. Manoim explains with his characteristic humor why Harber and Johnson were ideal for this campaign. Harber, he writes, was someone "who beneath the journalist exterior relished every opportunity for a good political fight, particularly when it involved phoning men of stature and putting impudent demands on them" (*Warned* 102). And Johnson, who had studied at Oxford University, was "the only member of staff who could put on a suit and not look as if it was the first time he'd worn one. . . . He could lunch at the Rand Club and know which fork to eat the hors d'oeuvres with. . . . The *Weekly Mail* needed a presentable Wasp, albeit a Wasp who happened to be Catholic" (102–3).

Within South Africa, the *Weekly Mail* courted two powerful constituencies. The first was the mainstream media. Manoim recounts the effort: "Relations between the 'alternative' and 'mainstream' press had never been cordial. Indeed, only a year before they had hit a low point when the Newspaper Press Union agreed in public with P W Botha that 'the revolutionary onslaught' demanded tighter media controls. The NPU's groveling so embarrassed the editors that this time round, every editor of an English-language South African newspaper signed a letter of protest. The *Star*'s Harvey Tyson, who surprised us by becoming an energetic supporter, tried to arrange a march of editors. There were no takers; editors prefer armchair protest" (*Warned* 103). This show of support was significant. As noted above, Botha had sought to drive a wedge between the mainstream and opposition press in that first meeting he had held with editors. In his statements, he reassured the mainstream press that they had little to worry about and that these regulations were designed for "revolutionary" newspapers such as the *Weekly Mail* and *New Nation*. As Abel rightly notes, "By intensifying repression, however, [Botha] increased solidarity between the previously compliant establishment press and the beleaguered alternative press" (304). By signing a letter of support on behalf of the *Weekly Mail*, the mainstream media made clear that the government's attempt to divide and conquer, a technique it had used with considerable success in the past, had not succeeded in this instance.[10]

The other powerful constituency the *Weekly Mail* appealed to within South Africa? Big business. Harber met with Harry Oppenheimer, who then arranged a meeting with individuals from South Africa's powerful mining industry, including Murray Hofmeyr, chairman of JCI (Johannesburg Consolidated Investments), and Michael Spicer, a prominent figure within the mining conglomerate Anglo American (Manoim, *Warned* 103). Both Harber and Manoim left this meeting without really knowing the extent to which these business leaders supported their cause. As discussed below, however, the South African business community provided crucial support to the *Weekly Mail*.

While the *Weekly Mail* appealed to powerful domestic constituencies, Harber and Manoim both realized that the apartheid government's real Achilles' heel was international pressure. Harber explicitly acknowledged this in an article he wrote at the time: "The only thing that may force Botha to rethink may be the threat that each action he takes against the press will meet with measured and carefully targeted counter-actions from the outside world. He would have to weigh his desire to suppress his critics against the costs of such reactions" ("We Are One" 3). And Manoim, when explaining why the *Weekly Mail* abandoned its legal approach, noted that they had decided instead to appeal to "international pressure," which he describes as "the last option" (*Warned* 109).

To try to garner international support, Harber and Johnson visited as many embassies as possible, and the officials at several were reluctant to meet with them. Manoim provides Johnson's description of their experiences: "Some of the embassies were loath to let us across the threshold. . . . The Japanese, for example, and also the Portuguese. It was blackmail, really, that got us in. We presented ourselves as a cause they couldn't honestly turn away. We'd say: 'Such-and-such an embassy has agreed to take a chance and back us'" (*Warned* 109). Even though certain embassies were "loath" to meet with Harber and Johnson, Manoim observes that "the most supportive were the British and the Americans" (109).

Manoim's claim regarding the British and Americans may rightly raise a legitimate question: How was such strong support possible at a time when Ronald Reagan was president of the United States and Margaret Thatcher was prime minister of the United Kingdom? Both leaders, after all, were extremely wary of the anti-apartheid movement and publicly adopted nonconfrontational approaches toward the apartheid government. Reagan's approach was described as "constructive engagement," whereas Thatcher's was referred to as "positive measures." On the surface, these governments would seem to be very far from "dependable allies" indeed. Despite the conservative orientation of Reagan and Thatcher, the *Weekly Mail*, one of the most stridently anti-apartheid newspapers in South Africa, ultimately obtained political *and* economic support from *both* the US and British governments. The fact that they were able to do so highlights the complex dynamics of power examined in chapter 2, specifically, the opportunities that decentralized governments present to those engaged in resistance.

The strong support the *Weekly Mail* received from the US government can be attributable to the tensions within the Reagan administration itself, as well as the tensions that existed between the Reagan administration and Congress, which, in turn, had an impact on decisions made within the Reagan administration. Edward Perkins, an African American diplomat appointed by Reagan to serve as the US ambassador to apartheid South Africa, provides a glimpse in his memoir into the infighting taking place within the Reagan administration regarding South Africa.[11] According to Perkins, "The extreme conservative right of the administration prevailed, and on July 22, 1986, the president delivered a conciliatory speech that might have been acceptable three years earlier, but now was seen as too little, too late. I know that the president was swayed in part by White House staffer Pat Buchanan and others who wrote a significant portion of the speech. What's more, the director of the Central Intelligence Agency, William Casey, seemed to be running his own foreign policy with the South African government" (249). Reagan's timid, conservative response to the South African government, which did not necessarily reflect a consensus within his own administration, was subsequently rebuked by Congress in a very public manner. In October 1986, Congress passed a bill calling for economic sanctions on the South African government, which Reagan subsequently vetoed. Congress, however, managed to muster the necessary two-thirds vote from both houses to override his veto, an extraordinary achievement, particularly given Congress's reluctance to override presidential vetoes on foreign policy matters.[12]

Those in the anti-apartheid struggle were quite aware, of course, of the rift that existed between the Reagan administration and Congress. Manoim recounted how he and other South African journalists at one point testified in front of Congress: "We were lobbying Congress. We sat in front of, I think it was the Wolpe Committee, along with people like Allister Sparks from what I remember. All I know is we turned around and saw two or three security police sitting right behind us! [laughter] We also talked to Ted Kennedy." While presidents obviously guide US foreign policy, Congress can also play a significant role, and those in the anti-apartheid movement were appealing to their many allies within the legislative branch.

In Reagan's desperate attempt to prevent the Senate from overriding his veto, he nominated Edward Perkins as the US ambassador to South Africa. The skepticism surrounding this appointment was easy to understand. A *New York Times* article at that time began by stating, "President Reagan, trying to win Senate support for his veto of South African sanctions legislation, today appointed Edward J. Perkins, a veteran black diplomat, as the new Ambassador to Pretoria" (Roberts).[13] Perkins recounts in detail the intense opposition he initially experienced by those in the anti-apartheid movement in both South Africa and the United States.[14] Those in the anti-apartheid movement perceived this appointment as mere window dressing to mask a fundamentally flawed approach toward the apartheid government.[15]

Perkins may have been appointed for quite cynical reasons, but once he actually began serving as the US ambassador, he took some notable public steps to register his opposition and, by extension, the opposition of the US government, to the apartheid government. For example, he describes how he joined religious leaders protesting the detention of children, despite the fact that the South African government had passed a "law making it illegal to either inquire about the status of jailed children or to protest their jailing" (320). For Perkins to support this protest publicly, in his capacity as the US ambassador, was significant indeed, since these religious leaders were "flagrantly disobeying the government" (320). Perkins not only attended this gathering but made certain to have the American flags displayed on his car to indicate he was doing so in an official capacity (321). At the service/protest, Perkins was filmed singing "Nkosi Sikelel' iAfrika." He writes in his memoirs that "it was great news that day: the American ambassador sang a condemned song. I became even more popular with the people after that" (321). For many who had initially been quite skeptical of Perkins, this act began to shift their views.[16]

In addition to this very public act, Perkins also sought to build relationships with black South Africans, including the person so instrumental to the founding of *New Nation*, Smangaliso Mkhatshwa. Mkhatshwa, similar to many other black leaders within the anti-apartheid movement, was initially skeptical of Perkins but eventually modified his position.[17] The relationship Mkhatshwa formed with Perkins proved useful when both he and Sisulu were detained by the government. When Senators David Boren and Sam Nunn visited South Africa at one point, they and Perkins met with P. W. Botha: "As I had asked them to do, Boren and Nunn protested the jailing of several people, including Father Mkhatshwa and journalist Zwelakhe Sisulu, son of Albertina and Walter" (379).

When Harber and Johnson appealed to the US embassy for assistance, therefore, they may have been appealing to an ambassador appointed by Reagan, but he was also someone who favored a more aggressive stance toward the apartheid government than did the more conservative members of the administration. Manoim describes the actions Perkins took on behalf of the *Weekly Mail*: "American ambassador Edward Perkins issued a statement: 'The United States deplores any attempt to censor the press, for its end result is to rob all citizens of their right to be informed.' He backed up that statement with a letter to P W Botha" (*Warned* 109).

Despite this public support, Harber described a relationship with Perkins that was polite and formal but not particularly close: "We did not have the same ongoing interaction with Perkins that we had with the British or the Canadians, for example. Ambassadors of the latter countries we met a few times, but Perkins we met just once. I recall it being a polite meeting with him being quite aloof and reticent" (personal email correspondence, 22 August 2014). Harber also described the strategic nature of their meeting with Perkins:

> We knew that freedom of expression was one issue he could and would embrace, so we avoided any other matters on which we might not see eye to eye and just focused on our situation. Closing our newspaper, we all knew, would increase pressure on his government to take a harder line on South Africa and make his job more difficult, so it was an easy case to present. If I remember correctly, it was a short meeting in which he did not need much convincing to say he would brief Washington and raise the matter with the South African government, though I don't remember him giving us any details. (personal email correspondence, 22 August 2014)

Harber's comments highlight the nature of the *Weekly Mail*'s strategic political approach. When requesting support from the US ambassador, they did not need to agree with every aspect of the Reagan administration's policy toward South Africa. This was strictly an issue of free speech. The Reagan administration may not have been a "dependable ally" on many issues related to the anti-apartheid struggle, but, on this particular issue, it was.

The support the US Congress provided after the government closed the *Weekly Mail* for one month was even more remarkable. Harber recalled receiving a phone call shortly after the government's announcement: "And there was an American Senator, whose name I'd love to remember, who got me on the phone. I mean, he caught me completely off guard, and said, "I'm going into the Senate now with a resolution. How much will you need to survive the month?" And I threw out a number of 70,000 rand—and of course I should have said 70,000 dollars! [laughter]. And he went in, and I got a phone call a few days later from the consulate to say 70,000 rand has been voted to assist you."[18] Before the *Weekly Mail* was closed by the apartheid government, therefore, the US ambassador sent a letter of support for the newspaper to the South African government, and after it was closed, it received financial assistance from the US Congress—all during the Reagan administration.

SOUTH AFRICAN BUSINESS, THE BRITISH GOVERNMENT, AND HIDDEN TRANSCRIPTS

The *Weekly Mail*'s political campaign reveals the significance of what James Scott describes as the hidden transcripts of power. Those engaged in resistance can meet with and make appeals to those in positions of power, but in the end they often do not have access to what transpires among power brokers behind closed doors. It is precisely this unknowability that accounted for what Shaun Johnson described in the introduction as the "knot of fear" that was pervasive among those working for opposition newspapers.

Moreover, certain constituencies of power could exert considerable pressure on the government in ways that were not publicly known at the time. It was not until much later, for example, that Harber and Manoim learned of the full extent to which the South African business community and the British government had lobbied on their behalf. Manoim explains in his book that "years later," Spicer, one of the businessmen from Anglo American with whom he and Harber had met, shared a copy of the letter that had been sent to Stoffel Botha on behalf of the *Weekly Mail*. Manoim cites a brief excerpt in his book:

> We are sure you agree that an enlightened society requires the greatest possible measure of press freedom and that South Africa's international position is severely damaged by an appearance to the contrary.... It is our impression that this newspaper covers the news in a legitimate albeit controversial way and expresses a viewpoint that is entitled to be considered. Its limited circulation and largely professional readership exclude any possibility of it posing a threat to the State. We believe the international repercussions were it to be closed down or otherwise restricted are likely to be out of all proportion to the real importance of the case. (qtd. in *Warned* 105)

The argument and tone are consistent with a letter coming from business leaders. After a brief ethical appeal concerning "press freedom," it ultimately made pragmatic arguments: the newspaper and its readers did not pose a genuine threat, and the costs of closing it would outweigh any perceived benefits on behalf of the government.

The actual arguments contained in the letter may have made some impact, but it was the power of those signing the letter that mattered most. Manoim rightly observes, "[I]t was the signatures at the bottom that were important: the chairmen of Anglo-American, JCI, Anglo Vaal, Barlows, AECI, Premier, Toyota, the Frame Group, First National Bank, Southern Life, and good few more. With hindsight, it was probably this private letter that caused Stoffel Botha to hesitate" (*Warned* 105). Indeed, this letter would most certainly have had a significant impact on Botha. It was not signed by anti-apartheid organizations already opposed to the government but rather by those with genuine economic power who made very pragmatic arguments. This letter was so significant that Harber at one point mentioned it during an interview, unprompted, when talking about their struggle to survive: "I mean, that [letter] was extraordinary."

The support the *Weekly Mail* received from the British government under Thatcher also reveals significant power dynamics that those at the *Weekly Mail* were not fully aware of at the time. Thatcher, as noted above, was perceived by many as being not sufficiently critical of the apartheid government.[19] Robin Renwick, the British ambassador appointed by Thatcher, however, paints a different picture of Thatcher. He notes, for example, how she once "lectured" Botha: "President Botha complained that he never received any credit for improvements that had been made in the conditions of black South Africans. In return he got a forthright lecture about the continuance of forced removals of black people from areas reserved for whites, and about the need to release Nelson Mandela" (*Journey* 185). Renwick also provides an anecdote about Thatcher's role in trying to prevent the collapse of a ceasefire signed between Namibia and South Africa in 1989: "But she warned Pik Botha [South Africa's foreign minister] in no uncertain terms that if the South Africans took unilateral action and used their air force, 'the whole world will be against you— led by me!'" (*Journey* 181). Renwick's accounts suggest that Thatcher did in fact express criticism of the apartheid government. But it was done in private.

Renwick, similar to Thatcher, was also quite complicated in terms of the anti-apartheid movement. With regard to economic pressure, he supported some but not too much: "In sending me to South Africa, Mrs. Thatcher knew that while I supported many sanctions which had been imposed, I did not support disinvestment" (*Unconventional* 112). Renwick claims that his opposition to British companies divesting was due in part to the positive example they set in South Africa, as well as his belief that disinvestment, even if it were to succeed in the short term, could have harmful long-term economic consequences for South Africa.[20] He thus supported the application of some pressure on the apartheid government but took a more cautious approach than others did at the time. During an interview, Shaun Johnson recalled Renwick very fondly. After noting that he was Thatcher's ambassador who opposed additional sanctions, Johnson described him as "intellectually brilliant," a supporter of "one person, one vote," and "very committed to freedom of information."

Indeed, Renwick proved to be one of the most significant and powerful allies of the *Weekly Mail*. When the newspaper was on the verge of being shut down by the government, Manoim notes, "Renwick also organised the trump card of the campaign, a diplomatic *démarche* from the entire European Community. A *démarche* is a formal letter of warning, one of the strongest forms of protest in the diplomatic book of ritual. Several countries were hesitant about joining in at first, *but the British view prevailed*" (*Warned* 110; emphasis added). Renwick, therefore, not only "voted for" this resolution; he championed it and actively persuaded others to do so as well.

That such ardent support came from the British was profoundly important. When the *Weekly Mail* was threatened with closure, they knew they had many stalwart allies, such as the Swedish government, which played an active and admirable role in the anti-apartheid struggle. By the late 1980s, support from the Swedes was certainly welcome, but as Manoim relates, even they recognized its limited value: "The Swedish government, not represented in South

Africa by an embassy[,] promised to protest formally, although, as one of their diplomats explained ruefully: 'We protest so often that they'll just file the letter where they've filed all our other letters—in the wastebin'" (*Warned* 109). Consider the signal that was sent to the South African government, therefore, when a member of the British government, officially representing Margaret Thatcher, took such a strong position on behalf of the *Weekly Mail*. In his memoir, Renwick explains why he believed his position carried significant authority: "It was made clear to the South Africans that I was going there as the Prime Minister's appointment[,] and that, I hoped, would give me some leverage with the regime: for they could hardly afford the complete withdrawal of her support, though they had been doing precious little to justify it" (*Unconventional* 112).

Manoim notes in his book that the details of Renwick's actions "were never revealed, even to the *Weekly Mail*" (*Warned* 110), but that he and Harber eventually received a letter from Renwick. Manoim quotes from it at length:

> In the second half of 1988, when you were threatened with indefinite closure, I did indeed mention this to Mrs. Thatcher,[21] and with her support, made strong representations to the Home Affairs Minister and other members of the South African government, including Pik Botha and Neil van Heerden. The European Community of Ambassadors also made a *démarche*, after your second warning, to the Foreign Minister. I think that this pressure, and particularly the knowledge that the Thatcher government would be strongly opposed, did help to ensure that you were suspended for only a month. (qtd. in *Warned* 110)

In addition to this extremely important act of support, Harber recalled other ways in which Renwick provided political support for the newspaper: "The British ambassador, I recall, made sure that there was a 10 Downing Street subscription, so he could go and say, 'You know, Mrs. Thatcher reads this newspaper [laughter].'"

Renwick also provided financial assistance to the *Weekly Mail* after it was shut down by the government. In his memoir, Renwick provides a rather cryptic description of the support he provided: "There were other ways in which we tried to show our support for those genuinely combatting apartheid. When the *Weekly Mail*, which was playing an invaluable role in exposing the abuses of the security forces, was suspended by the authorities, we helped to tide it over until it could resume publication" (*Unconventional* 124). Renwick does not specify in his book how, precisely, the British government helped to "tide [the *Weekly Mail*] over." But Harber did: "When we were closed down, Renwick arrived in our offices with a brown paper bag of cash for us. He said there would be no record of him having given this to us and we were not to mention it in public. It was not a huge amount of money" (personal email correspondence, 20 August 2014). Harber also noted in this correspondence: "A few years ago, I wrote to [Renwick] to ask if this story can now be told, and he said yes" (personal email correspondence, 20 August 2014). Harber and Manoim may have been unaware of the strong political support the South African business community and the British government had provided behind closed doors until much later—but they were obviously quite aware of this "brown paper bag of cash."

"WIN BY LOSING"

Despite their frantic efforts to stay alive, both *New Nation* and the *Weekly Mail* were ultimately closed by the government. While it may initially seem that the government "won" and these newspapers "lost," the reality was in fact much more complicated and provides an interesting insight into the complexity of power relations. First, the courts may have ruled that the government had the power to close *New Nation*, but the actual wording of the decision proved extremely damaging for the government. Specifically, the judge acknowledged, openly and bluntly, that Botha was engaging in political censorship that was in no way rooted in law. At one point, the judge argued, "I must point out that has got nothing to do with the wording of the Regulations; that arises because of censorship and the discretion of someone, in this case, a politician. And of course, censorship is very like a guillotine, and there is very little use in growing honeysuckle over a guillotine" (Curlewis 24). At another point, he writes, "While on this point let me say that the real deficiency in part of Applicant's representations . . . is not so much the alleged failure on his part to understand the thrust of the Regulations which is anyway irrelevant, but his failure to understand that he was dealing with the opinion of a politician and not a judgment of a Court of Law. *It is of course clear that censorship on the grounds set out in the Regulations is a political act*" (12; emphasis added). The apartheid government had taken significant pains to construct a system of censorship that it could present to white South Africans, and particularly the international community, as one grounded in "law": it crafted specific regulations; it appointed people to enforce these restrictions (who would use "science"); it issued warning letters to publications identifying the specific articles in violation of these restrictions; and it provided the opportunity for offending publications to respond in writing or in person. In his ruling, however, the judge undercut the entire façade, something that did not go unnoticed by the public. As Christopher Merrett observes, "Both court proceedings and the process to appeal to the Minister under the Emergency did, however, allow the public to see how muddled and arbitrary were the reasons for suspension" (*Culture* 143).

Indeed, if legal briefs and court decisions were given titles to capture the essence of their central arguments, Mahomed's legal response written for the *Weekly Mail* would have been "no rational principle," whereas the court's ruling would have been "in the opinion of the minister." The judge emphasized repeatedly throughout his ruling that the minister's opinion was the only relevant factor in determining whether or not an article contravened the regulations: "I must point [out] that whether there has in fact been systematic publishing in the periodical, is a matter of the Minister's opinion, whatever anyone else's opinion may be. In every case the matter must of course endanger public safety in the opinion of the Minister" (Curlewis 11). At another point the judge writes, "The problem for deponent is not the words used in the Regulations but that he does not know what will be the opinion of the Minister" (16). Later the judge writes, "It is no use asking rhetorically, would the call for the release of Mandella [*sic*] constitute promotion of the public image of the ANC. I decline to give any view on it because whatever I said or anyone else said, would be entirely irrelevant. If the Minister's opinion was in the affirmative, then that is enough and it would be offensive" (20). The court decision thus made abundantly clear the completely arbitrary nature of this system.

While the apartheid government may have succeeded in temporarily closing both newspapers, it clearly suffered a black eye in the process. In the wake of these closures, Stoffel Botha sought to assure members of Parliament about the legitimacy of his actions: "Botha defended newspaper suspensions, arguing that 'the procedure according to which action is taken against a publication is a long process and makes ample provision for such a publication to state its case and to decide what it wants to do'" ("Feisty Weeklies" 2). But in the final analysis, a closed newspaper is a closed newspaper, regardless of the intricacies of the process involved. This was something, as Merrett rightly notes, the international community fully grasped: "The esoteric details of the South African struggle are often difficult even for sympathetic foreigners, but the South African government's assault on freedom of expression and information touched on an international issue which was only too readily understood overseas, especially in an era when there was growing convergence on an understanding of human rights and the place of a free press" (*Culture* 148). In fact, David Dalling, a member of the South African Parliament from the Progressive Federal Party who was in the United States at the time the *Weekly Mail* was closed, went so far as to claim that closing this newspaper "did more damage to the image of South Africa than any single act of oppression" (Abel 299).

Richard Abel describes the aftermath of these closures "as one of many examples in which apartheid opponents sometimes 'won by losing'" (309). He offers the following trenchant analysis: "Two of white South Africa's proudest boasts have been a free press and the rule of law. These events [closing *New Nation* and the *Weekly Mail*] tested both pretensions and found them empty. Government attacked and ultimately suspended the few papers brave enough to assert their freedom. The judiciary offered little protection against this assault" (304). The concept of "winning by losing" during apartheid applied to more than these two opposition newspapers. It was clearly demonstrated, for example, by a political cartoon published shortly after the release of Mandela from prison. It depicted a gigantic Mandela towering over an extremely tiny prison, one that barely reached his knees. Two prison guards, even smaller than the prison, stand next to Mandela, and one says to the other, "We sure showed him!" This is not to suggest that the closure and reopening of *New Nation* and the *Weekly Mail* were in any way comparable to the release of Nelson Mandela. But a similar dynamic was certainly involved. In the process of trying to "punish" these newspapers, the apartheid government served only to enhance their credibility and popularity with their readers, with the anti-apartheid movement within South Africa, and with powerful constituencies abroad.

OVERALL MOMENTUM

Just as those at *New Nation* and the *Weekly Mail* recalibrated their tactics when faced with closure, the government similarly recalibrated its means of repression in the wake of this public relations fiasco. Instead of generating controversy by closing newspapers, the government resorted to an approach it had previously used: creating as many constraints as possible that were less visible to the public. A Committee to Protect Journalists report published in 1990 observed, "The government changed its strategy for controlling political coverage in 1989, relying less on drastic government action like media closures and more on court procedures. The lower-profile tactics took the sting out of public opposition to the government's consistently repressive press policies" (13). An Index on Censorship briefing paper, "South Africa: Court Cases against Critical Journalists and the Background," made a similar observation about the government's strategy in the wake of the embarrassment it experienced after closing these newspapers: "Their answer: use the courts. Go through normal and legal channels, and the action will appear to be fair and proper. . . . It may be a tedious process but the public will be less upset" (2).

The government, therefore, engaged in a calculated process of low-level legal harassment. Index on Censorship described the new approach as follows: "So you get your bureaucrats to scour these papers. Go back six months, go back a year, go back five years, do whatever you have to do, but find instances when they broke the law. (That's the easy part, because emergency regulations are so numerous, vague and wide-reaching that everyone breaks them from time to time, either purposefully or in error)" (2). That is precisely what the government did. In 1989, the government brought the following charges against the journalists working for the *Weekly Mail* and *New Nation*:

> Harber and Franz Kruger of the *Weekly Mail*, for "publishing details of the circumstances and treatment of detainees" (Index on Censorship 4)
> Harber and Jo-Ann Bekker of the *Weekly Mail*, for "publish[ing] the circumstances of detainees in June, 1987" (4)
> Harber of the *Weekly Mail*, "charged under the Internal Security Act for quoting African National Congress leader Harry Gwala" (Committee to Protect, 1990 113)
> Thami Mkhwanazi of the *Weekly Mail*, "charged under the Internal Security Act for quoting African National Congress leader Harry Gwala" (116)
> Gabu Tugwana, acting editor of *New Nation*, "charged under the Internal Security Act with quoting a 'listed' person, Harry Gwala, in December of 1988" (118)

Some of the cases listed above were based on articles that were two years old. Clearly the government did not view these articles as any kind of threat but rather were seeking to harass these journalists and make their jobs as onerous as possible.[22]

The stakes involved with this new approach were not as severe as closure, but the new tactic nevertheless created genuine hardships. First, the trials required the newspapers to expend resources defending themselves (Index on Censorship 3). Second, if the editors and journalists were found guilty, they ran the risk of harsh fines and sentences and could become "criminals." Moreover, as the Index on Censorship rightly noted, "[e]ven if the courts [go] no further than to hand out suspended sentences, an editor with this hanging over his head will find it much more difficult to operate under the State of Emergency" (3).

Neither the closure of the *New Nation* or the *Weekly Mail* nor the government's new approach for harassing newspapers served to successfully subdue either newspaper. In fact, even though *New Nation* had been suspended for the full three-month period allowed for by the regulations, it came back as strident as ever. According to Abel, "An advocate familiar with the case 'could not believe what [*New Nation*] was publishing. The closure . . . had precisely no effect whatsoever on the editorial content . . . [which] displayed to me an attitude of what I can only describe as open defiance'" (301). One can only imagine the reaction of Stoffel Botha and his assistants when they examined the first copy of *New Nation* after it resumed publication—only to realize that the closure "had precisely no effect whatsoever."

Far from weakening *New Nation* and the *Weekly Mail*, the closures seemed, paradoxically, to embolden them. Merrett rightly argues that both newspapers "emerged strengthened by the experience" (*Culture* 143). Both newspapers remained financially solvent, and their circulation figures actually increased after their closures (143). Moreover, the readership of both was even more committed and supportive, as demonstrated by the many letters of strong support that appeared in each newspaper when they resumed publication.

The period surrounding the closures of these newspapers illuminates the complexities of power for those engaged in long-term resistance. As noted in previous chapters, writing space did not open and close in a linear fashion but rather was constantly expanding and contracting due to a whole host of factors. There were both victories and defeats for those working on these opposition newspapers, and the question was which side ultimately had the most

momentum and would prevail. Howard Barrell, when reflecting on the tumultuous period of the late 1980s, offered the following analysis:

> We know that the initiative is with us. We also know, the more sensible
> amongst us know, that the state has not yet extended anything like its capacity
> to punish us. That's clear. The question, of course, is whether it has the will to
> do so, which, now with hindsight, we know it didn't. And also internationally
> and diplomatically, it might have been very difficult for it to do so. So, you know
> there is a sense in which we created a space, we occupied it. The state can reoc-
> cupy it, it can set about to reoccupy it, certainly it has the ability to reoccupy
> it, and it can set us back for five or ten years. But in five or ten years, or three or
> four years, we'll come back even stronger. I mean, that's how we're feeling at
> that point. And I don't think that that is bravado.

There is considerable evidence to show that Barrell's analysis was, in fact, not
mere bravado.

After Stoffel Botha temporarily closed five newspapers, not only did every
single newspaper continue to publish afterward but other opposition newspapers, such as *New African* and *Vrye Weekblad*, began to publish as well (Index
on Censorship 2). Closing opposition newspapers did not lead to fewer opposition publications; it led to more. A report by Index on Censorship explained
why: "One reason for this growth was that the government was restrained in
its attacks by the level of public outcry, locally and internationally. . . . It faced
the wrath not just of hundreds of thousands of readers, but of foreign governments, international anti-censorship groups, church leaders, trade unions and
businesses" (2). The anti-apartheid movement at a certain point seemed to
have reached a tipping point by the late 1980s: more internal resistance led
to more crackdowns; more crackdowns led to more condemnation; more condemnation made it more difficult for the government to crack down on subsequent internal resistance.

We now know that the clock was running out for the apartheid government.
In November 1989, Botha seemed sufficiently flustered that he informed *New
Nation* "that it might be closed again—this time around without the benefit
of three warnings" (Committee to Protect, 1990 13). But three months later,
in February 1990, de Klerk unbanned the African National Congress, the Pan
African Congress, and the South African Communist Party and released Nelson Mandela from prison. It would be four long, violent years before South

Africa experienced its first democratic election in 1994. But in terms of official government censorship, February 1990 represented a decisive moment. Manoim described in personal correspondence the period between 1990 and 1994 as one that was "utterly chaotic" but also as a time when "apartheid-era statutes . . . dropped right away." He wrote, "So if one narrows matters down to formal government restrictions alone, this was about as free as it ever got" (personal email correspondence, 4 May 2009). During this time, the government also dropped its charges against the *Weekly Mail*. According to Harber, "Emergency restrictions fell away immediately, as did the many court cases we had running where we were accused of breaking the regulations." In terms of legal restrictions, Harber described this period as "a free-for-all" (personal email correspondence, 5 May 2009).

CONCLUSION

New Nation and the *Weekly Mail* were not the only opposition newspapers targeted by the government. Merrett provides a comprehensive overview of the publications that received one or more warnings from the government between 1987 and 1989: *Work in Progress, Die Stem, Sowetan, South, Grassroots, Out of Step, Saamstaan, New Era, Between the Lines, Azania, Al Qalam,* and *Iziwelethu* (*Culture* 125). Moreover, the government also closed the following publications: *South, Grassroots,* and *New Era* (124). While this chapter has examined the legal and political tactics of two opposition newspapers, many publications experienced the stress of being warned and, in some instances, closed by the government. An analysis of the resistance of *New Nation* and the *Weekly Mail* during this tumultuous time, however, does yield some important insights into the challenges and opportunities for those engaged in resistance.

One challenge for those at *New Nation* and the *Weekly Mail* was determining when they needed to adjust and adopt new tactics in response to the government's actions. Were their current tactics working? Would they continue to work given recent developments? If not, what new tactics should be used? When they did shift tactics, they often did so with considerable uncertainty. As Harber noted when explaining the *Weekly Mail*'s decision to move away from a legal approach and embrace a more overtly political one, "But we stood by it, rightly or wrongly."

Moreover, as noted above, these opposition journalists were often acting in the dark since they had so little access to the dynamics of power taking place behind closed doors. They could appeal to business leaders and to members of foreign governments, and they may have left such meetings with vague assurances of support. But how would such assurances actually translate into action? How firm would the support actually be? How seriously would those in the government take it? All of this was ultimately unknowable.

Yet a third challenge: trying to determine, in real time, the longer-term implications of "victories" and "defeats." In other words, do certain moments represent an example of two steps forward and one step back? Or do they represent an example of, to borrow the title of one of Lenin's works, one step forward and two steps back? When *New Nation* was closed for three months and the *Weekly Mail* was closed for one, it was clearly a step back. It is only now with the benefit of hindsight that we know it was an example of two steps forward and one step back.

While those engaged in resistance face many challenges and uncertainties, the closure of these newspapers also highlights some of the unexpected opportunities that may be available. This was particularly true for the *Weekly Mail*, which received considerable support from some unlikely sources: the US government, the British government, and the South African business community. As noted in chapter 2, structures of power are not monoliths, and thinking of them as such may veil some genuine opportunities. Ronald Reagan clearly did not provide strong public support for the anti-apartheid movement, but even during the Reagan presidency there were nevertheless sites of power within the US government that could be harnessed strategically. Similarly, Margaret Thatcher did not display the kind of firm public resolve toward the apartheid government that many wished she would have. But she and her representatives did provide important support for those at the *Weekly Mail* behind closed doors when they desperately needed it.

The powerful business interests that provided a letter of support for the *Weekly Mail* may have also seemed a surprising source of support at the time. Benjamin Rabinowitz, a successful South African businessman and an early, crucial, ardent supporter of the *Weekly Mail*, described the cautious political approach of many within the business community: "You take the average businessman. They'd never speak out against the government. They certainly wouldn't speak out publicly. Business prospered very nicely, white business, in the old days." Appealing to prominent business leaders for support, therefore, may have at first seemed counterintuitive. But while many business leaders may have been politically conservative and/or cautious, there were neverthe-less those who opposed apartheid on moral and/or pragmatic grounds. More-over, there were vastly different levels of power within the business commu-nity. Business owners dependent on government contracts were obviously in a much more vulnerable position in speaking out than leaders of mining compa-nies and multinational corporations. Rabinowitz may have been correct in his analysis that business leaders "wouldn't speak out publicly." But some power-ful business leaders were willing to speak out privately.

The apartheid government's attempts to construct what Václav Havel referred to as a "pleasing illusion" provided another opportunity. The apart-heid government took elaborate steps to construct a censorship apparatus and engage in a public relations campaign to depict its censorship as being grounded in law and less onerous than in other countries. Botha, for example, argued in an interview shortly after the media restrictions were issued that since South Africa's "demographic make-up clearly falls within the Third World category, it is remarkable that it does conduct a very lively partial democracy" (Schneider 22). For the apartheid government, it was critical that they not be perceived as violating "Western values" too brazenly.[23]

Manoim described in an interview and Mandela describes in his autobi-ography the right-wing apologists from other countries who either tried to paint the anti-apartheid movement as negatively as possible ("terrorists," "communists," etc.) and/or who supported the kind of bogus arguments made by the apartheid government. But the more the government and its apolo-gists sought to create this illusion, the more awkward it became for the gov-ernment to engage in outright censorship. Manoim explained: "It was very important to the South African government, particularly in its relationship with the Thatcher and Reagan governments, to present itself as a reasonable and open democratic government. The right-wing British and American jour-nalists used to come here [and] used to point out that the South African press was free to criticize the government, and did so on a daily basis, unlike news-papers elsewhere in Africa. And there was a very important image that [the government] had to cultivate: This is a democratic society." There was thus a curious paradox in terms of apartheid apologists: the more they sought to promote the South African government as legitimate, the more awkward it

became for the government to crack down on opposition newspapers exposing its illegitimacy.

The brilliance of *New Nation* and the *Weekly Mail* was the way in which
their resistance exposed this illusion. As noted in the introductory chapter,
the Committee to Protect Journalists report of 1983 posed the following question when analyzing the South African National Press Union's decision to sign
an agreement with the apartheid government to engage in self-censorship:
"Might it not be better to require the government to use its punitive power
to enforce its laws restricting the press? At least then the government would
pay some price—in the form of public stigma—for restricting the press" (55).
The fallout generated for the apartheid government after it closed *New Nation*
and the *Weekly Mail* clearly answered this question in the affirmative. Harber
observed that Stoffel Botha was trying to "dress up his actions in legalistic finery" but that these efforts were only "a thin cover for his naked power." When
the government closed *New Nation* and the *Weekly Mail*, it showed the world
what these opposition journalists and those in the anti-apartheid movement
had known all along: the emperor had no clothes.

CONCLUSION

Hope, in this deep and powerful sense, is not the same as joy that things are going well, or willingness to invest in enterprises that are obviously headed for early success, but, rather, an ability to work for something because it is good, not just because it stands a chance to succeed. The more unpropitious the situation in which we demonstrate hope, the deeper that hope is. Hope is definitely not the same thing as optimism. It is not the conviction that something will turn out well, but the certainty that something makes sense, regardless of how it turns out.

VÁCLAV HAVEL, *DISTURBING THE PEACE*

The central argument of this book is that writing space provides a useful framework for understanding and explaining the tactics that writers—and collectives of writers—develop when engaging in resistance. Writing space is fluid and ever changing, and the extent to which it expands or contracts is ultimately determined by, in Havel's words, the "thousands of interactions between the world of the powerful and that of the powerless" (*Disturbing* 182). In this particular context, the apartheid government constrained writing space when it could do so without incurring too many costs but often pulled back when it determined that the costs might be too high.

Every successful tactic of resistance examined in this book can in some way be traced directly to a broad and diverse range of power dynamics. Three of the more significant include the following: the massive political resistance occurring within South Africa in the 1980s, the international pressure exerted on the apartheid government, and the challenges the apartheid government faced in trying to respond to this domestic and international pressure while simultaneously projecting a mask of legitimacy. These dynamics of power did not exist in isolation from one another but intersected in complex ways—and all had implications for writing space.

Many of those interviewed addressed, unprompted, the larger context of political resistance during the late 1980s. Shaun Johnson noted, "It would be a gross injustice of the *Weekly Mail* or the *New Nation* to hold themselves up as *the* catalyst. It was a much bigger thing. The UDF was happening, the trade unions were happening. But it was a very important one—it was really important, much more important in retrospect than we realized at the time." Anton Harber made a similar point: "Don't forget this [resistance] was happening in all aspects of society. The unions, the UDF, they were doing exactly the same. They were saying, 'We can get away with this, we can get away with that, we can push this,' and every act of defiance tried to take things a bit further. If you looked at the End Conscription Campaign, that's what they would do." In short, there was widespread resistance within the country and the South African government had only so many resources at its disposal to respond. Drew Forrest, a journalist at *New Nation*, observed, "But by that stage, you see, the ruling elite had sort of lost confidence in itself, and no longer had the kind of commitment to start cracking down left, right, and center. . . . It was a function of lack of confidence, lack of capacity. The whole situation just became more and more difficult over time to keep the state together." The *Weekly Mail* and *New Nation*, therefore, were not operating in a vacuum but rather were part of a much larger culture of resistance.

At the same time this was occurring, the international community was exerting considerable and sustained pressure on the apartheid government. Prior to the mid- to late 1980s, there had been various flashpoints that led to international condemnation of the South African government: the massacre in Sharpeville in 1960, the Soweto Uprising of 1976, and the murder of Steve Biko in 1977. But the expressions of outrage triggered at these moments simply did not compare with the global anti-apartheid movement that existed in the mid- to late 1980s. Grassroots activists, politicians, unions, church groups, academics, and artists from around the world applied sustained pressure in the form of several boycotts: cultural, sport, and academic. Moreover, activists targeted various institutions within their respective countries—colleges and universities; businesses; local, state, and federal governments—to divest from South Africa. All of these power dynamics, of course, were well beyond the control of those who worked for the *Weekly Mail* and *New Nation*. But they could develop tactics to capitalize on the government's vulnerabilities in the face of such intense pressure, particularly given the apartheid government's intense desire to project a mask of legitimacy.

Why were these newspapers able to publish so many articles that seized upon the protected space of courtrooms? Because the apartheid government sought to demonstrate that it was governed by the rule of law. In the process of doing so, it allowed journalists to publish, as appendix B reveals, massive amounts of information concerning a whole range of issues that the government wished to conceal: death squad activity, torture, police links to vigilantes, and the many abuses committed by members of the police and security forces. Courtrooms also provided journalists opportunities to quote those whom the government sought to silence. Howard Barrell captured perfectly the reason that this opening existed when he explained how he and other journalists were able to quote at length the statements of Steve Biko, a person who had been banned for years, simply by attending his political trial: "Justice had to be seen to be done, even if it was South African justice." Moreover, while the highest levels of the South African judiciary ultimately failed to check executive abuses of power, particularly during the states of emergency, a handful of progressive judges struck down, albeit temporarily, some of the earlier emergency restrictions that temporarily opened space. Those in the executive were thus in a bind. They obviously disliked these openings provided by the courts, but how could they close them without undermining the government's already fragile legitimacy?

Similar dynamics accounted for journalists' ability to publish information shared in the protected space of the South African Parliament. If the South African government claimed that it had "democratic" institutions, it could not prevent the public from learning about statements made on the floor by members elected by white South Africans. Censoring statements and responses to questions would defeat the very purpose of such an institution.

The government's concerns with legitimacy also facilitated the legal tactics these newspapers developed. The government would have been quite happy had publications simply avoided even mentioning the ANC, but as David Dison observed, the government's position was as follows: "We are a legitimate government. We pass our laws. Law making was preserved in Parliament." It thus passed a law forbidding publications from "actively promoting" the ANC in an effort to stifle opposition voices, justifying this action, as governments often do, on the basis of "protecting" the country from a "threat." Rather than issue a blanket ban on mentioning certain organizations, the government instead drafted a law that created a massive gray area, one that newspapers such as *New Nation* and underground members of the ANC such as Howard Barrell were more than willing to exploit.

The forms of violence used—and not used—against journalists were also linked to the government's concerns about legitimacy and had a significant impact on writing space. The use of subversive rhetorical tactics, for example, was facilitated directly by the apartheid government's public denials of the assassinations and torture it was in fact using. When journalists used allusions and strategic enthymemes to imply strongly that the government was in fact using death squads, it placed the government in an extremely awkward position. To challenge the newspapers would only bring more attention to these accusations—which, of course, were true. To close newspapers for publishing articles related to death squads would seem to confirm the allegations.

Moreover, while the apartheid government's use of violence was formidable, it did not reach the levels of violence employed by other governments. Shaun Johnson's observation, previously cited, about the "strange legalism" that existed and how this was "completely different from some kind of crazy dictator who is just murdering people" accounts for why legal resistance was even possible. Cleverly playing with the law and devising tactics such as the use of the all-clear flag or black lines would simply not be tolerated in contexts such as North Korea or Saddam Hussein's Iraq. There is obviously a wide range of violence used by governments. In many democratic countries, governments do not target journalists for assassination or create a sense that this is even a possibility. In other contexts, of course, governments use massive violence against journalists and those engaged in resistance. As Noam Chomsky has observed, "The journal of the Salvadoran Jesuits quite accurately pointed out that in their country Václav Havel . . . wouldn't have been put in jail—he might well have been hacked to pieces and left by the side of the road somewhere" (*What Uncle Sam* 70). George W. Bush made a similar claim about the ruthlessness of Saddam Hussein, even if he expressed his point less than artfully: "I heard somebody say, 'Where's Mandela?' Well, Mandela's dead because Saddam Hussein killed all the Mandelas" (qtd. in "Mandela Still Alive"). While many, including television comedian/host Jon Stewart, had a good laugh about the president's penchant for verbal gaffes and how he seemed to imply that Saddam Hussein had killed Nelson Mandela and every member of his family, the point Bush was attempting to make is frighteningly real: in some contexts, governments use massive levels of violence against opponents. Instead of employing massive violence to curtail writing space, the apartheid government resorted to written rules—and this opened considerable space. As Shaun Johnson noted about the apartheid laws, including the emergency regulations, "For every clause, there's a loophole, you know. And with our lawyers' attitudes, it was always, 'It's arguable. We might lose it, but it's arguable.'"

This aggressive interpretation of the law, coupled with the elasticity of language, ultimately made the apartheid government's position untenable. Mikhail Bakhtin and reader response theorists such as Wolfgang Iser have convincingly demonstrated the active role that readers/listeners play in the construction of meaning. This had particular significance in a context in which opposition journalists were conveying meanings in oblique and coded ways. Ismail Mahomed, for example, made the following argument in his legal brief responding to the government's allegation that a *Weekly Mail* article had "promoted" the image of the South African Communist Party (SACP): "Thus for example the claim that the Young Communist League was able to give an explanation for the condition of the 'oppressed and exploited' masses is deliberately put in quotation marks and the purpose appears to be to draw attention to the exaggerated and simplistic nature of the claim made" (80). Note Mahomed's claim "the purpose *appears* to be." He needed this qualifier because the ultimate meaning of this single sentence could be interpreted in any number of ways, depending on the reader in question. A conservative white South African might read this article as evidence that the newspaper was in fact trying to promote the views of the SACP by including this statement from the Young Communist League. A progressive South African critical of the government but skeptical of the SACP might read such a statement in the ironic manner suggested by Mahomed. And someone within the SACP might read such a statement non-ironically and as an expression of a fundamental truth. Something as simple as the strategic use of quotation marks demonstrates the multiple interpretations of articles, paragraphs, sentences, phrases, and even individual words. In the end, it was simply impossible for the apartheid government to construct a framework that could consistently and coherently adjudicate the boundaries of what it deemed acceptable expression.

While the *Weekly Mail* and *New Nation* were able to expand their writing space considerably, the possibilities for opposition journalists should not be overstated. The apartheid government was, in fact, able to curtail the publication of a significant amount of information as a result of its censorship restrictions. One question I asked everyone during the course of my interviews concerned the size of the gap they believed existed between what they wanted to write and what they were able to write. Their answers were revealing.

"THE GAP"

A small handful of writers thought that the gap, for them personally, was not particularly large. Ben Maclennan, a journalist I interviewed who did not work for the *Weekly Mail* or *New Nation*, claimed that he essentially wrote the stories that he wanted to write: "I can't think of anything that I haven't actually written because of these laws. I can't remember a single instance where I actually had a story, and I felt, 'My god, these laws—I won't even bother to write it.' Part of my way out was to leave it to my publications, to the editors, to do the gatekeeping for me. But I can't ever remember holding myself back from actually writing the story." In other parts of the interview, Maclennan noted there were instances in which editors did not publish his stories because of the restrictions, and he also qualified his remarks somewhat regarding the effects these restrictions may have had on him as a writer: "It's possible I might have done some internal censorship, particularly stories dealing with the police or prisons, to make sure the story got published or issued. But I can't, I doubt whether those were of major significance to the story." Phillip Van Niekerk, who wrote for the *Weekly Mail* and who eventually became the editor, expressed similar sentiments. For Van Niekerk, the biggest challenge, examined at greater length below, was obtaining information in a society obsessed with secrecy. Once he obtained the information, however, Van Niekerk claims the censorship restrictions did not have a major impact on the articles he wrote: "You know, again, the difficulty was getting the information. The difficulty was finding out what was really going on. But once you had it, as I said, I just don't think I ever knowingly censored myself. In fact, I always pushed it a little bit, you know, sort of pushed it as far as you could go."

Most of those interviewed, however, claimed that the gap between what they wanted to write and what they were able to write was very large. Kerry Cullinan, who also wrote for *New Nation*, stated, "There was a huge gap. Pushing the limits meant publishing a bit more information than maybe somebody else, but at one stage, we considered having a whole list of stories that had been killed that week because of censorship. We just wanted to have a headline for all these stories that, you know [were not published]. A lot of stories just never saw the light of day." Amrit Manga of *New Nation* concurred: "Oh, it was a huge gap. It was a huge gap. I think it would be correct to say it was an unbridgeable gap. Even though we tried all these different methods of getting around, circumventing the law, there was a hell of a lot that we were unable to say." Manga provided some specific examples of the stories Cullinan alluded to: the massacres committed by Koevoet in Namibia, the government's involvement in the train massacres occurring in the northern Transvaal, and the blowing up of buildings by government operatives.[1] He then provided another example:

> There were friends of mine, women, in one instance, a white woman who worked in the trade union movement who was detained for three months. And once she came out of detention, she told me this story of how she was repeatedly raped while in detention. There was nothing we could do. We couldn't write a word about that. . . . These were white cops that would go in there and say, "You have sold out and you've gone to the other side." She happened to be Afrikaans speaking. There was no way you could get around that story. The lawyers would say, "Where is your evidence?" And you'd say, "There she is." But it's her word against ten special branch detectives.

As Manga observed, "So you had those kinds of stories, and they were really gruesome tales to be told. And no one ever wrote them."

David Dison, the attorney for the *Weekly Mail*, concurred with Manga and Cullinan that the gap was quite large: "The context was, the touchstone was, What could you get away with? So it was pushing the margins to the nth degree. But there was a hell of lot that we had to take out. I mean, there was a hell of lot that you just couldn't do." Moira Levy, a journalist for the *Weekly Mail*, agreed: "It was big—it was a big gap." She elaborated on the nature of the restrictions and the profound impact they had on her and others writing at the time: "It's so easy to forget how scary it was and how repressive it was.

You know, it was so all-embracing and I think even though there was a great effort to break the bounds and push the barriers that much further, I think we really set out with those constraints in mind. I think we were hugely constrained."

Kerry Cullinan reflected on the insidious nature of these restrictions and the effects they had on her as a journalist. Specifically, she explained how she simultaneously tried to flout these restrictions as much as possible but then felt guilty when the government cited many of her articles when it closed the newspaper:

> And when *New Nation* got taken off the streets for three months, it was a huge shock to receive the notification from the police identifying the stories that were problematic, because stories that we thought were okay were suddenly—I mean there was this long, long, long list of stories, and a lot of them were mine. I felt so guilty and responsible in a way, even though it wasn't my fault. But I really felt, you know, we are off the streets for three months and it's my fault. You did internalize that kind of guilt and I thought maybe I should have been more careful. But how on earth are we to know that they would take offense to these [articles]? Because the law is so enormous—they could interpret it any way and they could say, "We just don't like it." And that would be that.

One can only imagine the enormous frustration these opposition journalists must have felt. Even though they refrained from publishing several stories, the government nevertheless claimed they were publishing too many problematic articles.

In the process of answering the gap question, many journalists identified issues not directly related to the censorship restrictions. Van Niekerk, as noted above, argued that secrecy and the inability of journalists to penetrate the hidden chambers of the government were the primary reason for the gap that existed between what was happening and what was reported:

> I think the biggest gap was actually getting the information. I mean, we were living in the 1980s in a society where the state had become more and more murderous. If you look at what Vlakplaas was doing, if you look at what Koevoet was doing in Namibia—very little of that was getting reported.[2] And that's the gap. Any normal society, well, those kind of things don't happen in

the first place, but if they did, they'd be written about. So we just didn't have access to that information.

Van Niekerk acknowledged that opposition newspapers exposed at least some of this information, but overall he offered a bleak assessment: "But I think out of everyone, I mean, the *Weekly Mail, New Nation,* and *Vrye Weekblad,* did get close to that story, and by 1989, we had already gone a long way when the Coetzee stories broke.[3] If you look at what the TRC found, they confirmed a lot of stuff. But if you really look at what was going on totally in our society, we were essentially in the dark. We were like a little pinprick of light, but the overwhelming shade was darkness." Dison concurred that government secrecy constituted a significant constraint that contributed to the size of the gap. He explained how *Vrye Weekblad* was closed for publishing a story about members of the government who had "supplied poisons for killing activists" and how the newspaper "was closed down, just on that." But in conversations he subsequently had with Max du Preez, the editor of the newspaper, Dison recalled, "Max du Preez said to me, 'It's much worse than this. There's a hell of lot more that we got from these guys.'"

Dison then reflected on the ways in which the constraints of secrecy and official censorship worked in tandem:

> I think the gap was—I think it was a very small group of educated people who knew what was going on, and some of them were in the media, so they would get it into the media. The black activists knew what was going on—unionists, UDFniks, civic association people—they knew, so they were telling sympathetic journalists and writers what was happening, and they were trying to get it into the *Mail* and various other things. And I think a small fraction of that was getting out. It was a very small fraction.

Van Niekerk's metaphor, "a little pinprick of light," and Dison's repetition of "a small fraction," using "very" the second time for emphasis, indicates that these newspapers did provide information that mainstream newspapers refused to touch. It would require the Truth and Reconciliation Commission, however, to uncover and expose the full and terrifying criminality of the apartheid government.

In addition to governmental secrecy, Drew Forrest identified another issue that contributed to the gap: the limited ability of these small newspapers to cover the government's crackdown taking place across the country, particularly in smaller, more isolated communities. He explained:

> The point about the emergency is that it swept up tiny townships across the country. We weren't just dealing with Soweto anymore. It was, you know, tiny little communities with their little townships. They were exploding all over the place, and those people had no contact for the most part. And so the police had a much freer hand there, you see, than they did in this area. You know, if something happened on the East Rand, it would have at least reached the attention of the media. But all these tiny townships that exploded in this period, one after another, it was this massive thing, and why it became so difficult for the state to contain. So what I'm saying is that huge amounts of stuff were not reported not only because we knew of it but didn't dare report it—that was part of it. But a lot of it was that it was just not known.

These small opposition newspapers, therefore, simply did not have the resources to monitor events taking place throughout such a large country.

A letter from Elijah Letswalo published in the *Weekly Mail* supports Forrest's claim. Letswalo initially praises the *Weekly Mail* and writes, "Your newspaper has become one of the few reliable sources of information about the reality of life in South Africa." He then observes, "But I am saddened by your newspaper's apparent complicity in the conspiracy of silence about repression in the far Northern Transvaal, where the security forces are dominated by conservative elements." Letswalo then proceeds to list several instances of detentions occurring in that area. Beneath this letter is the following response from "The Editors": "Thank you for bringing these detentions to our notice. There was no 'conspiracy of silence.' We depend on human rights groups for such information, but [due to] the size and remoteness of areas such as yours, Emergency restrictions and other factors mean the information is not always complete" (Letswalo).

Several journalists, in fact, addressed the impact that limited resources had for both the *Weekly Mail* and *New Nation*. Irwin Manoim explained, "There was an enormous amount that wasn't getting covered, not only because of the censorship but because of the inability to create the necessary news apparatus. In other words, there must have been staggering amounts that we didn't cover." Janet Wilhelm of the *Weekly Mail* identified specifically how lack of resources limited the ability of the newspaper to close the gap even more:

> Essentially what happened was I got a whole lot of information but didn't have the time to get enough of it, to consolidate it, to write about it. So the fact that it was never written about was also due to economics. It had to do with the fact that the *Weekly Mail* did not have the money. To get [the story] at the time, when things don't make sense: "Why is this guy doing that and why is that one … ?" To actually put together stuff like that so you can print it and it won't fall apart, you're talking about working on it for a few months. They didn't have the money.

Ryland Fisher of the *New Nation* made a similar argument: "It was a tremendous gap. *Ja*, it was. But you know, you had the legal situation, but there were lots of other factors. *New Nation*, apart from the legal problems, they had the problem of not having enough resources, not having enough money to actually do their job properly. And that's also limiting." One of the ironies, of course, was that the *Weekly Mail* and *New Nation* desperately wanted to challenge the government but did not have sufficient resources to do so, whereas mainstream newspapers had considerably more resources but lacked the will to aggressively challenge the government. Ryland Fisher observed that *New Nation* would have never been created if "the papers with the resources would have done their job properly." For those at the *Weekly Mail* and *New Nation*, the gap between what they wanted to publish and what they were able to publish was thus larger than they would have wished. But that fact in no way diminishes the many genuine accomplishments of both newspapers.

ACCOMPLISHMENTS OF THE *WEEKLY MAIL* AND *NEW NATION*

An inextricable link existed between censorship and maintaining apartheid, a system designed to benefit a minority of the population within South Africa. The government needed to prevent white South Africans and the outside world from learning about the inherent violence of the system itself, as well as the overt forms of violence it used to maintain it. Nelson Mandela's preface to a collection of essays by André Brink addresses this very issue: "The imposition of silence was a powerful tool in the oppressive arsenal of apartheid. Through a myriad of measures it attempted to keep untold the story of the suffering it inflicted [and] throttle the cries of anguish emanating from the victims of its brutalities" (vii–viii). One of Brink's essays, "State of Emergency," which he wrote in 1986, made a defiant call to writers to challenge what he described as "deadly silence" imposed by the government: "You are confident that you have finally reduced us to silence. But you have not. There may be a temporary silence in the land: the silence of prison walls so thick that you cannot see the blood on the inside or hear the muffled screams. But that blood, those screams, have a way of filtering through into the pen of writers. I appeal to the writers of my land to bear witness. We shall not be silent forever. We have history on our side. We have truth on our side" (*Reinventing* 23). Brink's challenge "to bear witness" was certainly embraced by those writing for the *Weekly Mail* and *New Nation*. As noted in previous chapters, and particularly as shown in appendix B, both newspapers chronicled in extensive detail the abuses committed at the time by the apartheid government.

The imposed silence, of course, was linked to isolation. In the process of enforcing its policy of "apartness," the South African government was quite successful in keeping white, black, coloured, and Indian communities isolated from one another. In fact, not only were the four "racial" groups isolated from each other but black communities were separated from one another as well. This was due both to geography and to the sheer size of South Africa, as well as the government's policy of separating black communities on the basis of ethnicity. One simply cannot overstate the importance, therefore, of these national newspapers that linked spaces and communities within the country. Both Zwelakhe Sisulu and Amrit Manga emphasized the isolation many black South Africans felt within their local communities, as well as the importance of chronicling the resistance taking place throughout the country. *New Nation* served, in Sisulu's memorable phrase, as a "transporter of shared experience." Amrit Manga explained, "We tried to give the perspective that this is a national problem. Obviously, that helped bring people together if [they] understand [they] have a common struggle."

The *Weekly Mail*, as previously noted, served as the transporter of *un*shared experiences for its white readers. Many black South Africans would have been quite aware of what took place in white spaces, since they spent so much time working in them as domestic servants and laborers. But the vast majority of white South Africans had very little or no idea about what took place within black spaces. Other than police officers, most white South Africans, even those critical of apartheid and who supported black aspirations, did not spend time in the townships.[4]

The opening scene of the film *Cry Freedom* conveys powerfully and visually the ways in which violence in black spaces was invisible to most whites. The movie opens with police raiding and destroying an informal settlement. Police roar into the settlement on trucks and proceed to use massive violence. They beat people, tear down shacks, and arrest people. Dogs are barking, people are screaming, children are crying, shacks are burning, and at one point a police officer rips the shirt from a fleeing woman while she resists, an action clearly implying that she will be raped. Following this scene of horror, there is an abrupt transition to the actor who plays Mamphela Ramphele. She turns on the radio when she wakes up and listens to a "report" of this incident on SABC. The announcer claims that the police entered Crossroads, which he describes as "an illegal township near Cape Town," and then says, "After warning the squatters to vacate the area in the interest of public health, a number of people were found without work permits and many are being sent back to their respective homelands. There was no resistance to the raid and many of the illegals voluntarily presented themselves to the police." The announcer then states, "In other news," and proceeds to discuss an upcoming match of South Africa's rugby team, the Springboks (Attenborough). This jarring juxtaposition of the violence that took place on screen with this sterilized news report (if a report would have even documented such an incident) conveys powerfully the limited awareness most white South Africans possessed who obtained their news from mainstream media sources.

In addition to linking spaces, both newspapers also served as a vital connection for anti-apartheid groups within South Africa. The numerous restrictions on movement and association within South Africa made it extremely challenging for like-minded individuals and groups to organize politically. In fact, one of the central objectives of the media restrictions imposed during the states of emergency was to further constrain communication among those in the anti-apartheid movement. Christopher Merrett writes, "For political activists of the 1980s, a major memory of the declaration of the national State of Emergency in June 1986 is of isolation, lack of information and abundant rumour. . . . The prevailing climate was of uncertainty, and even fear: apartheid society, already fractured along racial lines, proved highly susceptible to a disruption of the flow of information" (*Culture* 114). Many journalists discussed the vital ways in which the *Weekly Mail* and *New Nation* linked anti-apartheid forces within the country. Tyrone August, for example, explained, "In a sense, if you were part of the anti-apartheid struggle, at one stage or another, you would have to cross paths with *New Nation*. I'm not trying to say that it was the home or the center of the anti-apartheid struggle. But in terms of the information network, I think it played a central role. It had sort of a decent readership outside of Johannesburg as well, and it was reaching people who weren't necessarily catered to before." Ryland Fisher discussed how *New Nation* consciously directed itself toward the political leadership within the anti-apartheid movement: "The *New Nation* reached leadership people in communities and organizations. Lots of those people took guidance from *New Nation*—they were informed by *New Nation*, they read the views of their leaders in *New Nation*, and they then passed those views on to other people. So you can't actually quantify the impact of a paper like the *New Nation*. It's very difficult. But I do think it played a hell of an important role." Shaun Johnson noted that the *Weekly Mail*, which did not consider itself to be "within" the anti-apartheid movement, nevertheless was extremely important for those who were: "It was required reading for everybody within—I guess, the most loyal readers would have been those within the UDF and those within the security police! [laughter]."

During an interview, Stoffel Botha criticized this role that newspapers such as the *Weekly Mail* and *New Nation* played: "I would like to remind the journalism profession of the accusation that the media have become more than observers of the scene. They have become participants, as someone said—and I quote—'on the great battlefields of perceptions where modern conflicts rage as much as they do in the steamy jungles or shantytowns.' They are the field commanders" (qtd. in Schneider 26). Botha's claim that opposition newspapers were the "field commanders" of resistance was, of course, nonsense. But he was partly correct: newspapers such as the *Weekly Mail* and *New Nation* were in fact playing a vital role for those in the anti-apartheid struggle.

Moreover, both newspapers aggressively challenged the government's efforts to silence political opponents it had banned, particularly the ANC. Ben Maclennan, the journalist who claimed that he did not feel overly constrained by the censorship restrictions, observed that the gap for him was most noticeable with regard to stories about the ANC: "I suppose the major restriction we felt at the *Sunday Post* was the fact that we couldn't report what the ANC was actually saying. *Ja*, okay. That was an important one—there was a big gap there." The *Weekly Mail* and *New Nation* aggressively provided a forum for such voices, albeit in different ways, for different audiences, and for different purposes.

Anthony Holiday, a journalist who wrote for the *Cape Times*, while simultaneously working underground as a member of the South African Communist Party (SACP), offered compelling insights about the necessity of providing information about the ANC in apartheid South Africa. Holiday was eventually arrested and spent six years in prison. When asked about the relationship between his roles as both journalist and someone distributing underground material for the SACP, Holiday responded,

> For me, informing my readers, as any professional paper needs to do, was telling them that the ANC was in their country—and that was important. Remember the censorship laws stopped you from doing almost anything. And the duty is primarily to inform. It seemed to me that my role as revolutionary and my role as a decent professional journalist were absolutely coincidental. It was not, "Okay, here am I, the underground communist, I must get this name in [an article]." No. I thought it was very important that people know these things. Surely it was.

To support his claim about the importance of accurately informing South African citizens, Holiday specifically mentioned the apartheid government's decision to deploy troops to Angola in an effort to stop what he sarcastically referred to as the "communist wave." Ivor Powell describes the apartheid government's almost surreal ability to keep this fact hidden: "[T]he SADF [South African Defence Force] conducted a whole war in Angola during the 1980s without the South African public at large ever knowing about it. The Defence Act, apart from other relevant legislation, made it impossible for news reports ever to tell the truth" ("Most Censored" 26). After noting how the government managed to conceal an invasion and war in another country from the public, Holiday exclaimed, "That is *insanity!*" He explained:

> We would have had a far easier transition if there hadn't been this bloody press censorship. People would have had a far more realistic view of the issues. Suddenly a man [de Klerk] gets up, and he gives the whole fucking show away! I'm

amazed that it didn't come apart right there and then. There were a couple of times where it nearly did come apart. You can't do that to people. You can't go on telling them that you've destroyed these people [the ANC and SACP]— "They're destroyed. It's all right, it's all right." But it's not all right! You can't go on doing things like that to people. And it's a journalist's job to see that people are sanely informed. So when I point out [in my newspaper articles] that the ANC has this history, it has been around a long time, I'm doing no more than informing the public.

An excerpt from Holiday's obituary, published in the *Guardian*, confirms the role he played as a journalist: "His breach of professional ethics—having a hidden political agenda while working as a journalist—seriously embarrassed his employers at the *Cape Times*, but his newspaper work was acknowledged to have been strictly professional" (Shaw).

Journalists for the *Weekly Mail* also commented on the importance of providing accurate reporting on political groups such as the ANC. Van Niekerk explained: "I think that [the *Weekly Mail*] was one newspaper that reflected very clearly what the ANC was saying, that didn't take the idea that this was a terrorist group, this is an illegitimate group of people who have no support. You know, it said something different." Irwin Manoim claimed this was one of the *Weekly Mail*'s more important contributions: "I think one of the key things we did was to put opposition black leaders into the public realm. I mean, up until then, there would have been hardly any newspaper coverage whatsoever. We actually made them into public figures, at least in the white community. And that was quite important."

Moira Levy concurred that the *Weekly Mail*'s more serious coverage of the ANC played a significant role: "The ANC had been conveyed in the sixties and seventies—the ANC and especially the Communist Party—as the bogeyman, the fearful monster out there," and it was essential, she explained, "to strip the fear, the mysticism, and the bullshit basically." This was essential, she argued, for a certain segment of whites:

Whites—influential decision makers, power brokers, the people who were in big business—needed to be informed that the ANC was going to be your next government. So that was an important role that the *Weekly Mail* played. *New Nation* and *South* were popular papers and very self-consciously trying to appeal to the masses. That was important. But the masses knew what was going on. There were always reservations about the elitist nature of the *Weekly Mail*—it was difficult to read, you needed the time and education to actually get through the newspaper. But at the same time, it *had* to be that audience, because if they had tried to popularize it, they would have alienated those important readers. [The *Weekly Mail*] had an important constituency. It was a constituency, you know, who had been linked with the Progressive Federal Party [a liberal white political party] but was skeptical about it and couldn't see it taking the country any further. It had to be won over and needed someone to tell them how and what was going on. So I think, in that sense, it [the *Weekly Mail*] had a very important role to play.[5]

These dynamics within the white community explain in part why many political observers were so pessimistic in the late 1980s about the future prospects of South Africa. The white political opposition within the country had no realistic chance of defeating the National Party in elections, and the obvious alternative to the National Party, the ANC, had been portrayed for decades to white South Africans as terrorists and communists. As Levy observed, that was why it was so important "to show that the ANC is the only viable alternative, really." She continued: "I think also, the converse, to show that the state is not functional. The apartheid state could not last. It was posing a real threat. Its policies were not only morally wrong but they would jeopardize the economy and jeopardize the future of the country." Trying to shift the thinking of those within the white community, particularly, in Levy's words, the "power brokers," was extremely important—and also extremely challenging given the censorship restrictions.

Another role both newspapers played was serving to signal to ANC supporters within the country that the ANC leadership was in fact shifting tactics. Shaun Johnson discussed the complex political dynamics of the period: "In 1989, you're at a stage in South Africa where the government is saying, 'We will fight this group of communist terrorists until the end.' And nobody's got any reason to believe that they're going to change. Why should they? It's been like this for our entire lifetimes. On the other hand, the leftist core of the UDF and everybody else is saying, 'We will fight this to the death. No compromise. No negotiations.' The once forbidden word: negotiations. It was not acceptable on the left." Mandela, however, had been engaged in secret negotiations with the government, an action he did not even share initially with his ANC colleagues on Robben Island. This represented a fundamental shift in tactics for the ANC, one that needed to be conveyed to its supporters. Again, Shaun Johnson: "So suddenly, you're saying, and this is not addressed to the right wing, this is addressed to the left wing: negotiations are now being talked about. Tactics will begin to change. So the sacred cows, that you fight the revolution, no negotiation with the apartheid state—Mandela had moved way beyond that and understood that you could actually negotiate this revolution." Given that the ANC was banned, articles that conveyed the shifting tactics of the ANC were extremely important for sympathizers inside the country.

For all of these reasons, the ANC, as previously noted, thought highly of both newspapers. As Shaun Johnson observed, "We had quite amateurish contacts with Thabo [Mbeki,] in exile, and the whole range of ANC people in London, Lusaka, and Dar es Salaam. And the message that was coming back from them was, 'This stuff is so important. Don't blow it.'" Perhaps the best evidence of the fondness the ANC, particularly Mandela, had for *New Nation* is contained in an article appearing in the *Mail & Guardian* in May 1997 entitled, "*New Nation* Publishes Its Final Edition": "Constantly in financial trouble, *New Nation* was sold to Nthato Motlana, who also owns the *Sowetan*—and who reportedly bought the paper under instruction from Nelson Mandela, who had a soft spot for it."

These newspapers also served as a symbol of hope for those opposed to the apartheid government. It was simply devastating for progressive South Africans when the liberal *Rand Daily Mail* was closed. The fact that other newspapers sought not only to fill this void but challenged the government even more aggressively was profoundly inspiring for many. Janet Wilhelm, a journalist from the *Weekly Mail*, observed, "Just launching it [the *Weekly Mail*] was pushing a boundary because the government was delighted when the *Rand Daily Mail* was closed. And it was an act of defiance. Well, we're going to go on writing about what's going on in the black areas." Not only were these newspapers launched, but they managed to survive, publishing week in and week out. Moira Levy observed, "We did achieve things. We really did. For example, we achieved things by coming out each week. I mean the *Weekly Mail* came out and *South* and *New Nation* all came out week after week, and had important information, and were not banned that often. I think that was an achievement." Drew Forrest expressed similar sentiments about *New Nation*, particularly after the government detained Zwelakhe Sisulu: "I think it was probably assumed by the state that the newspaper would just collapse without the editor. In fact, we managed to keep it going under a form of collective leadership.

It was riven with conflict and all the rest, but yeah, that was a sort of victory in a way. Despite the detention of the editor, we still managed to put the thing out. And in fact we brought it forward almost as an act of defiance." The fact that these newspapers were launched and continued to publish provided a glimmer of hope in an otherwise bleak context.

Havel describes the significance of public acts of defiance in contexts of oppression. He recalls one particular example in communist Czechoslovakia when citizens signed a petition calling for the release of certain political prisoners. Even though the prisoners in question realized that the petition had limited practical value, they were nevertheless extremely heartened by this act: "But knowing that people knew about them, that someone was on their side and did not hesitate to support them publicly, even in a period of general apathy and resignation: this was of irreplaceable value" (Havel, *Disturbing* 175). Smangaliso Mkhatshwa's observation about *New Nation*, which applied equally to the *Weekly Mail*, identified a similar dynamic: "My overall impression is that the *New Nation* was really a blessing to the people that were involved in the struggle for liberation. It gave hope to many people. It morally encouraged people to go on with the struggle for liberation." For black South Africans in particular, it must have been, in Havel's words, of "irreplaceable value" to read the *Weekly Mail* and realize that "people knew about them," and to read *New Nation* and realize that "someone was on their side and did not hesitate to support them publicly."

The ANC's submission to the Truth and Reconciliation Commission, "The Role of the Media under Apartheid," which highlights the many accomplishments of "the independent press," specifically noted this role played by opposition newspapers such as the *Weekly Mail* and *New Nation*: "They restored dignity to communities which had been ravaged by apartheid." The amount of suffering created by apartheid was, in a very real sense, incomprehensible. Creating and enforcing a culture of silence surrounding this violence only compounded the sense of violation. Writing about the realities of black South Africans during apartheid was not only a political act but a deeply humanizing one as well. As Kerry Cullinan explained, "Basically, it was giving a voice to people who didn't have any voice at all. You know, you're a person, and you shouldn't have been treated like that—you've been treated like nothing. But your story is important."

The passion readers felt for the *Weekly Mail* and *New Nation* was amply demonstrated in the many letters both newspapers published. After those at the *Weekly Mail* published their first edition, they were flooded with letters of praise and gratitude. A few representative examples convey a sense of these feelings. P. Hollard of Krugersdorp wrote, "The toothless apologetic *Star* etc. just makes me despair. I am a lonely and very old widow and the [*Rand Daily*] *Mail* was my greatest companion after the death of my husband. I now feel lost and deprived of the truth and justice in this country. I'm South African born, but what a mess they have made of this happy land. May God bless your undertaking on behalf of the TRUTH." Nakempe E. Ramaphoko wrote, "[The *Rand Daily Mail*] was the voice of the voiceless. You spoke for me and all peace loving South Africans. Like what you used to do, please speak for the jobless, the hungry, the starving masses, the 'criminals' (in the Nats dictionary) and sundry. I am very pleased for you are showing us that you are not prepared to lie down and die. Goodbye propaganda, welcome the truth and justice again." Many letter writers also clearly shared the *Weekly Mail*'s sense of humor. When the *Weekly Mail* published its now famous front page with the black lines, one reader wrote, "Congratulations—you certainly made your point. EA Cogill, Waterkloof, Pretoria. P.S. Scrap this if it's likely to get me 10 years in jail—at 86, I really can't take the time off. EAC." And when the *Weekly Mail* was threatened with closure, Patrick Muller from Durban wrote, "How many white South Africans does it take to change a light bulb? None. They prefer being kept in the dark."

New Nation received similar letters, including one consisting of an imaginary dialogue with the newspaper:

Dear Editor: This is how I imagine a conversation between the *New Nation* and a reader.

Reader: I love you *New Nation*—you are my life, a real eye-opener, a paper for the people.

New Nation: How can I tell you love me?

Reader: Even if you double your price, I will still buy you.

New Nation: I am not interested in your money. I am only interested in knowing if you have learnt something from me.

Reader: Yes, I have learnt many things from you.

New Nation: If you really love me, tell other people about me, tell them what you have learnt from me. You must become a talking *New Nation*. Each one, teach one . . .

Reader: Now I realize that I have been contributing to our oppression by my silence and inactivity. I have also realized that as a talking *New Nation*, I will continue operating when Botha has banned you. People's education is the key to freedom.

(Reader is joined by other readers who shout): "We are the *New Nation* and the *New Nation* is the people!"

The heartfelt attachment of this particular reader reveals how *New Nation* had become much more than a newspaper: it sparked his political consciousness and inspired him to resist, even if the government should ban the newspaper. Other letters published by *New Nation*, including one written in the form of a praise poem, convey similar levels of admiration, respect, and even, as the letter above demonstrates, love.

Given the many accomplishments of the *Weekly Mail* and *New Nation*, particularly during apartheid, one interesting question to consider is the following: To what extent did the resistance of these newspapers constitute a genuine threat to the government? Havel's insights are particularly instructive on this point: "The power structure, whether it wants to or not, must always react to this pressure to a certain extent. Its response, however, is always limited to two dimensions: repression and adaptation" (*Power* 83). When prominent members of the South African business community argued in their letter to the government that the *Weekly Mail* should not be closed, they were essentially recommending adaptation: "Its limited circulation and largely professional readership exclude any possibility of it posing a threat to the State" (Manoim, *Warned* 105). Ken Owen, editor of *Business Day*, claimed that the government should not close the *Weekly Mail* because it was essentially irrelevant. He described the *Weekly Mail* as "'radical chic' rather than revolutionary," stating that "[i]ts political coverage is stylish, sophisticated, frequently clever, and aimed at an elite market. It is probably inconsequential" (qtd. in Battersby).

Havel's analysis regarding the threat Aleksandr Solzhenitsyn posed to the former Soviet Union, however, challenges the assumptions of the business leaders and Owen. As Havel rightly notes, Solzhenitsyn was expelled from the country "not because he represented a unit of real power, that is, not because any of the regime's representatives felt he might unseat them and take their place in government" (*Power* 43). Rather, Havel argues, Solzhenitsyn posed a different kind of threat: "For the crust presented by the life of lies is made of strange stuff. As long as it seals off hermetically the entire society, it appears to be made of stone. But the moment someone breaks through in one place, when one person cries out, 'The emperor is naked!'—when a single person breaks the rules of the game, thus exposing it as a game—everything suddenly appears in another light and the whole crust seems then to be made of a tissue on the point of tearing and disintegrating uncontrollably" (43). In the same essay Havel elaborates further on the nature of the threat posed by opposition writers: "In the post-totalitarian system, therefore, living within the truth has more than a mere existential dimension (returning humanity to its inherent nature), or a noetic dimension (revealing reality as it is), or a moral dimension (setting an example for others). It also has an unambiguous *political* dimension. If the main pillar of the system is living a lie, then it is not surprising that the fundamental threat to it is living the truth. This is why it must be suppressed more severely than anything else" (40). Havel's observations, based on his analysis of resistance to the communist government of Czechoslovakia, I would argue, apply to apartheid South Africa as well.

First, opposition newspapers such as the *Weekly Mail* and *New Nation* were providing information critical of the government week in and week out both to South Africans and to the international community. Moreover, they were challenging mainstream newspapers with much larger circulations to acknowledge stories they may not otherwise have covered. Their ability, in Irwin Manoim's words, to "embarrass" the mainstream press was extremely important: "I think [the opposition press] played a key role almost as an embarrassment factor to the mainstream press. The mainstream press was going through a period where it [sought to] pretend nothing was going on. So forcing issues into the public domain was important." Shaun Johnson of the *Weekly Mail* agreed: "We set out, quite intentionally, to shame the mainstream media by breaking stories that they could not possibly ignore." A letter published in the *Weekly Mail* provides tangible evidence of how opposition newspapers did indeed shape coverage in mainstream newspapers:

> I have just finished reading the October 10 issue of *Financial Mail*. It included an article on the National Security Management System network which is enveloping the country. What the article failed to do, however, was acknowledge its debt to the *Weekly Mail*: the article virtually echoed the facts which were presented in much more depth in the *Weekly Mail*, October 3–6, 1986. It is gratifying to see how, in a period when the mainstream press is developing an ever greyer personality, that the *Weekly Mail* has developed into such a fine example of courageous journalism. The money I spend on a *Weekly Mail* sub-

scription is more than offset by the money I save in no longer buying a morning daily. (MacDonald 12)

When this issue was picked up by the *Financial Mail*, it obviously reached many more readers and enhanced the impact of this particular exposé.[6] The Truth and Reconciliation Commission report commented specifically on this role played by opposition newspapers: "Throughout the period under review, the alternative media—some of it commercial, some not—attempted to challenge what was depicted in the mainstream press. Their continued revelations exposed the timidity of the bigger publishing houses in challenging the government and accelerating change" (vol. 4, 178). By occasionally nudging mainstream newspapers with much larger circulations to cover certain stories that they otherwise might not, the impact of the *Weekly Mail* and *New Nation* at times extended well beyond their own readerships.

The aggressive and more brazen defiance of these newspapers, I would argue, also posed a genuine threat to the government. As David Dison observed, "So, you know, if I were Botha, I would have also closed down the *Weekly Mail*. Because basically, it was a 'fuck you' sign. It was in his face. The *New Nation* was like that [too]." If these newspapers continued to defy the government's restrictions and it did not respond, how long could the government maintain credibility? How long might it take for other newspapers, watching these opposition newspapers challenge the government and push these boundaries week in and week out, before they, too, began to challenge the restrictions more aggressively? One can argue that the government overreacted by closing *New Nation* and the *Weekly Mail*, given their small circulations relative to the overall population of South Africa and also given that the censorship restrictions successfully prevented the publication of considerable information. But Havel's insights and Dison's observation reveal that the government, while of course acting unethically, may not necessarily have acted irrationally when assessing the potential threat of these newspapers.

But closing these newspapers also posed a threat for the government. Dison offered the following insightful analysis concerning the states of emergency:

The downfall of the Nationalist Party was the emergency because the emergency was the end of their legitimacy. Once they had to proclaim emergency laws that were decrees, it was an illegitimate regime. Before that, they had the kind of trappings of a legitimate regime. There was law and legalism, there was defamation, there were statutes—okay, there were statutes about "communism" and "promoting unlawful organizations" and that kind of thing. But it was very difficult for them to censor information per se unless they had straight decree powers to ban the publishing of information. I think once the emergency was proclaimed, everybody knew, the activists knew, the game was over. It was going to be a hard one. From 1985 to 1990, there was a lot of death and destruction in the townships, and there was a lot of death in detention, and there was a lot of strife. But it was the last kicks of a dying regime because their legitimacy was gone.

Indeed, the government's attempts to preserve the mask of legitimacy during the emergency bordered on the surreal. Merrett cites two humorous examples of Orwellian doublespeak used at the time by government officials: "There is no ban. It just will not take place until further notice," and "We do not have censorship. What we have is a limitation on what the newspapers can report" (qtd. in *Culture* 115). This is precisely why the court's ruling that denied *New Nation*'s appeal was so significant. The judges, by claiming that the "minister's opinion" was the only relevant factor, exposed for all to see that these regulations were not "law." It is worth repeating David Dalling's assessment that the government's decision to close the *Weekly Mail* "did more damage to the image of South Africa than any single act of oppression" (qtd. in Abel 299).

The impact of these two newspapers extended beyond the struggle against censorship during apartheid. One can also point to some significant accomplishments of these newspapers after the apartheid government fell. First, the training program that the *Weekly Mail* initially developed in part to obtain funding from outside sources trained several journalists, who then went on to prominent journalistic careers in democratic South Africa. Moreover, these newspapers certainly inspired future journalists. Nic Dawes, who served as editor of the *Mail & Guardian*, reflected in his final column as editor about his experiences working with the newspaper. In one section Dawes writes, "In 1985, my father began to bring home copies of the *Weekly Mail*, an utterly new kind of newspaper to me. It crackled with energy. There was the energy of outrage, of refusal to remain silent in the face of the emergency and the direct secrets of the state, but also of assertion—that the struggle was rocks and detentions and fear, but also theatre, and music and the joyous hope-filled defiance of apartheid."

Second, those who read the *Weekly Mail* and *New Nation* were better pre-pared for some of the shocking revelations of the Truth and Reconciliation Commission. The Committee to Protect Journalists report of 1983 noted the many ways the system of censorship affected all South Africans, including white South Africans: "whites are substantially disenfranchised by restric-tions on the press because they are denied the right to know much of what their government is doing" (77). This is precisely why the revelations of the TRC were so devastating for many whites, especially those who obtained their news primarily from SABC or mainstream newspapers. David Dison explained:

> And I think that's one of the biggest problems that we have in the country today [1999] is that white people and advantaged people were actually denied the truth right through that period. I think the classic measurement of that is the Truth Commission. Because what the TRC has done for those whites, those who had to actually confront what happened, it was like, "Wow." My par-ents and their generation, they were people who were not Nats, they were not apartheid people. My father was a sort of right-wing liberal, like the Tories, fol-lowing the English tradition. That whole group of people were fairly horrified by what came out in the Truth Commission.

Even some who wrote for the *Weekly Mail* and who actively tried to expose the atrocities of the apartheid government admitted to feeling somewhat overwhelmed by the sheer scope of the information provided by the TRC. Shaun Johnson explained: "In fact, in many cases, to my astonishment, the state was more evil than we believed—and we believed it was evil!"

Although most South Africans did not know the full scope of the hor-rors during apartheid, the *Weekly Mail* and *New Nation* provided consider-able information about what was happening. Anyone who read the *Weekly Mail* and *New Nation* on a regular or semiregular basis, for example, would have learned that political activists were being murdered, both in and out of detention; prisoners were being tortured on a regular basis; police and security forces were engaging in countless abuses of South Africans; and the government was turning a blind eye, and most likely working with, vigi-lantes who were targeting and killing UDF supporters. Benjamin Rabinow-itz, who contributed financially to the *Weekly Mail*, observed, "The *Weekly Mail* was showing terrible things that were going on in this country. They were publishing [this]. Other papers weren't. . . . Now what's come out of the Truth and Reconciliation Commission is horrendous. It's no use saying, 'We didn't know.' The *Weekly Mail* gave at least some inkling of what was going on. They ran really courageous stories." Harber, in an essay he wrote after the fall of apartheid, concurs: "The result, after the collapse of apartheid, is that South Africans, even the most reactionary whites, cannot say 'We didn't know.' The only ones who did not know the full horror of apartheid were those who chose not to" ("Censorship" 154). As Shaun Johnson rightly noted, even progressive South Africans who were against apartheid may have been surprised at the full extent of the apartheid government's crimes uncovered by the TRC. But it would have been difficult for someone to claim they were completely blindsided by the TRC findings unless, as Harber notes, they chose not to know.

Yet another legacy, particularly of the more politically independent *Weekly Mail*, was that it had provided a forum for a broad expression of ideas. As Van Niekerk explained, "Because what the *Weekly Mail* was doing was setting up what would happen afterwards, which is a fight for an open society. It's not only the propaganda war but the fight for, in a broader sense, the kind of values that the society must contain. So you want a democratic society and an open society—and I think fighting for those things made a huge difference." Van Niekerk's observation is particularly relevant for the years between 1990 and 1994. During that stage, Mandela had been released and various political parties had been unbanned. However, there was still massive violence throughout the country as it sought to make the transition to democracy. During this turbulent period, the *Weekly Mail* periodically published debates featuring very long statements, on a host of issues, from various parties across the political spectrum. In a county in which the range of debate had been severely constrained for decades, the ability to read extensive policy statements on vital subjects from a wide range of political perspectives was fundamentally new—and fundamentally essential—for a country trying to establish democratic norms.

One final legacy. As noted in the introduction, the plight of opposition journalists in apartheid South Africa was in many ways unique to that time and place. And in many other ways, these journalists are part of a much larger, inspiring tradition. Adam Hochschild's description of the journalists and political activists who exposed the horrifying crimes of King Leopold's forces in the Congo is also entirely fitting for those who worked for the

Weekly Mail and *New Nation*: "The movement's other great achievement is this. Among its supporters, it kept alive a tradition, a way of seeing the world, a human capacity for outrage at pain inflicted on another human being, no matter whether that pain is inflicted on someone of another color, in another country, at another end of the earth" (305). This tradition existed long before apartheid South Africa and continues to this day. One need only consult the Committee to Protect Journalists' website to learn of the many courageous men and women throughout the world who have been threatened, detained, and killed in their effort to challenge power and chronicle human rights abuses. Human rights abuses inevitably will continue, and, just as inevitably, there will be those willing to take the risks necessary, in Brink's words, "to write it down."

THE IMPLICATIONS OF WRITING SPACE AND TACTICS OF RESISTANCE FOR OTHER CONTEXTS

As noted in the introduction, one of the objectives of examining two opposition newspapers in apartheid South Africa was to reflect on whether the tactics of resistance used in this particular context may have implications for writers in other contexts as well. Each context of course will be unique, but based on the resistance of the *Weekly Mail* and *New Nation*, some questions to consider regarding the nature of tactics that might be available for writers in other contexts include the following:

To what extent does the government use violence and/or threaten to use violence as a means of silencing writers?

To what extent can loopholes be found within existing laws that restrict expression?

To what extent is the government willing to enforce all of the laws at its disposal to restrict writing space?

To what extent is the judiciary independent and able to constrain executive excesses?

To what extent is the governmental bureaucracy centralized and to what extent can writers strategically harness specific sites within it for their advantage?

To what extent is the government concerned with projecting itself as legitimate to its own citizens and the international community?

To what extent can opposition writers align with powerful elites within the
country who may also wish to expand writing space?

To what extent is the government vulnerable to international economic
and/or political pressure?

To what extent might international events affect domestic political dynamics that could open writing space?

To what extent can technology be harnessed to expand writing space?

In terms of the final question, technology was not necessarily as relevant for
the *Weekly Mail* and *New Nation* in terms of writing space as it currently is
and will be for opposition writers in the future. As noted in chapter 1, because
of the limited financial resources of both newspapers, personal computers and
laser printers played a crucial role. Manoim claimed the *Weekly Mail* would
not have existed had it not been for this technology. Once these newspapers
began publishing, however, technology did not necessarily play a central role
in determining the available writing space. In other words, the *Weekly Mail*
and *New Nation* produced hard copies of their newspapers, and the government either did or did not crack down.

The struggle for writing space will continue to play itself out in the realm
of print, of course, but the battle has shifted to new technologies: the internet,
social media, and so on. Reporters without Borders, for example, describes the
following developments that took place in Iran in 2011: "In January 2011, the
authorities finished setting up the first Iranian cyberpolice to strengthen their
control of the Internet. On 20 May 2010, Ebrahim Jabari, an Islamic Revolutionary Guard Corps (IRGC) commander, officially confirmed the creation of
an Iranian 'Cyber Army' which has already cracked down on online networks
deemed 'destructive,' and arrested hundreds of netizens." Moreover, the Chinese government has sought to impose greater restrictions on the internet.
An editorial appearing in the *New York Times* on 30 January 2015 claimed,
"Under the guise of improving security, the Chinese government is clamping
down on technology companies and further limiting the access its citizens
have to information that is not sanitized by the Communist Party" ("China's
Self-Destructive"). Specifically, Chinese officials are beginning to crack down
on virtual private networks (VPNs), a tactic many in China have used to circumvent censorship: "Dissidents, researchers, businesses and professionals

have long used V.P.N.s to access information beyond China's borders, and the government previously seemed to tolerate the practice" ("China's Self-Destructive"). Despite the government's claims that the new restrictions are designed for "improving security" and are necessary to "fight terrorism," the editorial writers draw the obvious conclusion: "With these new moves, Chinese leaders are trying to increase government control over communications in order to suppress dissent" ("China's Self-Destructive"). As with Iran, the site of struggle and the means of resistance and oppression have shifted in significant ways since the days of the *Weekly Mail* and *New Nation*. In terms of the overall dynamic, however, the struggle seems quite familiar: innovations that increase writing space are met with new restrictions, new restrictions will generate new forms of resistance, new forms of resistance will generate new restrictions, and so on.

The answers to the questions posed above can provide a general sense of, to use James Scott's words, the "arts of resistance" opposition writers may be able to devise. In contexts in which the government does not restrict expression through the use of overwhelming violence and has at least some concern about its legitimacy, writing space will be contested. Again, the number and nature of constraints that inhibit writing space will be unique in each context, but one can nevertheless point to writers who have used tactics very similar to those used by opposition journalists in apartheid South Africa. By highlighting these connections in contexts as diverse as the former Soviet Union, Iraq, Iran, Chile, and the United States, I am not implying any moral equivalence among these nations. Nor am I suggesting that writers in apartheid South Africa imitated the tactics of others or vice versa. It is always possible that writers obtain inspiration and ideas from elsewhere, but it is equally possible, and perhaps more likely, that the tactics of resistance writers develop are in response to the specific constraints they face. When Manoim explained the decision to use black lines in the *Weekly Mail*, for example, he described it more as an epiphany arrived at during the course of a very stressful evening prior to publication, not because he recalled that other publications in other countries had used such an approach. Michel de Certeau writes, "But it is not enough to describe individual ruses and devices. In order to think them, one must suppose that to these ways of operating correspond a finite number of procedures (invention is not unlimited and, like improvisations on the piano or on the guitar, it presupposes the knowledge and application of codes), and that they imply a *logic of the operation of actions relative to types of situations*"

(21; original emphasis). What follows, then, are some examples that reveal the "logic of operation" of writers struggling to expand their writing space in very different situations.

First, writers in other countries have developed variations of what Irwin Manoim called "oblique speak." The precise form that oblique speak assumes varies considerably depending on the context in question. J. M. Coetzee, for example, discusses the approach once used in Russia: "As I have pointed out, the practice of embedding social criticism in literary commentary—a practice fostered by censorship—had a long history in Russia" (*Giving Offense* 128). Moreover, oblique speak was even used in a context as terrifying as Saddam Hussein's Iraq: "Many texts on approved subjects like ancient Mesopotamia, the Baghdad-based Abbasid Empire, pre-Islamic Arab poetry and Iraqi folklore contained within them a set of 'hidden texts' in which Iraqi intellectuals sustained a rich, if covert, political discourse. An Iraqi intellectual could, for example, criticize Nebuchadnezzar's rule in a scholarly work, but the intelligentsia could read, between the lines, an attack on Saddam Hussein" (E. Davis). Both examples, which echo the efforts of opposition journalists in apartheid South Africa, show ways in which writers conveyed meanings without explicitly stating them.

There is one notable difference between these examples and the kind of oblique speak used by those at the *Weekly Mail* and *New Nation*, however. In the former Soviet Union and in Saddam Hussein's Iraq, oblique speak was used primarily by and for a small, elite audience, whereas the oblique speak used by opposition journalists in apartheid South Africa was much more accessible to general readers. This important difference can be traced to the fact that the apartheid government was more constrained in its responses to opposition writers. Saddam Hussein, perhaps the ideal example of what Shaun Johnson described as "some kind of crazy dictator murdering people," was not bound by such restraints.[7] In contexts of extremely violent oppression, oblique speak, for obvious reasons, will be quite oblique. This highlights, as Scott notes, the challenge that faces those who use such an approach: how to convey messages sufficiently coded to escape notice of the oppressors but not the intended audience. Even in the most daunting contexts in which the audience for oblique speak may be relatively small, it is still inspiring that writers can construct meaning subversively.

Similar to opposition journalists in apartheid South Africa, opposition journalists in Iran have seized upon opportunities created by the Iranian government's efforts to promote itself as legitimate. For example, they have capitalized on high-profile political trials for the purposes of embarrassing the government. John Burns covered for the *New York Times* the court case of Abdullah Nouri, a reformist cleric who was charged and ultimately convicted by conservative forces within the Iranian government in 1999: "The courtroom became the best platform the reformers have ever had, producing day after day of banner headlines in the reformist newspapers that have proliferated across Iran, and making Mr. Nouri even more popular than before" ("Court Silences"). In fact, the coverage of this trial was such an embarrassment for the Iranian government that it took steps to close this space: "Mr. Nouri had no opportunity to speak to reporters after the sentencing, which was held behind closed doors, apparently after the court decided that it had been a mistake to open the two-week trial to the news media. That decision, made in an attempt to show that Mr. Nouri was being given a fair trial, backfired when Mr. Nouri dominated the hearings" ("Court Silences"). The decision to have an open trial for Nouri, which was part of the Iranian government's attempt to show that he "was being given a fair trial," echoes Howard Barrell's observation that Biko's trial was an attempt to display "South African justice." If governments hold trials in secret and deny media coverage, they risk losing legitimacy; if they conduct open trials, they provide opportunities for political opponents and opposition journalists.

Yet another strong similarity between apartheid South Africa and Iran in the 1990s: the attempts by opposition journalists to hold their respective governments accountable to the law. Elaine Sciolino describes how "the conservatives, who control the Judiciary, obviously have more power to use—and abuse—the laws" and then observes, "[b]ut the reformers are refusing to fold under the pressure; they are using both the pages of their publications and the courtrooms to challenge the way laws are interpreted" (255). These dynamics are also noted by Susan Sachs in her *New York Times* article "Iran Reformers Feeling Pressed by Hard-Liners." Abdollah Ramezanzadeh, an advisor to Mohammed Khatami, a reformist president of Iran, explained: "Before Mr. Khatami's election in 1997, they would just go to an editor and say, 'Close.' . . . This time they closed the papers according to the law, even though the law is questionable. . . . We live in a third-world country, yet our opponents have dealt with us very calmly compared to what happens in the countries around us. . . . The reform movement has actually forced the opposition to play by the same rules" (qtd. in Sachs). The fact that the Iranian regime at least went through the motions of adhering to rules in the late 1990s, even though these rules may have been unfair, provided opportunities that do not exist for writers in contexts with no rules at all. By challenging the government, the opposition in Iran may have lost most, if not all, of these cases. As in the case of opposition writers in apartheid South Africa, however, it is important to keep challenging the regime to adhere to the rule of law, if only to expose, in Havel's words, the mendacity of the system. Moreover, Ramezanzadeh's claim that "our opponents have dealt with us very calmly compared to what happens in the countries around us" reveals that these opposition journalists were not targeted with the same levels of violence that have been used in other contexts. Whether or not governments actually believe they are legitimate or whether they cynically try to promote the appearance of legitimacy is perhaps less relevant for opposition writers than the fact that such concerns present meaningful opportunities for resistance.

In Chile, journalists utilized international political dynamics for the purposes of expanding their writing space in ways that parallel the dynamics of apartheid South Africa. When Gen. Augusto Pinochet was in power, he ruled with an iron fist and once bragged that "not a leaf shakes in Chile without my knowledge" (qtd. in Krauss). When Pinochet eventually lost a plebiscite and was forced to step down, he obtained immunity for himself before doing so and thus remained untouchable within Chile for the many crimes his government had committed. When Pinochet traveled to England, however, a Spanish court handed down "charges of gross human rights violations during his 17 years in power" (Krauss). These charges were made possible because Pinochet's regime murdered citizens from other countries, including Spain and the United States, in addition to the thousands of Chileans his regime tortured and murdered. The British government arrested Pinochet in October 1998 because of the warrant issued by the government of Spain but ultimately did not turn him over to Spain. In January 2000, the British government concluded that the ailing Pinochet was not fit to stand trial and allowed him to return to Chile.

The arrest of Pinochet and the international uproar it caused had a profound impact on the writing space within Chile. According to one report, "Suddenly, the taboo subjects of disappearances and torture became the daily grist of the news media as journalists covered the charges made against him by prosecutors in Spain, Belgium, France and other quarters" (Krauss). There are, of course, considerable differences between this example and the dynamics that existed in apartheid South Africa. During apartheid, of course, no former head of state was ever detained by another country and charged with crimes against humanity. But as Harber explained, international political dynamics, such as the sanctions debate that took place on the floor of the US Congress, did open writing space that opposition journalists in South Africa capitalized upon. Chilean journalists did not write about the numerous human rights abuses committed by Pinochet's government after he stepped down because doing so was still considered taboo. After he was detained in the United Kingdom, his seeming invulnerability was shattered, and, as a result, his government's many crimes became the "daily grist" for Chilean newspapers. The debates and dynamics that occur within politically and economically powerful countries, therefore, can at times present tangible opportunities for opposition writers in other countries.

In terms of the United States, many of the tactics used by those at the *Weekly Mail* and *New Nation* resonate strongly with the tactics of resistance used in the past, when current safeguards for free speech did not yet exist. Floyd Abrams writes in *The Soul of the First Amendment*, "Until well into the twentieth century, censorship was rampant. It was as if the First Amendment had yet to be written" (30). He cites numerous examples to support his claim, such as an article that appeared in the *New York Times* in 1909 about an incident that took place in Spokane in which authorities "seized 'every copy' of the *Industrial Worker*, the house organ of the Industrial Workers of the World, for reporting about the 'alleged experience' of a prisoner in the county jail. According to the city, the article was libelous. 'The papers,' the *Times* reported without comment, 'will be burned'" (30).[8]

During this period of overt censorship in the United States, Margaret Sanger, an outspoken advocate for contraception in the early twentieth century, was banned from personally speaking at a Ford Hall Forum event in the city of Boston in 1929. Sanger employed a variation of the tactic used by those at the *Weekly Mail* and *New Nation*: she had someone else summarize her speech. Sanger stood on stage with a gag over her mouth while Arthur Schlesinger Sr. read her words: "You all know that I have been gagged. I have been suppressed. I have been arrested numerous times. I have been hauled off to jail. Yet every time, more people have listened to me, more have protested, more have lifted their own voices" (Sanger). This was a particularly inspired and layered form of resistance. In addition to the fact that Schlesinger's participation allowed Sanger to express her ideas, the gag she wore over her mouth served simultaneously to comply with, draw attention to, and ultimately ridicule the injunction against her. This tactic, similar to the ways in which opposition journalists had others summarize speeches and comments made by banned individuals, makes an important symbolic statement as well: governments can silence individuals, but it is significantly more difficult to silence ideas.

The publication of the Pentagon Papers, one of the most significant moments in the history of American journalism, reveals the ways in which those opposed to the Vietnam War attempted to use the protected space of Congress as a means of revealing information to the American public. The Pentagon Papers, commissioned by Secretary of Defense Robert McNamara, were the result of a massive study of the Vietnam War produced for policy makers with national security clearance. Daniel Ellsberg, a military analyst and an initial supporter of the war who eventually turned against it, recalls, "It occurred to me that what I had in my safe at Rand was seven thousand pages of documentary evidence of lying, by four presidents and their administrations over twenty-three years, to conceal plans and actions of mass murder. I decided I would stop concealing that myself. I would get it out somehow" (qtd. in Trzop 10). Since it was classified, however, it was illegal for him to provide it to others who did not have sufficient clearance. Even if he could somehow get it in the hands of others, the legal status of publishing this classified information was unclear.

Ellsberg eventually managed to provide three copies of the Pentagon Papers to journalists: one to the *New York Times* and two to the *Washington Post*. Ellsberg requested that Ben Bagdikian from the *Washington Post* deliver one copy to a sympathetic member of Congress. Bagdikian provided the extra copy to Sen. Mike Gravel from Alaska. The initial plan was for Gravel to read the Pentagon Papers on the floor of the Senate—a protected space similar to Parliament in apartheid South Africa—so that this classified information would then form part of the Congressional Record. Once it was part of the Congressional Record, it could then be cited by newspapers. Gravel was hoping to set the record for the longest filibuster, but he eventually broke down after reading for several hours due to fatigue and what he described as emotional exhaustion. Gravel explained, "I came to the passage about metal crashing through bodies . . . [a]nd it welled up in me" (qtd. in Trzop 14). Although Gravel was unable to read these documents on the Senate floor, as a member of Congress he could still officially submit this information into the Congressional Record. His attempt to do so was frustrated, however, by Sen. Jennings Randolph from West Virginia, who "refused to authorize payment of a stenographer for a public record" of these documents (14). The attempt to use the protected space of Congress, therefore, was ultimately unsuccessful.

The Pentagon Papers were eventually published, however, as a result of a landmark Supreme Court decision, *New York Times Co. v. United States*. The *New York Times* and the *Washington Post* began publishing excerpts from the Pentagon Papers without the protection they otherwise would have had if this material had been successfully entered into the Congressional Record. The Nixon administration immediately filed an injunction against further publication on the grounds that publishing this material jeopardized national security. The Supreme Court, however, ruled that the injunction was unconstitutional. Justice Hugo Black wrote, "Every moment's continuance of the injunctions against these newspapers amounts to a flagrant, indefensible, and continuing violation of the First Amendment" (qtd. Trzop 11). Similar to opposition journalists in apartheid South Africa, journalists in the United States sought to use the protected spaces within their highest legislative body for the purposes of publishing information the executive branch sought to conceal. One notable difference between these contexts, of course, was that the Supreme Court of the United States exerted its independence and defied the will of the executive in a way that the highest courts in apartheid South Africa never did.[9]

Writers in the United States today enjoy considerable First Amendment protections, but there are still constraints that inhibit writing space, specifically with regard to the massive amount of material deemed "classified" by the government. In the process of trying to dislodge this information, individuals and groups have developed tactics, similar to those examined in chapter 2, in which they exploit the decentralized nature of the vast governmental bureaucracy. Specifically, the Freedom of Information Act (FOIA) has been an important means by which individuals and groups within the United States pry classified information from government hands. The website of the National Security Archive at George Washington University, for example, describes its success using this approach: "50,000 targeted Freedom of Information and declassification requests to more than 200 offices and agencies of the U.S. government that have opened more than 10 million pages of previously secret U.S. government documents."

Even when documents are released to the public, however, they are frequently heavily redacted. As Scott Shane of the *New York Times* explains, "In every nook of the national security agencies, redactors labor anonymously. The federal Information Security Oversight Office says 460 million pages of previously classified records have been made public since 1996, usually after a markup by the overworked gnomes of declassification" ("Spies"). For requesting documents from the government, therefore, the National Security Archive has developed the ingenious tactic of requesting the same document from two separate agencies. Given the very subjective nature of the redaction criteria, documents are seldom "redacted the same way twice" ("Spies"). By requesting the same document from two different sources, the National Security Archive, if it is lucky, achieves the following result: "The first redactor decides the top half of the page is too dangerous for release; the second redactor decides to delete the bottom half. It all becomes public" ("Spies").[10] This appraoch may not always produce such an ideal result. Given the challenge bureaucrats face when trying to apply the redaction guidelines to actual documents, however, requesting the same document from different sites within the bureacracy almost certainly ensures that more information will be released.

Publishers within the United States have also issued material containing black lines to indicate to readers that the government has censored material. One of the earlier examples of this approach, according to an article appearing in the *New York Times*, "dates back to 1974 when 'The C.I.A. and the Cult of Intelligence' by Victor L. Marchetti and John D. Marks appeared with 168 redactions on view" (Shane, "Spies"). Since that time, this tactic has been used in the United States for publishing some high-profile books. Valerie Plame Wilson's memoir, *Fair Game: How a Top CIA Agent Was Betrayed by Her Own Government*, features black lines throughout its pages. Wilson recounts how her cover as a CIA agent was blown by members of the George W. Bush administration after her husband, Joe Wilson, revealed the bogus nature of President Bush's claim in the lead up to the US invasion of Iraq that Saddam Hussein had sought to obtain uranium from Niger. The Central Intelligence Agency redacted several portions of her memoir. Mohamedou Ould Slahi's *Guantánamo Diary* was also heavily redacted by the government, which Slahi's publisher, the Back Bay Books imprint of Little, Brown reveals to the reader. In this memoir, which was a national best seller, Slahi recounts his experiences after he was arrested in Mauritania shortly after 9/11. Slahi, a victim of "extraordinary rendition" by the US government, was "flown, blindfolded, shackled and diapered, to Bagram Air Base in Afghanistan, for two weeks of interrogation" (Danner). He was eventually sent to Guantánamo Bay, where he "suffered months of strictest isolation, weeks of sleep deprivation, extremes of temperature and sound, and other elaborate tortures set out in a 'special plan' approved personally by Secretary of Defense Donald Rumsfeld" (Danner). Rather than simply noting in a preface or introduction to these books that material had been censored by the government and then publishing the nonredacted material, both Wilson's and Slahi's publishers instead published the text with black lines.

While those at the *Weekly Mail* used black lines as a form of subversive *self*-censorship, the material in Wilson's and Slahi's memoirs was in fact censored and redacted by the US government itself. There are, however, striking similarities in both contexts. First, it is still possible in rare instances to determine individual redacted words. As Scott Shane notes in his review of *Guantánamo Diary*, "Even the book's redactions are a tedious reminder of the government's frequent haplessness" ("From Inside Prison"). He explains:

> Much black ink was expended, for instance, to try to keep readers from learning that some of Mr. Slahi's Guantánamo interrogators were women. Why the censors decided their gender should be secret is anybody's guess. Still, they missed enough feminine pronouns that their efforts at cover-up were undone. Another dubious redaction draws a rare outburst of sarcasm from Larry Siems, who edited the book. . . .When a guard tells him not to worry because he'll soon be home with his family, Mr. Slahi writes, "I couldn't help breaking in [redacted]." Mr. Siems comments in a footnote, "It seems possible, if incredible, that the U.S. government may have here redacted the word 'tears.'" ("From Inside Prison")

Because of inconsistent redactions throughout the text and/or the context of certain passages, it is thus possible at times to determine some words that have been redacted.

As in the case of apartheid South Africa, this is the exception, because more often than not the black lines do successfully conceal the redacted material. The publishers of both Wilson's and Slahi's memoirs, however, developed various tactics for the purposes of, as the *Weekly Mail* noted in one of its headlines, "peeling away those black stripes." Simon and Schuster, Valerie Plame Wilson's publisher, hired Laura Rozen, a journalist who had "never signed an agreement to have her words vetted by the agency," to write an afterword in which she provided "many of the facts that the C.I.A.'s Publications Review Board cut from Ms. Wilson's text" (Shane, "Spies"). Simon and Schuster thus used the tactic employed by opposition journalists in apartheid South Africa and by Margaret Sanger: have someone not restricted by the government convey information on behalf of someone who is.

In terms of *Guantánamo Diary*, Larry Siems, the book's editor, provides compelling footnotes throughout the text containing information he obtained from other sources that allow readers to make an educated guess about the nature of the material hidden beneath the black lines. Siems addresses this issue in the section "Notes on the Text, Redactions, and Annotations":

> Because it depends on close reading, any process of editing a censored text will involve some effort to see past the black bars and erasures. . . . These notes represent speculations that arose in connection with the redactions, based on the context in which the redactions appear, information that appears elsewhere in the manuscript, and what is now a wealth of publicly available sources about Mohamedou Ould Slahi's ordeal and about the incidents and events he chronicles here. Those sources include declassified government documents obtained through Freedom of Information Act requests and litigation, news reports and the published work of a number of writers and investigative journalists, and extensive Justice Department and U.S. Senate investigations. (xv)

By consulting such a broad range of material, Siems is able to provide details that either help reveal information that might be hidden by the black lines and/or serve to corroborate Slahi's claims.[11]

Finally, even when it is not possible to determine the words, or even guess at the content contained in redacted passages, the black lines provide, as Manoim observed, a "visual metaphor." They serve as a stark reminder of government insecurities and possible criminality, and they raise an obvious question for readers: What are they hiding?[12]

Several of the tactics used by those at the *Weekly Mail* and *New Nation*, therefore, resonate quite strongly with the United States. Because protections for free speech have become much more meaningful and robust over time, the primary constraint inhibiting writing space in the United States today pertains to material classified by the US government, both in terms of accessing the material and also in publishing it in the event it is leaked. A decision made during the Clinton administration and upheld during the subsequent Bush administration has had a significant impact in terms of opening writing space. Beginning on 1 January 2007 government documents twenty-five years old or older will be declassified every year "unless agencies have sought exemptions on the ground that the material remains secret" (Shane, "U.S. to Declassify"). The facts concerning the amount of material affected by this decision are simply staggering. According to Shane, "Gearing up to review aging records to meet the deadline, agencies have declassified *more than one billion pages*, shedding light on the Cuban missile crisis, the Vietnam War and the network of Soviet agents in the American government" ("U.S. to Declassify"; emphasis added).

While those who support freedom of information were generally encouraged by this policy, it is important to acknowledge some important caveats. First, there is still a process by which the government can conceal a considerable amount of information if they seek exemptions. Second, there is a considerable lag—twenty-five years—between the time this material is produced and when it can be accessed by historians, journalists, and writers. Finally, as Steven Aftergood, of the Federation of Scientists, observes, "It is going to take a generation of scholars to go through the material declassified under this process" (qtd. in Shane, "U.S. to Declassify"). What facts concerning some of the most momentous incidents in recent US history might be lurking in the more than one billion documents released?

Another significant issue within the United States: the extent to which those who obtain classified information leaked to them can publish it without sanction. The Justice Department under President Obama, for example, considered issuing a subpoena to compel James Risen of the *New York Times* to reveal the source that provided him with classified information about a covert US program targeting Iran. As the Justice Department was weighing this course of action, Aftergood observed, "If the government proceeds and pursues the subpoena, especially if Risen goes to jail or is fined at some intolerable level, it will deal a withering blow to reporting that runs against the government's wishes" (qtd. in Mahler). Even though the Obama administration ultimately decided not to subpoena Risen and compel him to reveal his source, the fact that it so publicly and so seriously entertained this possibility for such a long time conveyed a message to those who might in the future consider publishing stories containing classified information.

One final observation concerning writing space and the political climate following the 2016 US presidential election. Every president in recent history has had an adversarial relationship with the media, but with the possible exception of the Nixon administration, President Trump's public attacks on the press differ in kind from statements made by recent presidents. Trump has called journalists "'liars' and 'sick people' who are 'trying to take away our history and our heritage,'" and he has also repeatedly used the term "fake news" to denounce media accounts critical of either him or his administration (Rieder). Most ominously, he has referred to the media as "the enemy of the American people." As Republican senator Jeff Flake observed in a speech delivered on the Senate floor, "Mr. President, it is a testament to the condition of our democracy that our own president uses words infamously spoken by Josef Stalin to describe his enemies. It bears noting that so fraught with malice was the phrase 'enemy of the people,' that even Nikita Khrushchev forbade its use, telling the Soviet Communist Party that the phrase had been introduced by Stalin for the purpose of 'annihilating such individuals' who disagreed with the supreme leader" (Phillips). There are disturbing parallels between Trump's attacks on the media and the ways in which apartheid officials savagely attacked South African newspapers, especially opposition newspapers such as the *Weekly Mail* and *New Nation*. In the apartheid context, these attacks were used in part to justify censorship. Norman Manoim's observations are worth repeating: "The government never wanted the public to know that newspapers were writing the truth about them and it [the government] was stopping the truth. They wanted to say, 'These people are lying. . . That's why we're censoring, not because they're telling the truth—these people are liars.'" Given the strong free speech protections that exist in the United States today, Trump's comments are not necessarily intended to provide a justification for censorship. He does not have that power. Rather, his attacks would seem to represent an attempt to discredit critical reporting of him and/or his administration and to help create a context in which a shared reality grounded in facts and evidence no longer exists.[13]

Despite the vast differences among the examples cited above, one can nevertheless draw some general conclusions. First, there are indeed legitimate reasons for governments to maintain some secrets. Few people, for example, would want governments to provide online access to information about the science, technology, and materials necessary to construct nuclear weapons or weapons of mass destruction. Floyd Abrams explores the complex decisions newspaper editors face when trying to determine when classified information should be released to the public and when doing so may have adverse implications for national security and/or may jeopardize lives.[14]

While there are legitimate reasons for not revealing certain information, governments, including the US government, also use "national security" for the purpose of classifying information that may be embarrassing, unethical, and/or illegal. Such information may include, but is not necessarily limited to, the following: engaging in deception in the lead up to wars (e.g., about the Gulf of Tonkin incident before the Vietnam War escalation and about weapons of mass destruction before the invasion of Iraq), kidnapping ("extraordinary rendition"), torture ("enhanced interrogation"), and attempted or actual assassinations of other world leaders.[15] Writers, editors, attorneys, and various organizations have collectively and creatively managed to reveal a considerable amount of classified information, but, as noted above, however, a massive amount remains concealed from the public.

|||||||||||||||||||||||||||||||||||||||||||||||||||||||

To conclude, I will address one question I have grappled with during the many years I have worked on this project: How were those who wrote for the *Weekly Mail* and *New Nation* able to muster the courage to write in such an uncertain and frightening context? During my interviews, I asked many writers how they felt when the government began to target their newspapers aggressively. At one level, the government's opposition served as a source of motivation. Clive Cope, when asked how he responded to all of the ways the government sought to prevent the publication and distribution of the *Weekly Mail*, said, "Oh, absolutely, it spurred us on. You know, it strengthened our resolve. There's no doubt."

This may have been true for many, but it was also certainly true that the government's actions caused tremendous stress and anxiety. Harber observed, "When you think back on it, we lived with an incredible level of harassment that I don't think we realized at the time what stress it was putting on us. It was all those things: living with bugged telephones, living with the expectation of— that anything could happen at any moment." Drew Forrest noted, "So it was, *ja*, an incredibly stressful period. I think probably the most stressful in my journalistic career." Sefako Nyaka of the *Weekly Mail*, who was living in Soweto, which he described as a place of "total fear," had to leave his residence because of death threats. And Zwelakhe Sisulu, who was detained "for 735 of 1056 days (70 per cent) of his paper's existence" (Merrett, *Culture* 127), provided a stark reminder to everyone about what could happen to them. In court papers filed on Sisulu's behalf, his attorneys described the many and profound hardships he experienced as a result of his detention (Jana).[16]

While the costs of resisting the apartheid government could be quite high,

the prospects for success were not. Václav Havel has spoken and written eloquently about the genuine risks that those engaged in resistance assume. In
one interview, he stated, "In the article you refer to, [the writer Milan] Kun-
dera took me to task for talking so much about risk—I believe he even counted
the number of times I used the word. Yes, I used it frequently—it's a stylistic
fault that I'm ashamed of—but I'm not ashamed of having drawn attention to
the fact that risk is a lack of *a priori* assurance of success" (Havel, *Disturbing*
176). It is difficult to overstate how truly grim the situation was in South Africa
in the late 1980s. The apartheid government, after all, had been in power since
1948. For those writing for these opposition newspapers, they had lived their
entire lives under this system. And P. W. Botha provided no sense, either to
South Africans or the world, that he planned to engage in the kind of significant, meaningful compromises necessary to resolve the political crisis. On the
contrary, he declared states of emergency and engaged in even more oppression. As Mark Mathabane writes in the preface to his memoir *Kaffir Boy*, published 1986, "The youths of my generation have become more militant, the
tools of repression have become more numerous and sophisticated and black
schools and ghettos have become centers of social protest and bloody conflict with police and soldiers. South Africa has entered its darkest hour" (xii).
Indeed it had.

Hence my question that had been with me when I interviewed these journalists and one that had remained with me the many years I have delivered
conference papers, published articles, and worked on this book: How did these
writers muster the necessary courage to act, given the very high risks involved
and the low prospects for success? Havel's discussion of "hope" perhaps provides some insight:

> Hope, in this deep and powerful sense, is not the same as joy that things are
> going well, or willingness to invest in enterprises that are obviously headed for
> early success, but, rather, an ability to work for something because it is good,
> not just because it stands a chance to succeed. The more unpropitious the situ-
> ation in which we demonstrate hope, the deeper that hope is. Hope is definitely
> not the same thing as optimism. It is not the conviction that something will
> turn out well, but the certainty that something makes sense, regardless of how
> it turns out. (*Disturbing* 181)

A statement made by Ryland Fisher captures the essence of Havel's idea of hope and conveys perhaps the sentiments of the many journalists who wrote for the *Weekly Mail* and *New Nation*, as well as those who engaged in the anti-apartheid struggle in some way. When describing what motivated him to write for *New Nation*, Fisher explained the fervent desire he and so many others at the time had to create a more just and humane South Africa: "We wanted to change our country." Then he added, "If you asked us at the time whether we thought that was possible, we probably would have said, 'Not really. But we'll try.'"

Appendix A
KEY APARTHEID
CENSORSHIP STATUTES

THE SUPPRESSION OF COMMUNISM
ACT (1950) AMENDED TO THE
INTERNAL SECURITY ACT (1982)

This law prohibited publications from advocating communism, but as Alex Hepple observed in a publication written during apartheid, "the definitions of 'communism' and 'communist' are so wide as to embrace the objects of non-communist and anti-communist parties and groups. In the very nature of apartheid in South Africa, those who energetically or actively fight against apartheid are suspect and consequently liable, sooner or later, to fall foul of this law" (25). Franz Kruger concurs, writing that communism was "so widely defined as to include almost any opposition to the government" (*Word Wars* 19). There was one provision of this law that was particularly onerous for both the *Weekly Mail* and *New Nation*, one they sought constantly to circumvent: the prohibition against quoting anyone who had been listed or banned by the government.

THE PUBLICATIONS ACT

This statute established publication committees and the Publications Appeal
Board, which were entities given the power to ban texts containing politically
or sexually inappropriate material. In the course of their existence, these
committees ultimately reviewed and banned thousands upon thousands of
"texts," ranging from books, poems, plays, newspaper articles, songs, films,
advertisements, and even T-shirts. *New Nation* in particular had to contend
with publication committees objecting to articles that had appeared in the
newspaper.

THE POLICE ACT

This law prohibited newspapers from publishing articles about the police that
were "untrue" and for which journalists did not have "reasonable grounds"
to establish the truthfulness of their claims. As Kruger notes, however, "The
onus of proof is on the newspaper, but the exact meaning of 'reasonable
grounds' has not been determined by the courts" (*Word Wars* 20). By the time
the *Weekly Mail* and *New Nation* began publishing, an informal agreement had
been reached with the government that allowed newspapers to publish articles about the police as long as they allowed the Police Service to respond and
then published these responses at the end of the article.

THE PRISONS ACT

In many ways similar to the Police Act, this law prohibited newspapers from
publishing "any false information concerning the behaviour or experiences
in prison of any prisoner or ex-prisoner concerning the administration of
any prison, knowing the same to be false, or without taking reasonable steps
to verify such information" (Ludman 82). This act placed an overwhelming
burden on journalists to prove that their stories did not contain "any false
information." The charges brought against the *Rand Daily Mail* in the 1960s
demonstrated how the government could use this law against newspapers.
Barbara Ludman, a journalist on the *Weekly Mail*, referred to this case when

writing about the *Weekly Mail*'s efforts to publish feature articles about life on Robben Island:

> In the mid-1960's, the *Rand Daily Mail* had published a series of articles about conditions in South African prisons. The newspaper had taken elaborate steps to verify its information—a steady stream of ex-prisoners, even prison warders, had signed affidavits, had been cross-examined relentlessly by the newspaper's lawyers, had stuck to their stories through thick and thin. It wasn't enough. The state trotted out more than a hundred of its own employees to say the prisoners were lying. Reporter Benjamin Pogrund and editor Laurence Gandar sat in court day after day for eight months. They were convicted, and fined. After that no newspaper would touch a prisons story. (83)

The *Weekly Mail* and *New Nation* had some success publishing articles about the awful conditions in prisons—the physical and psychological torture prisoners experienced, the hunger strikes engaged in by prisoners—but there were also many instances in which they were simply not able to report abuses they knew were taking place.

THE CRIMINAL PROCEDURE ACT

This law presented yet another constraint for newspapers seeking to expose the abuses of the police. As Anton Harber explains, "section 205" of this act was used against journalists "in order to force them to reveal their sources" ("Censorship" 151). This provision often made people very reluctant, for obvious reasons, to go on record for a particular story.

THE KEY POINTS ACT

This was perhaps the most Kafkaesque apartheid restriction. According to Harber, this particular statute "made it a serious offence to photograph 'key points.' One would assume that newspaper editors would have to be told what these 'key points' were so that they could avoid publishing illegal material, but no, it was too dangerous to tell them—if a list fell into the wrong hands, it would identify targets for our enemies. One could only know the 'key points' one could not photograph if one photographed them—and was prosecuted" ("Censorship" 148). When asked how journalists were supposed to know something was a key point without an actual list, Pat Sidley explained, "Well, you'd have to have called someone in charge on the night [some] thing blew up to find out what was going on, and somewhere along the line, some senior would then phone the newspaper and say 'key point.' And then you knew automatically what was missing, which was the whole story. Finished. Very irritating." In other words, if the ANC's Umkhonto we Sizwe militants did successfully destroy a "key point," this legislation could be used to prevent the public from knowing about a successful act of ANC sabotage.

THE PETROLEUM PRODUCTS ACT

Given that an oil embargo had been placed on South Africa and the country does not have bountiful oil deposits, the issue of fuel consumption was very sensitive for the government. This act thus restricted "information on the source, manufacture or storage of any petroleum products" (Kruger, *Word Wars* 21–22).

Appendix B
INFORMATION REVEALED USING THE PROTECTED SPACE OF THE COURTS

<hr>

The first column of each chart in this appendix (and subsequent ones) contains the newspaper headline and journalist (if provided); the second column contains extracts from the article. Here the extracts provide sufficient language from the article to demonstrate how the newspaper used the courts and court documents to publish this information.

DEATH SQUAD ACTIVITIES—*WEEKLY MAIL*

"Court Told of Secret Police Death Squad," Sahm Venter	"Details of a secret police hit squad of 'African National Congress defectors,' called the Askari Group, emerged in the Cape Supreme Court yesterday. Bongani Abednego Jonas, 31, the 'Mr. X' who refused to give evidence for the state against the 14 accused in the Yengeni terrorism trial, told the court he was shot by a member of this group. The work of Askaris, or the A-team as security policeman Major du Toit called them, was to 'go around the township acting on information from the security police to seek out and kill their former colleagues.' ... There are at least two units of this group operating in South Africa. One is led by a Sergeant Balletjies and is based in Pretoria. The other, a Cape unit, operates from East London and covers the area from Cape Town to the Wild Coast, the court heard" (3).

"Death Row Policeman Tells of SB 'Hit Squads,'" Ivor Powell	"A former security policeman on death row yesterday claimed he was part of a police death-squad that brutally killed leading human rights activist Griffiths Mxenge. Butana Almond Nofomela, who was granted a last-minute stay of execution last night, claimed in an affidavit that he was one of four South African security policemen who killed Mxenge under orders from senior officers in the force eight years ago. Nofomela said in the affidavit that he was partially responsible for eight other political killings ordered by superior officers and that all but one of the victims were connected to the African National Congress. It was unclear at the time of going to press whether the confession was genuine, or merely a well-hatched plot to escape the noose waiting for Nofomela early this morning. If it is shown to be true, it will be the first major lead to emerge from the series of political assassinations in recent years. In his affidavit, Nofomela gave a detailed description of the Mxenge killing and implicated police officers, including a brigadier and a captain. According to sources in Natal, Nofomela's account ties closely with the facts of the case" (1).

DEATH SQUAD ACTIVITIES—*NEW NATION*

"ANC Trial to Reopen Following Askaris' Evidence"	"The trial of two alleged ANC members will be reopened in January next year and secret state witnesses reex-amined following the exposure of police involvement in clandestine death squads.... Eugene de Kock was recently suspended from the police force following alle-gations that he was in command of a secret police death squad. It is not clear whether the De Kock mentioned by the state witness in the Nyembe/Abrahams trial and Eu-gene de Kock, named by self-confessed assassin Almond Nofomela, are the same people" (1).

POLICE KILLINGS—*WEEKLY MAIL*

In addition to covert death squads, there were numerous instances in which police killed activists or suspected activists.

"Court Hears of 'Death Threats,'" Anton Harber	"Supreme court application this week threw new light on the death of the four Duduza youths who were blown up by hand grenades last week. Nicholas Shata, of Duduza, applied to the court for protection because he said he had reason to believe police had killed his colleagues and they had threatened to kill him as well. This was the first such account of the mysterious hand grenade blasts. It directly contradicted suggestions from the police that the four died when attempting to bomb targets in the township" (3).
"Court 'Finds' Lost Riot Dead," Sefako Nyaka	"The death of a child affected by teargas and the extraordinary discovery of two more bodies in the government mortuary has taken the toll from the Mamelodi police shooting from the official count of 16 to 19.... One of the bodies, that of Moses Motsei, was only found after the intervention of the Pretoria Supreme Court" (1).
"Inquest Hears of Baton Beating," Gavin Evans	"Former Soweto student leader Bongani Khumalo was shot by police who then beat him with sjamboks, batons and rifles until he collapsed, the Johannesburg Inquest Court heard yesterday. Sylvia Mampumelelo Fihla, a close friend of Khumalo, was giving evidence on the death of the former Cosas leader in Soweto on September 13 last year. Her evidence contrasted sharply with the police explanation of the shooting" (2).
"The Many Deaths of Raditsela," Gavin Evans	"The policeman who arrested former trade union leader Andries Raditsela insisted in the Johannesburg Magistrate's Court this week that he had at all times treated his prisoner 'gently and with care, in order not to harm him.' ... Although seven witnesses, including four policemen, have stated they saw Wiese striking Raditsela to the ground, Wiese has consistently denied this, insisting that policemen were careful not to hurt him" (5).

"Raditsela: Dispute over 'Leading Questions,'" Gavin Evans	"Wiese denied all allegations that he had thrown Raditsela to the ground and hit him, kicked him or pushed him into the Casspir [a large military-type truck used by the South African police]. . . . Earlier the court heard that Raditsela was lying in a semi-conscious state on the floor with his face swollen and a red mark on the left side of his forehead while Wiese was 'filling out forms.' In a statement read to the court, Frans Tsotetse said that on entering the police station . . . he noticed the detained trade unionist lying on his stomach and unable to stand up. One of his eyes was swollen and red, he had urinated and soiled his trousers, and he had recently vomited, Tsotetse said. . . . In another statement quoted by Streicher, Mrs. Mamatong Anna Raditsela, the trade unionist's mother [said,] . . . 'Andries was clearly unable to stand up and I asked whether someone in this condition should not be taken to the hospital. One of the policemen replied: "Hy gaan doodgaan, hy gaan vrek" (he's going to die). . . . Constable Theophilus Albert Joubert said in a statement that he noticed Raditsela trying to raise himself on his arms several times, but he fell every time, hitting his head against the floor. He said Raditsela was also vomiting profusely. Asked to comment on these statements, Wiese said he had noticed nothing unusual about Raditsela's condition and ascribed his vomiting to drunkenness" (5).
"Court Told of 'Media Slanting,'" Jo-Ann Bekker	[Opening sentence of article]: "'I have shot a bit,' the young riot policeman told his headquarters in a radio message after firing the shots which killed a Soweto student in September 1985. The radio transcript was released in the Rand Supreme Court yesterday at the end of the state's case against Detective Constable Jacobus Johannes Laubscher, 22, of Hillbrow. He has pleaded not guilty to murdering two Soweto schoolboys but yesterday admitted firing the shots which killed Spencer Simelane and Thuso Godfrey Phuroe, both aged 17" (3).

"Police Admit Liability for Langa Massacre," Jo-Ann Bekker	"In what amounts to an admission of liability, the Minister of Law and Order has paid out R1,3 million to 51 people injured or widowed in the 'Uitenhage massacre' of March 21, 1985. The payment is accompanied by a rare concession notice which states the minister 'unconditionally pays the sum of R1,3 million.' 'It means the police have admitted they acted wrongfully and negligently and that this was the cause of the incident,' a Johannesburg attorney said. 'It means the police are open to charges of culpable homicide'" (1).
"Inquest Raps Policemen for 'Trojan Horse' Shootings," Moira Levy	"Police who killed three Cape youngsters in the 1985 Trojan Horse shooting were negligent, a Cape Town inquest court found yesterday. Magistrate D. Hoffman also described police evidence as 'unreliable and evasive,' and rejected police claims that they had fired because they feared their lives were in danger. The incident—which was filmed by an American network—caused an international outcry. The image of police leaping out of crates on the back of a truck and firing pump action shotguns at a crowd, which included young children, became a symbol of South African repression that flashed throughout the world" (1).
"Two Police Guilty of Murder," John Perlman	"Two policeman, one of whom said he believed he had been acting against African National Congress members, were yesterday found guilty of two counts of murder and one of attempted murder in the Rand Supreme Court" (1).
"We Watched Father Beaten to Death, Say Family," Gaye Davis	A young Cape political activist died of severe head injuries this week hours after allegedly being brutally beaten by police for at least 30 minutes in front of eyewitnesses. Witnesses—including the victim's common-law wife— have drawn up affidavits telling how they saw police in George, in the southern Cape, beat and kick Andile 'Ace' Kobe, 22, for no apparent reason. After using sjamboks and boots to assault him for some time—and sjamboking people who tried to stop them—police allegedly dragged him to a police van and drove him to a police station. The witnesses were prevented from entering the station, but for at least 20 minutes they heard Kobe screaming from inside, apparently being beaten" (3).

"Police Accused of Killing Student Leader," Si Ngomane and Karen Evans	"A security policeman yesterday identified two of his colleagues as the killers of Daveyton student leader Caiphus Nyoka last year. The policeman, Sergeant AH Engelbrecht of the Benoni Security Branch, identified the killers as Sergeant Stander and Sergeant Marais. He was giving evidence at the terrorism trial of Daniel Ntsoseng and Moses Mahlangu" (3).

POLICE KILLINGS—*NEW NATION*

"Living in Fear"	"A nineteen-year old youth who saw his friend gunned down by council police, has asked for protection because he fears that the same fate will befall him. In an affidavit, Luvuyo Popo of Walmer township, in Port Elizabeth, said they were watching a game of golf when some young girls shouted at them to run because the police were coming in their direction.... 'He [Rasta] was approximately twenty paces away from me, I heard him asking for forgiveness. There were two black officers who hit him with fists and sjamboks,' Popo said. He said he saw one of the officers draw a gun and shoot Rasta in the stomach. The two officers then hit him again. The second officer then pushed Rasta away, drew his gun and shot Rasta in the head at close range" (2).
"Vlok Sued for R2M"	"Two Uitenhage residents have filed civil claims for more than R1,5-million against Law and Order Minister Adriaan Vlok. The two test cases—the biggest claims yet against the police—follow the shooting of mourners on March 21, 1985, in which 21 people died and more than 30 were injured" (1).
"Interrogation Victim 'Taken Out,' Says Cop"	"A witness in the trial of two police-men appearing in the Grahamstown Supreme Court on charges of murder, assault and defeating the ends of justice, this week agreed that the actions of one of the accused amounted to murder. And for the second time in the six-week trial, a police witness has admitted that the two accused had decided to 'take out' (execute) a suspect who had been injured and was bleeding badly following an interrogation session. Constable Raynard Fourie was testifying this week at the trial of Constable David Patrick Goosen (26), and Warrant Officer Leon de Villiers. The two have been charged with two counts of murder, two of assault, and one of attempting to defeat the ends of justice" (4).

"'Kani Had His Hands above His Head, and the Cop Kept Shooting'"	"The Rev. Cameron Kani was holding both hands above his head and staggering backwards as a policeman fired a volley of shots at him, a 15-year-old boy who watched the incident through the window of a garage told a Wynberg Inquest Court yesterday. . . . The boy said a Special Constable had said Kani 'shot a white policeman.' 'I found this story strange as I had never seen a firearm in the house and I don't believe Kani had one.'" [final sentence of story]
"'We Killed Mntonga'"	"A Ciskei security policeman this week admitted in the Ciskei Supreme Court that he and one of the six accused were responsible for the death of Idasa border co-director Eric Mntonga" (2).
"Cop Kills Student"	"A Standard 10 Vryburg student was allegedly shot down by a municipal policeman at the weekend. Mervin Oupa Wilkinson had just come from a church service when a municipal cop, LL Maleboge, who was said to have been drunk at the time, allegedly shot and killed him. Wilkinson was due to write his final examinations in a few weeks. He was waiting for his parents in front of the Huhudi police station when the shooting took place. In a sworn affidavit, Elliot Ofentse Moratane, who was with him at the time of the shooting, said the incident took place at about 6 pm while they were waiting for transport to their home in Coleridge" (2).

TORTURE—*WEEKLY MAIL*

"In Their Own Words: The Affidavits of Ex-Detainees," *Weekly Mail* reporter	"'They forced my legs open by beating the inside of my thighs with sjamboks and attempted repeatedly to kick me in my private parts.' 'They beat me with a sjambok on my back and chest and smashed my toes and head with a short wood stick.' 'Four black policemen forced me to hold a chair above the heads of the detainees while I was forced to crouch in an uncomfortable position.' These are the words of former emergency detainee Mr. Vusumi George of Motherwell, Port Elizabeth. His affidavit and others in support of last week's Supreme Court application brought by Dr. Wendy Orr, a Port Elizabeth district surgeon, and 43 others persuaded Mr. Justice Eksteen to grant an interim order restraining the police from assaulting detainees in Port Elizabeth prisons" (13).

"On Medicine: The Words of Wendy Orr," Patrick Laurence	"Wendy Orr, the young district surgeon whose affidavit detailing evidence of police assault on detainees made her the focus of national and international attention, is an unlikely heroine.... Her 35-page sworn statement was cardinal to an unprecedented decision by the Supreme Court granting an interim order restraining police from assaulting detainees in two prisons and all future detainees in two magisterial districts in the Eastern Cape.... Recalling her examinations of detainees, she said in her affidavit: 'An inordinately large proportion of them complained to me that they had been assaulted by the police. They presented symptoms consistent with their complaints, mostly severe multiple welts, bruising and swelling.' Many South Africans have long suspected that detainees are tortured, but Orr is the first doctor employed by the state to present detailed and comprehensive *prima facie* evidence of its existence" (4).
"Almost 100 'Torture' Affidavits"	"The Port Elizabeth torture case took another step forward on Wednesday when 93 affidavits from detainees alleging horrific assaults were handed in to the court.... For example, Dennis Neer, general secretary of the Motor Assemblers and Components Workers Union, alleged he was beaten while still in his prison bed, taken on a nightmare ride in the back of a police vehicle during which teargas was sprayed at him and then assaulted so badly in prison that 'I could not stand the pain. I admitted everything, pleading only that they should stop,' he said.... Other allegations in this week's hearing were that detainees were whipped with quirts, forced to eat their own hair, forced to eat splinters from a broken pickhandle, [and] had chemical irritants thrown over their bodies.... The lawyers are hoping for a ruling preventing the SA Police from ever assaulting detainees. The case has been remanded until February 4" (2).

"Christmas Eve Order to Halt Cell Beatings," Carmel Rickard	"An urgent Christmas Eve Supreme Court application by an Umlazi widow has barred the police from assaulting her detained son. Victoria Mabaso brought an urgent appeal for an interim interdict, claiming that her 16-year-old boy, Fakizi Masondo Mabaso, was in hospital, having undergone emergency surgery to his testicles after alleged police assaults during interrogation. Mabaso brought the application against the Minister of Law and Order and it was granted in chambers by Justice Leon. Emergency regulations forbid the publication of details of the condition of Emergency detainees, even if revealed in court. Mabaso's case can only be reported because he is held under 'normal,' non-Emergency security legislation" (10).
"Court Okay to Cell Inspection," Anton Harber	"In an unusual behind-closed-doors judgement, an East London Supreme Court has established the right of detainees to a court order to search a police station if there is evidence they have been tortured. . . . The application, made by six former detainees, also revealed startling allegations of brutal torture, particularly the use of severe shock treatment" (2).
"Molly Blackburn," Moira Levy	"The last affidavits recorded by Molly Blackburn and Brian Bishop—sworn statements alleging police brutality and the torture of children in the Oudtshoorn township of Bongolethu—were released this week in Cape Town, less than a month after the two were killed in a car crash. . . . Several affidavits claim police repeatedly fired teargas into closed police cells. . . . 'When they sprayed teargas, they locked us in a closed cell. Some of us fainted and some of us vomited. I vomited.' . . . In a statement signed by Brian Bishop, a 12-year-old Veronica Ngalo claims she was shot in the back by a policeman. She still has the bullet embedded near her spine, and doctors warn she may be paralysed if it is removed. . . . [There are] affidavits from an eight-months-pregnant woman who was imprisoned for three days with 'inadequate medical care' and from parents of a youth who was shot and then imprisoned after his release from hospital, although the bullet was never removed" (5).

"Court Okays 'Torture' Search of Cells," Pippa Green	"The Cape Supreme Court has granted four alleged torture victims an order allowing torture victims and their attorneys to search two Peninsula police stations for torture instruments. The judgement, handed down by a full bench of the Cape Division, is believed to set a legal precedent in South Africa. The four Cape Town men, Alfred Siphia, Mxolisi Howard Stofile, Zweltsha Malinge Mhluthwa and Alfred Moyishikile Dyanti, applied for an 'Anton Pillar' order allowing them to search the Gugulethu police stations without prior warning to the police.... The application by the four men followed spells in detention during which they claimed they had been subjected to various forms of torture, including suffocation and electric shock treatment" (3).
"Another Day. Another Treason Witness," Lauren Gower	"A state witness in the Delmas treason trial said this week that he had contemplated suicide during nearly four months of police interrogation. The witness, a former Azapo member, who was giving evidence in camera at the trial, told the Delmas Circuit Court that during his detention he had been interrogated from 8am to 4pm. He also admitted to having been assaulted while in detention. After this admission, counsel for the defence made application to the court that the witness reveal where and by whom he was interrogated, but this was never allowed" (5).
"Policemen Fined for Nair Assaults," Carmel Rickard	"Two Durban Security policemen were convicted and fined this week for assaulting UDF leader Billy Nair in detention. W/O Johannes de Wet and Sergeant Gary van Sluys were both found guilty of assaulting Nair during his detention last year, leaving him with a perforated eardrum and eye injuries" (9).
"About-Face from a Key State Witness," Jo-Ann Bekker	"The evidence in camera of a key state witness in the Delmas treason trial was dismissed this week after the witness, a young woman, admitted she had invented it to satisfy interrogators who had assaulted her in detention.... Before she retracted her evidence on Wednesday, the state witness... told the court that one of the accused, Patrick 'Terror' Lekota, and others had taught a group of Tumahole residents how to make petrol bombs. Under cross-examination, however, she said she had signed a statement containing this evidence only after being sjambokked and interrogated in detention by nine policemen" (9).

"Court Told of Dead Foetus Found in Cells," Jo-Ann Bek-ker	"Two telephone conversations and a brief meeting at Kroon-stad Hospital provided the foundation for a startling court application brought before the Orange Free State Supreme Court yesterday to stop police allegedly torturing Emergency detainees. According to the claims, which were emphatically denied by the police, the police punched, slapped and used electric shocks on more than 30 detainees held at Heilbron Police Station. A pregnant woman aborted after she was al-legedly punched in the stomach" (4).
"Watson Witness Tells Court: 'I Was Tortured,' Peggy Killeen	"A key state witness says he was tortured by security police before confessing to setting fire to the home of the Watson brothers, Port Elizabeth's anti-apartheid rugby heroes[,] on their instructions.... He told the court security police took him to an 'unknown place' on August 1. A bag was pulled over his head, his arms and legs were tied and he was tortured and assaulted until he confessed to burning the house" (4).
"SAP Pay Out for Ex-Detainee," Shaun Johnson	"South African Institute of Race Relations researcher Monty Narsoo has received R5 000 from the South African Police—more than five years after he was allegedly tortured while in detention. The out-of-court settlement was made 'without prejudice'—meaning that the defendant, the Minister of Law and Order, has not admitted liability" (2).
"Stofile's Wife Tells of Beatings," Ncedo Ntamnani	"The wife of detained UDF official Rev Arnold Stofile told her domestic servant she had been assaulted so badly while in police detention that she urinated on herself, it was al-leged in papers before the Bisho Supreme Court" (4).
"Prisoners Beaten—Policeman," Jean Sutherland	"A police officer this week told the Windhoek Supreme Court awaiting-trial prisoners had been assaulted in custody.... Investigating officer WO van den Hoven told the court he had seen a Captain Ballach of the police's special counter-in-surgency unit (Coin)—formerly known as Koevoet—assault at least three of the accused" (5).

"Torture? Of Course, Policeman Tells Court"	"A security policeman stood in the Windhoek Supreme Court this week and blandly gave dramatic and unprecedented details of how his colleagues routinely torture Swapo suspects. Although there have been many allegations of such abuses before, this is the first time that someone within the security forces has confirmed it publicly. 'You thrash (a prisoner) until he cracks—points out what has to be pointed out,' was how Warrant Officer Nikodemus Nampala described the attitude of the security branch" (1).
"'Beatings' Officer Tells Court of Christian Duty," Jean Sutherland	"An officer of the feared SWA Police counter-insurgency unit (Coin, formerly known as Koevoet) this week admitted in court, without batting an eye, that he had severely beaten detainees. Another police office said he had concealed the beatings from his commanding officer—and a third said that although 'as a Christian' he found it difficult to beat prisoners, he had found it his 'Christian duty' to explain to one suspect the connection between punishment and repentance" (6).
"Captain on Eight Assault Charges," Jeremy Bernstein and Peter Auf Der Heyde	"The former commander of Fort Beaufort police station appeared in the local magistrate's court this week on eight charges of assault. Captain Gerrit Grobblaar's appearance is a sequel to an investigation in nearby Tinus township by lawyers, during which 34 affidavits were forwarded to the Minister of Law and Order detailing police behavior in Fort Beaufort during 1985 and 1986" (2).
"Youths Tell of Cell Beatings," Gaye Davis	"Cape Youth Congress members have alleged brutal beatings and sexual harassment by special constables who, they claim, held them for several hours at Nyanga police station after breaking up a Cayco meeting in a house in the KTC squatter settlement. The allegations are contained in 11 affidavits filed in the Cape Town Supreme Court this week" (5).

"Inquest Gives Rare Glimpse," Vusi Gunene	"For the first time since the imposition of the 1986 State of Emergency, the court is hearing startling oral evidence about detention conditions—allegations which, but for their status as court records, could not be published.... Led by E Roodt, Kekana told the magistrate Marule had 'considerable injuries' when he was placed in the same cell with him at the Dunnottar police station near Springs. 'His entire face was swollen and in particular, his left eye was very swollen. The inside of that eye was very red. He also had many strip marks on his back of his arms,' said Kekana. Mofokeng said a Captain Schlebush agreed that Marule would be taken to a doctor the following day. The doctor said Marule would be taken to hospital. However, 'that evening Marule collapsed in the toilet. Foam was coming out of his mouth. He was pulled up and placed on the bed. The intercom to the reception was not on. The cells then made noise. When our cell did contact the reception and the warders were told that Marule was sick, the warders replied over the intercom words to the effect that 'Julle lieg, julle kaffers, slaap'" ["You lie, you kaffirs, sleep"] (3).
"Court Hears of 'Panel Beating' for Dead Detainee," Jeremy Bernstein	"Hours after 18-year-old Wheanut Mlungisi Stuurman was detained for questioning by members of an 'unrest unit,' he was taken to a 'quiet place' to be tortured and then murdered, a police witness this week told the Grahamstown Supreme Court. For the second time in the six week trial, police witnesses have told the court that Stuurman had to be taken out (executed) after he had been 'panelbeaten' during an interrogation session.... The last man arrested, Stuurman, was taken to a 'quiet place for questioning' near a sewerage works at the Fish River. However, Fourie later conceded that the only reason Stuurman was taken to a 'quiet place' was to torture him further, as it was obvious that continued questioning would not help" (3).

"Held Mokaba Claims He Was Tortured," Jo-Ann Bekker	"The detained president of the South African Youth Congress, Peter Mokaba, was kept chained to a chair for days by his police interrogators, it was alleged in a Pretoria Supreme Court application this week. The urgent application for an interim order restraining the police from assaulting Mokaba and directing a magistrate and district surgeon to visit him was brought by his sister, Mapula Mokaba. The respondents, the Minister of Law and Order and the Commissioner of Police, are opposing the order" (3).
"Court Told of Black Hole of 'Kei," Carmel Rickard	"Five Transkei prisoners say they have been kept in grossly overcrowded cells, 24 hours a day for more than five months, and have asked that the supreme court order the practice to stop. The urgent application is being made by the five against Transkei's minister of justice and prisons and commissioner of prisons. They asked the court to declare a number of alleged irregularities at Umtata's Wellington Prison are illegal" (6).
"Ebrahim: My Brush with SA's Angels of Death," Vusi Gunene	"Senior African National Congress member and 'Bethal' treason trialist Ismail Ebrahim broke his silence this week— in a statement alleging systematic South African state terrorism, police fabrication of evidence and torture 'to the point where I nearly lost my mind.' The statement was made to the head of the Community Agency for Social Enquiry, Mark Orkin, who presented it to the court as part of his evidence in mitigation of sentence. Ebrahim had previously refused to testify. . . . Ebrahim says his abduction was followed by 'police torture to the point where I nearly lost my mind. My two co-accused were also brutally tortured. It is horrifying to note how widespread these tortures are'" (6).
"'From a Police Locker, I Heard Two People Screaming,'" Thandeka Gqubule	"A man who slept in the same room as Caiphus Nyoka on the night the student leader was killed has made startling allegations of torture by the South African Police. Exodus Gugulethu Nyakane, 21, of Wattville, this week gave evidence before a packed court during the inquest into the death of Nyoka." [This is followed by several long quotes from testimony about how police burned prisoners' hair and poured boiling water down their backs and about the screams heard of other torture victims in adjacent rooms] (4).

"Asvat Trial Accused Tells of Shocks," Cassandra Moodley	"An accused in the Asvat murder trial this week alleged police electrocuted him, 'pulled a tube (that of a car tyre) over his face' and forced him to make a statement confessing to the murder of community doctor Dr. Abu Baker Asvat. Zakhele Mbatha, 21, was giving evidence during a trial-within-a-trial in Rand Supreme Court where he and Thulani Nicholas Dlamini, 20, are appearing on seven charges relating to murder, robbery and unlawful possession of firearms and ammunition. Last Friday counsel for Mbatha, Wayne Hutchinson, challenged the admissibility of a statement made by the accused to a policeman because it was 'procured under duress and he was told what to say. Therefore the contents are false,' Hutchinson said" (4).
"Youth Describes Detentions, Assaults in 'Torture-Mobile,'" Ivor Powell	"Among other allegations in his affidavit Zondi claims that: He was detained on three separate occasions by the occupants of the Husky and tortured, threatened with death and various forms of physical violence, including being pushed off the edge of a cliff. . . . Among other forms of torture, physical and psychological, he was subjected to electric shocks; suffocated to unconsciousness by means of a plastic tube being drawn over his head; beaten with sjamboks and fists; and threatened with firearms. He also reported coughing blood as a result of assaults. . . . His allegations are supported by a medical report made after examination subsequent to one of Zondi's detentions, as well as a number of other sworn affidavits submitted by community activists who were allegedly also subjected to tortures by the occupants of the red Husky. These other affidavits also allege beatings, tube-tortures and electric shocks; the details are in close agreement with those supplied by Zondi" (3).

TORURE—*NEW NATION*

"Police Torture Claims Mount"	"The government could face a series of court actions around allegations of torture and assaults of emergency detainees. This has emerged following allegations of 32 hours of torture in an affidavit submitted to the Pretoria Supreme Court by lawyers acting for Father Smangaliso Mkhatshwa, SA Catholic Bishops' Conference secretary general.... In his affidavit, Fr Mkhatshwa says he was blindfolded and driven to a place 50 minutes from the Hercules police station in Pretoria. All he could hear before being tortured, he says, were whispers, moving furniture and folding paper. 'As someone poured water into a container, another said: 'Don't fill it, you will drown him, man....' His buttocks and genitals were exposed, he says. 'He (the interrogator) ordered me to sing two freedom songs of my choice. I obliged. Then the real grilling began.'... During his interrogation, he alleges: He was left standing on the same spot for at least 30 hours, blindfolded and in handcuffs, and was not allowed to drink or go to the toilet. His genitals and buttocks were left exposed for at least 29 hours. A 'creepy creature or instrument was fed into my backside. From there it would move up and down my legs and invariably end up biting my genitals. When I cringed with pain they would laugh.' He also says shots were fired twice just above his head. The European Community's executive commission has deplored Fr Mkhatshwa's long detention and the 'brutalities' it said he suffered" (1).
"State Opposes Detainees' Application"	"Two community leaders have filed urgent applications before the Port Elizabeth Supreme Court asking the court for interdicts restraining the police from assaulting them while in detention" (3).
"Louis Le Grange Sued—Again. 'We Were Beaten'"	"Three Turfloop student leaders are demanding R90 000 from the Law and Order Minister Mr. Louis le Grange for alleged assault by three security cops while in detention.... The students said that the assault took place while they were being interrogated on their activities on campus" (5).

"Minister Faces R10 000 Claim"	"An East London man is suing the Minister of Law and Order for R10 000 after a policeman allegedly strangled him with a piece of wire.... The policeman then fetched another man and tied a piece of wire to his hand and another man's neck. 'One of the policemen put his weight between us on the wire, and the wire strangled us,' he added. 'This continued until I lost consciousness'" (2).
"'Assaults': Prison Interdicted"	"Horrific details of the treatment of child detainees in Johannesburg's Diepkloof prison are contained in affidavits tabled in the Rand Supreme Court last week. The affidavits were presented during an application for an urgent interdict restraining prison service members at the Diepkloof Prison from assaulting or threatening to assault detainees. The interdict was granted yesterday" (1).
"Court Reins in Blackjacks"	"A Duncan village woman has been granted an urgent interdict restraining municipal police from assaulting her son, an employee of the Black Sash in London" (3).
"A Victim of Horror Speaks"	"One of the victims of the current terror campaign described in a sworn affidavit nearly 24 hours of terror at the hands of the security forces.... 'We were ... taken in hippos [Hippo, a make of armored personnel carrier] to a camp at Emagesini (Kwaggafontein). There, we were locked in a room throughout the night.' He alleged that during that period, they were assaulted.... 'The next day, some of us were taken to a remote area, where we were assaulted and interrogated" (1).
"I Was Detained, Tortured, Released and Redetained"	"An executive member of the Duncan Village Residents Association this week described in court how he was assaulted and tortured in detention in 1985.... Jordaan said he saw other people being assaulted in the police station the following day. 'That night I was taken to a certain office in which there were two policemen,' he said.... 'They then started assaulting me. I lost consciousness after getting electric shocks. When I came to, I was assaulted by a big security policeman who said I was going to tell the truth.' Jordaan said he was taken to hospital after the assault, and that he had to be carried to court during their first appearance because he could not walk. Even now, I cannot stand for more than 30 minutes because of the assaults,' he said" (3).

"Cops Assaulted Us, Potsdam 4 Tell Court"	"The Bisho Supreme Court this week reserved judgment in an application by four Potsdam residents seeking an order preventing the Ciskei police from assaulting them. In their application, Mondli Febana, Quntsu Leleki, Dennis Madolo and Velile Dasi alleged continued assaults by the Ciskei police and vigilante attacks on their homes" (5).
"Ebrahim Treason Trial: Doctor's Shock Assault Claims"	"Injuries consistent with assault were 'not uncommon' among political prisoners and detainees, a former district surgeon told the Piet Retief treason trial this week.... Holden also testified that he had on occasion examined three political detainees who had allegedly been tortured with electric shocks to their genitals.... Holden was giving evidence following Dladla's claim that he was tortured, assaulted and slapped by police at the Sandton police station after his arrest in June 1986 and forced to make a confession. Holden examined Dladla on June 24, about two days after his arrest, and found that he had a perforated eardrum 'caused by trauma.'... The court was also told that Pretorius [a police officer] had tortured Dladla by covering his head with a mask which made it impossible to breathe.... Dladla also claims to have been repeatedly tortured with electric shocks while his legs were down. But when the interrogators considered the torture too weak, a policeman suggested that something stronger should be tried, it was alleged in court. ... Dladla was then taken to another room where his face was covered with a red tube, his clothes removed and his legs tied to a stool. He was questioned and when he denied allegations made by the interrogators, the tube was tightened and he felt electric shocks being applied to his armpits and his genitals. Dladla was also allegedly told that if he did not cooperate he would be killed and no one would know about it" [final sentence of article] (1).

"Detainees 'Used to Trap Activists'"	"Detailed allegations that police assaulted detainees and then used them to set traps for wanted political activists were made in the Pretoria Supreme Court this week. Appalling prison conditions and violent assaults and torture in KwaNdebele were also alleged. . . . On his treatment at the hands of his interrogators, Phatlane alleges: He was handcuffed on [a] number of occasions and left in a sitting or standing position for lengthy periods without sleep. On occasions he went without food or water for more than a day. He was punched, struck with a cold drink bottle all over the upper part of his body and kicked. On one occasion he was assaulted until he fainted. He was subjected to electric shocks for 10 minutes at a time. 'The pain was unbearable. I screamed continuously and almost subsided into unconsciousness'" (1).
"Lawyers See Ciskei 'Torture Chamber'"	"A bloodstained t-shirt and a rag used to gag and blindfold detainees were found inside a security police torture room after lawyers searched sections of the Zwelitsha police station this week. The examination of at least six rooms in the police station was conducted after the Ciskei Supreme Court granted an order to two former detainees allowing them to conduct the search. . . . According to one of the detainees, a very high-ranking security police officer, known only as Major Ulana, took the lead in torturing him. Electrodes were attached to various parts of their bodies during the torture, the detainees claimed. One of the detainees said in his affidavit that he was blindfolded and tightly strapped to what appeared to be a chair before being subjected to electric shocks. He claims that a rag was stuffed into his mouth when he screamed. The torture was extremely painful, the detainee claimed, adding that he had lost consciousness when subjected to the electric shocks" (1).

"Former Detainee Talks of Torture"	"A former detainee described in the Durban Supreme Court yesterday how he was given electric shocks during interrogation by members of the security police.... On the first day of his arrest on August 27, 1985, [Eugene Vusi Dlamini] said, he was taken to the room where he was made to sit on a chair. He said his arms and legs were strapped to the arms and legs of the chair and he was blindfolded and gagged. Water was then poured over his head and he felt a few drops pour on to his feet. He said he was shocked on his neck, wrists and ankles, the second time for about two to three seconds. Dlamini lost consciousness after being assaulted by the six policemen who were present" (1).
"ANC Members Tell of Abduction and Torture"	The following is taken from an affidavit given by Sydney Jabulani Msibi, a guard of Oliver Tambo, who was abducted and tortured by the police: "... I was punched, slapped, beaten with a thick belt, my head hit against the wall and my toes stepped on as the interrogators forced information out of me. ... They continued the interrogation until I lost consciousness.... During the evening interrogation, cigarette butts were nipped on my face and an attempt was made to set my hair alight. A tyre was put on my neck and a threat made to necklace me. I lost consciousness on two occasions and on each time splashed with water."

POLICE LINKS TO VIGILANTES — *WEEKLY MAIL*

"AG to Rule on 'Chief with a Whip' Claims," Gavin Evans	"Affidavits detailing alleged assaults by KwaNdebele leaders—including Chief Minister S S Skhosana—on Moutse residents on New Year's Day have been sent to the attorney general, who will decide whether to prosecute. According to affidavits sworn by five residents, Skhosana and two colleagues—KwaNdebele Interior Minister Piet Ntuli and the Education Minister, referred to only as Mr. Kunudu—personally took part in assaulting more than 200 Moutse residents abducted by vigilantes.... According to one resident, Mtuli personally beat some of the men with a sjambok while a white policeman and three black policemen looked on" (6).

"Court Acknowledges Violence Allegations," *Weekly Mail* reporter	"A Supreme Court yesterday for the first time acknowledged allegations that community councilors were involved in violent vigilante actions and were being protected by members of the South African Police. The Eastern Cape Supreme Court in East London yesterday issued orders against three Fort Beaufort community councilors and an SAP sergeant. The councilors were restrained from assaulting two children and the policeman, Sergeant Sijila of the Fort Beaufort police station, was ordered to stop preventing the lodging of assault complaints or prejudicing investigations. Nolwandle Mathe ... saw the three community councilors—Taya Nzima, Sithombo Mbewu and Makwezi Gabashe—emerge from her house. She found her son lying on the floor, crying loudly and bleeding from the stomach. Her son told her that the men had entered a bedroom where he was sleeping and hit him with sjamboks and sticks. When she attempted to report the matter, Sgt Sijila had told a junior policeman not to take the statement and had said her children would continue to be beaten" (1).
"Journalist Sues over Sjambok Attack," Pat Sidley	"*Weekly Mail*'s news editor Anton Harber is suing the Minister of Law and Order for damages in the first of a series of actions arising from assaults on journalists during the first elections for the House of Delegates in 1984. Harber, who was the *Rand Daily Mail*'s political reporter, was assaulted by a group of vigilantes outside the Lenasia polling booth on election day, August 28, 1984. He told Johannesburg magistrate's court this week that police not only neglected to help him, but acted in concert with the assault, in that they assaulted colleague Gary van Staden from *The Star*" (9).
"Advocate Links Police to De'Ath Death," Jean Le May	"Affidavits handed into the Cape Town Magistrate's Court yesterday alleged that George De'Ath was killed by witdoeke [black paramilitary known for their white arm- or headbands] vigilantes acting under orders from or with the compliance of police. This evidence was advanced at a preliminary hearing by Jeremy Gantlet, the advocate acting for De'Ath's family. If it were accepted, it could lead to an inquest finding that culpable omission on the part of the South African Police led to the cameraman's death" (1).

"'I Watched a Man Burn a Tent While Police Stood By,'" Gaye Davis	"A doctor this week described watching a witdoeke vigilante set alight a tent housing refugees in the KTC squatter camp, near Cape Town—while a Casspir stood by and 'did absolutely nothing.' Dr. Mark Blecher, 26, was giving evidence in the Cape Town Supreme Court on behalf of the 21 KTC families and the Methodist Church in Africa, who are suing the minister of law and order for R312 000 for damages incurred in June last year when witdoeke razed about 70 percent of the settlement" (5).
"Register Hints at Police Link to Vigilantes," Jo-Ann Bekker	"A police 'operations register' contained evidence suggesting policemen had been involved in attacks on Alexandra activists, the Rand Supreme Court heard this week. This information emerged during the cross-examination of the former Alexandra station commander, Colonel Ambrose Dickenson, by lawyers for eight Alexandra treason trialists. The lawyers claimed the attacks on activists' homes on April 22 last year began soon after a senior black policeman made an entry in the operations register, stating that black policemen wanted to march into the township because one of their colleagues had been robbed. A subsequent entry in the register records that 70 to 88 men 'possibly black policemen' were standing in front of a burning house" (3).

POLICE LINKS TO VIGILANTES—*NEW NATION*

"Bandits Had SAP Backing"	"The South African Police and Witdoeke vigilantes worked hand in hand in 1986. The armed vigilantes, who were responsible for the killing of hundreds and destruction of property, were officially regarded as a 'home guard, to act against stone-throwing youths.' This emerged during the cross examination this week of Major Dolf Odendaal, second-in-command of the Peninsula Riot Squad, during a Supreme Court action brought by the Methodist Church and 21 KTC families who lost their homes during vigilante action in June 1986" (1).

"Police Sat Back ... as Vigilantes Assaulted Hundreds, Rang in Curfew, Court Is Told"	"Shock claims of collusion between police and the right-wing vigilantes were heard this week in the Cape Town Supreme Court. The court was told that: ... Police had been present when vigilantes assaulted people at the offices of the local administration board. Police had been unwilling to deal with cases relating to the vigilantes. Vigilantes acted in concert with the police by pointing out people whenever there were incidents of unrest. The claims of vigilante-police links—which echo those of residents in townships across the country—concern the township of Zolani, outside Ashton in the Boland" (1).
"Vigilante Rampage: Vlok Sued"	"Residents of KwaNobuhle township, near Uitenhage in the Eastern Cape, are to sue Minister of Law and Order Adriaan Vlok for hundreds of thousands of rands following the alleged connivance of the police in a vigilante attack on the community in which three United Democratic Front members were slain. . . . The lawsuit is a sequel to the January 4 attack on KwaNobuhle residents by Ama Africa vigilantes, who left behind a trail of death and destruction. . . . In support of their claims, the residents allege that vehicles belonging to and manned by members of the SA Police were present in KwaNobuhle during January 4 when the attacks took place. They add that certain acts of violence were committed by the vigilante group in the presence of policemen. The letter also claims that police vehicles at various times traveled in close proximity to the armed group which marched through the township" (1).
"Alex Vigilante Violence ... Cops' Role Questioned"	"The possible involvement of policemen in vigilante attacks on Alexandra residents in April last year was raised again this week—this time during the Johannesburg Supreme Court treason trial of eight Alex youths. Among the exhibits in the trial is an 'operations register' from Wynberg police station which records events on the night of April 22 last year. It reports the presence of between 70 and 88 people, 'possible black policeman,' in an area where gunfire, burning cars and houses and assaults on residents were recorded. These scenes were also reported by security force Casspir 88C on April 22 when township residents allege they were attacked by vigilantes and police. Nowhere in this and two other entries on the violence do the police report any intervention except notifying the fire brigade" (1).

"Police 'Escorted Inkatha Murder Mob'"	"Police and soldiers escorted armed Inkatha men into the Ashdown township, near Pietermaritzburg, and stood by as they stabbed a man to death, attacked residents and stoned homes, it has been alleged. According to affidavits supporting a Supreme Court application, nothing was done to disarm or restrain the Inkatha group.... One of the affidavits says that 'the perpetrators of the violence have been able to act without any restraint from the SAP.' It also alleged that vehicles transporting armed Inkatha men were escorted by the SADF and SAP. This group is alleged to have stabbed Mandla Mbatha to death. A resident[,] who witnessed the police escorting the alleged murderers, described in detail how the crowd attacked houses and residents" (1).

MISCONDUCT BY POLICE AND MILITARY PERSONNEL—*WEEKLY MAIL*

"What the Clerics Told PW," *Weekly Mail* reporter	"Allegations that a 59-year old Graaff Reinet woman was sjambokked by Security Forces as she lay sick in her bed were among reports leading clergymen shared with State President PW Botha on Monday. Three sworn statements—two from women in Graaff Reinet, and one from a 70-year-old Cradock woman, who claims she was raped by two white soldiers—were handed to Botha by a delegation of clergymen, headed by Anglican Archbishop, the Rt Rev Phillip Russell.... Mariana [Qomoyi], who was 8 and a half months pregnant, was whipped across her stomach and back. 'Her stomach bled and her dress showed the blood stains,' said the statement.... Annie Gilbert, aged 47, from Graaff Reinet, described in an affidavit how a policeman shot her 20-year-old son George as he entered the house. Earlier the policemen had told her son, who was working in the yard, that: 'Botha het gese ons can julle doodmaak soos vliee' (Botha has said we can kill you like flies). The statements, made to Brian Bishop, were sworn to in front of PFP MPC's Di Bishop and Molly Blackburn. Judge Nathaniel R. Jones, a United States Circuit Judge, was present when the statements were taken, Bishop says" (1).

"Rape Claims Grand-mother in Hiding"	"A 70-year-old Cradock woman, whose allegations that she was raped by two white soldiers was among those handed to State President PW Botha, is 'hiding in fear of her life.' The elderly woman's affidavit, alleging that she was forced into a hippo driven by soldiers and raped on a roadside by two of them, was widely publicized after it had been handed over to the State President by a church delegation headed by Archbishop Phillip Russell. The woman claimed last week she had gone into hiding 'in fear of her life' after a hippo had come to her house three times in a day" (6).
"Strange Case of the Mystery Glass-Smashers," Own Correspondent, East London	"Startling claims of security force members stoning cars have emerged from Duncan Village, near East London. In one incident, a bottle was thrown at a pedestrian, bruising his hip. Other reported incidents have involved the stoning of parked cars. In an affidavit made available to *Weekly Mail*, a resident said he had been woken up at about 2am on September 4 by the noise of a truck he believed was a military vehicle because he had seen policemen and soldiers climb off (6).
"Press Embargo on Claims against SADF," Jo-Ann Bekker	"In a dramatic interim judgment on an urgent application brought this week by the Krugersdorp Residents' Organisation against the South African Police and Defence Force, the Minister of Law and Order and of Defence gave undertakings that their members would not commit 'unlawful acts' in Krugersdorp's townships, and an embargo was placed on the publication of affidavits supporting the application. Rand Supreme Court judge Justice Goldstone said the more than 100 supporting affidavits contained allegations 'of a particularly grave nature' concerning the conduct of members of the police and the Defence Force in the township of Kagiso 1 and 2 and Munsieville. . . . Justice Goldstone described the embargo on the contents of the affidavits as 'a most unusual procedure' and said the decision to withhold papers before an open court had not been taken lightly" (9).

"I Saw Police Fire at Kids, Says Lawyer," *Weekly Mail* reporter	"A Johannesburg advocate has given an eyewitness account of the incident in White River this week when police opened fire on a large crowd of schoolchildren, saying there was no apparent justification for the shooting. Advocate Lawrence Tonkin said in a statement yesterday that the shooting, which has provoked worldwide indignation, came with no warning to the crowd to disperse. His account—that the children were not uncontrollable, that he saw no teargas being fired—directly contradicted the police version. . . . Tonkin decided to issue a statement—an extraordinary action for a member of his profession—with special permission from the Bar Council" (1).
"Court Hears of Police Beatings in Classrooms," Jo-Ann Bekker	"Papers before the Free State Supreme Court have lifted the veil on Security Force activities in black schools during the first two months of the Emergency, when reports on their actions were restricted. While the police have told the Supreme Court that they were deployed in schools to prevent unrest, parents and a teacher from Parys' Tumahole township have accused them of conducting daily assaults on schoolchildren. . . . The application for an order stopping Security Forces from continuing the alleged assaults was brought two weeks ago. However, the details were embargoed until Wednesday to allow the replying affidavits to be filed" (2).
"I Let Police Punish Pupils, Says Principal," Jo-Ann Bekker	"Corporeal punishment, one of the chief grievances of black students in last year's countrywide school boycotts, is being carried out by the Security Forces in Parys under the Department of Education and Training's new disciplinary measures, according to papers before the Free State Supreme Court. And, although Parys principal Jafta Mokgotle Mogashoa denied the broad allegation, he has admitted instructing a policeman to punish a pupil who allegedly insulted a policeman. Mogashoa described how a policeman had lashed Standard Nine student James Mathamelo, 20, four times with a plastic cane on his buttocks while another policeman 'restrained the deponent when he resisted the punishment'" (2).

| "Ex-Soldier Tells Court of Orders to Beat People," Mike Loewe | "A conscript in the South African Defence Force, giving evidence in support of [a] conscientious objector, yesterday told how an army major had ordered troops to assault township residents because the police were 'ineffectual.' . . . [Steven Louw] gave a detailed account of incidents of misconduct he had witnessed during active service from June 1985 to June 1986. [Louw], a first-year student at the University of Witwatersrand, said that while performing service in the Eastern Cape, the major had ordered the troops to 'beat up blacks.' . . . Among the things he saw troops doing were: Using catapults with stones against residents to provoke 'action.' Placing a 10-year-old boy in a small 'bin' behind a Buffel [military vehicle]. A Corporal then beat the boy with a stick. Blackmailing shebeen [illicit bar] owners into providing them liquor. Breaking up fences for firewood. Driving at a congregation as they left a Sunday church service and then teargassing them. Hiding among township houses while a Buffel was driven about in a manner which it was hoped would provoke action. Conducting high-speed trips through the townships in order to give residents locked in the 'bin' (the back of the truck) a 'joy ride.' Assaulting residents using sticks cut from trees because troops were not issued sjamboks" (1). |
| "The Proud Soldier Who Changed His Mind," Mike Loewe | "National servicemen serving in the townships craved for action involving violence and found it mainly to beat up blacks, according to a former 'parabat,' Steven Louw. The parachute battalion soldier last week gave evidence in mitigation for classified conscientious objector, Phillip Wilkinson. For the first time they can be published as they form part of the court record. Louw told of fist, boot, stick and catapult attacks on residents in four townships. . . . On another occasion while on a foot patrol, a man who gave a salute managed to get away and a small boy was apprehended. Louw's fellow troop 'started to hit and interrogate him. When I saw this I went over and pushed him away. . . . I asked him why he was hitting the boy . . . his words to me were 'Prevention is better than cure'" (5). |

"Soldiers' Trial Reveals Plan to Discredit ECC," Gaye Davis	"A covert defence force campaign to discredit the End Conscription Campaign was revealed in the judgement of three national servicemen in Cape Town this week. . . . In his judgement, Dempers said that during cross-examination, the commanding officer of Communication Operations at Western Province Command Headquarters in Cape Town's Castle, Colonel JJ Claassen, had conceded that there was an SADF campaign to discredit the ECC in order to undermine its goodwill—in the sense of its ability to attract members and funds" (1–2).
"SADF Threw Fake ECC Pamphlets from 'Copter, Court Hears," Moira Levy	"The South African Defence Force's secret campaign against the End Conscription Campaign involved a series of operations using false number plates, phony addresses and [a] commercial helicopter commissioned by the army without the knowledge of the minister of defence. This was heard in the Cape Town Supreme Court last week in an urgent application brought by Hein Monnig, 24, Peter Pluddeman, 25, and Desmond Thompson, 20" (2).
"At Last, ECC Able to Reveal Bar on SADF," Gaye Davis	"A Supreme Court order restraining the South African Defence Force from harassing and interfering with the End Conscription Campaign has been in effect for almost a month—but details of it can only now be published. This is the latest development in legal action the ECC is taking against the SADF—details of which have, until now, been shrouded in secrecy by virtue of *in camera* orders requested by the SADF" (3).

"Schoolboys Claim: We Were Flung into a Grave," Carmel Rickard	"Two Durban schoolboys are to lay charges with the police and claim damages after members of South African Defence Force allegedly assaulted them, threw them into a newly-dug grave and shoveled sand on top of them. The two boys, one of whom was taken to hospital after the alleged incident, have given statements to their lawyers who are to lay charges and investigate their legal action. . . . He was told to get in [the grave] but refused and there was a scuffle. Eventually he was pushed in by two soldiers, one of whom got in as well and made him lie down, again assaulting him. . . . 'As the soil hit my face I tried to sit up and the soldier shoveling the soil into the grave then got into the grave and began to assault me with his fist on my head and upper torso. . . . I feared that I was being buried alive. This fear, with the pain I was experiencing, caused me to begin screaming for help. The soldier who had first assaulted me then got into the grave and kicked me in my face and told me to shut up, otherwise he would kill me" (2).
"Pensioner Tells How He Was Told to Thrash His Own Son," Gaye Davis	"A pensioner has described how he was taken to security police headquarters in De Aar in the Northern Cape and allegedly forced to beat his son with a sjambok. Simon Voko's allegations are contained in an affidavit backing a supreme court application by the De Aar Youth Congress (Dayco) for an order restraining police from unlawfully assaulting, detaining or intimidating its members" (5).
"Riot Police Shot ANC Seven 'in Self-Defence,'" Gaye Davis	"A Colonel who investigated the shooting by police of seven alleged African National Congress guerrillas in Gugulethu in 1986 was criticized by a Wynberg magistrate this week. Magistrate G Hoffman blamed Colonel Fanie Brits for the court's inability to hold a proper inquest soon after the deaths" (11).
"Soldiers Tell of Maseru Attacks," *Weekly Mail* reporter	"Two SADF soldiers told the Pietermaritzburg Supreme Court this week how they had attacked alleged ANC bases in Maseru residential area in December, 1982, 'eliminated' the male occupants and seized numerous documents. . . . Both witnesses said women and children were present in the houses they raided during the pre-emptive strike, but in the words of Heyns, 'We tried, as far as possible, to keep them out of the line of fire'" (page unreadable from copy).

| "Keepers of the Peace Are the 'Very Cause of Our Fears,'" Carmel Rickard | "A Supreme Court application to protect residents of Mpophomeni has spotlighted the role of the South African Police in Natal's political violence. The application to protect the residents of this township near Pietermaritzburg against alleged unlawful police activity was brought by a number of residents, three local ministers and the National Union of Metal Workers of South Africa (Numsa). They asked for an order restraining police from unlawfully assaulting, threatening, harassing or intimidating residents of the township" (7). |

MISCONDUCT BY POLICE AND MILITARY PERSONNEL—*NEW NATION*

| "Minister to Pay Damages" | "The Minister of Law and Order has agreed to pay damages to three Mooi River textile workers who were arrested and interrogated about a consumer boycott last year—and charged with failing to produce their dompasses [government passes colloquially termed "dumb passes"]. The charges were withdrawn on September 27. In an out-of-court settlement with Durban's Legal Resource Centre (LRC), the Minister has agreed to pay the men R750 each. He will also pay legal costs" (5). |
| "Court Told of Police 'Attack' on Home" | "The wife of one of three executive members of the Port Elizabeth Black Community Organisation (Pebco) who have been missing for two years this week told the Port Elizabeth Supreme Court that her house had been attacked and damaged by policemen. Mrs. Hashe told the court that her husband had disappeared on the night that he, Godolozi and Galela were supposed to see someone at the airport. The following night, her house was attacked by policemen, she told the court. She alleged that teargas was fired into the house, youths who were looking after her had been assaulted by police and that she had fallen and fainted during the attack" (3). |

"More Harassment Claims against 'Kitskonstabels'"	"The conduct of 'kitskonstabels' and municipal police has come under the spotlight again in the Cape and Eastern Transvaal. Allegations of harassment, intimidation, assault, theft and sexual abuse committed by kitskonstabels were made in the Cape Town Supreme Court this week by Cape Youth Congress (Cayco) members, who applied for an urgent interdict restraining the police, especially the kitskonstabels, from interfering with the organisation's meetings" (3).
"They Came in the Dark"	"Abducted top African National Congress (ANC) member Ebrahim Ismail Ebrahim, alias Roy Zaheer, this week gave a picture of the dramatic events surrounding his kidnapping from Swaziland to South Africa last December 15. This was in the form of an affidavit presented in court at Komatipoort" (18). [After this brief opening, the entire page of the newspaper contains the copy of the affidavit filed by Ebrahim. In the course of his story, he reveals how South African policemen came to the home he was staying at in Swaziland, tied him up, blindfolded and gagged him, and threatened to kill him if he shouted. They then took him across the border into South Africa against his will. During this ordeal, Ebrahim claims he had a conversation with one of his abductors, who told him stories about how the police had allowed one prisoner in the past to escape so that he could become a police informant, and when he "betrayed" the police, he "was subsequently killed." Ebrahim was eventually taken to the offices of the Pretoria security police, where he was told by other police officers that they had abducted other activists who had been living in Swaziland, and they also mentioned how they were able to turn one of these activists into a police informant.]

"Soldiers Beat Us, Say Youths"	"A terrifying account of assaults and interrogation with the use of a live snake emerged following the brief detention of at least seven youths in the St. Wendolins area near Durban two days before the municipal elections. Armed soldiers allegedly forced a number of youths to lie on their backs, then stood on their stomachs, beat them all over their bodies and questioned them about their 'leaders' and the whereabouts of firearms. The interrogators also put a live snake around one of the youth's neck during his brief detention. These are some of the allegations made in affidavits that were presented to the South African Defence Force (SADF) by the Progressive Federal Party (PFP) in Durban" (1).
"I Lied, Says Witness"	"One of the three activists who were due to be hanged today was convicted on evidence of a key state witness who had lied in court because of pressure from a security branch cop. Security police also visited the witness in September this year and warned him that if he involved himself in the petition for clemency, they would see to it that he be hanged in place of the condemned activist. This was alleged in an affidavit in support of an urgent application for a stay of execution for Paul Tefo Setlaba, a member of the Colesberg Youth Organisation. The application was unsuccessful. . . . The state witness, Xolile Bonase, who was 16 at the time of the trial, allegedly told a Charles Myaba that security police had told him exactly what to say in court or he would hang in the place of Setlaba" (1).
"Policeman Admits He Fired on Crowd"	"A former police lieutenant told the Supreme Court yesterday that he was forced to open fire in a crowd of people attacking a truck, and that he emptied his magazine because of the intensity of the attack. Willem Jacobus Smit was giving evidence in the R39 000 damages action brought against law and order minister Adriaan Vlok by Eveline Nomtshongwana, who was shot in the neck during the incident" (2).

"Weapon Planted on ANC Guerrilla's Body"	"A cop admitted in a Wynberg Inquest Court this week that someone must have planted the firearm next to the body of an alleged ANC guerrilla before a photograph, now being used as an exhibit in the hearing, was taken. . . . Mbelo's admission came a day after another cop, a Sergeant Wilhelm Bellingham, denied that he had planted weapons on one of the alleged guerrillas" (2).
"New Swazi Link to Hit Squads"	"A Commissioner of Police in Swaziland helped organise the abduction of an ANC member, now a police spy, from a jail near Manzini in August 1986. This is the latest claim made by self-confessed assassin Almond Nofomela. He says in an affidavit that a Major De Kock had told him and other members of the squad that the mission in which police spy Glory Lephosa Sidebe, known as September, was abducted, was organised with the commissioner of police of Swaziland" (1).
"Minister Pays Up"	"The Minister of Law and Order this week made an out of court settlement of R1170 to a Soweto resident in Port Elizabeth, whose shack was flattened by a hippo during unrest September 7 last year. In the papers which were to come to court, Amos Mbuli (36) alleged that the driver of the hippo drove negligently or alternatively drove into the shack deliberately" (2).

Appendix C
ANC TESTIMONY CONVEYED USING THE PROTECTED SPACE OF THE COURTS

WEEKLY MAIL **EXCERPTS**

"ANC Songs in Court as Passtoors Convicted of Treason," Pat Sidley	"Helene Passtoors, convicted yesterday of treason, said she found it no less strange for a foreigner like herself to work for the African National Congress 'than Americans or South Africans coming to liberate my parents in my country in World War II.' Passtoors, wearing the green, black, and gold colours of the ANC, was speaking in mitigation of sentence shortly before being found guilty of treason and not guilty of terrorism.... On her youth, [Passtoors] said that talk of Nazism and the resistance dominated her memory. 'The point made by adults was that we should know and understand how we were liberated from evil, we should know it should never, never happen again,' she said" (1).

| "A White Woman Tells Why She Joined Umkhonto," Jo-Ann Bekker | "Marian Sparg, a former journalist who was sentenced to 25 years imprisonment yesterday on charges of high treason and arson, told the Witwatersrand Supreme Court she had acted as a soldier for the banned African National Congress (ANC). The 29-year-old Rhodes University graduate is the first white South African woman known to have served as a member of the ANC's military wing, Umkhonto we Sizwe. . . . She said she regarded herself as a patriot rather than a traitor: 'Even as a white South African I do not owe any loyalty to a government which is clearly not based on the will of the people,' she said. . . . Shortly after her arrest in March, certain newspapers described Sparg as a lonely, overweight person who turned to revolutionary politics out of a desire to belong. It was an image difficult to reconcile with the woman who spoke in confident, measured tones about her political commitment. . . . The death in detention of black consciousness leader Steve Biko that year horrified her, Sparg added, as had the reaction of most whites around her, 'who simply did not seem to care.' Biko's death set her thinking about violence and pacifism. . . . However, she said, she did not regard herself as a violent person. 'I still maintain the hope that white South Africa and the Botha government will come to its senses and realise the conflict can be solved at a conference table. But it should not expect the ANC to suspend violence without a similar undertaking from the Botha government" (3). |

"ANC Accused Tells of *Witdoeke* in Crossroads," Gaye Davis	"The story of how a young man came to join the African National Congress unfolded in the Cape Town Supreme Court this week as Joseph Ngoma, convicted of terrorism under the Internal Security Act, gave evidence in mitigation of sentence. Ngoma's story began with his parents' extreme poverty. The family's staple diet was 'sweet water, bread and stamp mielies' [pounded corn] and he was 15 years old before he ate his first piece of buttered bread, he said. In 1976, when he was 17 and a Std 9 pupil at Langa High School, near Cape Town, he saw his friend shot dead by police after about 1 000 students marched on the Langa police station to ask for the release of fellow students. They were carrying placards reading: 'We are not fighting. Release our fellow students. Please don't shoot.' ... Two youths, who went to negotiate with police, were told the students would be released and that the marchers should return home. 'As we turned our backs the police started shooting. My friend was killed and other students injured. I picked up a bullet as big as my finger as a memo of that day.' Events at Crossroads squatter complex last year when thousands of shacks were razed was a further spur. 'I saw with my own eyes a certain warrant officer Barnard issuing arms to the so-called witdoeke. I also witnessed soldiers moving along with the so-called witdoeke burning the shacks of the people of Crossroads.' ... Gladwin Mabengeza, a 35-year-old scooter driver and father of six who was earning R 95 a week at the time of his arrest, ended his plea in mitigation by asking the bench: 'I wonder what you would do, my lord, if you were in my position in our country?'" (3).

"Mr. X, the ANC Commissar, Explains Why He Suddenly Changed His Mind," Gaye Davis	"Explaining why he had waited until he was in court before announcing his refusal to testify, Mr. X spoke calmly, without passion. In his blue suit, he was the image of the personnel manager he might have been in different circumstances. He did it because he was afraid—'of falling on a piece of soap . . . or from the 10th floor or down a flight of stairs,' he said. Driving home the point, he said he was afraid he would end up having a brain operation or that he would 'leave someone cold'—a reference to former justice minister Jimmy Kruger's comment on the death in detention of black consciousness leader Steve Biko" (10).

NEW NATION EXCERPTS

"I Can See Neil Agett Hanging"	"Unless things change radically, Helene Passtoors, mother of four, will be a free woman in 1996—ten long years. . . . To understand her beliefs, one must look at her history. Born during World War Two, tales of the resistance and lessons of fascism and nazism loomed large in her early life. It should 'never, never be allowed to happen again.' . . . 'I had a very, very strong duty to help the ANC. It was a general human rights duty to fight fascism. I would like to remind you that part of the party in power now, the National Party, was on Hitler's side during the Second World War,' she told the court. She said she wanted to be able to face her children. 'I owed it to my children. They were born in Africa and saw the things that I did. The time would come when they would say, 'Mama, it's nice you say all these things, but what have you actually done?' . . . The crowd was enthralled by her strong stance and clapped repeatedly when she refused to implicate anyone else, or disclose information about Joe Slovo [leader of the South African Communist Party]. . . . Eventually, defiantly wearing ANC colours, which she knitted in prison and shouting 'Amandla' and 'Victory' to a supportive crowd, she kissed her family and was led down to begin her sentence" (page unreadable from copy)

Appendix D

NEW NATION ARTICLES ON ANC ACTIVITIES ABROAD

"ANC Hails Shultz Talks"	"The African National Congress has welcomed the United States' new policy of dialogue with the organisation following this week's talks between the ANC and the US Secretary of State, George Shultz. An ANC spokesman, Tom Sebina, said in Lusaka that the US had now finally publicly recognized the ANC as a major factor in the search for solutions to the apartheid problem" (8). [A picture of Shultz appears next to this article with the following caption underneath: "George Shultz: his talks with Oliver Tambo are seen as a 'public recognition' of the ANC's vital role in achieving settlement in SA" (8).]
"Back Frontline States— ANC"	"The African National Congress (ANC) has called on members of the Organisation of African Unity (OAU) to stand by frontline states in condemning the South African government's 'violation of their territorial integrity and sovereignty.' The ANC's chief representative in Dar es Salaam, Stanley Mabizela, made the call at the OAU Council of Ministers meeting in the Ethiopian capital" (8).

"ANC to Consider 'Truce' Deal"	"The African National Congress is considering a 'truce' deal made by the Commonwealth's Eminent Persons Group, in a bid to halt the escalating violence in the country. The proposals apparently call for peace talks between the South African Government and the ANC that would be followed by the release of Nelson Mandela and the unbanning of the ANC" (1).
"Tambo Visit"	"The President of the African National Congress, Oliver Tambo, has arrived in Yugoslavia for a three-day visit, according to news sources. Tambo was due to meet Yugoslav leaders to review the situation in South Africa during his stay, the official Tanjug news agency reported" (8).
"ANC Out in Force at Summit"	"The African National Congress is mounting a massive political presence at next week's summit of the 101-member Non-Aligned Movement (NAM) in Harare, indicating the supreme importance of the struggle in South Africa attached to the meeting" (8). [Pictures of prominent ANC leaders surround this article, including one of Oliver Tambo with his fist clenched in the ANC salute. The week after this conference, *New Nation* featured a large picture of Oliver Tambo and Joe Modise on the front page with the following caption: "After hours of talking it was time for a break: African National Congress president Oliver Tambo with Joe Modise, the commander of the ANC's military wing, Umkhonto we Sizwe, at the eighth summit of the Non-Aligned Movement last week. Leader after leader slammed South Africa's racist policies at the summit" (1).]

Appendix E
BIBLE READINGS FROM THE RELIGION PAGES OF *NEW NATION*

"Don't be afraid of your enemies; always be courageous, and this will prove to them that they will lose and that you will win, because it is God who gives you victory." Phil 1:28, 25 September 1986, p. 14

"Their armies advance in violent conquest, and everyone is terrified as they approach. Their captives are as numerous as grains of sand. They treat kings with contempt and laugh at high officials. No fortress can stop them—they pile up earth against it and capture it. Then they sweep on like the wind and are gone, these men whose power is their god." Habakkuk 1:9–11, 9 April 1987, p. 14

"And now you rich people, listen to me! Weep and wail over the miseries that are coming upon you! . . . You have not paid any wages to the men who work in your fields. . . . You have condemned and murdered innocent people, and they do not resist you." James 5:1–5, 30 April 1987, p. 14

"They do not speak in a friendly way, instead they invent all kinds of lies about peace-loving people." Psalms 35:20, 4 June 1987, p. 14

"So then, as the body without the spirit is dead, so also faith without action is dead." James 2:26, 2 July 1987, p. 14

"Listen to the groans of prisoners, and by your great power free those who are condemned to die." Psalms 79:11, 9 July 1987, p. 16

"The boots of the invading army and all their blood-stained clothing will be destroyed by fire." Isaiah 9:5, 12 November 1987, p. 12

"When I speak of peace, they are for war." Psalms 120:7, 19 November 1987, p. 12

"Evildoers frustrate the plans of the humble man, but the Lord is his protection." Psalms 14:6, 10 December 1987, p. 12

"May they be defeated and terrified forever; may they die in complete disgrace." Psalms 83:17, 18 February 1988, p. 12

"When good men come to power, everybody celebrates, but when bad men rule, people stay in hiding." Proverbs 28:12, 14 July 1988, p. 15

"The dragon gave the beast his own power, his throne, and his vast authority." Revelation 13:2, 21 July 1988

"They laugh at other people and speak evil things; they are proud and make plans to oppress others." Psalms 73:8, 9 March 1989, p. 14

"He chose for us the land, where to live, the proud possession of his people, whom he loves." Psalms 47:4, 22 March 1989, p. 12

"How much longer must I wait? When will you punish those who persecute me?" Psalms 119:84, 18 August 1989, p. 18

"Proud men are coming to attack me; cruel men are trying to kill me—men who do not care about God." Psalms 54:3, 8 December 1989, p. 18

Appendix F

POLITICAL ISSUES COVERED IN THE RELIGION PAGES OF *NEW NATION*

Issue	Headlines
Allegations of governmental abuses	"Church Hits Out at Killings"; "'Solve the Bombings—or You'll Be Blamed'"; "Bugging Device Found at Church after Night Raid"; "Assassinations Inquiry Call"
Conscription	"ECC [End Conscription Campaign] Church Group Launched"; "Bishops Call for Draft Law Changes"; "Church Support for Objectors"; "Mother Objects to SADF [South African Defence Force] Call-Up"
Death penalty	"Death Row Ministry"; "Church Supports Tutu's Call for Reprieves"; "Hurley Calls for End to Hangings"
Defiance of emergency restrictions	"Church Leaders Threaten to Defy Emergency"; "Campaign to Go Ahead Despite the Emergency"; "Churches Call for Civil Disobedience"; "Priests Plan to Defy Funeral Restrictions"
Detention	"Serving God Led Him to Jail"; "Prayer Plea for Those Held"; "Detentions Call to Bishops"; "Bishops Express Sympathy for Detainees"
Economic sanctions	"No 'U-turn' on Sanctions"; "Support for Sanctions"; "US Lutherans Back SA Disinvestment"

Education	"Denial of Free Education a Violation of Human Rights"; "Call to Solve Education Crisis"
Forced removals/ homelessness	"Christmas Focus on Durban Homeless"; "Forced Removals Highlighted"; "Home Is a Right Not a Privilege"; "Church May Back Homeless"; "Hurley Slates Weenan Evictions"
Foreign policy— criticism of South African government	"Horrors of War in Region Come under Spotlight"; "Church Accuses SA of Not Honouring Nkomati Accord"
Hunger strikes	"Call for Catholics to Support Hunger Strikers"; "Focus Is on Hunger Striking Detainees This Good Friday"
Media restrictions	"Signs of the Times"; "Communication Is Key to Liberation"
Women's rights	"Women Unite"; "Women in Politics"
Workers' rights	"God's Message to Workers—and Bosses"; "Worker Struggle 'Part of Salvation History'"; "Uniting the Gatherers of the Crops"; "Ministers Back Soweto Strikers"

NOTES

INTRODUCTION

1. There are no in-text citations or endnotes detailing my interviews, but the names of all interviewees and the dates and location of all interviews are provided in the Works Cited.

2. Prior to his detention, Zwelakhe Sisulu had also been banned for a period in the early 1980s, when he was active in Media Workers Association of South Africa (MWASA), a union for black journalists. The Committee to Protect Journalists in a 1983 report revealed the onerous restrictions that were placed on Sisulu at that time: "Former MWASA President Zwelakhe Sisulu, whose father Walter is serving a life sentence with banned African National Congress leader Nelson Mandela, must get special permission to go to Cape Town on those rare occasions when he is permitted to visit his father. He must fly, despite the expense, on the theory that he could organize political meetings on the train. Sisulu's banning orders had to be amended because he was living with his mother Albertina who was also banned, and conversation between banned persons is prohibited. The amended orders allow conversation between Sisulu and his mother. The banning orders prohibit him from entering any factory, educational institution, or church. On weekends and public holidays he is under house arrest. He is not permitted to have visitors at his home" (25–26).

3. In many ways, this tension between individual rhetors and larger dynamics of power dates back to the rhetorical theories developed in ancient Greece. Aristotle offered many insights that continue to be useful for speakers and writers to this day, but neither he nor other classical rhetoricians focused extensively on the ways in which power constrains individual rhetors and how it affects their rhetorical situations. In fact, one concern sometimes raised about classical rhetoric is that it not only fails to theorize adequately about power but that it is itself implicated in elitist power relations. Moreover, the debates within writing studies that occurred in the 1980s between those conducting empirical research, perhaps best represented by the work of Linda Flower and John R. Hayes, and those who challenged some of the underpinnings of this research, such as Patricia Bizzell and James Berlin, are a manifestation of this tension. Subsequent scholarship sought to preserve the unit of analysis of early empirical research—individual writers—while also focusing on those moments in which writers negotiate imbalances in power. Ellen Cushman, for example, in her book *The Struggle and the Tools*, examines the linguistic practices of Quayville residents for the purposes of providing "an upclose account of the tight connection between agency and social structure as individuals maneuver through asymmetrical power relations" (xii). Shirley Wilson Logan's *We Are Coming: The Persuasive Discourse of Nineteenth-Century Black Women* and Jacqueline Jones Royster's *Traces of a Stream: Literacy and Social Change among African American Women*, meanwhile, focus on nineteenth-century African American women rhetors for similar purposes.

4. In *The Literature Police*, Peter McDonald also uses the term "space" when analyzing the ways in which the South African government censored literature. Part I of his book, for example, is actually entitled "Creating Spaces/Guarding Borders."

5. In many ways, the nature of writing space mirrors Bakhtin's description of the centripetal and centrifugal forces, acting upon language, that are constant, fluid, and saturated in power relations.

6. The collective nature of resistance necessary for expanding writing space is also consistent with considerable scholarship within writing studies. Thomas P. Miller and Joseph Jones examine this dynamic in a *College English* book review entitled, "Working Out Our History," in which they examine the following texts that focus on the important role women rhetors played in the black liberation struggle in the United States: Jacqueline Jones Royster's *Southern Horrors and Other Writings: The Anti-Lynching Campaign of Ida B. Wells* and *Traces of a*

Stream: Literacy and Social Change among African American Women; Jacqueline Bacon's *The Humblest May Stand Forth: Rhetoric, Empowerment, and Abolition*; and finally, Shirley Wilson Logan's *With Pen and Voice: A Critical Anthology of Nineteenth-Century African-American Women* and *We Are Coming: The Persuasive Discourse of Nineteenth-Century Black Women*. Miller and Jones observe that "[t]hese works suggest that our discipline's historical frame of reference is evolving beyond surveys of isolated individuals to reconceive of rhetoric as an art of collective agency rather than as individual persuasion" (425).

7. I am tremendously indebted to the scholarship of Deborah Brandt in my effort to make this link between the "micro" and the "macro." Specifically, Brandt's ideas concerning sponsorship illuminate the very real connections that exist between individual literacy practices and the larger economic, political, and historical forces that shape them: "Sponsors are delivery systems for the economies of literacy, the means by which these forces present themselves to—and through—individual learners" (19). Her ideas, in turn, challenged me to reflect on the links that exist between individual writers and the forces that serve both to constrain and foster their resistance.

8. Writing space encourages us to consider that some forms of government-imposed constraints exist for writers in every context, and again, with the exception of the most extreme situations, writers can engage in resistance with varying degrees of success. Rather than creating a binary of "censorship" versus "no censorship," therefore, writing space suggests more of a continuum. The North Korean government, which provides no writing space within the public transcript, exists at one end. At the other end of the spectrum, the US, Canadian, South African, and many European governments allow for a much wider but not unlimited range of expression. Located between these two ends of the spectrum are governments in places such as Russia, Venezuela, Iran, and Turkey, which, similar to apartheid South Africa, constrain writers much more significantly than democracies but not to the same extent as North Korea.

9. André Brink provides only a brief list of some of the writers banned by South African censors in his essay "Censorship and Literature":

> Among the literary corpses on the battlefield of about 20,000 titles prohibited in South Africa—*excluding* those of our entire generation of black writers silenced, with a single stroke of a bureaucratic pen, in the early 1960s and forced into exile—are names like Carlos Castaneda, Francoise Mallet-Joris, Emile Zola, John Updike, Robert Penn Warren, James Baldwin, Erskine Cald-

well, Jack Kerouac, Junichiro Tanizaki, William Styron, J. P. Donleavy, Vladi-
mir Nabokov, Henry Miller, Alberto Moravia, Mary McCarthy, Brendan Behan,
Nathanael West, Guy de Maupassant, André Pieyre de Mandiargues, Colin Wilson, Jean-Paul Sartre, Alain Robbe-Grillet, William Burroughs, Jean Genet,
Bernard Malamud, etc., etc., etc. (45)

10. *Grassroots* was produced and distributed primarily within Cape Town, whereas
    Saamstaan was produced and distributed primarily in the Southern Cape.

11. Drew Forrest claimed, "I think at its peak, we were never sure, I think we sold
    60,000. It was always unclear what the actual circulation figures were." Switzer
    and Adhikari also cite a similar circulation figure of 60,000 (46). One can safely
    assume, therefore, that the number of South Africans reading the *Weekly Mail*
    and/or *New Nation* on a weekly basis was in the hundreds of thousands given
    that a single edition would have been read by several people, due in part to the
    financial situation of black South Africans at that time.

12. At one point during my research, I had strongly considered examining both
    newspapers up to 1994, the year South Africa became a democracy and Man-
    dela was elected president. The primary question guiding my research, however,
    pertained to how writers circumvent government-imposed restrictions, and in
    terms of this issue, 1990 did represent a seismic shift. When asked to compare
    the challenges the *Weekly Mail* faced in the 1990–94 period with those between
    1985 and 1990, Harber responded, "I am not sure it is helpful to say whether the
    pressures of the latter period compare to the former. They were substantial, they
    were serious, they were difficult, but they were of a different order. Apples and
    oranges, as we say, even here" (personal email correspondence, 31 May 2009).
    Due to the timeframe I had decided to examine, I do not address some of the
    major stories published by these newspapers between 1990 and 1994, including
    the *Weekly Mail* articles on "Inkathagate." This explosive exposé revealed that
    Chief Mangosuthu Buthelezi, who publicly opposed the apartheid government
    and was viewed by many conservatives within the United States more favorably
    than the ANC (which had close ties with the South African Communist Party),
    was actually receiving payments from the apartheid government.

13. I conducted one interview with the editor of *New Nation*, Zwelakhe Sisulu, and
    two interviews each with the founders of the *Weekly Mail*, Anton Harber and
    Irwin Manoim. I subsequently had email correspondence with both Harber and
    Manoim and conducted a joint follow-up interview with them in the summer of
    2013. In addition, I was able to interview the lead attorney who worked with the

Weekly Mail, David Dison, as well as one of the lead attorneys for *New Nation*, Norman Manoim, brother of Irwin. I had the privilege of interviewing Father Smangaliso Mkhatshwa, the remarkable Catholic priest who helped secure funding for *New Nation* and who was serving as the deputy minister of education for South Africa in 1999. Finally, I of course conducted interviews with several of the journalists who wrote for these two newspapers.

14. When interviewing journalists, for example, I asked questions designed to elicit information concerning legal and extralegal constraints. The questions I posed to attorneys were based on the specific tactics they developed for evading the censorship restrictions. In addition to asking them about the finer points of the law, I asked them to describe the process of working with journalists and the extent to which they thought they were successful in conveying the intent and meaning of the original draft that journalists had produced. When I interviewed the person responsible for soliciting advertising for the *Weekly Mail*, Marilyn Kirkwood, or the person at *New Nation* who served as the liaison to the Southern African Catholic Bishops' Conference, Father Mkhatshwa, I focused less on matters pertaining to censorship legislation and more on the complex relationship that existed between the newspaper and its financial sponsors. Finally, the editors were concerned not only with the legal and economic constraints; they were also the ones, as noted above, who tended to be the targets of the extralegal harassment. I thus tried to elicit as much information as possible concerning all of these constraints during my interviews with Harber, Manoim, and Sisulu.

15. To avoid confusion in the text between Irwin Manoim, cofounder and coeditor of the *Weekly Mail*, and his brother Norman Manoim, I always use Norman's full name ("Norman Manoim") when referring to him. Since I cite Irwin Manoim so frequently, I refer to him either by his full name or as simply "Manoim" in sections where I am focusing on the *Weekly Mail* and am clearly referring to Irwin.

16. I had also initially wanted editors and journalists to perform "read-aloud protocols" with articles they had written during my interviews, a method used in writing studies in which writers read their work out loud and then comment upon significant choices they had made when composing that particular piece. Given that these journalists were writing on a weekly basis and that I was showing them articles they had written many years ago, it was understandably difficult for the first few journalists with whom I tried this approach to recall with any certainty the specific decisions they had made when writing a particular article. I thus determined early in the process to abandon read-aloud protocols and instead to conduct general interviews.

CHAPTER 1. "THAT'S HOW NUTTY IT WAS"

1. In the 1970s, for example, Donald Woods and Helen Zille helped uncover the story that Steve Biko, despite the government's claims that he had died as a result of a hunger strike while in detention, had in fact died of a brain hemorrhage as a result of a savage beating from the police. Donald Woods, the editor of the *Daily Dispatch*, whose story is depicted in the Hollywood film *Cry Freedom* (1987), was eventually banned by the apartheid authorities and had to leave South Africa in order to publish his book about the murder of Steve Biko. Tony Heard, the editor of the *Cape Times*, conducted an interview with the president of the African National Congress, Oliver Tambo, and published it shortly after the state of emergency had been declared in 1985. According to Merrett, Heard's interview with Tambo was "the first interview with an ANC leader to be published inside South Africa for a quarter of a century" (*Culture* 138). Of course, this directly contravened the censorship statutes, and the authorities subsequently charged Heard with violating the Internal Security Act, charges that were later dropped. Moreover, when the government began to target opposition newspapers such as the *Weekly Mail* and *New Nation*, the editor of the *Star*, Harvey Tyson, played an admirable role in trying to rally support from other mainstream newspapers on behalf of the *Weekly Mail*. There were, of course, many other examples of courageous acts on the part of journalists and editors within the mainstream who tried to circumvent or defy the censorship restrictions.

2. The authors of this Committee to Protect Journalists report, after questioning the NPU's approach, acknowledged the complexity of the situation: "In raising this question, of course, the delegation is mindful that individual newspapers and journalists would inevitably suffer if they tested the resolve of the government of South Africa to limit what may be published. In addition, it may be argued that more may be published through such self-censorship agreements between the press and the government than if the press refused to enter into such agreements and attempted to defy the government. The choices confronting the press in South Africa are not easy" (1983, 55–56).

3. In its submission to the Truth and Reconciliation Commission, the ANC was also quite critical of the South African mainstream press: "The South African media was, and is, a powerful institution. . . . The African National Congress believes that one of the greatest shortcomings of the commercial media was *its failure to use this power and influence to bring pressure on the apartheid system.* As disseminators of information, the commercial media failed to resist cen-

sorship and encroachments on its freedom. Instead, it chose to either willingly comply with the conditions laid down by an illegitimate government (in the case of the Afrikaans-language press) or to apply self-censorship" (in the case of the English-language press) through a range of agreements ("Role of the Media" 14; original emphasis).

4. Sidley's observations about the SABC refer to the televised news on the South African Broadcasting Corporation. The South African government actually did not allow television into the country until 1976, and when it finally did, the news, not surprisingly, was tightly controlled. Rian Malan, in his memoir *My Traitor's Heart*, provides his assessment of how SABC news shaped public opinion: "The South African Broadcasting Corporation dwelt lovingly on terrorist bombings in Paris, ethnic riots in Sri Lanka, and IRA knee-cappings in Belfast, as if to say, look, things are tough all over. It had very little to say about the ongoing mayhem in the townships, though. If it addressed the subject at all, it was to blame Communist agitators, who were said to be inciting children too young to understand what they were doing to sacrifice themselves in senseless acts of arson and violence" (159).

Robin Renwick, the British ambassador to South Africa during the late 1980s, offered this anecdote in his memoirs: "P. W. Botha on one occasion flew into a ferocious rage over the evening television news, telephoned the producer and had the news changed before the end of the programme!" (*Unconventional* 125). Ryland Fisher of *New Nation* offered perhaps the best description of the SABC with his seemingly tautological but insightful claim: "You must also understand that we were reporting in a context where the state broadcaster was exactly that: it was the state broadcaster."

5. Merrett writes, "The reason for the timing of the event [declaration of the first state of emergency] is still subject to speculation. Harber mentions the heightened unrest around Soweto Day, the recent cancellation of an All Black rugby tour, and the raising of the SACP flag (for the first time in such a public fashion) at the funeral of the Cradock Four" (*Culture* 113).

6. Drew Forrest explained: "When the state of emergency was first declared, the whole climate actually was one of fear and loathing. People were really scared. I can remember, for example, I was living in Yeoville [section of Johannesburg] at the time, hearing that the emergency had been declared, and thinking that I'm not going to stay in the house tonight, because there was the possibility that the cops are going to arrive. I just got in my car and drove around Johannesburg, for a long time, not wanting to come back."

7. Images coming out of apartheid South Africa in the 1980s and those coming out of the American South during the civil rights movement were strikingly similar in the ways they tarnished each government's international reputations. According to the PBS documentary series *Eyes on the Prize*, when Bull Conner ordered fire hoses and dogs to be used on protesters in Birmingham, Alabama, the televised images were particularly damning: "Photographs appeared in newspapers throughout the world, and the Birmingham story was told in many languages. The Russian newspaper *Pravda* ran a cartoon of police intimidating a black child. The federal government worried about America's image in other parts of the world" (Crossley and DeVinney).

8. The regulation prohibiting journalists from conveying the events that took place at "scenes of unrest" issued in November 1985 was particularly sweeping. It forbade

> any person from photographing, filming, or recording, as well as broadcasting or distributing within or outside South Africa any film, photograph, drawing, or sound recording, of any public disturbance, disorder, riot, public violence, strike, or boycott; or any damaging of property; or any assault on or killing of a person; or any person present at or involved in any of these activities; or any conduct of a force or member of a force with regard to the maintenance of the safety of the public or the public order or with regard to the termination of the state of emergency. (Cooper et al., *Race Relations Survey: 1985* 460)

9. According to the apartheid government, a subversive statement was one that

> discredited or undermined compulsory military service or which incited or encouraged members of the public or was calculated to have the effect of inciting or encouraging members of the public to
>
> take part in unrest . . .
> resist or oppose any member of the cabinet[,] . . . the government, or any official of South Africa . . .
> take part in a boycott action against a particular firm or against firms . . .
> take part in acts of civil disobedience . . .
> stay away from work or to strike unless it was in accordance with the Labour Relations Act of 1956 . . .
> attend or take part in any restricted gathering. (Cooper et al., *Race Relations 1986* 841)

10. To capture the full bleakness and desperation, Perkins writes in his memoirs

that this period in South Africa's history reminded him of the time he had witnessed a trapped female raccoon. Rather than allow herself to be captured, the mother proceeded to eat her young: "I felt this paralleled the Afrikaners' position when I was there—we were approaching a time when the Afrikaners would emulate the mother raccoon and say, 'This is the end for us, and we will now destroy everything we have accomplished, *along with the blacks.*' I thought it quite likely that they were considering using small-scale nuclear weapons on some of the townships, even with the knowledge that they would also be destroyed in the process. Intelligence information provided to the embassy would later confirm my suspicion" (280; emphasis in original).

11. Robin Renwick, the British ambassador to South Africa at the time, relates in his memoirs, "Like Mrs. Thatcher, neither I nor anyone else I knew warmed to P. W. Botha on this or any other occasion. His domed head and tinted glasses gave him a sinister appearance. He was in the habit of receiving me in a study lit only by his desk lamp, conjuring up images of what it must have been like calling on Hitler in his bunker. He was prone to furious rages, and his Ministers were terrified of him" (*Unconventional* 114). Renwick notes that Botha not only alienated world leaders and diplomats but even members of his own political party: "By this stage, he had long since ceased to listen to the advice of anyone except his security chiefs. [. . .] His party no longer were consulted and, I discovered, many leading Afrikaners deeply resented what they regarded as his determination to turn the government of South Africa into a Latin American–style military *junta*, complete with death squads" (114). Edward Perkins, the American ambassador, describes in his memoir his first meeting with Botha. After telling Botha that he planned to tour the country, Botha responded, "I don't want you getting involved in our affairs" (287). When Perkins responded that he needed to learn about South Africa by meeting a broad range of people so he could represent the US government to the best of his ability, Botha, he writes, then "stuck his finger in my face. 'Didn't I tell you that I don't want you to get involved in our affairs?' His two aides were shaking because they realized he had gone beyond the norms. When he put his finger in my face, it was like putting his finger in Reagan's face. He ranted on before he finally caught himself and ended the meeting" (287). Sen. David Boren, in the preface to Perkins's memoirs, praises Perkins at length in part because "I observed his incredible self-restraint and personal dignity in the face of racial insults hurled at him in a private meeting with then President P. W. Botha" (xvi).

12. There are countless individual stories to support these claims. Edward Perkins,

the US ambassador, described in his memoir some of the hardships that Percy Qoboza experienced: "He was a brave, outspoken critic of apartheid who had been persecuted, harassed, interrogated, and imprisoned for his vehement press attacks on the government, which had shut down two newspapers he edited. When the government began to crack down on black journalists, he remembered coming to work to find that nine reporters had disappeared, as if wiped off the face of the earth. He never saw some of them again" (403).

13. One of the more horrifying practices was "necklacing," which consisted of filling a tire with gasoline, putting it over a person's head, and setting it on fire.

14. When I asked Harber about Webster's killing and if that had an impact on him, he responded, "David Webster was such a shock to the white Left that had a level of immunity greater than the black Left. That's why Webster shook everyone up." Also, Amrit Manga of *New Nation* recounted that many white women political activists were raped in prison because they had "gone to the other side."

15. Amrit Manga, while never detained, recounted a chilling moment he experienced late one evening:

> I would be driving home and there would not be a soul on the street. And it's terrifying. I used to be terrified. There was a day, I mean, I still wouldn't be able to explain what this was all about, but as I drove down the street in Joburg, heading home, a car pulls out of the side street behind me. I get to a robot [traffic light]. It's red, so I'm waiting and this car pulls in front of me. This is the time you hear these tales of people getting shot and all kinds of things. The car pulls up in front of me, and here are these two guys, big, burly white chaps talking on their two-way radio. He checks my plates, gets back into his car, and this robot turns green, and I'm unable to go. And I'm thinking, do I reverse and try to run away? I said no, that would be stupid. So I sit there, it changes red again, goes green, and there is this car. And I'm sitting [there at] 2:00 a.m. in the morning— there's not a soul in sight. And the guy just wags his finger at me and I go on my way. And for the next month or so, I didn't write anything naughty! [laughter].

Manga was able to joke about this incident when interviewed, but his comment that "for the next month, I didn't write anything naughty," is revealing. Of course Manga more than likely did write "something naughty" given the nature of *New Nation*, but it is significant that he joked about this scary moment of intimidation in relation to the decisions he would make as a writer.

16. The Truth and Reconciliation Commission notes that torture was not used by the apartheid government at first. Joe Slovo testified as follows: "However firm

the old type of policemen were . . . they were not torturers. . . . In a sense, up to about 1960/1, the underground struggle was fought on a gentlemanly terrain. There was still a rule of law. You had a fair trial in their courts. Nobody could be kept in isolation. Up to 1963, I know of no incident of any political prisoner being tortured" (vol. 4, 195). That all changed. According to the TRC, "It was widely believed by many political activists of the time that, in the early 1960s, a special squad of security policemen received special training in torture techniques in France and Algeria and that this accounted for a sudden and dramatic increase in torture" (195). In addition, the TRC noted the following about the use of torture: "It is further believed that, in the early 1980s, joint co-operation agreements between South Africa, Argentina, Chile, and Taiwan led to further training opportunities and an exchange of ideas and experiences" (196).

17. Crowe recalled a story, humorous in hindsight, about how she managed to get a warning to Sisulu:

> Right outside our offices, because it was all glass, down in the streets . . . there was a group of journalists underneath our window, in particular, Peter Magubane, a South African photographer, very well known. . . . And I was drinking coffee and pretending to the police that I was just drinking coffee and looking down underneath and I threw my spoon to attract attention so that they would warn Zwelakhe not to come into the building. So I threw the spoon, which was only about one floor down, and it banged [Magubane] on the head [laughter]. Oh, he was furious! So he finally looked up and I said, "Don't let Zwelakhe come in. We're all under arrest." So they managed to get word to Zwelakhe, who I think had driven down our street but who was told by people in the area to get the hell out of there. So he did. And he went into hiding. In fact, we all went into hiding for a number of weeks, just went into different people's homes.

Eventually, the police released *New Nation* staff. According to Crowe, "Their powers could not keep us for more than twelve hours or something. They would have had to arrest us, and effectively, they weren't really looking for us. They were looking for Zwelakhe and they wanted our files."

18. The police could engage in other forms of harassment that, in the words of Pat Sidley, a *Weekly Mail* journalist, were "irritating more than anything else." One example she provided: "Slashing tires—when I was nine months pregnant [laughs]. In the boot, where I would have gotten my spare out of, I couldn't get into because it was quite high off the ground and my pregnant tummy wouldn't— and it was midnight and it was in the Alexandra township." When asked if she

was certain it was the police, Sidley responded, "Absolutely. No doubt at all." Although Sidley laughed about this incident and described it as "irritating more than anything else," it could have in fact been quite dangerous to be stranded in the Alexandra township at midnight during the turbulent and violent 1980s.

19. Clive Cope recalled the threats he received when the *Weekly Mail* ran a story about "petty apartheid" laws (segregated park benches, pools, and so on) that the apartheid government at one point had repealed in an attempt to demonstrate its commitment to "reform." Shortly thereafter, black journalists working for the *Weekly Mail* went to a small town to write a story based on their experiences after the repeal of these laws. Because Cope was the office manager, the vehicles these journalists traveled in were registered in his name. Cope recalled, "Suddenly I got a death threat on the telephone. These guys said, 'We're coming to get you,' just when the article appeared. 'We're going to come and shoot your brains out.'" After receiving these threats, Cope explained, "We put a guard on my house. *Ja*, we had a twenty-four-hour guard on our house."

20. Indeed there was widespread admiration and respect for both Harber and Manoim for taking this initiative in the wake of the closure of these two newspapers. Many sang their praises, unprompted, in the course of providing answers to other questions. David Dison, who was their primary attorney, observed, "Between Manoim and Harber, they were such geniuses. I mean Manoim was exactly my contemporary at school, and he was a writing genius. And he is a writing genius. He won the writing prize at school. He was a serious talent. Plus he was, you know, the designer. Harber was really the network guy—he was the connected reporter. And they were a fabulous team." Drew Forrest, whom I interviewed about his experiences at *New Nation*, said of the *Weekly Mail*, "I mean, there were very skilled journalists there. A guy like Irwin Manoim is one of the most skilled journalists in the country. I have boundless respect for him." Forrest later described Manoim as "one of the kindest people on earth. There's a genuine fellow-feeling there."

21. In Manoim's book there is a picture of Harber and Manoim holding up a copy of one of their front pages. Manoim's caption captures the sense of exhaustion evident on both their faces: "It is early 1987 and the editors, in the words of one visiting reporter, have 'sandblasted eyes.' Eighteen months of late-night stress lie behind" (*Warned* 106). Manoim then quips of their longish hair "and there is no immediate prospect of a quick visit to the barber" (106).

22. Phillip van Niekerk commented at length about the complexities of this relationship between the *Weekly Mail* and the ANC:

Our advocacy was a human rights advocacy and that human rights happened to
coincide with the liberation movement. But if it flipped around, as in the case
of Winnie [Mandela], or in the case of the ANC camps in Angola and Tanzania,
we would write quite tough stuff about that as well. Okay, so ours was sort of a
general principle of human rights, whereas the *New Nation* was more secretly
advocating the liberation movement. That is a critical difference. I'm not sure
everybody at the *Weekly Mail* felt the same way that I did. There were a lot of
people at the *Weekly Mail* who specifically advocated the liberation movement.
But the way I justified it to myself, I'd say, "Well, it's human rights. And that's a
valid kind of reporting anywhere in the world."

23. When asked what he thought about journalism aligned with political organizations, Manoim responded, "We considered it to be highly problematic. I had
some personal experience with [that on] some of the other newspapers I worked
with. Because you ended up, you know, there were frequently internal tensions
inside unions which would be suppressed by those publications, or they would
run the leadership line. I mean it was about, very infrequently, lying to your
membership in support of the current leadership cadre. We didn't support that.
There were journalists on our staff who did, so there were frequently arguments
about that."

24. This dynamic, of course, is not confined to apartheid South Africa. In *Necessary Illusions*, Noam Chomsky discusses in his analysis of the *Daily Herald* in
England the importance of having the "right kind" of audience, namely, those
with economic power. The *Daily Herald*, part of the labor-oriented press, had
a huge audience, approximately "five times as many readers as the *Times* and
'almost double the readership of the *Times*, the *Financial Times* and the *Guardian* combined'" (24). Nevertheless, this newspaper was unable to survive financially, which he discussed in an interview with Bill Moyers: "That journal and
other social democratic journals disappeared, primarily because of standard
market pressures. They couldn't get advertising. Their advertising rates were
too low because they had the wrong kind of readers. They couldn't reach capital markets for support, not because they didn't appeal to people, but because
they had the wrong ideas. They disappeared. Now there's no conspiracy in that.
Those are the workings of power" (44).

25. Mkhatshwa, a longtime vocal critic of apartheid, was detained in 1976 for 136
days, and he received a five-year banning order in 1977 that placed him under
house arrest from 6:00 a.m. to 6:00 p.m. In 1982, the authorities extended his

banning for three more years. In 1983, he was arrested for "subversion" and spent four months in prison (Nyaka, "It's Trouble" 8). Mkhatshwa was detained again in 1986, and this time he was tortured. His account was conveyed in a *New Nation* article, "Police Torture Claims Mount," a summary of which is provided in appendix B under the heading "Torture—*New Nation*."

26. Marilyn Kirkwood, responsible for obtaining advertising for the *Weekly Mail*, explained how many people in the South African business community were reluctant to advertise in the *Weekly Mail* because they perceived the newspaper as too radical and too focused on black South Africans. If the *Weekly Mail*, as Kirkwood joked, generated a "fright factor" for potential advertisers, *New Nation* would have generated a "terror factor." A newspaper with a black editor, mostly black journalists, targeting the black community, and aggressively challenging the government was simply never going to receive the necessary advertising revenue in apartheid South Africa. Without the funding provided by the Catholic Church, therefore, this newspaper would have never been founded and would have never survived. The decision by the South African bishops to fund *New Nation* caused considerable strife within the South African Catholic Church.

27. Amrit Manga, for example, spoke at length about the lack of bylines. For starters, Manga explained that many of those who wrote for *New Nation* were not necessarily "seasoned journalists" but rather those "who had come and who had lived the struggle in their communities. They're not journalists. We brought them into the newsroom and we got them to write." This, Manga explained, had implications for some of the writing that was produced: "To turn their work into something that we would then be able to print, something that was readable and accessible to everyone, a lot of work had to go into it. So it would go through a process. At any one point, you would have three or four people looking at one piece of writing. So in a real sense, it wasn't just one person that wrote any one story." Manga explained that this process was used for his articles as well, even though he had years of experience as a journalist: "Even my analysis, if I put it all together at the end of the day, it wasn't all my work. I would take ideas from a whole range of people and we would have lots of play with Zwelakhe as the editor, and then put it all together. And that kind of stuff doesn't come out of one office—somebody sits in a corner and then thinks up all these ideas. It was very much a collective effort. It was true of the entire paper." Tyrone August concurred: "The people who established the *New Nation* were trying to develop some kind of collective journalism to try to

get away from the individual scoop, that kind of mentality. I think they were trying to do something very different." August also commented on the security concerns: "I don't think it was the main consideration, but I think there was a security consideration as well." Cullinan agreed: "There was a deliberate policy not to give bylines, and part of the reason for that was it was protecting journalists so the state never knew who wrote what, and from that point of view, we were protected."

28. Ryland Fisher explained:

> *New Nation* was aimed almost at leadership within these communities. Even though we tried to keep the writing fairly simple, you know, it wasn't a popular paper in the sense of a tabloid, where you have your page-3 girls and you keep your story short, and in that way, you draw more people, more readers. [Populist newspapers] get [readers] by using popular mechanisms and then you spread the gospel. *New Nation* was never like that. The people who read *New Nation* knew what it stood for, and a lot of them were people who had a certain level of literacy and education.

One flashpoint for *New Nation* pertaining to this issue: the depiction of women. The newspaper did not feature what Sarah Crowe described as the "page-3 Dolly Birds," a common practice of tabloids in many countries. As Amrit Manga explained, this would have been inconsistent with its political views of gender equality. Manga related a story concerning this issue based on an interaction with Govan Mbeki, a prominent member of the South African Communist Party imprisoned on Robben Island and also the father of Thabo Mbeki, South African's second democratically elected president after Mandela:

> Govan Mbeki had just been released from jail. We went to see him as well, and he made an incredibly interesting comment. We said, "What do we do?" He said, "You know what you do? On page 3, you put a bikini-clad girl on it. That's what you do." And he says, "When these chaps, when these police, open this paper, they see this and they're not going to read the bloody thing." So there were, I mean from all angles, a sense that we had to do it more strategic. We had a position on general equality that conflicted directly with what he believed. I mean, there would have been a revolt in the *New Nation*'s newsroom had we done that, but this is what he suggested we do.

The possible success of Mbeki's suggestion seems doubtful. By the time of his release, *New Nation* had already garnered a reputation as a radical, opposition newspaper, and it seems unlikely that images of "bikini-clad" women on page 3 would have successfully deflected the attention of the police.

29. Those writing for *New Nation* were mindful that English was not the first language for many of their readers. Amrit Manga on the many complexities of writing in English:

> We were always very conscious of the fact that the audience we were addressing were not sophisticated in English, so we tried to write as simply as we could, which, in a sense, came naturally because the people that wrote were equally unsophisticated [with English]. None of us were necessarily schooled in the English language. No one did masters, PhDs in English. English wasn't necessarily the home language. So we wrote very simple English. . . . I know that people in the trade union movement had lots of white activists who had come from the Left. Very sophisticated people [such as] Alec Irwin, and they made the comment that the *New Nation* distinguished itself because it was able to express all these complex issues in a very simple way.

30. *New Nation* sought to convey information about these abuses not only to black South Africans but to an international audience as well. Drew Forrest made the following observation: "I'm sure [*New Nation*] was read by the embassies. And it probably would have been read by foreign correspondents operating in the country. The idea would have been to get that kind of perspective and as much news as that kind to the outside world. I mean, there was major pressure on the government at the time. And that's why they introduced the emergency regulations, because they wanted to put a damper on the kind of negative publicity that was going to the outside world."

31. A similar dynamic is currently playing out in China. In an NPR report broadcast on 2 June 2017, Beijing correspondent Anthony Kuhn responded as follows when asked if there are protests in China today: "Certainly. There are protests all the time. But they are not about making the central government more democratic. They're about resolving specific issues, and it's been this way for years. They're about local corruption, they're about demolition of homes, they're about people getting swindled out of their money by fraudsters, they're about pollution, they're about crooked cops. These are all local issues and the government has been very effective harnessing technology to make sure these people do not link up, making sure they do not use social media to organize street protests."

32. Drew Forrest explained why he also did "not have a problem" with advocacy journalism:

> I do think it is important to present both sides of the story and be journalis-
> tically fair and that sort of thing. And I think under normal conditions—and
> you've got normal conditions in this country at the moment pretty much, you've
> got a free press—those are the rules that ought to apply. But in a situation where
> one side cannot have its say, I don't have any problems with advocacy and with
> pushing a line. Because often now, [people] poke fun at the alternative media
> and that they basically "betrayed" certain basic journalistic principles and that
> sort of thing. I don't know if under those conditions that [this criticism] is jus-
> tified.

33. The hatred of the government and the police for these newspapers was so extreme, Ryland Fisher explained, that "sometimes people would be arrested for being in possession of the paper [*New Nation*]." When I asked him how that was possible given that *New Nation* was not a formally banned publication, he explained that "[w]ithin the state of emergency, the police had tremendous pow-ers and they could argue that, you know, *New Nation* published subversive arti-cles and if they caught you with subversive literature, they could just detain you if they wanted to. And in some cases they did." Merrett cites one documented case: "In November 1988, a Lebowa youth was arrested at a bus stop for reading *New Nation*" (*Culture* 125). In his book *You Have Been Warned*, Irwin Manoim cites an article published by Carmel Rickard in 1988 describing how a youth was beaten for having a copy of the *Weekly Mail*: "A high school pupil covered in bruises walked into the *Weekly Mail*'s Durban bureau and claimed he had been beaten by a KwaZulu policeman for being in possession of the 'World' section of the *Weekly Mail*" (86). According to Rickard's report, when the youth told the police he had purchased the *Weekly Mail* "in town," the police claimed "he was lying and it was a 'communist newspaper'" (86).

34. The Apple ad featured images of a completely oppressed society as a Big Brother-like figure speaks from a giant screen. A young, athletic woman is then shown running toward the Big Brother visage, and before she is captured by the pursuing police, she flings her sledgehammer and shatters the screen. A voice-over then states, "On January 24th, Apple Computer will introduce Macintosh. And you'll see why 1984 won't be like *1984*."

35. Manoim describes in an essay he wrote, with the clever title "Voortrekkers of Tech," how he developed the idea to use this technology. He was looking through

a magazine that featured an ad for an Apple laser printer that explained how "laser printers may one day eliminate the need for expensive typesetting equipment, darkrooms, chemicals and skilled technicians, says the magazine. And, it occurs to me, make it possible for people with almost no money to produce a newspaper" (71).

36. Unfortunately, Manoim's love for Apple products was not reciprocated. At the time, Manoim explained his "relationship with Apple was one of unrequited love.... I was obsessed with their products, read every Mac magazine or technical manual I could lay hands on (not easy in sanctions days), evangelised on their behalf, which is why *New Nation, South* and the unions all adopted the same system" (personal email correspondence, 3 November 2014). Manoim's commitment and gratitude toward Apple was so intense that he actually decided to write to them: "I wrote a letter to Apple in the US to tell them how their marvelous computers were aiding the heroic struggles of the anti-apartheid alternative press. Six months later I received a letter asking me not to correspond with Apple again" ("Voortrekkers" 72). Apple's response to Manoim's letter is indeed baffling. Why would a corporation, especially one that advertised its product as one that facilitated resistance to oppression, *not* embrace the *Weekly Mail*? As Manoim explained, "I wrote to them in the hope of arousing their enthusiasm, Apple having a reputation (unwarranted?) for being sympathetic to leftish causes. I think the letter was accompanied by copious explanations and examples of our work" (personal email correspondence, 3 November 2014). Manoim also noted that they "were very conscious of Apple being the good guys" (personal email correspondence, 3 November 2014). Apart from supporting the *Weekly Mail* on moral and ethical grounds, one would have thought supporting opposition newspapers in apartheid South Africa would have been in Apple's self-interest: here was a newspaper using one of its products to resist arguably the most despised government in the entire world at the time, particularly in the eyes of many of Apple's customers in the United States and western Europe. It was a potential marketing campaign that did not require the fiction of George Orwell. Manoim could only speculate about Apple's cold, impersonal response to his letter and their unwillingness to provide any assistance. He observed that he "may even have addressed the letter direct to Steve Jobs. (Unaware that perhaps he'd been pushed out somewhere around that time)" (personal email correspondence, 3 November 2014). Instead of getting a response from Jobs or a top-ranking executive, Manoim recalled, "I don't recall the precise wording of the disappointing response, but it came from some minor underling, ignored the

content of my letter and told me either that they did not deal with South Africa or to address future correspondence to a European subsidiary" (personal email correspondence, 3 November 2014).

CHAPTER 2. "IN THE INTEREST OF THE PUBLIC"

1. In one section of his memoir, Mathabane recalls a conversation he had with Helmut, a German living in apartheid South Africa who befriends Mark. Helmut claims, "[T]his whole thing [apartheid] reminds me of what Hitler did to my country. . . . There could yet be another Holocaust in the world" (279). Mathabane responds:

> I think a Holocaust is taking place right now in this country. There are no gas chambers or ovens this time, but black people are dying by the tens of thousands. Just look at the black infant mortality rate. This country has the best medical facilities in the world—Christiaan Barnard performed the first heart transplant here. It exports food—but just look at the government's homeland policies of breaking up families and carting women and children to deserts where there's no food. And what are homelands if not open-air concentration camps? Just look at the murder rate in the ghettos. Because people aren't allowed to work without permits and passes, they kill each other in order to survive. And finally, just look at what is happening to the black man's mind: loss of self-esteem, apathy, mental illness. What does all that add up to? Genocide. (279–80)

2. Bloemfontein was, and is, one of the three capital cities in South Africa and serves as the nation's judicial capital.
3. "The consequence for some applicants and witnesses was in turn assassination, at which point the system of recourse to legal process for publicity began to lose popularity" (Merrett, *Culture* 139).
4. MK is the abbreviation used for Umkhonto we Sizwe, or Spear of the Nation, the armed wing of the ANC.
5. André du Toit writes, "It is thus safe to say that currently the political component amounts to *well over half* of all the material subjected to publications control" (83; original emphasis).
6. In fact, Gilbert Marcus, from Wits University's Centre for Applied Legal Studies, claimed that the committees had a "deliberate and almost contemptuous disregard of the guidelines laid down by the PAB" ("Lawyer Claims" 5).
7. The Rivonia Trialists were those members of the ANC's armed wing, the MK,

who were put on trial in 1963–64. They were charged with treason and faced the death penalty. It was at this trial that Mandela delivered his famous speech that concludes with "it is an idea for which I am prepared to die."

CHAPTER 3. "OBLIQUE SPEAK"

1. Shirley Wilson Logan notes in her book how nineteenth-century African American women utilized allusions in many of their speeches. The advantages of allusions are perhaps obvious in contexts where there are clear threats for writers/speakers, such as violence, imprisonment, and the like.

2. Adriaan Vlok testified before the Truth and Reconciliation Commission, saying, "Mr. Botha . . . told me . . . 'I have tried everything to get them [the Council of Churches] to other insights, nothing helped. We cannot act against the people, you must make that building unusable'" (vol. 2, 291).

3. The *Weekly Mail* and *New Nation* were not the only newspapers that used coded language. Merrett recounts the following incident: "Inkatha members rode into Ashdown on police vehicles in the course of an attack: foreign reporters risked deportation by dispatching full accounts, but locally only a broad and highly codified version was acceptable. Journalists wrote about 'armed white men,' 'white men wielding whips,' 'shotgun-toting men dressed in tracksuits,' and 'people running away holding jerseys to their mouths,' which was interpreted by the alert as a teargas attack by the police and kitskonstabels on township dwellers. Even this elicited abusive phone calls from conservative whites" (*Culture* 130).

4. Given the seemingly inexhaustible list of rhetorical terms, there may be terms other than "subversive enthymeme" to refer to this tactic of indirection. "Significatio," for example, is defined as "to imply more than is actually stated" (Lanham 138). "Schematismus" is defined as "circuitous speech to conceal a meaning, either from fear or politeness, or just for fun" (Lanham 136). While fear was an important consideration for these journalists, they were certainly not using this form of oblique speak because of "politeness" or "fun." There could, of course, be others, but in the final analysis I prefer "subversive enthymeme" for two reasons. First, the enthymeme is a well-known rhetorical term that has generated considerable scholarship; second, "subversive" captures an important essence of this particular tactic.

5. Sometimes there were no bodies to recover. One practice used by members of the security forces was to burn the body completely so there was no evidence of the assassination. Dirk Coetzee related the following in his testimony to the TRC:

The burning of a body to ashes takes about seven hours, and whilst that happened we were drinking and even having a braai [barbecue] next to the fire. Now, I don't say that to show our braveness, I just tell it to the Commission to show our callousness and to what extremes we have gone in those days ... the chunks of meat, and especially the buttocks and the upper part of the legs, had to be turned repeatedly during the night to make sure that everything burnt to ashes. And the next morning, after raking through the rubble to make sure that there were no pieces of meat or bone left at all, we departed and all went on our way. (vol. 2, 235)

In many instances, the TRC was able to recover the bodies of those who had gone missing based on information provided by those applying for amnesty. In situations where the body was burned, there was obviously nothing for the victims' families to recover.

6. Joe Slovo, the leader of the South African Communist Party (SACP), was the number one white enemy of the apartheid government. His wife, Ruth First, was a prominent activist who had been detained by the South African authorities and spent extensive periods of time in solitary confinement. She eventually left South Africa but remained active in the anti-apartheid struggle. In 1982, she was murdered when members of the apartheid security forces sent a letter bomb to her office in Mozambique.

7. There was also a darker and more sinister use of oblique speak in apartheid South Africa with regard to security force action. The Truth and Reconciliation Commission revealed how those operating in the shadows of the apartheid government often used oblique speak and veiled rhetoric as well: "Nowhere in any of the SSC [State Security Council] documents is a clear and unambiguous definition provided for any of the terms *elimineer* (eliminate), *neutralisser* (neutralise), *fisiese vernietiging* (physical destruction), *uithaal* (take out) or *ander metodes as aanhouding* (methods other than detention)" (vol. 2, 274). As Pik Botha explained to the commission, the use of this language led to the following dynamic: "Members of the security forces would have interpreted a phrase like 'wipe out the terrorists' to include killing them, and unless the senior command structures of the security forces made sure that all ranks understood the distinction between a person who is directly engaged in the planning and execution of acts of violence threatening the lives of civilians on the one hand, and political opponents belonging to the same organisations as the terrorists on the other

hand, lower ranks would probably not have made that distinction on their own" (vol. 2, 274). Oblique speak, therefore, was used not only by opposition journalists but also by those ordering assassinations of activists. Oblique speak—similar to rhetoric and technology—is morally neutral. Its value ultimately depends upon how it is used.

CHAPTER 4. "A HOPE IN HELL"

1.. Norman Manoim of *New Nation* agreed: "To the extent that one understood what these guys were saying, most of the time, I think you knew how their heads worked. But sometimes, what looked like quite an innocent article may have been objected to—I mean, we didn't see it in this way. And we were worried about this article, and they don't seem to see it. So certainly their own gloss on this was sometimes confusing."

2. Nyaka seemed to have a distinct advantage over other journalists in that he actually lived for a period with David Dison, the main attorney from the *Weekly Mail*, an expert on the censorship restrictions: "We had a guy called David Dison, and I was living with him in the same flat. We would talk about this, he would tell me, listen this means that, this means that, you know, just discuss it." Nyaka went to live with Dison when his life was threatened in the township where he lived.

3. Harber's analysis of how a system of censorship over an extended period of time can cultivate self-censorship is echoed in an observation made by Aluf Benn, editor in chief of *Haaretz* newspaper. Benn explained the ambiguous role that military censors play for journalists in Israel. On the one hand, censors can provide a layer of protection because newspapers cannot be prosecuted by the government for conveying "sensitive information" if it has been approved by the censor. On the other hand, the military censors can also induce, in Benn's words, "self-censorship": "They [journalists] know some stuff will not see the light of day. So why bother even researching it?" (qtd. in Abramson).

4. The idea that the laws created by governments can be illegitimate, and therefore opposed, is one that has of course been expressed in many contexts from a variety of perspectives. In Martin Luther King Jr.'s "Letter from Birmingham Jail," he invokes both theology and philosophy to make a critical distinction between "just" and "unjust" laws. King argues that one has a moral obligation to defy unjust laws. Archbishop Óscar Romero discussed this idea in a theological context when he made his passionate appeal to members of the death squads in El Salvador: "No soldier is obliged to obey a law contrary to the law of God. In

the name of God, in the name of our tormented people, I beseech you, I implore you; in the name of God I command you to stop the repression" (qtd. in Dickey). Noam Chomsky examines this issue from a secular perspective, using the concept of "better justice" to determine which laws citizens should and should not follow. In a moderated discussion he had with Michel Foucault, Chomsky stated,

> The concept of legality and the concept of justice are not identical; they're not
> entirely distinct either. Insofar as legality incorporates justice in this sense
> of better justice, referring to a better society, then we should follow and obey
> the law, and force the state to obey the law and force the great corporations to
> obey the law, and force the police to obey the law, if we have the power to do
> so. Of course, in those areas where the legal system happens to represent not
> better justice, but rather the techniques of oppression that have been codified
> in a particular autocratic system, well, then a reasonable human being should
> disregard and oppose them, at least in principle; he may not, for some reason, do
> it in fact. (Chomsky and Foucault, 181)

The attempts by those at the *Weekly Mail, New Nation,* and other opposition newspapers in apartheid South Africa to oppose the illegitimate media restrictions may have been viewed as "radical" at the time. But they certainly appear now, as Chomsky notes, as the actions of "reasonable human being[s]."

5. Labor unions such as COSATU served as major sources of legal opposition to the regime, given that the apartheid government had officially banned so many political parties, including the ANC, the SACP, and the Pan African Congress.

6. Merrett provides the various warnings that newspapers printed for their readers. He lists a total of thirteen examples. Some are quite short, such as *South*'s warning: "You have the right to know." Others, such as the one used in the *Sunday Tribune,* were lengthier: "Severe restrictions have been placed on newspapers. These make it increasingly difficult to report on unrest-related matters. This newspaper, however, will continue to provide the most balanced information that it can" (qtd. in *Culture* 145). Despite the different wordings used, all of these warnings clearly served the same purpose.

7. The *Weekly Mail* was not the only newspaper to block out text to indicate to readers that certain information could not be revealed publicly. As Merrett observes, "Newspapers appeared with heavy black lines through censored portions; *Ilanga, Weekly Mail,* the *Star,* and the *Sowetan* all used blank spaces, and

the last ran a blank box instead of a leader. The *Weekly Mail* of 20 June 1986 used black lines and white space, axing photographs, an article, and a cartoon. Such indications of censorship were themselves banned in July" (*Culture* 116).

8. Manoim describes in his book the interaction with the police the first time the newspaper was printed with the black lines:

> It was after midnight when two visitors arrived, burly men in blue jeans and tackies, with big bulges under the armpits of their plastic jackets. No one needed to ask who they were. They wanted to buy copies of the paper. One of them took out a wallet and counted out change. "Take it. It's free," said Harber. But no, the policemen insisted on paying. We stood and watched as they read through the paper, slowly, methodically, every article. In silence. We looked for flickers of emotion: a scowl, a smile, anything that betrayed what they thought. Nothing. The men stood and read for thirty minutes. Just over a minute spent studying each of the twenty-eight pages. Then they announced that they were leaving. "How does it look to you?" said Harber with feigned cheerfulness. "It looks all right," the man said. "Our lawyers went over every word." "Yes. I can see that they did. Goodnight." (*Warned* 67)

9. Performing a toyi-toyi was a popular form of resistance that consisted of individuals jumping up and down, holding their fists in the air, chanting, and singing in unison. It is very impressive to observe, particularly when large numbers of people perform it together.

10. Judge Richard Goldstone, one of the most progressive judges during apartheid, issued several rulings that curbed the excesses of the government. He subsequently prosecuted Serbian war criminals on behalf of the UN, was named by Mandela to serve on the Constitutional Court after South Africa became a democracy, and helped to produce for the UN a report, subsequently very controversial, that criticized both Hamas and Israel for potentially committing war crimes.

11. I am aware of the masculine pronoun in this sentence, but judges in apartheid South Africa were all men.

CHAPTER 5. "THE NATS BELIEVED IN LEGALISM"

1. Manga described this process from the journalists' perspective: "They [the lawyers] were not at all innovative. As I said, they were very conservative in instructing in the letter of the law. So we would suggest ways of getting around:

'What if we said it this way? Is there a possibility of getting around it? Or what if we said it that way?' It never worked, but those were the kind of things that we tried."

2. In terms of who had actual authority concerning what was and was not published within the pages of *New Nation*, the editor or the attorneys, comments from interviews paint a mixed picture. Ryland Fisher described a relationship similar to the one described by Harber at the *Weekly Mail*. Fisher claimed, "In fact, what the lawyers said was ultimately, 'It's up to you guys. You must make a decision. We can only advise you.'" Others, however, indicated considerably more deference to the attorneys. Manga stated that while journalists would "actually push [attorneys] and made all kinds of suggestions," in the end, he claimed, "I think nine times out of ten, we would respect their views." Drew Forrest concurred: "Look, there would be some discussion about it. But I think everybody accepted that [Norman] Manoim was the person who understood the law, particularly the implications of the security legislation, better than anybody there, and nobody was really in a position to really argue with him. So if he ordered something to be removed, it would be removed."

3. Indeed, Mandela was concerned about people's unrealistic expectations of him when he was released from prison. As Bill Keller observed in a *New York Times* column, "In 1994, shortly after Nelson Mandela was inaugurated as the first president of all South Africans, one of the local newspapers ran an interview with him under a huge, boldface headline: 'MANDELA: I'M NOT "MESSIAH."' That this would be considered banner news testified to the degree of myth and the unreality of expectations that attended the man."

4. White South Africans were not the only ones who had a negative view of Mandela and the ANC before the end of apartheid. In 1986, 180 members of the US Congress voted against a resolution that called both for the release of Nelson Mandela and for formally recognizing the ANC. One of those who opposed that resolution: Rep. Dick Cheney. When he became George W. Bush's running mate in 2000, Cheney defended his vote against this resolution: "[A]t the time [the ANC] was viewed as a terrorist organization and had a number of interests that were fundamentally inimical to the U.S." (qtd. in Gonzalez and Goodman). Bill Clinton, who developed a close personal friendship with Mandela during his presidency, subsequently said of Cheney's vote, "[I]t takes your breath away" (qtd. in Lewis).

5. The government had good reason for preventing members of the ANC from expressing their views freely. Mandela also describes in his memoir the inter-

actions he and his ANC colleagues had with the prison guards at Robben Island: "He [the warder] even began to ask questions about the ANC. By definition, if a man worked for the prison service he was probably brainwashed by the government's propaganda. He would have believed that we were terrorists and Communists who wanted to drive the white man into the sea. But as we quietly explained to him our nonracialism, our desire for equal rights, and our plans for redistribution of wealth, he scratched his head and said, 'It makes more bloody sense than the Nats'" (419).

6. A variation of Hall's ideas has been examined by many scholars of journalism who have written extensively about the concept of "framing."

7. The *Weekly Mail*, it should be noted, also published articles that sought to challenge the conventional view many white South Africans had at that time of Mandela and the political prisoners on Robben Island. They accomplished this primarily by having those who had a personal relationship with Mandela describe him in their own words. "My 15 Years on the Island with Mandela," by Eddie Daniels, a former political prisoner, contains the following statement: "It is said by the government that Nelson is a terrorist. He is no terrorist. He is a kind, honest, humble and peace-loving man. Nelson is a family man. He has been pushed into this position and, being a man of caliber, he has accepted it" (14). Another example includes "The Nelson Mandela I Know: By His Minister," written by the Reverend Dudley A. Moore. In Moore's letter, he describes the fact that he has "regularly administered the sacrament of Holy Communion" (12) to Mandela and mentions some of the theological discussions he has had with him. Moore also addresses the question that was an obsession of white South Africans and many international observers at that time: Was Mandela a "communist"? Moore writes that Mandela "would probably admit that he is influenced by some of the teachings of Marx," but he then concludes, "The man Mandela that I know just cannot be a communist" (12). The closing paragraph of Moore's letter captures the central purpose of these personal accounts: "I have written this letter because I believe the people of our country ought to know something about the man. What I have written is not what has been reported to me by others. It is my own personal knowledge of the man, Nelson Mandela" (12).

In addition to these articles, the *Weekly Mail* published a groundbreaking series written by a former political prisoner, Thami Mkhwanazi, about his days on Robben Island. The first one, "Mandela Today: As Told by a Colleague Who Spent Three Years in Prison with Him," appeared on the front page of the 7

August 1987 edition. There were at least four major articles subsequently written by Mkhwanazi about Robben Island. Harber explained that there were two
objectives of publishing this series: "I think we were aware that we were doing
two things at that time. The one was that we were going into prisons for the first
time. But the other was that we were trying to give a human face to the Robben
Islanders, to Mandela, Sisulu, and so we were, as I recall, we were very conscious
of the political force of doing this, of making Mandela more than a name." As
noted in chapter 1, Harber and Manoim were not interested in promoting the
ANC and Mandela per se but instead were interested in providing perspectives
of them that the government sought to suppress with its censorship restrictions.

8. J. B. Marks was a prominent member of the ANC and the Communist Party.

9. In addition to being quoted in the article's opening, Zuma is quoted elsewhere in
   the article:

> "We know that the press talks about soft targets, but the ANC has never
> talked about soft targets."
>
> "We are not a racial organization. We are fighting a war of liberation against
> the apartheid system and against colonialism of a special type."
>
> "When the ANC was formed, it pursued the path of non-violence. It con-
> tinued for decades. All those years the ANC wanted to resolve the conflict
> peacefully. The response of the regime has been very violent, with massa-
> cres, bannings, and killings. . . . So the question of violence did not originate
> from the ANC but from the government." ("ANC Men" 1)

10. The other article covering this trial, "ANC Policy Outlined," contains additional
    statements from Zuma. At one point, Zuma claims the ANC is not hostile to
    whites, and he then proceeds to read from ANC official statements, which *New
    Nation* quotes word for word:

> Once more, we call on our white compatriots, and especially the youth, to break
> ranks with the apartheid system to refuse to serve in its armed forces and no
> longer to mortgage their future to a racist system that is doomed to destruction.
> . . . To our white compatriots we say, as the Botha regime prepares to celebrate,
> in your name, the ignoble history of a system that has been categorised as a
> crime against humanity, what are you going to do? You have the possibility to
> contribute decisively to redress an historical injustice that has persisted over
> three centuries. (5)

When Zuma read this statement at length, he must have known that progressive newspapers would publish this information as part of his testimony,

much as they did with Mandela's courtroom statements. While several newspapers would have covered this trial, *New Nation* clearly framed its coverage to promote the ANC as much as possible.

11. Susan Rabkin was pregnant when she was arrested, and she actually gave birth while in prison. Because Rabkin was a citizen of the UK, she was eventually released, whereupon she immediately began to work with the ANC and SACP in exile. When her husband, David, was eventually released, he, too, left South Africa and joined the MK. He was accidentally killed while receiving military training. He was thirty-seven years old.

12. The UDF-ANC conditions included the following: "the release of all political prisoners"; allowing the return of all exiles to South Africa; "the unbanning of the ANC and all outlawed organisations"; the withdrawal of the security forces from the townships; repealing all laws "restricting free speech and assembly and press freedom"; and lifting the state of emergency ("Talk to Botha" 7).

13. Later in "Hit the Hit Squads," the journalist provides a historical overview of other assassinations of top ANC leaders in exile, including Joe Gqabi, and indicates the links to the South African government in that killing: "The Zimbabwean government and the ANC said South African agents were responsible for Gqabi's murder" (2).

14. Later in his interview, Taylor makes a startling claim about how and why his perspective began to change: "I saw a film, I think it was about in '89, 1990, *Mississippi Burning*, which was also about apartheid. It made quite an impression on me, especially the involvement of the police in the assassination of activists. I started realizing that that's actually not what policing is all about; it should rather be about protection than assassination. After that, I read Nelson Mandela's autobiography, and it changed my whole perspective" (Reid and Hoffman).

15. Edward Perkins, the US ambassador, claims that the Dutch Reformed Church also used a passage from the Acts of the Apostles as well as the story of Babel to justify apartheid: "The church's interpretation was 'Who has the right to bring together people that God has separated?' From these two scriptures the Afrikaners concocted a witches' brew of theology" (282). In Mark Mathabane's memoir *Kaffir Boy*, he recounts a conversation he had with a white South African friend who explained the socialization he experienced as a child during apartheid: "I never felt guilty about it at all. I was told God wanted us to live that way; that was why he made us white. I was told that you blacks deserved to be our servants because that's God's way of punishing you for the sins committed by your ancestor, Ham" (291).

16. The decision by the bishops to support *New Nation* caused considerable tension within the South African Catholic community. Sarah Crowe recalls that "for the suburban type, I think, they were uncomfortable. They were uncomfortable that church money was being used for what they would have seen as propaganda, political propaganda." Kerry Cullinan also recalled this opposition: "My father's Catholic, okay, so, there was this very conservative Catholic newspaper that would come out, and they were very critical of the *New Nation* stuff. And it was a bit awkward for him, having a daughter who was working for this newspaper that was supposedly tearing apart the Catholic community, which I think it was."

In addition to "the suburban types," there was more organized and more politically extreme opposition to *New Nation* from far-right groups within the Church. Father Mkhatshwa explained:

> What was actually very interesting was that there was, if I remember correctly, a small, right-wing fringe Catholic organization. . . . Now those [were] a real bunch of fascists who would turn a blind eye to the P. W. Botha regime oppressing people and so on. They didn't worry too much about that. But if the Catholic bishops issued a statement that was very critical of the regime, they would be the first ones to, you know, attack the bishops. So it was attacking the *New Nation*—that it was a communist, horrible newspaper and so on.

Later in his interview, Father Mkhatshwa discussed this opposition again: "For all it was worth, let me also just mention in passing, Bryan, that with very few exceptions, the groups or individuals within the Catholic Church that were critical of the *New Nation* were the whites. I hardly ever remember black groups or coloured groups or Indian groups coming out and attacking the *New Nation* and so forth. Why? Simply because, very broadly speaking, you know, the nonwhites were the ones that felt the pinch and tended to be sympathetic to what the *New Nation* was writing."

17. Catholics living under other violent and oppressive contexts have made similar arguments. Christopher Dickey, in an article that examines the assassination of Archbishop Óscar Romero, writes about a Salvadoran Jesuit, Rutilio Grande, who observed that "if Jesus of Nazareth were to come to El Salvador . . . [he] would be arrested and 'crucified all over again.'" Dickey notes, "Shortly afterward, Grande and two others with him were murdered."

18. Whether or not the pope fully supported the bishops' decision to fund *New*

Nation may not have been as clear cut as the newspaper suggested. The Vatican, for example, was quite critical of leftist clergy in South and Central America who lent their strong support to leftist movements. Given that *New Nation* actively promoted the ANC, which worked so closely with the South African Communist Party, it was certainly possible that the Vatican could have criticized the South African bishops for funding *New Nation*, particularly given the strong backlash from many white South African Catholics concerning the funding of this newspaper. Father Mkhatshwa explained: "You see, this crowd, I know for a fact that they used to send stuff to the Vatican—you know, look what the bishops' conference is sponsoring and tolerating." For the *New Nation*, the crackdown from the Vatican fortunately never came. Father Mkhatshwa explained: "But I don't think the Vatican, as Vatican, officially ever really made any pronouncement on this [funding of *New Nation*]. But I would imagine, because we also have a right-wing element within the Vatican, probably some of them were saying, "What are these bishops sponsoring now? [laughs]." But officially, to the depths of my recollection, I don't think they ever made any such pronouncements either for or against." Sarah Crowe also commented on this: "Interestingly enough, for some reason, if you compare the Vatican's involvement in South America and their involvement here, it was much less obvious."

James Carroll, a former priest who has written extensively on the Catholic Church, including his award-winning *Constantine's Sword: The Church and the Jews*, suggested in an interview several possible reasons why the Vatican did not crack down on the South African Catholic Church in the same way that it did in South and Central America. First, while Mkhatshwa and the South African bishops were clearly acting in an overtly political way by funding *New Nation*, they were not as formally and fully immersed in the political power structures of the anti-apartheid movement as some of the Catholic clergy were in political structures in Central America. For example, the Cardenal brothers, two priests serving in Nicaragua, not only supported the Sandinistas but were actually serving in the Sandinista government. Another possible reason the Vatican did not crack down: South and Central America were, as Carroll noted, practically "papal territory" in a way that South Africa was not. While Protestantism is currently on the rise in South and Central America, Catholicism has been and continues to be dominant. The Catholic Church in South Africa, on the other hand, was and is a minority church and probably was not, in Carroll's words, on the "Vatican's radar" in quite the same way as countries in South and Central America. Carroll also mentioned in passing how the Vatican had funded a publication produced by Solidarity in Poland during the Cold War. This is speculative, but to what extent would it have been awkward for the Vatican to denounce Catholic funding of an anti-apartheid newspaper in South Africa while simultaneously funding an anticommunist publication in Poland? Finally, it should be noted that Pope John Paul II publicly criticized the system of apartheid in May 1985 in an address at the World Court in The Hague. He was thus on record as opposing the system of apartheid.

19. The entertainment section, for example, consistently featured articles on anti-apartheid art. Moreover, the "Learning Nation" section, particularly the pages created by the History Workshop, provided another means of promoting the anti-apartheid struggle. Such an overview, of course, would have never been provided in apartheid schools. Even *New Nation*'s sports section was framed politically and featured many articles that examined the sports boycott of South Africa. Rob Nixon writes about the dramatic impact the international sport boycott had on white South Africans: "In a 1970 survey, white South Africans ranked the lack of international sport as one of the three most damaging consequences of apartheid—a melancholy statistic, but an index, nonetheless, of how deep the boycott cut" (139). *New Nation*'s sports pages examined these boycotts in articles such as "The Objective: The Total Isolation of SA Sportsmen" and also highlighted the political dimension of sports within the country. Specifically, it provided coverage of sports under the authority of the South African Council on Sport (SACOS), a sports body advocating nonracialism in sport.

While *New Nation* maintained ideological consistency by covering the South African Council on Sport, Drew Forrest questioned whether this was the best strategic decision for the newspaper:

> I mean, even the sports section, looking back on it, it was crazy. We were look-
> ing for a mass audience and we should have been writing about mainstream
> soccer, because that's what most black people are interested in. But in fact, it
> was all the fringe sports that were represented by the South African Council
> on Sport. You know, SACOS is the kind of radical, alternative, political sports
> body. It was pushing for nonracialism in sport, but it was really pretty much
> a fringe organization. But it had the right line, so in fact, we were promot-
> ing SACOS because SACOS was a federation—they had their own code, and
> their own cricket affiliate, and their own rugby affiliate, and the rest of it. And
> we promoted those like mad even though they were not the national soccer

league, which was apolitical, where the big and popular clubs fell. We did not touch those.

20. The apartheid government employed the common tactic of oppressive regimes elsewhere by using members from oppressed communities to help enforce its laws. The role of black police officers in apartheid South Africa was extremely complex: some black police were in fact quite abusive whereas some used their positions to provide strategic assistance to members of the black community.

21. Janet Wilhelm of the *Weekly Mail* explained how she had strategically used the racist attitudes of an editor at a mainstream newspaper where she had once worked. Specifically, she described how she wrote extremely critical articles about various homeland leaders: "The racial sensibilities of the editor made it possible for you to attack those homeland leaders because they were black. So you could say really nasty things about them, and I'd do it and he didn't mind that because he didn't differentiate. He wouldn't pick up the difference between the ANC or the guys who ran Bophuthatswana or the Transkei or KwaNdebele. So when I was writing about the homelands, I got away with saying the most outrageous, almost defamatory stuff about them. And he just let it all through." For the apartheid government and its supporters, reports of abuses by black South Africans actively involved in supporting apartheid structures were quite complicated. On one level, they could reflect poorly on the overall system of apartheid. On another level, they could be viewed as further justification for white rule.

22. This political movement in support of the ANC was significant because the ANC, while popular, was by no means the only political organization opposed to the apartheid government, nor was its approach, particularly its alignment with the South African Communist Party, universally shared. The Pan African Congress, a black nationalist party that broke from the ANC, and the Inkatha Freedom Party, a Zulu-based political party, were directly competing with the ANC.

CHAPTER 6. "MAKE ONE HELL OF A NOISE"

1. P. W. Botha's justification for implementing the states of emergency, quoted at length here, provides a fascinating insight into the apartheid government's worldview at the time:

> We have too often experienced how organisations and even governments in
> the Free World undermine our efforts by extending naïve moral, political and

material support to the forces of revolution, and this despite the fact that the
ANC and its followers stated unequivocally that they are committed to revolutionary violence. Dr. Henry Kissinger made the following meaningful remark in
this regard in his book *Years of Upheaval*: "When the crying need is for an assertion of authority, our advice usually dilutes it. And hard-pressed governments
beset by an implacable domestic enemy are often reduced to paralysis by advice
which they know is dangerous if not disastrous but which they dare not reject.
This was the fate of Nguyen van Thieu, as it was later of the Shah of Iran." I wish
therefore to forthrightly say to the outside world: We have seen clearly what
happened in Angola, as well as in Vietnam, Nicaragua, Kampuchea, Afghanistan, and Iran. We will consequently not allow our heritage of more than three
hundred years to be placed needlessly on the altar of chaos and decay. . . . The
government appeals for national and international understanding for the strict
actions which have been decided upon and again confirm its commitment to
the principle of broadening of the democracy in the Republic of South Africa.
(237–38)

Botha's defiant statement is significant on many levels: how it situates
South Africa within the larger Cold War context; how it reveals the siege mentality and the existential threat felt by those within the apartheid government;
and how it invoked Kissinger's phrase, "an assertion of authority," to justify its
repression. Kissinger's euphemism, "assertions of authority," raises but does
not answer some troubling questions about the specific tactics that should
accompany such "assertions": Detention without trial? Censorship? Violence
against demonstrators? Torture? Death squads?

2. The complex interplay between international and domestic political dynamics
also serves to explain the somewhat intangible yet very real importance of "profile." In other words, the more that individuals within South Africa were promoted internationally, the greater protection they generally had from the government. This is precisely why the report of the media conference held in London in
March 1988 recommended the following steps: "There is a small charmed circle
of black leaders the government appears not to dare seriously touch, and that circle is charmed because those people are very well known in the world outside.
The more we mention the names of Zwelakhe Sisulu and others, the more reluctance there will be by Pretoria to take the next move" (Margolis 15).

3. In his book *You Have Been Warned*, Manoim humorously describes what it was
like to work with Mahomed, who was clearly a legal force:

He did not leave his seat, either to talk on the phone or take notes, both of which
tasks were left to minions—ourselves included—who scurried around the room
in search of various pieces of paper the master required. Mahomed talked con-
tinuously and excitedly, a stream of legal-talk punctuated with bewildering
jokes, court-room gossip and sudden commands: "Gilbert, get me Colman, J in
Northwest Townships vs the Administrator" or "David, get me all the morning
newspapers for the past month." Now and then someone would try to interject a
sentence or two, before being cut off by another Mahomed barrage. (98)

4. Before he even addressed the specific articles cited in the warning letter,
Mahomed made an astute observation that undercut the government's justification for granting Stoffel Botha the power to close newspapers. As noted above,
Botha claimed the new system to regulate the press was needed in part because
the South African legal system was not equipped to deal with these issues in
a sufficiently timely manner. As Mahomed observes, however, "the elaborate
structure of Regulation 7A providing forewarnings, hearings and preliminary
procedures deprives the occasion identified by Regulation 7A of the quality of
urgency" (9). In other words, if these newspapers were really as dangerous as
the government claimed and the need to act was so urgent, why construct such
an elaborate, time-consuming process?

5. Mahomed also makes an appeal based on elitism when discussing the possible
effects *Weekly Mail* articles could have on their readers: "[A] further relevant
fact to be taken into account is the quality and sophistication of the likely reader
of the WEEKLY MAIL. . . . It attracts a particular sector of the population who can
afford the cover price. . . . Many of the individual paragraphs of annexure 'A' bear
the stereotyped wording of similar notices served upon other newspaper publishers with a vastly different quality of readership and sophistication" (19). It
is possible and even likely that Mahomed was appealing to the racism of conservative whites within the government. In short, the government's biggest fear
was that the black majority would rise up in revolution. Even though the *Weekly
Mail* had a significant number of black readers, by describing *Weekly Mail* readers in this coded way—well-educated whites of a certain class—Mahomed may
have been signaling to the government that it need not fear the readership of the
Weekly Mail as much as the readership of other publications.

6. Merrett rightly captures the government's fear regarding the "legitimation of
'unlawful organisations'" (*Culture* 122) to explain the government's response
to articles written about the ANC, even those that may be critical: "Thus, ANC

condemnation of necklacing [and] gay criticism of the ANC . . . all worried the authorities because they encouraged people to think of anti-apartheid organisations as bodies to be taken seriously by the South African public" (122–23). This dynamic explains Stoffel Botha's response to a question that appeared in *Leadership Magazine*. He was asked, "If I interviewed Oliver Tambo, if I critically examined him on such issues as press freedom under another government, and I then went to the State President for his comments and I wrote a balanced story, would that be acceptable?" (qtd. in Schneider 36). Botha's response: "No, it will not be. It will elevate Tambo to a status he doesn't deserve" (36).

7. To demonstrate the selective application of these regulations, Mahomed provided example after example of comparable articles that had appeared in other newspapers that the government did not object to. In terms of the *Weekly Mail* article about Oliver Tambo, Mahomed cites an article from the *Cape Times* not cited by Botha: "It is difficult to understand what is the rational principle or the objective criteria which determine that a description of Mandela as being by far and away the most popular political figure in South Africa with a potential for forging national unity does not promote the public image of an unlawful organisation and some of its current leaders but the kind of profile pertaining to Tambo in the *WEEKLY MAIL* to which objection has been taken, does" (44). Regarding the government's objections to the *Weekly Mail* articles on the release of Govan Mbeki from prison, Mahomed cites the many newspapers that covered this story and notes, "An examination of some typical reports in the news media dealing with the release of Mr. Mbeki and a comparison of that analysis with the report in the *WEEKLY MAIL* objected to leave the *WEEKLY MAIL* totally perplexed as to why objection is taken to its reporting and permitted in other cases" (59).

8. When Norman Manoim, one of the attorneys for *New Nation*, was asked if he understood the government's objections to specific articles that appeared in *New Nation*, he responded, "Yes and no. [We wanted] to embarrass them for selective enforcement. There was no doubt that there was selective enforcement. They wanted to go for certain papers and they were not particularly bothered by the same article being run in a context of a conservative newspaper like the *Star*. If one wanted to embarrass these guys, [we'd] say, 'If you're saying this is law and this is enforceable, then you must apply it blindly and consistently.'"

9. Irwin Manoim offers an important insight that he and Harber obtained after a meeting with Botha to discuss their warning letters, an opportunity Botha never granted to those at *New Nation*. Manoim recounts how Botha, after exchanging pleasantries, took out some papers and started to read excerpts of

speeches Manoim and Harber had made while they were abroad. One excerpt came from a speech made by Manoim in which he claimed, "The warning letters show so little sign of a mind actually engaged in examination of the contents of the objectionable publication that they tend to produce more guffaws than alarm" (*Warned* 107). Botha then read a speech that Harber had made in London that, according to Manoim, "made some characteristically wild remarks" (107). Manoim recalls his and Harber's realization: "Slowly, we understood. The minister did not really care what the *Weekly Mail* said. Perhaps he'd never read the paper. What mattered was the embarrassment we were causing the country abroad. Not just to the country, to himself, personally. What really hurt, deep down, was the press did not take Stoffel Botha seriously. All our speeches ridiculed him, poked fun at the absurdity of his objections" (107). Manoim writes how the meeting came to an abrupt end when a bell rang, and Botha excused himself for lunch, shaking hands with both before leaving. Harber and Manoim remained in the room, and Manoim describes the scene: "Harber studied the rows of framed photographs on the walls. The minister with an arts council. The minister at the opera. The minister at a cultural gala evening. This was a man who prided himself on his sophistication and culture. And we were presenting him to the world as a dolt. There could probably be only one punishment for that" (107).

10. The *Weekly Mail* staff, in addition to gaining support domestically from South African newspapers, were also able to mobilize the support of media throughout the world. According to Abel, this effort included "an open letter to the State President from editors, writers, and media people in thirty-three countries"; "the Inter-American Press Association (representing more than 1,300 newspapers)" (Abel 290); "the American Society of Newspaper Editors . . . the International Press Institute, the World Press Freedom Committee, and the Committee for the Protection of Journalists" (Abel 295).

11. Perkins claims Secretary of State George Shultz and Chester Crocker, assistant secretary of state for African affairs, favored a harder line against the apartheid government and "wanted a speech that would put the president and the administration solidly in favor of doing the right thing: vigorously opposing the apartheid system, making proactive efforts to dismantle the system, working to ensure a non-racial government, unbanning political activity, and freeing Nelson Mandela" (249). That position, however, did not carry the day.

12. A *New York Times* article written at the time noted how Reagan had lobbied Congress aggressively not to override his veto for fear that "he would appear

weak and ineffective in Iceland in his upcoming summit with Gorbachev" (Roberts). Despite this plea, several Republican lawmakers, including Sen. Mitch McConnell, voted to override Reagan. McConnell explained he did so "with great reluctance," and Sen. John Chaffee, another Republican who voted to override, stated, "You don't like seeing a President's veto overridden, and it's unfortunate that it's come to this" (qtd. in Roberts). According to Perkins, Republican senators Richard Lugar and Nancy Kassebaum were considered "turncoats" by conservative members within the Reagan administration "because they not only had opposed the administration's South Africa policy, but also had led the sanctions bill through Congress" (265). Reagan did have his supporters, however. Sen. Jesse Helms argued, "The thrust of this legislation is to bring about violent, revolutionary change, and after that, tyranny" (qtd. in Roberts).

13. In an NPR report on Perkins years later, Perkins recounted how Secretary Shultz essentially conceded what was fairly obvious to everyone at the time. When Shultz called to offer Perkins the position, he told him, "There are people around the president who believe that it is time to send a black ambassador.... But not necessarily for the right reasons'" (Williams).

14. Perkins writes, "Even before I left Washington, I received word that the black leaders of South Africa had decided not to meet with me. They considered Reagan to be anti-black and the Reagan administration's constructive engagement policy to be favorable to the Afrikaner government.... One black leader in South Africa who was most determined to boycott me was Anglican Archbishop Desmond Tutu, Nobel Laureate and pastor of St. George's Cathedral in Cape Town. He refused my requests to call on him" (309). Perkins also described his meeting with Jesse Jackson at the time: "'Brother Perkins, I have come here today to ask you not to go.' He asked if I thought it appropriate for a racist president like Ronald Reagan to nominate the first black ambassador to South Africa" (263).

15. There was not, however, universal consensus within the anti-apartheid movement about how best to respond to Perkins. According to Perkins, Mandela had "urged black leadership to meet with me" (310), whereas Walter Sisulu, Zwelakhe's father and the person considered Mandela's closest confidant, disagreed and recommended from prison to his wife, Albertina Sisulu, that she not meet with Perkins. Walter may have disagreed with Mandela, but Albertina disagreed with Walter. Perkins writes, "Luckily for me, she ignored [Walter] and acted on her own. Within the first two weeks I was in South Africa, she came to the residence to dine" (310).

16. In the United States, an editorial in the *New York Times* stated, "We can't think

of many things that the Reagan administration has done in foreign policy that [merit] our thanks. President Reagan's appointment of Ed Perkins to be ambassador to South Africa ranks among those things that we think are exceptional" (qtd. in Perkins 322). Jesse Jackson stated, "Before Edward Perkins went to South Africa . . . I asked him not to go. I was wrong, and today I have told him so" (qtd. in Perkins 356). The response in South Africa was similar: "Archbishop Tutu was reported to have said to his aide-de-camp, 'If Ambassador Perkins keeps doing the things he's doing, it looks like we're going to have to meet with him'" (qtd. in Perkins 322). And much later, in 2002, Perkins described a meeting he had with the Sisulus: "Walter was frail, but mentally and politically astute as always. Before I left, he told me, 'I was wrong to tell her not to meet you.' Albertina was astounded. 'He has never said that to me before now,' she murmured" (qtd. in Perkins 311).

17. Perkins writes, "[Mkhatshwa] had made a decision not to deal with the American Embassy because he thought the Americans were sanctioning the white South African government. After about six months of watching my activities, he changed his mind and we met and our relationship grew ever more cordial. He became a valuable contact as we planned strategy to try and contribute to the elimination of apartheid" (343).

18. According to Harber, the way the *Weekly Mail* received this money was as follows: "I recall that the people from USAID Pretoria came and said they had been instructed to work out a way to give it to us, and it was given to us as training money" (personal email correspondence, 20 August 2014).

19. In his memoir, Perkins paints a rather unflattering portrait of Thatcher's meeting with Botha in 1986: "[T]he two of them met in the presence of South African ambassador Denis Worrall, who told me about the meeting. Thatcher was not forthcoming in condemning the South African government. When the meeting was over, Botha said, 'We have our work cut out for us. She wants us to hold the line.' Intentionally or unintentionally, Thatcher had conveyed the message that she did not want the South African government making any concessions to black political leaders" (383).

20. Renwick elaborates on his position: "I explained to Archbishop Tutu that we would continue to disagree about disinvestment, because I genuinely believed that many of those who disinvested were unlikely to return, but that he would find us determined and, I hoped, effective allies in the struggle against apartheid" (*Unconventional* 119).

21. The longest the government could have closed the *Weekly Mail* would have been

for a period of three months. Nevertheless, a three-month closure would have been disastrous, particularly in terms of the newspaper's revenues.

22. The case brought against Harber and Bekker, for example, involved the publication of an article that had incorporated sensitive information revealed on the floor of Parliament, generally considered a protected space, as explained in chapter 2. The article in question, "Detainee 'Barred from Seeing Psychologist,'" involved an activist, Emson Banda, who was experiencing such intense depression that the psychologist who treated him recommended his release because he feared he was suicidal. The security police not only failed to release Banda but claimed that they had the power to authorize whether or not Banda was allowed to see a psychologist. Bekker conveyed this story by using statements made on the floor of Parliament, but she was charged nevertheless, along with Harber as the editor, because the government argued that, "[i]n terms of the Emergency regulations, court proceedings dealing with the manner of arrest, treatment and circumstances of detainees were embargoed until final judgment" (Merrett, *Culture* 126). Since Bekker had written about a detainee's case in which a final decision had not yet been rendered, she was technically in violation of the regulation. To find such a technicality in an article that had been written two years previously indicated the extent to which these bureaucrats did indeed "scour the newspapers."

23. The Committee to Protect Journalists report published in 1983 rightly seized upon the inherent flaw in the argument that those in the apartheid government occasionally tried to make: "[T]here is an obvious cynicism in the government of South Africa's contention that, insofar as freedom of the press is concerned, it should be judged according to African standards. That portion of the South African population that enjoys the right to take part in formulating and implementing the laws of South Africa that restrict freedom of the press—that is, the 15 per cent of the population that is white—prides itself on being the heir to Western cultural traditions" (1983, 76). The apartheid government may have been able to ignore this argument when it was made by an organization to protect journalists, but it was harder to ignore when members of the US government made a similar claim. When the apartheid government imposed additional media restrictions during the state of emergency, the US embassy released a statement that read in part, "We are sorry to note the action removes South Africa from the code of Western values to which it professes to adhere" (qtd. in Abel 270).

CONCLUSION

1. Koevoet was a South African paramilitary organization that committed numerous human rights abuses in Namibia.

2. Vlakplaas was the paramilitary organization responsible for numerous political assassinations. Their activities were subsequently exposed at great length by the TRC.

3. Dirk Coetzee, a member of Vlakplaas, confessed his role as a death squad leader in 1989. *Vrye Weekblad*, the courageous opposition newspaper written in Afrikaans, broke this story.

4. André Brink opens one chapter of his novel, *A Dry White Season*, by describing how Ben du Toit, an Afrikaner schoolteacher, was planning to visit the family of a black janitor from his school who had been killed by the police. Brink notes this was the first time in Ben's life that he had traveled to Soweto. The fact that a white South African in his fifties had never visited Soweto, or any township for that matter, was remarkable perhaps only in the sense that it would have been so completely unremarkable.

5. Levy's analysis concerning the potential of alienating progressive whites by assuming an advocacy role for the ANC and/or the UDF was quite real. Benjamin Rabinowitz, an important and early financial supporter of the *Weekly Mail* who was adamantly opposed to the apartheid government, explained why he admired the *Weekly Mail* so much: "I didn't bother to read the other newspapers. I often had the view, and I'm sorry to say it, they were not impartial. I thought the *Weekly Mail* was objective. I thought they were objective whereas the others were beating a particular chord. The *Weekly Mail* wasn't scared to criticize across the board. These other papers were sycophantic vis-à-vis—it was the UDF in those days. I didn't need it."

6. This letter suggests another dynamic Johnson described: even when stories published in the *Weekly Mail* were challenged or refuted by the government on SABC, this situation would also constitute success. Johnson explained, "Because even if you got denials on the SABC, the issue is there—the issue is on the agenda."

7. An article by John Burns that appeared in the *New York Times* prior to the overthrow of Saddam Hussein, "How Many People Has Hussein Killed?," contains this chilling information:

> Mr. Hussein's [rule] has been a tale of terror that scholars have compared to

that of Stalin, whom the Iraqi leader is said to revere, even if his own brutalities have played out on a small scale. Stalin killed 20 million of his own people, historians have concluded. Even on a proportional basis, his crimes far
surpass Mr. Hussein's, but figures of a million dead Iraqis, in war and through
terror, may not be far from the mark, in a country of 22 million people.... "Enemies of the state" are eliminated, and their spouses, adult children and even
cousins are often tortured and killed along with them. . . . The terror is self-
compounding, with the state's power reinforced by stories that relatives of
the victims pale to tell—of fingernail-extracting, eye-gouging, genital-shock-
ing and bucket-drowning. Secret police rape prisoners' wives and daughters
to force confessions and denunciations. . . . Casualties from Iraq's gulag are
harder to estimate. Accounts collected by Western human rights groups from
Iraqi émigrés and defectors have suggested that the number of those who have
"disappeared" into the hands of the secret police, never to be heard from again,
could be 200,000.

8. In another section of his book, Abrams provides a lengthy list of the many times
in American history when the government infringed upon free speech:

> Shortly after ratification of the Constitution, the Sedition Act of 1798 was
> adopted, making criminal a good deal of criticism of the president and other
> high-ranking officials. That repressive law, adopted by the John Adams admin-
> istration, led to the jailing of more than twenty newspaper editors and was
> the single greatest frontal attack on freedom of speech in the nation's history.
> Abolitionist speech in the years leading up to the Civil War often led to its
> suppression and the jailing of the speakers. So did speech opposing that war
> after its commencement. Socialists and anarchists were jailed by the Wilson
> administration for their speech during World War I. The victims of the House
> Un-American Activities Committee and the antics of Senator Joseph McCar-
> thy and his colleagues still bear the scars of their mistreatment. More recently,
> the Obama administration engaged in repeated efforts to punish leakers of
> information to the press and to limit the ability of journalists to protect their
> confidential sources. (58)

9. The last and final twist to this story: the federal government finally declassified all seven thousand pages of the Pentagon Papers on 13 June 2011—*forty
years* after they were first leaked. A *New York Times* article explains the significance of the full declassification of this document: "Until now, the complete

text of the report—officially known as the Report of the O.S.D. Vietnam Task Force—has been as elusive to researchers as a clean copy of *Hamlet* has been to generations of Shakespeare scholars. The version Mr. Ellsberg provided to the press was incomplete. A book published by Beacon Press, based on a copy from Senator Mike Gravel, Democrat of Alaska, had missing sections. And a version published by the government was heavily redacted" (M. Cooper and Roberts). Prior to this decision to release these papers, there was debate among various archivists about whether or not to continue to redact "11 words" within these seven thousand pages. After some debate, the entire text of the Pentagon Papers was released—and the eleven words were not redacted (M. Cooper and Roberts).

10. According to this same article, the excessive and seemingly haphazard method of redacting documents has caused exasperation even among those generally supportive of national security agencies: "Senator Pat Roberts, a Kansas Republican who is usually friendly toward the spy agency, grumbled publicly about its editing of the 2004 Senate report on pre-Iraq-war intelligence. 'If the agency were classifying basically an elementary book and the book had, 'See Spot run,' it would redact 'Spot,' Mr. Roberts said" (Shane, "Spies").

11. In one part of Slahi's diary, for example, he describes how he eventually began to "hallucinate and hear voices as clear as crystal" (272) as a direct result of his torture. Siems writes in an explanatory note: "This is corroborated chillingly in government documents. According to the Senate Armed Services Committee, on October 17, 2003, a JTF-GTMO interrogator sent an e-mail to a GTMO Behavioral Science Consultation Team (BSCT) psychologist that read, 'Slahi told me he is "hearing voices" now.... He is worried as he knows this is not normal.... By the way ... is this something that happens to people who have little external stimulus such as daylight, human interaction, etc.???? seems a little creepy'" (Slahi 272).

12. In my experience teaching this material to students, the black lines evoke a range of responses: anger, frustration, and, not particularly surprising, a "forbidden fruit feeling" that only entices readers to want to read more. The use of black lines, which convey the clear message that the material is so "dangerous" that it needs to be censored, is not necessarily an effective deterrent for most readers, especially young adults.

13. According to an article appearing in the *New York Times*, "That leaves scholars like Ms. Goodwin [Doris Kearns Goodwin] to wonder whether Mr. Trump, in

elevating the art of political fabrication, has forever changed what Americans are willing to tolerate from their leaders. 'What's different today and what's scarier today is these lies are pointed out, and there's evidence that they're wrong,' she said. 'And yet because of the attacks on the media, there are a percentage of people in the country who are willing to say, "Maybe he is telling the truth"'" (Stolberg).

14. Abrams notes, for example, that Ellsberg, who leaked the Pentagon Papers, "refrained from sharing the three volumes that dealt with negotiations to end the war for fear that it might interfere with the very process of a diplomatic resolution" (124). Moreover, even after the court decision was made that allowed the *New York Times* to continue publishing the Pentagon Papers, "[a] decision, in fact, had already been made not to publish some of the documents. On further review the editors determined not to publish a few more and to continue to publish some others" (137). Abrams also provides several examples in which various newspapers, individual journalists such as Glenn Greenwald, and organizations such as WikiLeaks have made different decisions about what leaked material they ultimately decided to publish or to refrain from publishing.

15. Ewen MacAskill wrote an article published in the *Guardian*, "The CIA Has a Long History of Helping to Kill Leaders around the World." Some of the leaders mentioned in the article who were either targeted or actually killed by the US government include Fidel Castro of Cuba, Patrice Lumumba of the Congo, Rafael Trujillo of the Dominican Republic, Sukarno of Indonesia, and Ngo Dinh Diem of South Vietnam. According to this same article, President Ford signed in 1976 "an executive order stating: 'No employee of the United States government shall engage in, or conspire in, political assassination.'" MacAskill explains, "In spite of this, the US never totally abandoned the strategy, simply changing the terminology from assassination to targeted killings, from aerial bombing of presidents to drone attacks on alleged terrorist leaders. Aerial bomb attempts on leaders included Libya's Muammar Gaddafi in 1986, Serbia's Slobodan Milosevic in 1999 and Iraqi president Saddam Hussein in 2003."

16. Some of the many personal hardships this two-year detention had on Sisulu included the following:

> "It has had a devastating effect on his marital and family relationships; his family is able to see him for a few minutes at a time, about twice a month. He is not allowed to have physical contact with them, but must be content to communicate with them through thick glass and metal partition."

"Moreover, Mr. Sisulu has not been able properly to maintain his family and
  oversee his young children on a day to day basis."
"Not only has Mr. Sisulu been deprived of his liberty, but he has been subjected
  to . . . the severest of deprivations, namely solitary confinement or complete
  isolation from all persons, apart from officials of the State." (Jana)

WORKS CITED

Abel, Richard. *Politics by Other Means: Law in the Struggle against Apartheid, 1980–1994*. Routledge, 1995.

Abrams, Floyd. *The Soul of the First Amendment*. Yale UP, 2017.

Abramson, Larry. "'Prisoner X' Raises Questions about Israel's Secrecy." *National Public Radio*, 20 February 2013, www.npr.org/2013/02/20/172470387/prisoners-x-raises-questions-about-israels-secrecy.

"Alex Vigilante Violence . . . Cops' Role Questioned." *New Nation*, 10 September 1987, p. 1.

"All Eyes on the Charter." *New Nation*, 5 March 1987, p. 6.

"Almost 100 'Torture' Affidavits." *Weekly Mail*, 20 December 1985, p. 2.

"ANC Denial." *New Nation*, 9 October 1986, p. 1.

"ANC Hails Shultz Talks." *New Nation*, 29 January 1987, p. 8.

"ANC Members Tell of Abduction and Torture." *New Nation*, 15 December 1989, page unknown.

"ANC Men Tell Court of War." *New Nation*, 6 October 1986, p. 1.

"ANC Out in Force at Summit." *New Nation*, 28 August 1986, p. 8.

"ANC Policy Outlined." *New Nation*, 6 October 1988, p. 5.

"ANC to Consider 'Truce' Deal." *New Nation*, 9 May 1986, p. 1.

"ANC Trial to Reopen Following Askaris' Evidence." *New Nation*, 15 December 1989, p. 1.

"Apartheid Death Squads." *New Nation*, 4 February 1988, p. 7.

"'Assaults': Prison Interdicted." *New Nation*, 12 February 1987, p. 1.

"At Last: A Face Not Seen for 25 Years." *Weekly Mail*, 9 December 1988, p. 3.

Attenborough, Richard, director. *Cry Freedom*. Universal Pictures, 1987.

August, Tyrone. Personal interview. Johannesburg, South Africa, 6 May 1999.

"Back Frontline States—ANC." *New Nation*, 30 July 1987, p. 8.

Badela, Mono. "What Winnie Would Have Said to Wits (If They'd Let Her Talk)." *Weekly Mail*, 8 May 1987, p. 10.

"Bandits Had SAP Backing." *New Nation*, 20 October 1988, p. 1.

BANNED! *Weekly Mail*, 25 March 1988, p. 1.

Barrell, Howard. Personal interviews. Cape Town, South Africa, 4, 5, 11 March 1999 and 9 April 1999.

Battersby, John D. "Anti-Apartheid Paper Fights Government for Its Right to Fight." *New York Times*, 10 May 1988, www.nytimes.com/1988/05/10/world/anti—apart-heid-paper-fights-government-for-its-right-tofight.html?mcubz=3.

Bauer, Charlotte. "How It Works." *Weekly Mail*, 19 June 1987, p. 15.

Bauer, Charlotte. "In Search of the Light." *Weekly Mail*, 19 June 1987, p. 14.

Bauer, Charlotte. Personal interview. Johannesburg, South Africa, 17 May 1999.

Bauer, Charlotte, and Shaun Johnson. "The State vs. the State." *Weekly Mail*, 5 August 1988, pp. 16–17.

Bekker, Jo-Ann. "About-Face from a Key State Witness." *Weekly Mail*, 2 May 1986, p. 9.

Bekker, Jo-Ann. "Balaclava Men Seen at 'Cheeky' Explosion." *Weekly Mail*, 25 October 1985, p. 2.

Bekker, Jo-Ann. "Court Hears of Police Beatings in Classroom." *Weekly Mail*, 29 August 1986, p. 2.

Bekker, Jo-Ann. "Court Told of Dead Foetus Found in Cells." *Weekly Mail*, 21 November 1986, p. 4.

Bekker, Jo-Ann. "Court Told of 'Media Slanting.'" *Weekly Mail*, 6 March 1987, p. 3.

Bekker, Jo-Ann. "Held Mokaba Claims He Was Tortured." *Weekly Mail*, 22 April 1988, p. 3.

Bekker, Jo-Ann. "I Let Police Punish Pupils, Says Principal." *Weekly Mail*, 29 August 1986, p. 2.

Bekker, Jo-Ann. "An Illustrated Guide to Public Ignorance." *Weekly Mail*, 6 February 1987, pp. 14–15.

Bekker, Jo-Ann. "The Odd Cases of the Activists Who Vanished." *Weekly Mail*, 20 December 1985, p. 6.

Bekker, Jo-Ann. "Police Admit Liability for Langa Massacre." *Weekly Mail*, 31 July 1987, p. 1.

Bekker, Jo-Ann. "Press Embargo on Claims against SADF." *Weekly Mail*, 21 February 1986, p. 9.

Bekker, Jo-Ann. "Register Hints at Police Link to Vigilantes." *Weekly Mail*, 11 September 1987, p. 3.

Bekker, Jo-Ann. "A White Woman Tells Why She Joined Umkhonto." *Weekly Mail*, 7 November 1986, p. 3.

Bernstein, Jeremy. "Court Hears of 'Panel Beating' for Dead Detainee." *Weekly Mail*, 11 December 1987, p. 3.

Bernstein, Jeremy, and Peter Auf Der Heyde. „Captain on Eight Assault Charges." *Weekly Mail*, 27 March 1987, p. 2.

Boren, David. Preface. *Mr. Ambassador: Warrior for Peace*, by Edward Perkins and Connie Cronley. U of Oklahoma P, 2006, pp. xv–xvi.

Botha, J. C. G. "State of Emergency: Subversive Propaganda," Letter, 1 October 1987. Supreme Court of South Africa. *Catholic Bishops Publishing Company and The State President of the Republic of South Africa (First Respondent) and The Minister of Home Affairs and of Communications (Second Respondent)*, Annexure L, 1988.

Botha, J. C. G. "New Nation: Catholic Bishops Publishing: State of Emergency: Subversive Propaganda." Letter, 6 November 1987. Supreme Court of South Africa. *Catholic Bishops Publishing Company and The State President of the Republic of South Africa (First Respondent) and The Minister of Home Affairs and of Communications (Second Respondent)*, Annexure M, 1988.

Botha, P. W. "Before a Joint Sitting of Parliament." Address by State President, 12 June 1986, Director Liaison and Information, State President's Office, Cape Town.

Brandt, Deborah. *Literacy in American Lives*. Cambridge UP, 2001.

Brandt, Hans. "We're Backing ANC, Say Greens." *Weekly Mail*, 11 July 1986, p. 6.

Brink, André. "Censorship and Literature." *Censored: Studies in SA's Censorship Laws by Five Leading Writers*, edited by Theo Coggin, SA Institute of Race Relations, 1983, pp. 37–54.

Brink, André. *A Dry White Season*. 1979. William Morrow Paperbacks, 2006.

Brink, André. "State of Emergency." *Reinventing a Continent: Writing and Politics in South Africa*, Zoland Books, 1996, pp. 21–24.

Brink, André. "Visions of the Future." *Reinventing a Continent: Writing and Politics in South Africa*, Zoland Books, 1996, pp. 59–70.

Burns, John F. "Court Silences Iran Reformist with Jail Term." *New York Times*, 28

November 1999, www.nytimes/com/1999/11/28/world/court-silences-iran-re-formist-with-jail-term.html.

Burns, John F. "How Many People Has Hussein Killed?" *New York Times*, 26 January 2003, www.nytimes/com/2003/01/26/weekinreview/the-world-how-many-people-has-hussein-killed.html?mcubz=3.

"Campaigning for Truth, Justice, Freedom and Love." *Africa News*, vol. 29, no. 10, 16 May 1988, p. 5.

Carroll, James. Personal interview. Boston, Massachusetts, 15 September 2014.

"Censors Will Use 'Scientific' Procedures—Minister." *Star*, 3 September 1987. Supreme Court of South Africa. *Catholic Bishops Publishing Company and The State President of the Republic of South Africa (First Respondent) and The Minister of Home Affairs and of Communications (Second Respondent)*, Annexure F, 1988..

Certeau, Michel de. *The Practice of Everyday Life*. Translated by Steven F. Rendall, U of California P, 1984.

"China's Self-Destructive Tech Crackdown." Editorial. *New York Times*, 30 January 2015, www.nytimes.com/2015/01/31/opinion/chinas-self-destructive-tech-crackdown.html?mcubz=3&_r=0.

Chomsky, Noam. Interview by Bill Moyers. *A World of Ideas*, Doubleday, 1989.

Chomsky, Noam. *Necessary Illusions*. South End Press, 1989.

Chomsky, Noam. *What Uncle Sam Really Wants*. Odonian Press, 1992.

Chomsky, Noam, and Michel Foucault. "Human Nature: Justice versus Power." *Reflexive Water: The Basic Concerns of Mankind*, edited by Fons Elders, Souvenir Press, 1974, pp. 133–98.

Coetzee, J. M. *Giving Offense: Essays on Censorship*. U of Chicago P, 1996.

Coetzee, J. M. "Into the Dark Chamber: The Writer and the South African State." *Doubling the Point: Essays and Interviews*, edited by David Attwell, Harvard UP, 1992, pp. 361–67.

Cogill, E. A. Letter. *Weekly Mail*, 27 June 1986, page unknown.

Committee to Protect Journalists. *South Africa and Zimbabwe: The Freest Press in Africa?* Report, March 1983.

Committee to Protect Journalists. *Attacks on the Press: A Worldwide Survey, 1989*. Report, March 1990.

Cooper, Carole, et al. *Race Relations Survey: 1985*. South African Institute of Race Relations, 1986.

Cooper, Carole, et al. *Race Relations Survey: 1986, Part II*. South African Institute of Race Relations, 1988.

Cooper, Carole, et al. *Race Relations Survey: 1987/88*. South African Institute of Race Relations, 1988.

Cooper, Carole, et al. *Race Relations Survey: 1988/89*. South African Institute of Race Relations, 1989.

Cooper, Michael, and Sam Roberts. "After 40 Years, the Complete Pentagon Papers." *New York Times*, 7 June 2011, www.nytimes/com/2011/06/08/us/08pentagon.html?pagewanted=all.

"Cop Kills Student." *New Nation*, 27 October 1989, p. 2.

Cope, Clive. Personal interview. Johannesburg, South Africa, 17 May 1999.

"Cops Assaulted Us, Potsdam 4 Tell Court." *New Nation*, 16 July 1987, p. 5.

Corrigall, Jim. "Media." *Subverting Apartheid: Education, Information, and Culture under Emergency Rule*, IDAF Publications, 1990, pp. 8–28.

"Court Acknowledges Violence Allegations." *Weekly Mail*, 10 January 1986, p. 1.

"Court Reins in Blackjacks." *New Nation*, 30 April 1987, p. 3.

"Court Told of Police 'Attack' on Home." *New Nation*, 4 June 1987, p. 3.

Cronin, Jeremy. Personal interview. Johannesburg, South Africa, 5 May 1999.

Crossley, Callie, and James A. DeVinney, directors. "No Easy Walk." *Eyes on the Prize: America's Civil Rights Movement*, PBS, original air date February 1987.

Crowe, Sarah. Personal interview. Johannesburg, South Africa, 10 May 1999.

Cullinan, Kerry. Personal interview. Cape Town, South Africa, 16 June 1999.

Curlewis, Judge J. Judgment, Supreme Court of South Africa. *Catholic Bishops Publishing Company (Applicant) and The State President and others (Respondent)*. 3 March 1988.

Cushman, Ellen. *The Struggle and the Tools: Oral and Literate Strategies in an Inner City Community*. State U of New York P, 1998.

Daniels, Eddie. "My 15 Years on the Island with Mandela." *Weekly Mail*, 21 March 1986, p. 14.

Danner, Mark. "'Guantánamo Diary' by Mohamedou Ould Slahi." *New York Times*, 20 January 2015, www.nytimes.com/2015/02/15/books/review/guantanamo-diary-by-mohamedou-ould-slahi.html.

Davis, Eric. "Baghdad's Buried Treasure." *New York Times*, 16 April 2003, www.nytimes.com/2003/04/16/opinion/baghdad-s-buried-treasure.html.

Davis, Gaye. "ANC Accused Tells of *Witdoeke* in Crossroads." *Weekly Mail*, 5 June 1987, p. 3.

Davis, Gaye. "At Last, ECC Able to Reveal Bar on SADF." *Weekly Mail*, 22 April 1988, p. 3.

Davis, Gaye. "'I Watched a Man Burn a Tent While Police Stood By.'" *Weekly Mail*, 6 November, 1987, p. 5.

Davis, Gaye. "Mbeki Would Have 'Urged Unity.'" *Weekly Mail*, 18 December 1987, p. 3.

Davis, Gaye. "Mr. X, the ANC Commissar, Explains Why He Suddenly Changed His Mind." *Weekly Mail*, 21 April 1989, p. 10.

Davis, Gaye. "Pensioner Tells How He Was Told to Thrash His Own Son." *Weekly Mail*, 16 September 1988, p. 5.

Davis, Gaye. "Riot Police Shot ANC Seven 'in Self-Defence.'" *Weekly Mail*, 27 October 1989, p. 11.

Davis, Gaye. "SADF in the Dock." *Weekly Mail*, 2 September 1988, p. 1.

Davis, Gaye. "Soldiers' Trial Reveals Plan to Discredit ECC." *Weekly Mail*, 5 February 1988, pp. 1–2.

Davis, Gaye. "We Watched Father Beaten to Death, Say Family." *Weekly Mail*, 31 March 1988, p. 3.

Davis, Gaye. "Youths Tell of Cell Beatings." *Weekly Mail*, 19 June 1987, p. 5.

Dawes, Nic. "It's Time to Start a New Conversation." *Mail & Guardian*, 8 August 2013, p. 5.

"'Death Squad' Spectre Haunts UDF." *Weekly Mail*, 5 July 1985, p. 1.

"Death Squads Waging War in the Shadows." *New Nation*, 30 July 1987, p. 6.

"Detainees 'Used to Trap Activists.'" *New Nation*, 21 January 1988, p. 1.

Dickey, Christopher. "Why Pope Francis Wants to Declare Murdered Archbishop Romero a Saint." *Daily Beast*, 24 August 2014, www.thedailybeast.com/why-pope-francis-wants-to-declare-murdered-archbishop-romero-a-saint.

Dickinson, Emily. "Tell All the Truth." Poetry Foundation, www.poetryfoundation.org/poems/56824/tell-all-the-truth-but-tell-it-slant-1263.

"The Disappeared Ones." *New Nation*, 4 February 1988, pp. 6–7.

Dison, David. Personal interview. Johannesburg, South Africa, 2 June 1999.

"Ebrahim Treason Trial: Doctor's Shock Assault Claims." *New Nation*, 22 October 1987, p. 1.

"Emergency Made Simple." *Weekly Mail*, 12 December 1986, p. 1.

"Erudite Footsying around the Really Tough Question." *Weekly Mail*, 3 July 1987, p. 27.

Evans, Gavin. "AG to Rule on 'Chief with Whip' Claims." *Weekly Mail*, 24 January 1986, p. 6.

Evans, Gavin. "Inquest Hears of Baton Beating." *Weekly Mail*, 13 December 1985, p. 2.

Evans, Gavin. "The Many Deaths of Raditsela." *Weekly Mail*, 17 January 1986, p. 5.

Evans, Gavin. "Raditsela: Dispute over 'Leading Questions.'" *Weekly Mail*, 24 January 1985, p. 5.

"An Experience of Profound Joy." *New Nation*, 3 December 1987, p. 12.

"An Extraordinary Exchange in the House." *Weekly Mail*, 19 February 1988, p. 4.

"Feisty Weeklies under Fire." *Africa News*, vol. 29, no. 10, 16 May 1988, p. 5.

"The First Legal Photo of Nelson Mandela in 22 Years." *Weekly Mail*, 6 June 1986, p. 1.

Fisher, Ryland. Personal interview. Cape Town, South Africa, 11 June 1999.

"Former Detainee Talks of Torture." *New Nation*, 27 October 1988, p. 1.

Forrest, Drew. Personal interview. Johannesburg, South Africa, 14 May 1999.

Gage, John T. "Teaching the Enthymeme: Invention and Arrangement." *Rhetoric Review*, vol. 2, no. 1, September 1983, pp. 38–50.

Gonzalez, Juan, and Goodman, Amy. "Remembering Nelson Mandela: From Freedom Fighter to Political Prisoner." *Democracy Now!*, 6 December 2013, www.democra-cynow.org/2013/12/6/remembering_nelson_mandela_from_freedom_fighter.

Goshen, B. Letter. *Weekly Mail*, 28 June 1985, p. 14.

Gower, Lauren. "Another Day. Another Treason Trial." *Weekly Mail*, 14 February 1986, p. 5.

Gqubule, Thandeka. "Church Conference Defies Regulations." *Weekly Mail*, 1 July 1988, p. 5.

Gqubule, Thandeka. "Defiant Churches Await State's Response." *Weekly Mail*, 8 July 1988, p. 2.

Gqubule, Thandeka. "'From a Police Locker, I Heard Two People Screaming.'" *Weekly Mail*, 17 March 1989, p. 4.

Gunene, Vusi. "A Chilling Pattern to Activist Deaths." *Weekly Mail*, 29 January 1988, p. 1.

Green, Pippa. "Court Okays 'Torture' Search of Cells." *Weekly Mail*, 6 June 1986, p. 3.

Gunene, Vusi. "Ebrahim: My Brush with SA's Angels of Death." *Weekly Mail*, 13 January 1989, p. 6.

Gunene, Vusi. "Inquest Gives Rare Glimpse." *Weekly Mail*, 20 November 1987, p. 3.

Harber, Anton. "Censorship." *The Legacy of Apartheid*, edited by Joseph Harker, Guardian Newspapers, 1994, pp. 147–54.

Harber, Anton. "Court Hears of 'Death Threats.'" *Weekly Mail*, 12 July 1985, p. 3.

Harber, Anton. "Court Okay to Cell Inspections." *Weekly Mail*, 10 January 1986, p. 2.

Harber, Anton. "Five Crucial Areas the Court Set Aside." *Weekly Mail*, 1 August 1986, p. 8.

Harber, Anton. "Honour Outs Revolutionary Newsman." *Mail & Guardian*, 22 November 2013, https://mg.co.za/article/2013-11-21-honour-outs-revolution-ary-manoim.

Harber, Anton. Personal e-mail correspondence. 4 May 2009, 31 May 2009, and 20 August 2014.

Harber, Anton. Personal interviews. Johannesburg, South Africa, 4 May 1999, 13 May 1999, and 9 August, 2013.

Harber, Anton. "We Are One of the Last Few Voices." *Africa News*, vol. 29, no. 10, 16 May 1988, p. 3.

Havel, Václav. *Disturbing the Peace: A Conversation with Karel Hvížďala*. Translated from the Czech with an introduction by Paul Wilson, Alfred A. Knopf, 1990.

Havel, Václav, et al. *The Power of the Powerless: Citizens against the State in Central-Eastern Europe*. Introduction by Steven Lukes, edited by John Keane, M. E. Sharpe, 1985.

Hepple, Alex. *Press under Apartheid*. International Defence and Aid Fund, n.d.

Hirsch, Lee, director. *Amandla*. Interviews with Sophie Mgcina and Dolly Rathebe, Lionsgate, 2002.

"Hit Squads on the Rampage in Chile." *New Nation*, 4 February 1988, p. 6.

"Hit the Hit Squads." *New Nation*, 16 July 1987, p. 2.

Hochschild, Adam. *King Leopold's Ghost: A Story of Greed, Terror, and Heroism in Colonial Africa*. Houghton Mifflin, 1999.

Hollard, P. Letter. *Weekly Mail*, 14 June 1985, p. 16.

Holliday, Anthony. Personal interview. Cape Town, South Africa, 27 April 1999.

Hoy, David Couzens. "Power, Repression, Progress: Foucault, Lukes, and the Frankfurt School." *Foucault: A Critical Reader*, edited by David Couzens Hoy, Basil Blackwell, 1986, pp. 123–48.

"I Can See Neil Agett Hanging." *New Nation*, (day unknown) May 1986, page(s) unknown.

"I Lied, Says Witness." *New Nation*, 24 November 1988, p. 1.

Index on Censorship. "South Africa: Court Cases against Critical Journalists and the Background." Briefing paper, London, 1989.

Innes, Duncan. "A Book on Freedom by Unfree Authors." *Weekly Mail* 27 June 1986, p. 19.

"Interrogation Victim 'Taken Out' Says Cop." *New Nation*, 10 December, year unknown, p. 4.

"In Their Own Words: The Affidavits of Ex-Detainees." *Weekly Mail*, 4 October 1985, p. 13.

"Invisible Man." *Weekly Mail*, 26 September 1986, p. 7.

"I Saw Police Fire at Kids, Says Lawyer." *Weekly Mail*, 14 March 1986, p. 1.

"It Could Have Been Drawn from the Bible." *New Nation*, 25 June 1987, p. 14.

"It's Mandela and It's Legal." *Weekly Mail*, 27 November 1987, p. 14.

"It's Perfectly Legal—Only They Can't Say It." *Weekly Mail*, 25 March 1988, p. 2.

"I Was Detained, Tortured, Released and Redetained." *New Nation*, 28 May 1987, p. 3.

"I Was Threatened in Court—Detainee." *Weekly Mail*, 4 July 1986, p. 9.

Jana, Priscilla, and Associates (Attorneys for Mr. Sisulu). "Representations to the Minister of Law & Order for the Release of Mr. Sisulu."

"Jesus on Trial Today." *New Nation*, 16 March 1989, p. 12.

Johnson, Shaun. "Inside the Kine Consulate." *Weekly Mail*, 21 October 1988, p. 1.

Johnson, Shaun. Personal interviews. Cape Town, South Africa, 19 April 1999 and 28 April 1999.

Johnson, Shaun. "SAP Pay Out for Ex-Detainee." *Weekly Mail*, 19 December 1986, p. 2.

Johnson, Shaun. "Showdown as Editors Face Subpoena Threat." *Weekly Mail*, 2 June 1989, p. 3.

"Journalist Jailed for 'Silence.'" *Weekly Mail*, 15 December 1989, p. 3.

"Journalists [black line]." *Weekly Mail*, 20 June 1986, p. 2.

Judge, Dermod. Letter. *Weekly Mail*, 5 July 1985, p. 10.

"'Kani Had His Hands above His Head, and the Cop Kept Shooting.'" *New Nation*, 7 July 1988, p. 3.

Keller, Bill. "South Africa since Mandela." *New York Times*, 16 December 2012, www.nytimes.com/2012/12/17/opinion/keller-south-africa-since-mandela.html?mcubz=3.

Killeen, Peggy. "Watson Witness Tells Court: 'I Was Tortured.'" *Weekly Mail*, 5 December 1986, p. 4.

"Killings Don't Stop Liberation." *New Nation*, 30 July 1987, p. 7.

Kirkwood, Marilyn. Personal interview. Cape Town, South Africa, 2 March 1999.

Kockott, Fred. "I Saw the Shootings at the MAWU Rally." *Weekly Mail*, 21 November 1986, pp. 1+.

Krauss, Clifford. "Pinochet at Home in Chile: A Real Nowhere Man." *New York Times*, 5 March 2000, www.nytimes.com/2000/03/05/world/pinochet-at-home-in-chile-a-real-nowhere-man.html.

Kruger, Franz. "Arsonists Burn Union Offices." *Weekly Mail*, 8 August 1986, p. 3.

Kruger, Franz. *Word Wars: South African Media under the Emergency* (MA thesis). International Journalism to the City University, Graduate Center for Journalism, London, 1989.

Kuhn, Anthony. "Ahead of Anniversary, How Tiananmen Square Is Remembered in China." *Here and Now*, NPR, 2 June 2017, www.wbur.org/hereandnow/2017/06/02/anniversary-tiananmen-square.

Lange, Margreet de. *The Muzzled Muse: Literature and Censorship in South Africa*. John Benjamins, 1991.

Lanham, Richard A. *A Handlist of Rhetorical Terms*. 2nd ed., U of California P, 1991.

Laurence, Patrick. "A Murder That Raises the Spectre of Death Squads." *Weekly Mail*, 31 July 1987, p. 11.

Laurence, Patrick. "On Medicine: The Words of Wendy Orr." *Weekly Mail*, 18 October 1985, p. 4.

Laurence, Patrick. Personal interview. Johannesburg, South Africa, 10 May 1999.

Laurence, Patrick. "A 75-Year Thorn in the Flesh of White Power." *Weekly Mail*, 9 January 1987, p. 11.

"Lawyer Claims Special 'Political' Censor Board." *Weekly Mail*, 21 June 1985, p. 5.

"Lawyers See Ciskei 'Torture Chamber.'" *New Nation*, 7 July 1988, p. 1.

Le May, Jean. "Advocate Links Police to De'Ath Death." *Weekly Mail*, 10 April 1987, p. 1.

Letswalo, Elijah. Letter. *Weekly Mail*, 3 February 1989, p. 14.

Levy, Moira. "Inquest Raps Policemen for 'Trojan Horse' Shootings." *Weekly Mail*, 4 March 1988, p. 1.

Levy, Moira. "Molly Blackburn." *Weekly Mail*, 31 January 1986, p. 5.

Levy, Moira. Personal interview. Cape Town, South Africa, 3 March 1999.

Levy, Moira. "SADF Threw Fake ECC Pamphlets from 'Copter, Court Hears." *Weekly Mail*, 11 March 1988, p. 2.

Lewis, Neil. "President Criticizes GOP for Delaying Judicial Votes." *New York Times*, 31 July 2000, www.nytimes.com/2000/07/31/us/president-criticizes-gop-for-delaying-judicial-votes.html?mcubz=3.

"Living in Fear." *New Nation*, 6 November 1986, p. 2.

Lodge, Tom. "The Slovo Line on Private Investment." *Weekly Mail*, 14 November 1986, p. 13.

Loewe, Mike. "Ex-Soldier Tells Court of Orders to Beat People. *Weekly Mail*, 15 May 1987, p. 1.

Loewe, Mike. "The Proud Soldier Who Changed His Mind." *Weekly Mail*, 22 May 1987, p. 5.

Logan, Shirley Wilson. *We Are Coming: The Persuasive Discourse of Nineteenth-Century Black Women*. Southern Illinois UP, 1999.

"Long Live the People's Charter!" *New Nation*, 25 June 1987, p. 6.

"Louis LeGrange Sued—Again. 'We Were Beaten.'" *New Nation*, 6 November 1986, p. 5.

Ludman, Barbara. "Inside Mandela's Cell." *You Have Been Warned*, by Irwin Manoim, Viking, 1996, pp. 81–93.

MacAskill, Ewen. "The CIA Has a Long History of Helping to Kill Leaders around the

World." *Guardian,* 5 May 2017, www.theguardian.com/us-news/2017/may/05/cia-long-history-kill-leaders-around-the-world-north-korea.

MacDonald, Bruce. Letter. *Weekly Mail,* 17 October 1986, p. 12.

Maclennan, Ben. Personal interviews. Cape Town, South Africa, 13 April 1999 and 19 April 1999.

Madonsela, Keith, and Mzimkulu Malunga. "Uniformed Whites Linked to Firebombing." *Weekly Mail,* 28 July 1989, p. 2.

Mahler, Jonathan. "Reporter's Case Poses Dilemma for Justice Department." *New York Times,* 27 June 2014, www.nytimes.com/2014/06/28/us/case-of-james-risen-times-reporter-poses-dilemma-for-justice-department.html.

Mahomed, Ismail. "Representations to the Minister of Home Affairs and Communications Concerning the *Weekly Mail.*" 31 December 1987. Manuscript viewed at the library of the University of Witswatersrand.

"The Main Men." *New Nation,* 7 May 1987, pp. 6–7.

Malan, Rian. *My Traitor's Heart.* Vintage, 1990.

Mandela, Nelson. *Long Walk to Freedom: The Autobiography of Nelson Mandela.* Little, Brown, 1994.

Mandela, Nelson. Preface. *Reinventing a Continent: Writing and Politics in South Africa,* by André P. Brink, Zoland Books, 1996, pp. vii–ix.

"Mandela: Man of Mystery." *New Nation,* 13 February 1986, p. 6.

"Mandela Still Alive after Embarrassing Bush Remark." *Reuters,* 21 September 2007, www.reuters.com/article/2007/09/21/us-safrica-mandela-bush-idUSL21784 99420070921.

Manga, Amrit. Personal interview. Johannesburg, South Africa, 18 May 1999.

Manoim, Irwin. Personal email correspondence, 4 May 2009, 16 June, 2009, 21 August 2014, 3 November 2014, and 4 November 2014.

Manoim, Irwin. Personal interviews. Johannesburg, South Africa, 5 May 1999, 19 May 1999, and 8 August 2013.

Manoim, Irwin. "Voortrekkers of Tech." *25 Years of the Mail and Guardian,* Tafelberg, 2010.

Manoim, Irwin. "The Worst Monsters Are the Ones We've Invented." *Weekly Mail,* 21 March 1986, p. 18.

Manoim, Irwin. *You Have Been Warned.* Viking, 1996.

Manoim, Norman. Personal interview. Johannesburg, South Africa, 31 May 1999.

Margolis, Joe, editor. "South Africa: Controlling the News." Report of the Media Conference, Commonwealth Secretariat, London, 11–12 March 1988.

Mathabane, Mark. *Kaffir Boy: An Autobiography*. Touchstone, 1986.

"Mbeki: Still Steadfast as Ever." *New Nation*, 12 November 1987, p. 5.

McDonald, Peter. *The Literature Police: Apartheid Censorship and Its Cultural Consequences*. Oxford UP, 2009.

Merrett, Christopher. *A Culture of Censorship: Secrecy and Intellectual Repression in South Africa*. David Philip, 1994.

Merrett, Christopher. Letter. "'Endearing' Censor Is Just Another Apartheid Lackey." *Weekly Mail*, 26 June 1987, p. 10.

Mervis, Joel. *The Fourth Estate: A Newspaper Story*. Jonathan Ball P, 1989.

Miller, Thomas P., and Joseph Jones. "Working Out Our History." *College English*, vol. 67, no. 4, 2005, pp. 421–39.

"Minister Faces R10 000 Claim." *New Nation*, 20 November 1986, p. 2.

"Minister Pays Up." *New Nation*, 3 September, year unknown, p. 2.

"Minister to Pay Damages." *New Nation*, 4 December 1986, p. 5.

"Missing." *Weekly Mail*, 14 June 1986, p. 14.

Mkhatshwa, Smangaliso. Personal interview. Johannesburg, South Africa, 12 May 1999.

Mkhwanazi, Thami. "Mandela Today." *Weekly Mail*, 7 August 1987, p. 1.

Mkhwanazi, Thami, and Shaun Johnson. "Another Murder Riddle as Former Detainee Stabbed." *Weekly Mail*, 5 February 1988, p. 2.

Moodley, Cassandra. "Asvat Trial Accused Tells of Shocks." *Weekly Mail*, 27 October 1989, p. 4.

Moore, Rev. Dudley A. "The Nelson Mandela I Know: By His Minister." *Weekly Mail*, 27 September 1985, p. 5.

"More Harassment Claims against 'Kitskonstabels.'" *New Nation*, 18 June 1987, p. 3.

"Mystery Surrounds Mofolo Night Raiders." *New Nation*, 14 May 1987, p. 1.

Muller, Patrick. Letter. *Weekly Mail*, 21 October 1988, p. 10.

National Security Archive. "Accomplishments." George Washington University, http://nsarchive.gwu.edu/about/accomplishments.

"New Body Will Monitor Press." *Citizen*, 3 September 1987, pp. 1–2. Supreme Court of South Africa. *Catholic Bishops Publishing Company and The State President of the Republic of South Africa (First Respondent) and The Minister of Home Affairs and of Communications (Second Respondent)*, Annexure D, 1988.

"*New Nation* Now Unbanned." *New Nation*, 29 September 1988, p. 5.

"*New Nation* Publishes Its Final Edition." *Mail & Guardian*, 30 May 1997, https://mg.co.za/article/1997-05-30-new-nation-publishes-its-final-edition.

"New Swazi Link to Hit Squads." *New Nation*, 15 December 1989, p. 1.

Ngomane, Si, and Karen Evans. "Police Accused of Killing Student Leader." *Weekly Mail*, 29 April 1988, p. 3.

Nixon, Rob. *Homelands, Harlem and Hollywood: South African Culture and the World Beyond*. Routledge, 1994.

Ntamnani, Ncedo. "Stofile's Wife Tells of Beatings." *Weekly Mail*, 30 January 1987, p. 4.

Nyaka, Sefako. "Behind the Barricades." *Weekly Mail*, 24 April 1987, p. 1, 3.

Nyaka, Sefako. "Court 'Finds' Lost Riot Dead." *Weekly Mail*, 13 December 1985, p. 1.

Nyaka, Sefako. "The Day That Fell Off the Calendar." *Weekly Mail*, 20 June 1986, p. 14.

Nyaka, Sefako. "It's Trouble Once More for the 'Torture' Bishop." *Weekly Mail*, September 5, 1986, p. 8.

Nyaka, Sefako. Personal interview. Johannesburg, South Africa, 11 May 1999.

Nyaka, Sefako. "Shooting Victims Buried in Secret." *Weekly Mail*, 5 September 1986, p. 1.

Orsmond, Bishop Reginald. Replying Affidavit, Supreme Court of South Africa. *Catholic Bishops Publishing Company (Applicant) and The State President of the Republic of South Africa (First Respondent) and The Minister of Home Affairs and of Communications (Second Respondent)*. 24 January 1988.

Paris, J. Letter. *Weekly Mail*, 19 July 1985, p. 10.

"Peeling Away the Black Stripes." *Weekly Mail*, 22 August 1986, p. 12.

Perelman, Chaim, and L. Olbrechts-Tyteca. *The New Rhetoric: A Treatise on Argumentation*. U of Notre Dame P, 1969.

Perkins, Edward J., with Connie Cronley. *Mr. Ambassador: Warrior for Peace*. U of Oklahoma P, 2006.

Perlman, John. "Two Police Guilty of Murder." *Weekly Mail*, 31 March 1988, p. 1.

"Persons Known to Be in Detention since June 12." *Weekly Mail*, 20 June 1986, p. 4.

Phillips, Amber. "'Our Democracy Will Not Last': Jeff Flake's Speech Comparing Trump to Stalin, Annotated." *Washington Post*, 17 January 2018, www.washingtonpost.com/news/the-fix/wp/2018/01/17/our-democracy-will-not-last-jeff flakes-speech-comparing-trump-to-stalin-annotated/?utm_term=.0867839725 63.

Pinnock, Don. "Culture as Communication: The Rise of the Left-Wing Press in South Africa." *Race & Class*, vol. 31, no. 2, 1989, pp. 17–35.

Pinnock, Don. Personal interview. Cape Town, South Africa, 20 April 1999.

Plessis, Deon du. "Editors Briefed." *Pretoria News*, 3 September, 1987. Supreme Court of South Africa. *Catholic Bishops Publishing Company and The State President of the Republic of South Africa (First Respondent) and The Minister of Home Affairs and of Communications (Second Respondent),* Annexure E.

"Police 'Escorted Inkatha Murder Mob.'" *New Nation,* 18 February 1988, p. 1.

"Policeman Admits He Fired on Crowd." *New Nation,* 11 August 1989, p. 2.

"Police Sat Back . . . As Vigilantes Assaulted Hundreds, Rang in Curfew, Court Is Told." *New Nation,* 5 March 1987, p. 1.

"Police Torture Claims Mount." *New Nation,* 28 August 1986, p. 1.

Powell, Ivor. "Death Row Policeman Tells of Death Squads." *Weekly Mail,* 21 December 1990, p. 1.

Powell, Ivor. "Most Censored Society." *Limits of Liberty: Obscenity, Blasphemy & Hate Speech; How Much Can We Tolerate? Weekly Mail* and Guardian Film Festival, in association with the Mayibuye Center, University of the Western Cape, and the Anti-Censorship Group for the Limits of Liberty Conference, July 1993, pp. 13–26.

Powell, Ivor. "Youth Describes Detentions, Assaults in 'Torture-Mobile.'" *Weekly Mail,* 3 November 1989, p. 3.

"The Quotable Biko: 12 Years Later." *Weekly Mail,* 18 October 1985, p. 15.

Rabinowitz, Benjamin. Personal interview. Cape Town, South Africa, 8 April 1999.

Rabkin, Sue. Personal interview. Cape Town, South Africa, 19 March 1999.

Ramaphoko, Nakampe E. Letter. *Weekly Mail,* 21 June 1985, page(s) unknown.

"Rape Claims Grandmother in Hiding." *Weekly Mail,* 13 September 1985, p. 6.

"A Rather Fuzzy Picture." *Weekly Mail,* 24 February 1989, p. 6.

Reid, Frances, and Deborah Hoffman, directors. *Long Night's Journey into Day.* SnagFilms, 2000.

Renwick, Robin. *A Journey with Margaret Thatcher.* Biteback, 2013.

Renwick, Robin. *Unconventional Diplomacy in Southern Africa.* St. Martin's Press, 1997.

Reporters without Borders. "Iran." Last updated 20 January 2016, https://rsf.org/en/news/iran-2.

Rickard, Carmel. "Christmas Eve Order to Halt Cell Beatings." *Weekly Mail,* 9 January 1986, p. 10.

Rickard, Carmel. "The Court Clips the Commissioner's Media Power." *Weekly Mail,* 25 September 1987, p. 8.

Rickard, Carmel. "Court Told of Black Hole of 'Kei." *Weekly Mail,* 8 July 1988, p. 6.

Rickard, Carmel. "Disappointments, but Several Media Restrictions Go Out." *Weekly Mail,* 25 September 1987, p. 8.

Rickard, Carmel. "Gwala Sjambokked, Say Lawyers." *Weekly Mail,* 15 June 1989, p. 3.

Rickard, Carmel. "Keepers of the Peace Are the 'Very Cause of Our Fears.'" *Weekly Mail*, 5 May 1989, p. 7.

Rickard, Carmel. "New Catholic Paper Launched." *Weekly Mail*, 17 January 1986, p. 9.

Rickard, Carmel. "Policemen Fined for Nair Assault." *Weekly Mail*, 25 April 1986, p. 9.

Rickard, Carmel. "Schoolboys Claim: We Were Flung into a Grave." *Weekly Mail*, 8 July 1988, p. 2.

Rickard, Carmel. "The State's Attorneys Redo Their Homework." *Weekly Mail*, 19 December 1987, p. 13.

Rieder, Rem. "The World Is Watching Trump's Attacks on the Press." *CNN Politics*, 27 August 2017, www.cnn.com/2017/08/27/politics/donald-trump-media/index.html.

Roberts, Steven. "Senate, 78 to 21, Overrides Reagan's Veto and Imposes Sanctions on South Africa." *New York Times*, 3 October 1986, www.nytimes.com/1986/10/03/politics/03REAG.html?mcubz=3.

"The Role of the Media under Apartheid." African National Congress Submission to the Truth and Reconciliation Commission, 15 September 1997.

Rumney, Reg. Personal interview. Johannesburg, South Africa, 11 May 1999.

Rushdie, Salman. "Censorship." *Imaginary Homelands: Essays and Criticism: 1981–1991*, Granta, 1991, pp. 37–40.

Ryzik, Melena. "A Miracle in Shorts." *Carpetbagger: The Hollywood Blog of the New York Times*, 2 December 2009, carpetbagger.blogs.nytimes.com/2009/12/02/a-miracle-in-shorts/?mcubz=3.

Sachs, Susan. "Iran Reformers Feeling Pressured by Hard-Liners." *New York Times*, 25 April 2000, www.nytimes.com/2000/04/25/world/iran-reformers-feeling-pressed-by-hard-liners.html.

Said, Edward. "Foucault and the Imagination of Power." *Foucault: A Critical Reader*, edited by David Couzens Hoy, Basil Blackwell, 1986, pp. 149–56.

Sanger, Margaret. "Banned in Boston: The Silent Speech of Margaret Sanger." Ford Hall Forum Archives, www.fordhallforum.org/index.php?s=banned+in+boston.

Schneider, Martin. "The Last Word: Interview with Minister of Home Affairs and of Communication, Stoffel Botha." *Leadership South Africa*, vol. 6, no. 5, 1987. Supreme Court of South Africa. *Catholic Bishops Publishing Company and The State President of the Republic of South Africa (First Respondent) and The Minister of Home Affairs and of Communications (Second Respondent)*, Annexure H.

Sciolino, Elaine. *Persian Mirrors: The Elusive Face of Iran*. Simon and Schuster, 2000.

Scott, James. *Domination and the Arts of Resistance: Hidden Transcripts*. Yale UP, 1990.

"The Secret Slaughter without Boundaries." *New Nation*, 30 July 1987, p. 7.

"Sensible Voices from the Appeal Board." *New Nation*, date and page unknown.

"72 Hours of Terror." *New Nation*, 19 February 1987, p. 1.

Shane, Scott. "From Inside Prison, a Terrorism Suspect Shares His Diary." *New York Times*, 20 January 2015, www.nytimes.com/2015/02/15/books/review/guanta-namo-diary-by-mohamedou-ould-slahi.html.

Shane, Scott. "Spies Do a Huge Volume of Work in Invisible Ink." *New York Times*, 28 October 2007, www.nytimes.com/2007/10/28/weekinreview/28shane.html.

Shane, Scott. "U.S. to Declassify Secrets at Age 25." *New York Times*, 21 December 2006, www.nytimes.com/2006/12/21/washington/21declassify.html?mcubz=1.

Shaw, Gerald. "Anthony Holiday." *Guardian*, 17 August 2006, www.theguardian.com/news/2006/aug/18/guardianobituaries.pressandpublishing.

Sidley, Pat. "ANC Songs in Court as Passtoors Convicted of Treason." *Weekly Mail*, 16 May 1986, p. 1.

Sidley, Pat. "Journalist Sues over Sjambok Attack." *Weekly Mail*, 17 January 1986, p. 9.

Sidley, Pat. Personal interview. Johannesburg, South Africa, 10 May 1999.

Siems, Larry. "Notes on the Text, Redactions, and Annotations." *Guantánamo Diary*, by Mohamedou Ould Slahi, Little, Brown, 2015.

Sisulu, Zwelakhe. "By Zwelakhe." *Weekly Mail*, 9 December 1988, p. 13.

Sisulu, Zwelakhe. Personal interview. Johannesburg, South Africa, 20 May 1999.

Slahi, Mohamedou Ould. *Guantánamo Diary*. Edited by Larry Siems, Little, Brown, 2015.

Smith, Charlene. Personal interview. Wellesley, Massachusetts, 19 June 2015.

"Soldiers Beat Us, Say Youths." *New Nation*, 10 November 1988, p. 1.

"Soldiers Tell of Maseru Attacks." *Weekly Mail*, date and page unknown.

"Sol Plaatje." *New Nation*, 15 January 1987, p. 6.

"State Opposes Detainees' Application." *New Nation*, 11 September 1986, p. 3.

Stewart, Justice Potter. United States Supreme Court. *Jacobellis v. Ohio* (1964). Legal Information Institute, Cornell Law School, www.law.cornell.edu/supremecourt/text/378/184#writing-USSC_CR_0378_0184_ZC1.

Stolberg, Sheryl Gay. "Many Politicians Lie. But Trump Has Elevated the Art of Fabrication." *New York Times*, 7 August 2017, www.nytimes.com/2017/08/07/us/politics/lies-trump-obama-mislead.html?partner=rss&emc=rss&smid=tw-nyt-politics&smtyp=cur.

"Strange Case of the Mystery Glass-Smashers." *Weekly Mail*, 20 September 1985, p. 6.

Stuart, Kelsey. *The Newspaperman's Guide to the Law*. Butterworths Professional Publishing, 1990.

Sutherland, Jean. "'Beatings' Officer Tells Court of Christian Duty." *Weekly Mail,* 6 March 1987, p. 6.

Sutherland, Jean. "Prisoners Beaten—Policeman." *Weekly Mail,* 20 February 1987, p. 5.

"Suzman's Strange Tale of the Mirror-Glass Mini-Bus." *Weekly Mail,* 4 September 1987, p. 1.

Switzer, Les, and Mohamed Adhikari, editors. *South Africa's Resistance Press: Alternative Voices in the Last Generation under Apartheid,* Ohio U Center for International Studies, 2000.

"Talk to Botha? He Won't Let Us Talk to Ourselves." *New Nation,* 26 November 1987, pp. 6–7.

"Tambo Visit." *New Nation,* 3 September 1987, p. 8.

"Test Trial for Mandela Photo." *Weekly Mail,* 1 July 1988, p. 5.

"That Baffling Blank Centre." *Weekly Mail,* 16 January 1987, p. 6.

"They Came in the Dark." *New Nation,* 6 August 1987, p. 18.

Thompson, Leonard. *A History of South Africa.* Yale UP, 1995.

"Three Arson Attacks in a Night." *Weekly Mail,* 20 March 1987, p. 3.

Toit, André du. «The Rationale of Controlling Political Publications." *Censored: Studies in SA's Censorship Laws by Five Leading Writers,* SA Institute of Race Relations, 1983, pp. 80–129.

Tomaselli, Keyan, and Eric P. Louw. *Studies on the South African Media: The Alternative Press in South Africa.* Natal Witness Printing and Publishing, 1991.

"Torture? Of Course, Policeman Tells Court." *Weekly Mail,* 27 February 1987, p. 1.

"Torture: The Pain of Repression." *New Nation,* 11 September 1986, p. 6.

Truth and Reconciliation Commission of South Africa Report. Vol. 2, CTP Book Printers, 1998.

Truth and Reconciliation Commission of South Africa Report. Vol. 4, CTP Book Printers, 1998.

Trzop, Allison. *Beacon Press and the Pentagon Papers.* Beacon P, 2007.

"2,200 Babies in Jail, Coetsee Says." *Weekly Mail,* 6 March 1987, p. 1.

Van Niekerk, Phillip. "Dad Won't Believe His Son Escaped." *Weekly Mail,* 17 January 1986, p. 4.

Van Niekerk, Phillip. Personal interview. Johannesburg, South Africa, 21 May 1999.

Venter, Sahm. "Court Told of Secret Police Death Squad." *Weekly Mail,* 2 June 1989, p. 3.

"A Victim of Horror Speaks." *New Nation,* 21 May 1987, p. 1.

"Vigilante Rampage: Vlok Sued." *New Nation,* 18 June 1987, p. 1.

"Vlok Sued for R2M." *New Nation*, 16 July 1987, p. 1.

Walt, Vivienne. "'We Started Riding a Donkey and Ended on a Tiger.'" *Weekly Mail*, 24 July 1987, pp. 14–15.

Walzer, Michael. "The Politics of Michel Foucault." *Foucault: A Critical Reader*, edited by David Couzens Hoy, Basil Blackwell, 1986, pp. 51–68.

"Weapon Planted on ANC Guerrilla's Body." *New Nation*, 22 September 1989, p. 2.

"'We Killed Mntonga.'" *New Nation*, 1 December 1988, p. 2.

"Welcome Home Govan Mbeki." *New Nation*, 12 November 1987, p. 1.

"What the ANC Says about Negotiations with Pretoria." *New Nation*, 26 November 1987, p. 6.

"What the Clerics Told PW." *Weekly Mail*, 23 August 1985, p. 1.

Wilhelm, Janet. Personal interview. Johannesburg, South Africa, 28 May 1999.

Williams, Juan. "A Black Ambassador to Apartheid South Africa." *Morning Edition*, NPR, 24 October 2006, www.npr.org/templates/story/story.php?storyId=6369450.

Worden, Nigel. *The Making of Modern South Africa*. 2nd ed., Blackwell, 1995.

INDEX

administration, 208, 352n11, 353nn12–13,
354n16; and relations with black political
leaders, 353nn14–15, 354n17
Pietermaritzburg Supreme Court, 62
Pinnock, Don, 69, 123, 151, 166, 185
Pinochet, Augusto, 112–13, 256–57
Plaatje, Sol, 172–73
Poland, 180, 347n18
police: and abuses, 29, 32, 72–74; and abuses
in rural areas, 234; and *New Nation* raid,
3, 34, 327n17; and *New Nation* and *Weekly
Mail* hatred for, 333n33; and powers
under emergency, 28, 30 59, 195; and
Weekly Mail journalists targeted, 2, 327.
See also affidavits; all-clear flag; allusions;
Bellingham, Michael; black journalists;
black lines; *Cry Freedom*; Erasmus,
Paul; Gavin Evans; oblique speak; racial
arithmetic; rape; Sisulu, Zwelakhe; security
forces; subversive enthymemes; Taylor,
Eric; torture; Truth and Reconciliation
Commission; violence
Police Act, 22
Port Elizabeth, 49, 90, 97, 104, 143
Port Elizabeth Supreme Court, 90
Powell, Ivor, 78, 81, 120, 239
Pretoria, 166, 209, 244, 349n2
Pretoria Central Prison, 160
Prisons Act, 84–85
prisoner(s), 75, 196. *See also Cry Freedom*;
Mandela, Nelson; Mbeki, Govan;
Mkhwanazi, Thami; Prisons Act; rape;
Rivonia Trial/Trialists; Robben Island;
torture
Prison Service, 172, 342n5
Progressive Federal Party (PFP), 21, 90, 217, 241
protected space(s): and courts, 70–71, 75–78;
and definition, 69; and Parliament, 71–75
public transcript, 7, 94, 319n8
Publications Act of 1974, 22, 57, 78–81
Publications Appeal Board (PAB), 30, 57, 78–86,
90
publication committees, 79, 81
Publications Control Board, 78–79
Publications Control Directorate, 84

Qoboza, Percy, 326n12

Rabinowitz, Benjamin, 222–23, 249, 356n5
Rabkin, David, 77, 344n11
Rabkin, Susan, 13, 176, 344n11
radio, 53, 55–56, 70
Ramaphosa, Cyril, 149–50

Ramphele, Mamphela, 237
Rand Daily Mail: and black readership and
advertising, 41–42; and closure, 35, 37, 133,
242, 244; and Mandela's court speech, 76,
77; and *Weekly Mail* relationship, 35–36, 38,
42, 132
Rand Supreme Court, 66
Randolph, Jennings, 258
rape, 10, 48, 231, 237, 326n14, 357n7
Rathebe, Dolly, 165
Rather, Dan, 180
Ravan Press, 96
Reagan administration, 174, 208, 210–11,
353n12, 353n14, 354n16
Reagan, Ronald, 207–11, 222, 223; and
Congressional override of veto, 353n12. *See
also* Buchanan, Pat; Casey, William; Perkins,
Edward; Shultz, George
Release Mandela Campaign, 61, 62, 174, 176, 200
religion page (*New Nation*), 181–83
Renwick, Robin, 118, 213–15, 354n20; and
assessment of Botha, 212, 323n4, 325n11
repetition (as rhetorical device), 93, 106, 108, 115
Reporters without Borders, 252
revolution: and anti-apartheid movement, 50,
107, 175, 181, 239; and apartheid government
fear of, 350n5; and justification cited in
Botha's warning letters, 196, 203; and
justification for oppression, 113, 349n1;
and justification for targeting opposition
newspapers, 29, 80, 194–95, 205–6; and
Mandela negotiating instead of, 242
rhetoric: classical, 318n3; and space of
courtroom, 77. *See also* all-clear flag;
allusion; Aristotle; black lines; enthymeme;
indirection; oblique speak; performance;
repetition; subversive enthymeme; wide-
eyed innocence
Rhodesia, 109–10
Rickard, Carmel, 141, 333n33
Risen, James, 263
Rivonia Seven, 176
Rivonia Trial/Trialists, 84, 176–77, 355n7
Robben Island, 44, 89, 166, 241, 271, 331n28. *See
also* Mandela, Nelson; Mkhwanazi, Thami
Roberts, Pat, 358n10
Romero, Óscar, 338n4, 345n17
Romney, Mitt, 164
rooi gevaar (fear of communism), 51
Roomse gevaar (fear of Catholicism), 51
Royster, Jacqueline Jones, 318n3, 318n6
Rubicon Speech, 31
rugby, 27, 43, 323n5, 347n19

The Ultimate Manual: Beard Styles and Grooming Strategies (Trimmers and Beard Oil) To Transform Ordinary Whiskers into Man-tastic Facial Hair Fashion

by Jack Daytona

Introduction

When you are walking down the street and see a man with an awesome beard, what goes through your mind? In your head you are probably thinking, "I could never grow a beard like that." The truth is having a beard is a manly thing. It is like a rite of passage into the world of manhood. Stop being a baby! Get rid of those old razors and shaving cream. It's time to fully experience how to be a man that all the ladies drool over. Because let's face it, the ladies love the beard. You will be amazed at the attention you will get once that beard starts coming in.

It is time to stop thinking you can't and just do it! You will be glad that you did!

A well-groomed beard says a lot about you. How to be a man and how to do what a man is supposed to do which is grow a beard! From the thin and trimmed to the big and bushy, men with beards are taking over the world one beard comb at a time. Get over the idea that you could never grow a beard. Have you ever tried to grow one? It takes a whole lot of work. Do you think that you are ready for it?

What this Book will cover

This book is going to cover the ins and outs of the awesome man beard. The individuals who are cool enough to sport them and how to take care of them. From the history of the beard all the way to the various styles that make every beard unique. It will also talk about how the beard is way cooler than the mustache and how nutrition can even help you grow a beard.

So you will learn how to grow a beard, maintain a beard, love your beard, and worship it forever.

Sit back, relax, and learn all there is to know about having a man-tastic super beard.

Chapter 1: Why Grow a Beard?

The answer seems fairly obvious to those who already sport amazing man-tastic beards but for others some explaining is required. Have you seen some of the people who have beards? They are ultimately some of the coolest people on the planet, and did I mention that the ladies seem to dig it?

Everybody loves a guy with a beard. It is impossible not to see some dude walking down the street with a beard and thinking "man, that guy must be really cool." Even if you are not cool, you can look cool! If you have a baby face this is the perfect opportunity to show the world what you've got. There is nothing more awesome than a beard. Period. Here are some of the most common (and essential) reasons why you should stop being a big baby and just grow that beard already.

Great Men throughout History with Awesome Beards

First, let's take a minute to talk about some of the awesome beards in history. Some of them include rock stars, fictional dudes, and various different types of men from history. From Santa Clause to Jesus himself, it is hard to doubt the coolness of the beard even if you want to.

- Those dudes from ZZ Top have beards. Some of the longest, coolest beards I have ever laid eyes on. No matter how old those guys get as long as they have their beards and their guitars they will never be forgotten.
- Santa Clause. Yes, he's "fictional" but he is one of the most popular people in the entire world, "fictional" or not. He has

a lot of power and he is able to fly around in a sleigh above the world and deliver gifts, so everybody loves him. I am sure he has gotten a cookie crumb or two stuck in that beard.

- One of the greatest songwriters of all time, John Lennon had a beard later in his career. He is missed not only for his ability to write amazing songs with the Beatles, but for his ability to grow awesome beards.
- Forrest Gump. Even though he is a fictional character, wasn't Forrest much cooler after he ran across the country and had that crazy long hair with beard to match? At least I thought so.
- Jesus has a beard. I don't think this needs any explaining.

Various Other Reasons to Grow a Beard

Ok, as if the cool dudes with beards list above wasn't enough to get you to toss out your razors then maybe you need some more encouragement. There are so many reasons why beards are a necessity, so let's discuss some, shall we?

- The chicks dig it, yo. It is an absolutely fact that women love a guy with a big bushy beard. Whether it is well-kempt or a complete mess of a rat's nest on your face, she will love it. It makes you look manly, the ladies like manly. A man with a beard can easily scare away all the creepy dudes. For real.
- It is cheaper to have a beard. No more spending money on razors and shaving cream and all that other nonsense. Think of the money you will save simply by being awesome. When you have to by replacement razors you probably look at the price and lose your mind. Just be awesome.

- Ever get short on cash and need to rob a bank? Growing a beard is a great disguise, no one will ever suspect a thing. I'm kidding. Sort of.
- Having a beard gives you an excuse to be very lazy. It gives you an extra 20 minutes of sleep. By growing a beard you are being given the gift of time! Even though it takes time to grow it, by the time it is in full crazy mode you won't have to worry about getting up early to groom. Apparently you can rob banks and be lazy. Good day for you!
- Let's face the reality of the beard. Men who have long beards appear to be wiser, do they not? It is almost as if a beard is a sign of you having been around the block a few times. This kind of goes along with the idea that women dig beards. They also like dudes who are smart, or at least appear to be smart, at least.
- You will be glad you grew a beard if you live in an area where it gets crazy cold. The beard will keep your face warm. Who needs a scarf? You have a beard so you will be cozy all winter long.
- Beards are very manly. Football players, rock stars, even Jesus has a beard. It gives you a sense of manliness that you won't be able to find anywhere else. If you have a baby face then this is your chance to turn yourself into a real man...fast!

The Beard vs The Mustache

The only mustache that is cooler than a beard is Magnum P.I's mustache. It was cool, well-groomed, and gives the beard a run for its money. I hesitate when I say this because ultimately how could one mustache be cooler than all the beards in the world? Well, I guess it isn't. But Magnum P.I was pretty cool, right?

Look, there is nothing wrong with a good looking 'stache. If you can pull it off then by all means do it. But there is something about the beard that is a bit more rugged and manly. If you grow the mustache wrong then it ends up looking like a porn-stache. With a beard you don't have to worry about that. You can just let it grow and grow until gets all bushy and awesome. Nobody is going to care because your beard is tremendous. So beards are better, but facial hair in general is pretty trendy. But trendy isn't always manly, and those girls really do love a rugged and manly looking dude.

Chapter 2: Beard Styles

Just like with anything, beards come in various shapes, sizes, and styles. It depends on the shape of your face as to be able to figure out which is the right type of beard for you.

The Full Beard – This is the king of all the beards. If you are able to grow a full beard then it is highly recommended that you do so. Some men are not able to grow a full beard or can't pull it off due to the shape of their face. But this is the manliest beard you can get and it also the most awesome. It is thick, burley, and truly amazing.

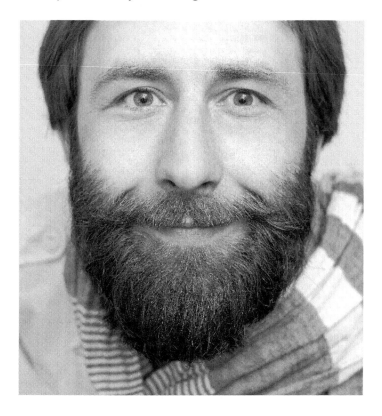

***The Goatee* -**The goatee is the little brother of the full beard. You want facial hair to hide your baby face but can't commit to a full beard. Maybe you're experimenting in college with facial hair or want to look like Shakespeare and be able to stroke your goatee while in deep thought.

Mutton Chops – This is an awesome look that is definitely making a comeback these days. The mutton chop beard is basically when you grow your sideburns long enough to connect to your moustache. The sideburns are typically thick and appear as though it could be a beard. Watch out for those sideburns, they are trying to fool you!

Barely There – These are the beards that we love to hate. They are pencil thin (aka the chin strap) and take way too much time to groom. If you are going to grow one of these beards you may as well not grow one at all. These are also sometimes called designer beards or "sexy stubble." You are not saving any time by having to get up super early and groom your skinny beard. Get over yourself, get a real beard!

Picking a Beard Style for Your Face

Believe it or not picking a beard style for your face is not always easy. Depending on the shape of your face, one type of beard could look amazing while the other one is a complete bust. Whether your face is round, long, skinny, or short, there are beard styles that will bring out the best in your face.

The Round Face – If you have a round face there are certain styles that simply work better for you. You are going to want to have more of a chin beard than anything else and do not grow bushy sideburns. Round-faced men tend to look better with goatees as opposed to beards.

The Long Face – This is going to be just the opposite of what we talked about round faces. If you have a longer face you should make sure your beard is fuller out on the side of your face and shorter around your chin area. This gives you a bit of width so your face won't look as long. Not that there is anything wrong with a long face!

The Square Face – This is another instance where you should try and grow a goatee as opposed to a full beard. You are going to want it to be shorter on the side and long in the front. The best idea is to go with a goatee or a long chin beard.

The Large Face – You are going to want to grow a full beard if you have a larger face. Anything that you grow that is thin or small will look out of sorts. Make sure your beard is full as well as your mustache.

The Small Face – Small face equals small amounts of facial hair. Do not overdo it with the full beard style. It simply will not work for your type of face. The beard will not be in proportion with the rest of your face and it just will not work.

The Oval Face – If your head is oval-shaped then you are the luckiest man alive. Apparently this is the best shape to have in order to grow an impeccable beard. There is no need to shape or groom just let it grow and it is going to look great.

Chapter 3: How to Grow a Beard Faster

Believe it or not there are ways that you can go about growing your beard faster and with ease. From food to over-the-counter products, there are about a million and one ways you can help speed the beard-growing process along. I bet you had no idea that food could help you grow a beard faster. This just keeps getting better and better!

Nutrition

Eating the right kinds of foods is a great way to grow your beard faster. If you are really impatient you need to add certain foods to your diet to help insure that you are going to grow the beard of your dreams. One way to make your beard grow super-fast is to add more protein to your diet. You will find high amounts of protein in foods such as eggs, meat, and salmon. So now you get to grow a beard, get lots of ladies, and eat lots of steak? It doesn't get much manlier than that!

If you don't like eating foods packed with protein then there are always supplements that you can purchase over-the-counter to help with your protein intake. Maybe you don't like steak and eggs. I am not sure many men would say no to eating a lot of steak, but everybody is different, that's for sure.

It may sound cliché' but drinking the ample 8 glasses of water a day will help speed the process along. Doing simple things like that and taking care of yourself sounds like common sense but you would be amazed at the people who need to hear it. One other thing that will help you grow a beard faster is to make sure you take care of your skin with the right products and get plenty of sleep at night. I can't even tell you how amazing all of this sounds.

Products

There are so many products on the market right now to help keep your skin looking awesome while preparing you for the beard that has yet to arrive, but it would take all day to list them all. One product that stood out to me was a product called Vita Beard. This product claims to give you all of the vitamins you need to grow a legendary beard. It is loaded with lots of B vitamins which are supposed to help your beard grow faster.

Beard Envy makes a product that comes in a kit that has a beard wash that hydrates your beard and adds protein to it to keep it soft and easy to comb. It also comes with a brush so you can comb through your beard after you wash it. This product is really cool because it is not tested on animals and it won't do any damage to your skin as there are no chemicals in it. That and it makes your beard look super-clean and super-healthy. You have to take care of that beast!

Since protein is supposed to help you grow a beard faster you can always make protein shakes to help you grow your beard. There are some other products by Doo Gro Mega that help your beard grow and become thicker. I suppose if you are having that hard of a time growing a beard I would try these products. But I would only try them as a last resort.

Chapter 4: Taking Care of Your Beard

If you want an awesome beard you have to know how to take care of it. Grooming is essential and so is keeping it clean. You never know what could find its way into the depths of your beard causing you to lose a Cheeto or something. There are things that men have found in their beards that they probably don't even want to tell you about. So keeping it well groomed is absolutely essential.

Trimming the Beard

If you don't know how to trim your own beard go and have someone professional do it. If you do plan on doing it on your own make sure you have a high quality beard trimmer. Not something bought in a discount bin at Wal-Mart. A real beard trimmer that keeps your full beard under control. Consider purchasing a cordless trimmer so you have easy access to it at all times.

One good tip is to never trim your beard when it is wet. Hair is always longer when it is wet so you do not want to cut off too much. Some men prefer to use the comb and scissors method to trim their beard. If you are experienced with this method, by all means, go for it. But leave it to the professionals. Beard trimmers are much easier to use and cause less of a hassle.

Don't ever trim your beard if you simply do not have the right tools to do the job. Might as well get the job done right or go purchase an awesome set of barber scissors or a pair of clippers. When using a comb it is always best to use a wide-tooth comb. Fine-tooth combs will work fine on mustaches but not on beards. If you have a three-way mirror that would be awesome. Then you can see every angle of your face so you can make sure that the beard is even.

If you do decide to use a comb and scissors make sure that you comb out your beard and only cut the hair that is on the outer part of the comb. It may take some practice, but you will get the hang of it.

When purchasing a beard trimmer make sure that it comes with a trimming guide that can easily be removed and adjusted. This will determine how closely you plan on trimming your beard.

Washing Your Beard

The beard is hair, ya know. So you have to wash it just like you wash the hair that is on your head. You might want to pick up a light shampoo as the hair on your beard can become sensitive. It is also best to use a conditioner if you have one. This will make it easy for you to comb out when you groom it. Rinse it out thoroughly as this could cause a dandruff problem and nobody has time for that.

When you dry your beard make sure you only wipe and pat it with a towel, but not too rough. Do not blow dry it! This could make things worse by causing your skin to dry out even more. Use a wide-tooth comb to brush out any tangles.

Beard Dandruff and Other Issues

Just like with any hair you are bound to get dry skin or dandruff. You can use regular dandruff shampoo on your beard to prevent dandruff from occurring. You can also purchase some beard oil to help keep dry skin at bay. It may cause some itching but a good beard oil or balm should help with that. There are products on the market such as "Beard Wash" that will help keep the dandruff away. But some good old Head and Shoulders should easily do the trick.

There are also some other products out there that might help with the beard dandruff. Beard oil is definitely the best product you can buy when it comes to dry skin in the beard. It can be embarrassing, but just like with regular dandruff, you can take care of business with no problem.

Dying Your Beard

Okay, it is inevitable, we are all going to go gray at some point. And yes, your beautiful beard can also go gray. Some men like having a little gray in the beard. It adds a little bit of rugged manliness to it. Other dudes simply cannot deal with the thought of having gray in their beards. You can always use a comb-in beard color that will get rid of the gray pretty fast. This isn't the method for everyone, but if you seriously cannot handle seeing gray in your beard there are tons of products on the market that can help you out.

Just for Men makes a comb-in hair dye product that is easy to use if you are embarrassed by your graying beard. It comes with a tiny brush where you can come in the color without getting it everywhere. Some men may think this is less manly, but hey, to each their own. It is recommend that if you plan on coloring your beard to grow it out for a couple of weeks before you do. This makes it easier to color and you will get less dye on your skin. Take a shower and make sure it is rinsed out thoroughly.

Shaving off Your Beard

If the time has come and you are ready to shave off your beard then there is a certain way you should go about it. Not sure why anybody would want to lose their beard, but whatever. If you are sporting a full beard, it is best to trim it down with clippers before you do a full shave. This will make your job much easier. Once you get it down to a manageable level, you can then shave it off with an electric razor. You also need to purchase a high-quality shaving cream, not the cheap stuff. That is a lot of hair that you are taking off your face, be careful! I don't know about you but I would be very sad if I lost my beard.

This may sound like a "girly" thing to say but you should always moisturize after you shave your beard completely off. Your skin has been covered by this big manly beard for quite some time and has not seen the light of day in many moons. You may have some excess dry skin or other issues that can be caused by having a man-tastic beard. It would be easiest if you simply did not shave it off at all!

Chapter 5: Beard Slang

Ahh, the ever so popular beard slang. Everybody uses it, because beards are the "in" thing right now. I wouldn't take offense to any of them if I were you. Most of them are quite hilarious and silly if you sit down to think about it. Here are some of the most common slang used for the righteous beard.

- Chin Curtain
- Fu Manchu
- Nose Neighbor
- Five o'clock Shadow
- Lip Wig
- Tom Selleck
- Sideburns
- Mouth brow
- Trash stash
- Crumb Catcher
- Peach fuzz
- Side locks
- Undercover brother
- Cookie duster
- Stubble
- Muttonchops

The list could go on and on. It is kind of cool to think that there are so many ways you can talk about someone's beard. What makes it truly cool is that the beard is so unbelievably awesome that one name for it simply won't do. My personal favorite is crumb catcher. You always gotta save some for later!

Chapter 6: Lets wrap it up

I am sure that seems like a lot of information to take in in such a short period of time. So I want to make sure you got the gist of what you should have learned out of all of this.

- Anyone can grow a beard. Stop making excuses and just do it!
- Discover the beard that is the best for the shape of your face and it will make all the difference.
- Take care of your beard and treasure it as if it were your first born.
- Beards are cooler than mustaches.
- Having a beard takes a lot of work but it is totally worth it.
- Chicks love beards.

If you learned at least that much then my job here is complete. Beards are the heart and soul of a manly man. He is rugged, handsome, cool, and can grow a beard, so he's awesome. Cherish the beard, love him, and he will love you in return.

13541881R00015

Printed in Great Britain
by Amazon.co.uk, Ltd.,
Marston Gate.